The Speaker's Handbook

Sixth Edition

Jo Sprague
San Jose State University

Douglas Stuart

THOMSON
™
WADSWORTH

Australia • Canada • Mexico • Singapore • Spain
United Kingdom • United States

THOMSON

™

WADSWORTH

Executive Editor: Deirdre Anderson
Publisher: Holly J. Allen
Development Editor: Eric Carlson
Assistant Editor: Nicole George
Editorial Assistant: Mele Alusa
Technology Project Manager:
 Jeanette Wiseman
Marketing Manager: Kimberly Russell
Marketing Assistant: Neena Chandra
Advertising Project Manager: Shemika Britt

Project Manager, Editorial Production:
 Mary Noel
Print/Media Buyer: Karen Hunt
Permissions Editor: Joohee Lee
Production Service: Vicki Moran, Publishing
 Support Services
Copy Editor: Thomas L. Briggs
Cover Designer: Carole Lawson
Compositor: R&S Book Composition
Printer: Phoenix Color, BTP

For more information about our products, contact us at:
Thomson Learning Academic Resource Center
1-800-423-0563
For permission to use material
from this text, contact us by:
Phone: 1-800-730-2214 **Fax:** 1-800-730-2215
Web: http://www.thomsonrights.com

ISBN 0-15-5046314

Wadsworth/Thomson Learning
10 Davis Drive
Belmont, CA 94002-3098
USA

Asia
Thomson Learning
5 Shenton Way #01-01
UIC Building
Singapore 068808

Australia
Nelson Thomson Learning
102 Dodds Street
South Melbourne, Victoria 3205
Australia

Canada
Nelson Thomson Learning
1120 Birchmount Road
Toronto, Ontario M1K 5G4
Canada

Europe/Middle East/Africa
Thomson Learning
High Holborn House
50/51 Bedford Row
London WC1R 4LR
United Kingdom

Latin America
Thomson Learning
Seneca, 53
Colonia Polanco
11560 Mexico D.F.
Mexico

Spain
Paraninfo Thomson Learning
Calle/Magallanes, 25
28015 Madrid, Spain

Brief Contents

Contents

Chapter 7. Audience Analysis   **75**

Chapter 8. Research   **88**

Chapter 21. Informative Strategies 271

Chapter 22. Persuasive Strategies 277

Preface

The Speaker's Handbook, Sixth Edition, is at once a reference guide for the individual speaker and a textbook for use in the public speaking course. It is a compendium of principles, examples, and exercises that covers the issues one commonly confronts in preparing and delivering a speech. What distinguishes *The Speaker's Handbook* from other books on public speaking, though, is its flexibility: Each of the thirty chapters stands by itself, so that speakers need consult only those parts of the book covering the aspects of speech-making with which they need further help.

About the Handbook Approach

In a sense, a book about public speaking is a contradiction. Public speaking is a lived, performed, embodied event that draws its special qualities from the immediate context, the personality of a particular speaker, and the response of a certain audience. Is there really any useful general advice about so specific an act?

Apparently so. For as long as people have felt the need to speak in public, they have turned to others for advice on how to do so more effectively. Early evidence from Egyptian tombs shows that leaders gave serious thought to the choices they faced in speaking to their followers. The oral tradition captured in Homeric legend hints that the giving and taking of this advice predated the written word. The increasing supply of information about the ancient cultures of China, India, and the Americas shows that these peoples had culturally distinctive ways of speaking, which some analyzed and discussed. These observers then formulated advice for others in their culture. Such advice usually came in two forms: Those who had vast experience as speakers told stories about what worked for them; others looked beyond what worked and theorized about why it worked.

Both forms of guidance are still present. Leading platform speakers write books about their experiences. The popularity of such books year after year suggests that people find benefit in the personal and experiential approach. At the same time, university libraries continue to accumulate academic treatises on rhetoric and communication. Here, too, the vitality of these lines of research after thousands of years suggests that much is left to be said and investigated.

There is a third form, one that we differentiate from both those kinds of books and place within another venerable tradition that is over two thousand years old. This form is neither a narrative account of personal success stories nor a scholarly theoretical tome. This is the *handbook*. The first written handbooks for speakers were probably produced by the Sophists in the Greece of 200 B.C.E. In any field, a handbook represents a particular blending of theory and practice displayed in a concise format. There are scouting handbooks, birding handbooks, managing handbooks, and meditation handbooks. In all these cases, a handbook is a distillation of the experience and theory of many people and many eras.

The particular usefulness of handbooks can be found in their characteristics.

Handbooks are brief.

They fit in a person's hand. They are supposed to be as small as practicable to remove the impediment of size for easy carrying, storing, and referencing. The implication of this is that we have tried to distill the most meaningful advice, avoiding bulking the book out. The sample speeches on the Web site are called on over and over again in the text in both examples and exercises. Putting in as many sample speeches as usual in standard textbooks, interspersed throughout the body of the book, would defeat the advantages offered by the handbook format. Cartoons and photographs, likewise, take up too much space.

Handbooks are reference books.

The contents of a handbook are meant to be used in any order. The progression of the chapters, as we have arranged them, is not random, but then again, a reader or teacher does not necessarily have to follow that order. We have written the chapters to be as self-contained as possible to make the book adaptable to the differing needs of its various users. Long before the information superhighway or menu-driven computers or the invention of the term *random access,* people liked to learn things as they needed them.

Adult learners have their own way of designing their learning programs, whether they are setting up a computer or understanding a new job. Most people who buy a computer do not take a course on how to use it. They try a few things, glance at the manual, and work until they get into trouble. Then they look at the manual again, but only for the specific information they need to get beyond the current problem. In effect, they don't worry about the things they don't have to worry about, but they won't know that a thing to worry about exists until they discover it. Public speaking is like that. Until people start speaking, they cannot be sure of all the areas in which they may need improvement. Therefore, users should approach this handbook with a spirit of flexibility, taking what they need in the order they need it. Each teacher brings to the classroom a different experience set and an understanding of the values, needs, and capabilities of the students who attend a particular institution. Therefore, each teacher may choose to assign chapters in an order that fits his or her perception of the best way to increase the skills of those students. Whether users are teachers, students, or professional persons, we think that they will find some benefit in every chapter of this handbook, but we don't dictate to them in what order they will find that benefit.

Handbooks are handy.

When people haul out the book that came with their computer, they want to find the section on changing printer types quickly, not read about the architecture of the system to find the bit that refers to communications between the computer and printer. A good user guide compartmentalizes related information and then tries to make that information as accessible as possible through a variety of pointers and references, using design tools to make things easy to find. We have included aids to let users get to where they want to be, from the quick index and checklists on the endpapers to the use of color and typeface weight in the text itself.

With this compartmentalization, users do not have to read everything at once. A student may be preparing to give an informative speech for a class and is thinking of including some humor. The student could jump ahead and read section **18a(4)**. It is not that long. A businessperson may be giving a presentation to the board on the adoption of new technology but feel uncertain if he or she has covered everything and in the most effective order. That person could read chapter **9** on transforming his or her ideas into points and chapters **21** and **22** on informative and persuasive strategies.

We do have a few specific recommendations, however, on preliminary steps that will help students and other readers get the most out of this book. First, such users should read chapter **1**. It provides an orientation to communication and helps them crystallize their self-definition as speakers. It helps them diagnose their skill level and gives them an approach to mapping out a skill-development plan for themselves. The format of this book is based on the assumption that speakers cannot be conscious of everything at once. In designing a skill-development program, speakers should *not* be conscious of everything at once. Trying to do everything in parallel will frustrate their purpose and inhibit their skill-building. As we say in **1d**, speakers should avoid being overly conscious of their manner of speaking or their message's exact language. But if a speech is different from just another conversation, as we also say, how do public speakers become *just enough more conscious* of the craft of speaking to improve their skill without breaking the conversational bond? The secret lies in having a very clear plan of what their priorities are and in deciding on a limited number of goals to pursue consciously at any one time. The handbook approach lets users pick one or two important skills to work on, and when those are mastered, move to another set.

About Writing This Book

We approached this writing task with an unusual combination of perspectives. In her thirty years of teaching public speaking, visiting the classes of other teachers, and consulting, Jo Sprague has observed that there are many "right ways" to approach a course. Doug Stuart, as a vice president of a technical and marketing publications department and a director of a creative development department, has learned how to take even the most complex material and make it clear and accessible to readers. It became evident to us that there was a need for a different kind of book on speaking, one based on what we knew about how adults learn. *The Speaker's Handbook* proceeds from the premise that people like to focus first on the area of greatest concern and then design their own learning experience outward from that point.

About the Sixth Edition

We have been gratified with the response to the first five editions of *The Speaker's Handbook*. And we are pleased that the handbook format worked for students and their instructors, as well as for people who give presentations in their business or community. In this edition, we have once again responded to user suggestions on how to make the information even more accessible. The sample speeches, once in an appendix, are now available on the *Handbook's* Web site. We have added a new chapter on listening that pulls together material previously dispersed throughout the book and adds several new recommendations for listeners. A second new chapter replaces Guidelines for Special Occasions and introduces the notion of speech *contexts* in their wide variety. The new chapter **23** presents the norms and expectations for several business, professional, political, civic, social, and ceremonial contexts. Perhaps more important, since no two contexts are alike, it guides readers through the steps they might use in analyzing any speaking context. It casts speakers as leaders who have the power to shape contexts in constructive ways and thus improve the level of discourse in society.

For this new edition, important new resources are now available:

InfoTrac® College Edition A free four-month subscription to this extensive online library is enclosed with every new copy of *The Speaker's Handbook*, Sixth Edition. This easy-to-use database of reliable, full-length articles (not abstracts) from hundreds of top academic journals and popular sources is ideal for opening whole new worlds of information and research. To help you use the this tool effectively, key exercises throughout the text are linked to InfoTrac College Edition.

The *SpeechMaker* CD-ROM, packaged free with every new text, brings together text, full-motion video, sound, and the Internet to create a dynamic exploration of the steps involved in the speechmaking process.

The Speaker's Handbook Web site, containing additional InfoTrac College Edition exercises, sample speeches, and Web links focusing on technology in communication, research, documentation, and more can be found at *http://www.communication.wadsworth.com.*

Thomson Learning WebTutor™ Advantage, 2.0 for WebCT and Blackboard is a Web-based teaching and learning tool that takes a course beyond classroom boundaries to an anywhere, any time environment. WebTutor for *The Speaker's Handbook* corresponds chapter-by-chapter and topic-by-topic with the book, including practice quizzes and online tutorials. Instructors can use WebTutor to provide virtual office hours, post syllabi, set up threaded discussions, and track student progress on the practice quizzes.

Instructor's resources include

Instructor's Resource Manual with Test Bank, by Jo Sprague, Doug Stuart, and Neeley Silberman has proved to be an invaluable resource for instructors. It features a wealth of teaching resources including discussions on issues in teaching public speaking, basic course materials including sample syllabi, speech outlines, critique forms, test questions, and much more.

ExamView is a fully integrated collection of test creation, delivery, and classroom management tools that feature all of the test items found in the *Instructor's Resource Manual.*

Finally, though we have received compliments on the inclusiveness of the first five editions, we strive to make each subsequent edition of the *Handbook* more attuned to the diversity of contemporary life. In our treatment of language, reasoning, and vocal and physical delivery, we attempt to show how social forces shape, and are shaped by, speech. What is appropriate, or clear, or persuasive constantly changes as society changes. The effective speaker will be open to the subtle cultural variations in speech situations. If there were no differences between people, communication would be unnecessary. If there were no similarities, it would be impossible. The great strength of oral communication is that its many dimensions offer people ways to seek out connections in the midst of difference; its immediacy allows for on-the-spot adjustments.

Acknowledgments

From the vantage point of this sixth edition we cast back in time to the first edition and once again acknowledge Peter Dougherty, who initially approached us with the idea for *The Speaker's Handbook*. The Wadsworth team for the sixth edition proved to be enthusiastic, attentive, dedicated, and professional—and through their efforts and vigilance made it easier for us to be enthusiastic, attentive, dedicated, and professional as well. Working closely with Deirdre Anderson, Executive Editor for Speech Communication, and Eric Carlson, Senior Development Editor, has been a pleasure. Along with Deirdre and Eric, others at Wadsworth who were involved in this edition are Mary Noel, Production Project Manager, Jeanette Wiseman, Senior Technology Project Manager, and Kimberly Russell, Marketing Manager. Vicki Moran, at Publishing Support Services, and copy editor Tom Briggs provided expert production guidance.

We are grateful to Becki Bowman, Dalton State College, Ellen Bremen, Darton College, Judith A. Deisler, Pasco-Hernando Community College, James E. Reppert, Southern Arkansas University, Laura L. Young, Southern Oregon University, and Tonette Long, Southern Oregon University, who provided helpful comments and suggestions for this edition. In addition, there are many loyal users of the *Handbook* who have generously shared their comments with us. Without them, we might have changed too much. Thanks for letting us know what works, as well as what can be improved. Neeley Silberman has once again provided great service by taking the lead on the sixth edition of the accompanying *Instructor's Resource Manual*.

Whenever a book revision comes into our lives it overlays an already complex set of responsibilities, interactions, and deadlines. Were it not for the combination of nudges, cheerleading, opinions, and creative selflessness from our partners, Gary Ruud and Samantha Schoenfeld, we might not have been able to untangle ourselves enough to give this project its due. For this, and much more, we stress our love and thanks.

Jo Sprague
Douglas Stuart

Part 1

Foundation

Introduction

C hances are, if you are reading these words, you will soon have the opportunity to give a public speech. This may be in the context of a public speaking class, or you may have picked this handbook up in the library because you need to give a presentation at work. Perhaps you are preparing to speak in front of the local council. Regardless, this is an "opportunity"; this is a good thing.

For some, the statement "you will soon have the opportunity to give a public speech" will sound like the equivalent of "you will soon have the opportunity to have a root canal." True, many people approach the idea of speaking in public with attitudes that fall somewhere between mild apprehension and utter dread. As widespread and real as such concerns are, we suggest that there is one thing worse than being called upon to give a public speech when you *don't* want to. This is not being able to give a public speech when you *do* want to. This latter situation plays out in scenarios like these:

- You attend a public meeting on an issue crucial to you and your family but are so intimidated by the articulate speakers on the other side, that you never speak up.
- You sit in class, knowing the answer to a question that is asked but lacking the confidence to raise your hand.
- You attend a business meeting in which colleagues are discussing a problem. You think you have some insights that could be part of the solution, but you can't formulate your thoughts clearly enough to present them.

- You would like to take on a leadership role in a work group or social group, but the position involves giving speeches, and you are paralyzed with fear at the thought.
- You are being interviewed for a job you really want and think you are qualified for, but you cannot seem to answer the questions without stumbling over words and rambling.
- You start to make a presentation on a topic you know well, but soon forget the key ideas and hastily bring the speech to a close.
- You listen to your friends telling stories of funny things that have happened to them and you are dying to share one of your experiences, but you are too shy to speak up.

It saddens us to know that situations like these exist. The individuals involved feel powerless and miss out on the attention and credit they deserve. More seriously, all of us miss out when voices are left out of the conversation because people lack the skill or confidence to participate in public events. A democratic society is structured around the free exchange of ideas so that people can listen to each other's views and select the best courses of collective action. Every citizen must be willing to contribute positively and also to speak up against oppression or infringement of rights. Organizations depend on participants to pool their expertise through communication. Our social connections and family bonds are cemented through storytelling and the sharing of personal feelings.

In addition to these societal and social benefits of becoming comfortable with and effective in public speaking, there are personal and professional benefits that accrue as well. Experience with analyzing information and expressing your opinions will not only increase your confidence in day-to-day activities but also help you get more out of your classes. Participating constructively in class discussions and applying the skills of preparation, organization, development, and presentation will enhance your learning experience.

Regarding professional benefits, a quick glance at job descriptions on the Web turns up phrases like "strong communication skills," "excellent verbal and written skills," "strong ability to motivate others," "strong written and oral communications skills required," and "excellent interpersonal and communication skills" with regularity. Clearly, familiarity with the skills you develop as a public speaker will help you get a job. After all, the candidate who can answer questions concisely and to the point, who can express ideas and desires in memorable ways, and who remains calm in a stressful situation will make the better impression. Once you get the job, you can use these communication skills to shape your career environment so that you gain personal satisfaction while being an effective and valued professional resource.

Except for situations obviously beyond the scope of a handbook (such as living in a tyrannical society in which free expression of ideas is viciously punished or being part of an organization or group in which those in power make speaking out against them a dangerous thing to do), the factors that inhibit people from speaking in public can be addressed through education and coaching. And effective speaking is a skill that almost everyone can learn. Why else do so many colleges and universities require or strongly recommend courses in public speaking? Why do thousands of people voluntarily join groups like Toastmasters International? Why do corporations and public agencies spend millions of dollars on presentation training?

As with any other skill (such as dancing, programming, or tree surgery), with public speaking, there are principles to be mastered, there is a need for concentration and practice, and there are benefits to working with a skilled teacher and supportive colearners. We have seen reticent speakers gain in confidence and poise. We have observed people who saw a speech as a list of points to be covered develop an exquisite awareness of how to engage an audience in the unfolding meaning of a speech. From people who absolutely hated preparing outlines of their speeches, we have heard testimonials of how they now use organizational tools in writing and speaking in college classes and in their professional lives. And, believe it or not, some of the most reluctant speakers have discovered that making a presentation can even be fun. They find it exhilarating to make a point so clear and compelling that they can see in listeners' faces that they have moved them. We all like to receive compliments and applause when a speech hits its mark. We enjoy a sense of effectiveness and value when our ideas are taken seriously and contribute to dialogues about our future. There is great joy and power in finding our voices in the public sphere.

Chapters **1–4** deal with some fundamental issues that underlie or inform the act of speaking in public. Examine your approach. *Understanding speaking* and the communicative resources you have at hand are the foundation on which you will build. Good *listening* habits enrich your experience, as both a speaker and an audience member. Whatever your reason for speaking, you should operate always within a framework of *speaking ethics*. *Overcoming fear of speaking* may be one of the first things you have to deal with, but this too can be mastered.

Chapter 1

Understanding Speaking

Understand that public speaking is the act of creating meaning with your listeners, and approach your role as a speaker by consciously combining communicative resources you already have at hand.

1a. Understand what it means to be a speaker.

For many people, the mental image that forms when they hear the words *public speaking* features a lectern, a podium or stage, and an auditorium—the components of a classic, capital-S Speech. This image can be frightening for some and invigorating for others. It is also very narrow. In this handbook, we deal with a wider picture of what public speaking means and of when a person becomes a speaker. This picture includes the capital-S Speech, and we hope that users of this book will become more skilled in that context, but it includes more. You are a speaker when you stand behind the lectern at an awards banquet, or when you approach the floor microphone at a planning commission meeting, or when you sit at a table with three other members of your work group and present your proposal for tackling some problem. You are a speaker in class, you are a speaker at work, and you are a speaker among friends and family. And in any one of these settings, you are a different speaker from the speaker you'd be in another.

Having said this—having broadened the context—we must also ensure that we do not become too broad. Not all oral communication in a group setting is public speaking. Perhaps the distinguishing characteristic of public speaking is that it is an event when a contract is reached among a group of people such that one person, the speaker, is given consent to direct the event.

Many people tend to think that a gulf separates speakers from listeners, with meaning being created by the former and transmitted to the latter. This can promote the erroneous view of an adversarial relationship between speakers and listeners: Audiences are made up of people who judge you or receive your thoughts or can be manipulated by you. Actually, communication theorists stress that meaning is socially constructed in a mutual transaction between speakers and listeners.

Looking at speaking this way does not relieve the speaker of certain basic responsibilities. This does not mean that every speaking situation is an improvisation. To uphold your end of the contract, you are obliged to invest energy into creating an effective and efficient event. You should understand that as speaker you are an originator and inventor—that you bring something uniquely "you" to the transaction and that this is not an option but a condition for effective speaking.

1b. Ground your approach to effective public speaking in a meaning-centered view of communication.

Of course, public speaking is a subset of the broader human activity called *communication*. Even in a practical handbook, it is worth examining your own assumptions about the nature of communication. Working from a view that is too narrow or mechanical will hinder your effectiveness as a public speaker.

(1) Do not confine your view of communication to information transmission and reception.

For decades after the dawn of the Information Age, *communication* was defined in terms of the clear transmission of information from a sender to a receiver. For some kinds of speaking and some aspects of speech preparation, this notion is very useful. (See **21**.) In general, though, comparing speaking with making a phone call or delivering a package has severe limitations. These metaphors tend to direct your thinking toward discrete, sender-controlled steps. "Giving a speech" becomes a matter of selecting ideas, packaging them, shipping them efficiently, and verifying their receipt. For most purposes, speakers are better served by embracing a more collaborative and complex model of communication.

(2) Think of communication as the joint creation of meaning.

The metaphor of collaborative creation evokes a very different set of images. Think about a group of filmmakers at work, or a software design team, or two textbook authors for that matter. At any given time, one individual may be putting forth ideas while the others listen and react. The end product is a composite that emerges from the interaction; it did not exist in any one person's mind at the outset. For us, the distinction between these two approaches to communication is not a trivial one. The shift in emphasis from messages (speaker controlled) to meanings (jointly created) has important implications.

Meaning is social.

This implies that no one individual, either sender or receiver, can control the "true meaning" of a statement. A speaker who has violated a social norm cannot get off the hook by saying, "I did not intend that to be offensive, so it wasn't." But neither can a single receiver unilaterally control what a statement or action really means. A thin-skinned listener is not justified in overreacting to a rather innocent comment by declaring, "I felt offended, so that statement was offensive." Most of us have been involved in these fruitless and frustrating arguments in which one person insists on his or her view of a communication event.

Meaning is contextual.

Similarly, few disputes about meaning are settled by pulling out a dictionary. This implies that words or messages alone cannot tell us the "true meaning" of the communication. *Context* is that which surrounds a text. Words take their meanings not just from a dictionary but from all that surrounds them as they were uttered. A message can be repeated verbatim, but its meaning will not be identical if the context has changed. Thinking about meaning this way takes into account when and where a statement was made, who was present, what happened previously, and what tone of voice and expression accompanied the utterance.

Meaning is contingent.

This implies, in turn, that no sentence or act frozen in time has acquired its "true meaning." What something means has to be interpreted within a chain of events. A speech may begin with an anecdote that initially sounds authentic but that is later exposed as an example of what the speaker opposes. Meaning becomes clear as it unfolds in the interplay between speaker and listeners. Often, we do not know what something meant until we reflect back on an entire encounter.

Ultimately, meaning is negotiated by discourse communities. In cases in which the "true meaning" of a message is contested, appeals to the words themselves, or to the speaker's intentions, or to the listeners' response have all been shown to be inadequate. Therefore, meanings are worked out over time by larger groups whose members share some common agreements and come to build others. What counts as sexual harassment in the workplace, for instance, is not settled by a single court case or congressional hearing. The meaning of the term is hashed out in speeches, columns, letters to the editor, and countless personal conversations. Groups whose meanings included every friendly comment found their definition rejected. So did those whose meanings excluded everything except direct physical assault. Gradually, a range of meanings of the term within contemporary U.S. culture came into general understanding. However, because these meanings are social, contextual, and contingent, they will continue to evolve.

1c. Approach public speaking by drawing on three familiar communicative resources.

Public speakers who approach communication in terms of creating meaning with their audiences are off to a good start. Think of all the times you have successfully created meaning with different groups of people, in different contexts, and on different topics. When you enter into the contract that designates you as a "speaker," you are not required to master a brand-new skill. Rather, your challenge is to adapt several communication skills that *you already have* in your repertoire: conversation, writing, and performance, as Figure 1-1 shows.

Take stock of the communicative resources already at your disposal, available for you to call into use as a speaker.

(1) Draw on your conversation skills.

In everyday conversations, you do certain things that make you effective. Probably you are relaxed and spontaneous, responsive to the situation and naturally expressive of your changing feelings. Your attention is centered on the person or people to whom you are speaking and on the general ideas you want to get across. You do not worry about your exact words because the event is highly interactive, with meaning clarified in the give-and-take.

Conversation is a form of risk taking—in that you are not sure of the outcome at any point. Usually, this uncertainty does not prevent you from conversing, even if you know that disagreements may occur. A lot of apprehension

FIGURE 1-1 Three Communicative Resources

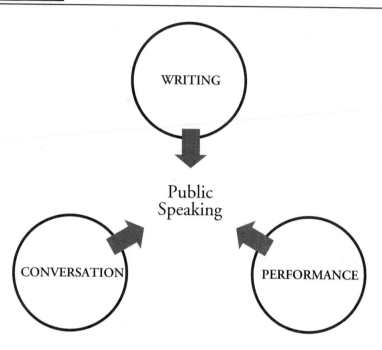

about public speaking can be dissipated if you carry this aspect of the conversational model into the speaking event.

One of the highest compliments a speaker can receive is to be called "conversational." The skills drawn from conversation that are useful to a public speaker include speaking in a comfortable and confident manner, listening to and taking in the perspective of others, and adapting constantly to feedback.

(2) Draw on your writing skills.

The written word enables you to distance yourself from your ideas and to freeze them on paper. This distancing allows you to craft and tinker—to experiment with alternative forms and play them out in your imagination. This takes much longer than a conversational exploration of ideas, in which the vague "you know what I mean" to a friend can substitute for quite a bit of written groundwork.

In writing, you pay close attention to word choices and organization to produce a carefully crafted message. Vocabulary is more precise than in conversation. You have the time to enjoy wordplay, to explore nuance, and to find elegant phrasing that makes the message unforgettable.

One benefit of writing is that it gives you the opportunity to put enough distance between you and your ideas to see them objectively, test them for logical coherence, and see how well they fit together. In writing, you can weave in multiple voices of authorities along with your own.

From writing, then, a speaker draws on the attention to language, the order of ideas, and the internal unity of the speech. Good writing means not settling for the first thing set down, but rather spending time polishing to achieve the most economical and forceful way of getting a message across.

(3) Draw on your performance skills.

Most people would say they are not performers because they have not starred in a Broadway show, a rock concert, or even a community theater production or company talent show. But this is a narrow definition of *performance*. Actually, we are all performers. In one sense, performance occurs whenever we *do* something, rather than merely think about it. So, you might plan a phone call to a friend and then perform it. When you play volleyball or tell a story to your family, you are performing. In this handbook, when we talk about your performance skills, we mean the ways you have learned to use certain physical qualities—tone of voice, gestures, movement—to create a focal point for a group.

To many, performance connotes drama and virtuosity: the electric "presence" of a violin virtuoso, the flash of a track star, or the understated passion of an actor in a revelatory scene. In context, and in appropriate forms, drama and virtuosity are not bad things for a speaker to manifest. Communication can be more complete if you do what you are doing well, with an awareness of the emotional needs of your listeners.

So strong has been the emphasis on conversation that *performance* has become a dirty word among speech teachers. This is because for some time performance was seen as an end in itself rather than as an essential human activity. To downplay the performative aspects of public speech is to deny the essential power that makes a speech more than conversation, more than an outline or transcript. *Performance* refers not to display or phoniness but to an enactment, one that creates an event between speaker and listeners that transcends the message or exchange of information. This transcendence is what makes people say, "You had to be there."

Performance skills useful to the speaker include the ability to pay attention to the entire effect, the knowledge of how to use setting and timing, and the capacity to turn a collection of individuals into a cohesive group. Performers know how to make use of all the senses. They tie together visual effects, lighting, sound, music, humor, and drama. They have a superb sense of timing and understand how to direct emotional buildup and choose the right moment for climax. Speakers can make use of these skills by learning to visualize the desired impact and carefully planning details that contribute to that overall impact.

(4) Combine some features of these three communicative resources for an effective speech.

Implicit in the descriptions of the positive influences of these three resources is the proposition that public speaking will not be successful if it omits the conversational, the compositional, or the performative qualities. A speaker needs the adaptation of conversation, the preparation of writing, and the engagement of performance to earn the undivided attention of an audience. This is not to say that each merits equal emphasis in all situations for all speakers. Understanding the positive qualities just described, you need to come up with a unique blend for each time and place. You also need to understand the negative side; 1c(5) describes some of the perils of leaning too heavily on any one resource.

How you combine these resources, or whether you are aware of them at all, depends on your level of consciousness of your competence (see 1d) or perhaps on the kinds of feedback you receive in your practice sessions (see 2 and 25). Starting with the assumption that, either through self-awareness or feedback, you are mindful of how you currently call on the three communicative resources, let's look at some things to consider as you decide how to combine them to create an effective speech.

Consider the demands of the situation and the expectations of the audience.

The type of speech and the situation determine how you blend the skills of communication in various speeches. Often, a formal occasion and a large audience require that a speaker give some of the writer's attention to word choice and overall unity. Moderating a discussion entails tapping the listening skills involved in conversation. A festive occasion may cry out for a larger-than-life demonstration.

Chapter 7 gives some suggestions on how to learn more about the people to whom you will speak. Chapters 23 and 29 present guidelines about occasions and situations.

Consider your own personality and distinctive speaking style.

Even on the same occasion and for the same topic, speakers will differ. It is not a mistake to rely on one resource over another if it is well matched to who you are and how you work best. For instance, if you are one of those speakers who is folksy and conversational and puts an audience at ease, you will draw most heavily on those skills. If you are a great storyteller or have a dramatic flair, you should use that resource to the extent that it is appropriate. If you know that you have trouble being spontaneous, let alone dramatic, in front of a group, you should work extra hard on developing the content of your speech so that your words and message bond you to your listeners.

(5) Avoid relying exclusively or excessively on any one of these resources.

A speaker needs to draw some behaviors out of all three of these domains. Though ratios may vary, it is just as bad to overuse conversation, writing, or performance orientations as to neglect them. Too much reliance on conversation leads to:

- uneconomical use of time and language
- spontaneous blunders
- failure to control delivery habits that might be distracting
- disorganization and repetition of points already made
- the tendency to go off on tangents and lose focus

Too much reliance on writing leads to:

- unnatural use of language and unnatural inflection—a "canned" sound
- lack of flexibility and an inability to adapt to an audience, with many missed opportunities for specific adaptation
- a one-way transmission of a message
- a focus on a general audience
- an almost inevitable tendency to read or memorize the text

Too much reliance on performance leads to:

- an opening for stage fright
- an egocentric, melodramatic exhibition that minimizes the transaction between speaker and listeners
- a credibility problem, with the audience doubting the sincerity of expressed emotions and, hence, also doubting the accuracy of facts presented

11

- the message getting lost in a stagy, overly planned speaking event
- the contrast to natural conversation, creating embarrassment for speaker and audience

1d. Understand the role of consciousness in skill learning.

We learn complex skills differently than we learn simple facts. A skill like public speaking involves the combination of a number of intellectual and physical operations. Most of these operations are already in your repertoire. You know how to breathe, how to raise and lower your voice, how to move your hands, how to define a new term, and how to group ideas into categories. What you may not know is how to put all of these skills together to make an effective public speech.

The learning of skills is said to progress through four stages:

1. *Unconscious incompetence.* In this stage, a person is not aware that he or she is making errors in some area and may even be unaware that some skill needs to be learned.

2. *Conscious incompetence.* A person in this stage has come to the realization that she or he is doing something ineptly and that there is room for improvement. In many cases, this awareness creates anxiety, which actually increases incompetence.

3. *Conscious competence.* In this stage, a person has taken a skill in which he or she feels incompetent, has improved, and now devotes a portion of consciousness to performing it competently. The absence of such vigilance is likely to mean a regression to more comfortable and familiar but less competent patterns. However, if the person perseveres, the awkwardness of the new behavior diminishes, and the need for self-monitoring lessens.

4. *Unconscious competence.* Now a person has integrated the learned skills well enough that she or he need not devote conscious attention to maintaining competence—it comes naturally. The skill becomes relatively effortless and maybe even fun. At this level, as a speaker, you can do more than merely talk; you are free to pay attention to audience response and to make spontaneous adjustments that enhance the quality of the communication.

A great deal of your communication behavior is unconscious. You do not think about how you move your lips to make sounds or why you speak one way with your friends and another with your boss. These may be areas of unconscious competence. At the same time, you may not be aware that you mispronounce "escape," twirl your hair when you are nervous, and often commit the fallacy of hasty generalization. These are examples of unconscious incompetence.

When do your communication behaviors receive your conscious attention? Usually when you are learning new skills or when you run into difficulties in communicating. As soon as a skill is mastered or a communication problem is solved, your behavior becomes unconscious again. This is a very efficient system. You are constantly freeing yourself to direct your conscious attention to something more challenging.

Being aware of this process is important because it makes it possible for you to be, as it were, conscious of your consciousness. As a developing speaker, you can set priorities for learning and decide where to focus your attention. Several of the misconceptions listed in **1e** can be understood in terms of this approach to skill development. The person who thinks speaking should be effortless (Misconception 2) usually wants to jump straight to Stage 4, unconscious competence, without going through the difficult process of discovering weaknesses and practicing new ways of communicating. The person who thinks speaking is impossibly hard (Misconception 3) does not trust that Stage 3, conscious competence, will eventually lead to Stage 4. In attempting to become conscious of what is usually an unconscious act, things may even seem to get worse before they get better. But if increased competence is the goal, the process is necessary, and it does pay off. Before you know it, the new, formerly awkward, behaviors are as habitual as the old ones—but they work better for you.

An imbalance in drawing on the skills of conversation, writing, and performance can result in an inappropriate focusing of consciousness. It can be beneficial to highlight one of the skill areas over the others at various stages while creating the speech (See 5.) However, if you rely on one skill area disproportionately, you place impediments in the way of becoming competent in speaking.

The person relying too heavily on the performance model is overly conscious of the physical and vocal delivery of ideas at the expense of the ideas themselves. The speaker holding this view who also sees herself as consciously incompetent can become paralyzed by self-consciousness and anxiety. At the other extreme is the speaker who is overly conscious of what he sees as competence in delivering a speech. He is so enamored with his own gestures and voice that the result is an affected and often showy style. His attention is on the presentation of self rather than on the presentation of ideas.

The speaker who relies too much on writing skills misdirects awareness in the opposite direction. She may think too much about what she is saying and very little about how she is saying it. Or he may go on talking to the formulas on the board while the audience snoozes, or become incoherent when someone asks a question that derails him from his intricately constructed train of thought.

The speaker who thinks little of writing and performance skills while concentrating on conversation can end up being very personable in a speaking event that covers little of substance. If a speaker, however, has been able to use writing and performing skills to develop the speech, the conversation skill can and should come to the fore during the speech itself.

To see a speech first and foremost as interpersonal communication should keep you from being disproportionately conscious of either your manner of speaking or the exact language of your message. In day-to-day interaction, you are usually conscious of very basic things: your reason or goal for speaking, the essential message you want to get across, your relationship with the other communicator, the response you are receiving. These are the same things you should be aware of when you speak in public.

1e. Beware of common misconceptions about public speaking that may interfere with efficient mastery of the skill.

There are many approaches to teaching public speaking and much folk wisdom about how effective speakers get that way. Mastery of speaking will come more quickly if you can avoid being affected by misinformation and oversimplifications.

Misconception 1: Good speakers are born, not made.

Some people do seem to be born speakers. In fact, they are people who have a number of component speech skills already in their repertoire or people who learn speech-related skills quickly. Regardless of appearances, no one is born an effective speaker any more than one is born a good tennis player or an accomplished violinist. Inborn predispositions and early learning mean that some people will learn faster and go further. However, anyone who has moderate coordination, adequate motivation, and sound instruction can learn to play a game of tennis or a simple tune on the violin. Similarly, virtually anyone can learn to give a clear, effective public speech.

Misconception 2: Good speaking should be easy right away.

When we watch world-class figure skaters, we are fascinated by the apparent ease with which they perform what we know are extremely difficult moves. However easy they make it look, we know that on our first time out on the ice we cannot immediately perform triple axels. We can understand that years of training, dedication, and discipline have gone into making it seem so effortless. Not everyone figure skates—but everyone communicates. We all have our share of good ideas and transmit them more or less successfully in our everyday encounters. This success may lead us to underestimate the difficulty in making the transition to more formal and public modes of expression. Many speakers think, "I know how to talk, so I must know how to give a speech." When they recognize this fallacy after a speech that fails badly, they become discouraged. In addition, the discouragement may be compounded by Misconception 3.

Misconception 3: Speaking will always be as difficult as it is when you are first learning it.

Preparing an oral message on a substantial topic for a live audience is demanding. When, at least initially, you must spend hours preparing for a short presentation, there is a real temptation to say, "Who needs it? I can't invest this much time and effort every time I have to talk before a group." Remind yourself that skills requiring effort and attention while being learned become much simpler, and almost automatic, once you reach a certain level of mastery. Remember how hard tying a shoelace was at first? Or driving? Or dribbling a basketball? Now that you have mastered one of these skills, you simply think of the goal you want to achieve; the individual operations necessary to reaching the goal happen on their own unless an unforeseen situation forces you to pay conscious attention. When you get discouraged with a speech outline that just will not fit together or with phrasing that keeps coming out wrong, remember: It *will* get easier.

Misconception 4: There are simple formulas for effective speaking.

Communicating with an audience is an incredibly complex and sophisticated act. Every public speaking event is unique. The speaker has a distinctive style and personality, the audience has idiosyncratic needs and preferences, and the situation differs from case to case. How these three factors interact creates the meaning in any speaking event. No one can give an all-purpose recipe for preparing or delivering a speech. With this in mind, be wary of books at the supermarket checkout stand or of one-day workshops that promise instant speaking success. The quickest way to do something is not automatically the best way. When you want to learn a skill well enough for it to become habitual, you obviously want to take the time to develop good habits. To return to the example of driving, you were fortunate if you were taught solid fundamental techniques. In the area of public speaking, we have some basis for agreeing on the fundamentals. Certain basic principles date back over two thousand years to Aristotle's *Rhetoric* and continue to be refined through social science research.

We have confidence in these principles. The advice in this handbook is based not on what is easiest or fastest but on what has proved to be the soundest. It is more difficult to do a thorough audience analysis than to prepare a speech for all occasions. It takes longer to develop a full-sentence outline than to jot down points in the order they occur to you. It is harder to sound conversational and look poised standing and speaking from notes than it is to read while leaning on a table. But, having learned these sound techniques, you will be more flexible and effective than if you had nothing but some all-purpose recipe.

Although the chapters of this handbook are written as prescriptions, you will not find simple dos and don'ts to apply automatically to every situation. The fundamentals of speaking are stated simply, but the application and combination of these principles depend on your good judgment in each speaking situation.

Exercise 1. Which misconceptions about public speaking do you think are most widespread? Which do you personally tend to hold? Are there other misconceptions of which you are aware?

Exercise 2. Identify a skill that you have mastered. For this skill, how did you progress through the four stages of skill learning?

Exercise 3. Can you think of an example in any area of your life in which you improved your effectiveness not so much by increasing your skill as by taking control of your consciousness and restructuring where you did and did not pay attention?

Exercise 4. What are some of your areas of conscious competence as a public speaker? Conscious incompetence? Unconscious competence? Can you speculate about some areas of unconscious incompetence or remember examples from the past?

Exercise 5. Assess the resources you have to draw upon as a public speaker by thinking about your strengths and weaknesses as a conversationalist, a writer, and a performer. Which of these areas promises to be the most transferable to your public speaking? Which of these areas will be difficult for you to transfer? Which resource might you tend to draw too much from as a speaker?

Exercise 6. What role do strong public speaking skills play in professional settings? Log on to your InfoTrac College Edition and perform a search for *public speaking*. Find an article that relates to public speaking in a profession. Summarize what the article says about the importance of public speaking within that occupation.

Chapter 2

Listening

Develop your skills as a listener to enhance your own speaking and to meet your obligations as an audience member.

2a. Recognize the relationship between effective speaking and listening.

Being a good speaker and a good listener go hand in hand. If you master the techniques in this "speaker's" handbook, we guarantee that you will be a better listener as well. You will be more appreciative of good speaking when you hear it, recognizing the art and craft that come into play to create a satisfying and successful speaking event. You will also be more critical of speaking that fails to measure up to the standards you set for yourself. At the same time, giving thought to your habits and attitudes as a listener will directly enhance your effectiveness as a speaker.

Throughout this handbook, listeners are cast as coauthors of every speech. A message does not really exist until it is received and shaped by a listener. The act of listening, though it seems to flash by, includes the reception of stimuli, the organization of them into usable chunks of sound, the identification of comprehensible words or phrases, and the interpretation of meanings. From this, it follows that listening is not something experienced passively. Rather, it is a complex set of actions that requires explicit attention and practice.

2b. Prepare to listen.

Though true impromptu speaking is exceedingly rare, people largely rely on impromptu listening. It may seem silly to talk about "preparing to listen," but taking the time to prepare before a situation that requires skilled listening is neither foolish nor necessarily instinctual.

(1) Banish distractions and get physically set to listen.

In our multitasking society, we all listen to the radio while driving, play computer solitaire while talking on the phone, or make shopping lists during a professor's lecture. So, when listening is a priority—when it should demand your full attention—you need to break that pattern. This means sitting up straight, looking at the speaker, and clearing away all materials except those needed for note taking.

(2) Stop talking.

As obvious as this advice sounds, many people enter situations in which they need to gain information and understanding from others, such as interviews, and then proceed to do most of the talking. And even when they stop talking, many listeners keep up a running internal commentary that hampers genuine listening as they focus on composing rebuttals. (See **2c.**)

(3) Decide on your purpose as a listener.

Are you listening to learn, to understand a new point of view, to evaluate a controversial argument, or to enjoy a narrative by a talented storyteller? These are four objectives out of many possible—and to achieve any one of them, or some other, requires different subsets of listening skills and approaches. As we show in **2c–2f**, your empathy, your curiosity, your critical analysis, your concentration—all come into play in different ways in different situations. Marshal the resources you need to draw on to meet your goal as a listener.

2c. When listening as an audience member, be both curious and critical.

When participating as an audience member, you do the speaker a disservice if you are so resistant to a message that you close yourself off to new ideas or different opinions. At the same time, you do *yourself* a disservice if you uncritically accept the ideas and information you encounter. Effective listeners navigate between these two extremes, balancing a charitable and open receptiveness against a critical assessment based on their real-life experiences and common sense.

(1) Show respect for the speaker.

Even if you disagree with a viewpoint or find a topic dull, recognize that speaking in public takes courage and effort. Give the gift of your full attention, and adhere to the courtesies of a public situation.

We encourage native speakers of American English to make a special commitment to respect nonnative speakers who may have an accent. Learn to listen past any unusual pronunciations or inflections that may be by-products of the speaker's original language. Remember that, in order to communicate with you, he or she has learned American English vocabulary, grammar, and syntax, and then has risked speaking publicly in that new language. In return, the only contribution required of you is to accustom your ear to a somewhat different pattern of sounds. In an increasingly multicultural society, developing an ear for various accents will serve you well in the workplace and community.

(2) Be open to the speaker's point of view.

We do not believe that it is possible to "suspend judgment" until a speaker has finished a speech. In fact, people cannot help evaluating everything they hear as they hear it. However, you can avoid a harshly critical attitude toward the speaker and make a conscious effort to substitute an attitude of curiosity. What exactly is this person saying? What led to that position? Presupposing that the speaker is sincere and well intentioned, how did he or she come to these conclusions? What assumptions were used to make sense of the information?

The discussion of reasoning (see **16a(1)**) suggests that the same data can be put together in ways that lead to highly divergent views. Get inside the speaker's world with this analytic approach, and one of two things will happen: You will be able to put your finger on the exact points you want ask questions about or refute, or you will find yourself changing, in ways small or large, to accommodate part of the speaker's view.

(3) Consciously follow the structure of the speech.

Try to identify the thesis, main points, supporting materials, and crucial links, whether these are explicitly stated or not. Discerning the structure aids your retention of content and your evaluation of its validity.

Unfortunately, not every speaker will be skilled at highlighting important points and providing clear transitions to signal relationships. To get the most out of a speech, you may need to rely on a mental template of an outline to structure the points you hear.

(4) Critically assess the speaker's claims.

As you listen to any speaker who makes a controversial claim, engage your critical thinking skills to test the validity of the argument. Ask yourself:

- Do the main points taken together justify the thesis? (See **9c.**)
- Is each claim stated clearly as a proposition that can be validated or rejected? (See **22b.**)
- Is this claim a proposition of fact, value, or policy? (See **22b.**)
- Is the support offered for each claim relevant to the point? (See **15.**)
- Does each piece of evidence meet the appropriate tests for examples, testimony, or statistics? (See **15.**)
- Are the links between the points logically drawn? (See **16.**)
- What premises are taken for granted without being stated? Are these assumptions valid? (See **16c.**)
- Are any fallacies present? (See **16f.**)
- Does the speaker misuse emotional appeals or substitute them for intellectual argument? (See **20d.**)

(5) At the designated time, ask questions.

"Bookmark" points you want to return to during the question-and-answer period. Be sure you ask genuine questions; do not give a speech, present an argument, or try to trap the speaker. Again, the spirit of curiosity should help you frame questions that deepen your understanding of what the speaker is trying to get across.

2d. When listening as a consultant to a speaker, use the principles of constructive feedback.

In one special situation, you agree to listen as more than an audience member and also to provide feedback on the decisions a speaker has made and the effectiveness of the presentation. This may occur during a practice session of a speech that is still in preparation, or it may take place after a speech has been given, with the goal of helping the speaker improve future presentations. (See **24a–24b.**) In either case, the role of critic/consultant requires a special blend of honesty and tact. The supportive critic bears in mind the fragility of partially formed ideas and the close connection between the speaker's speaking personality and her or his self-image. The following guidelines are for listeners who have been asked to give feedback.

(1) Start with the positive.

Acknowledge what the speaker has tried to do and how it has succeeded. (In working on the current edition of this book, we have relied on readers' suggestions of what to keep and what to change. Without their help, our attempts to "improve" this book might have boomeranged.)

(2) Make important comments first.

Try to communicate some sense of priority. There is no profit in refining the phrasing of a sentence if the whole point is going to be cut from the speech. Think first about whether the message makes sense and whether the overall strategy is effective. When those issues are settled, move on to the refinements.

(3) Be specific.

It is more helpful to say "You were discussing causes of the problem in Point 1 and then again in Point 3" than "This speech was disorganized." With positive comments as well, it's better to say "Comparing the greenhouse effect to the atmosphere inside a closed car really had an impact" than "The speech is great."

(4) Give suggestions, not orders.

Your comments should acknowledge the fact that your response is the reaction of just one listener and that others may differ. Also, recognize that some wonderful ideas can and should be rejected by a speaker because they simply do not fit her or his style. Bearing these things in mind, you might make a suggestion along the lines of "I have never cared for a big dramatic introduction, though I know it works for some people. Have you thought about . . . ?"

(5) Be realistic about the amount and kind of feedback a speaker can receive.

Always consider the speaker's feelings when deciding what to say and how to phrase it. There is no need to comment on aspects of a person's speech style that are tied to cultural identity. Also, some delivery problems are so obvious that viewing a videotape is a less embarrassing way to confront them. Others are so complex that a speech professional rather than a peer audience member could better address them.

Be aware of the time constraints a speaker faces. If you are giving feedback early in the development of the speech, you can make some major suggestions for revision. However, if the speech is in final rehearsal, it's probably too late to suggest going back to the drawing board. Try to offer a few suggestions that can improve this speech, rather than make the speaker wish there were time to prepare a different speech.

(6) Use the 90/10 principle.

This principle, developed by one of the authors in teaching interpersonal communication, states that people's weaknesses are rarely the *opposite* of their strengths. More often, they are the *excesses*. This awareness suggests a way of phrasing feedback: "The first 90 percent of quality A is a positive addition to your speech, but the last 10 percent of quality A begins to work in the opposite way." You are not suggesting that speakers eliminate a characteristic behavior, but that they hold it in check. Actual feedback phrased this way might sound like this: "Your informal conversational style works wonderfully for most of the speech, except that at one or two points it becomes so colloquial and casual that your credibility suffers a bit" or "Generally, the use of evidence is what makes this speech so compelling. Sometimes, though, the statistics are so dense that I find it hard to concentrate and wish that you would insert a down-to-earth example or a little of your own interpretation."

Exercise 1. The following statements might have been directed at a speaker during a feedback session. Revise them so that they better adhere to the principles of constructive feedback.

1. Your tone is too dogmatic.
2. Talk louder.
3. Your speech was interesting.
4. Take your hand out of your pocket. Use more humor. Your points don't prove your thesis.

2e. When gathering information for your speech, listen to optimize your learning.

In chapter **8**, we cover seeking information from other people as you research your speech. Effective listening in these situations will enable you to reach a deeper understanding of your topic and to use your time more efficiently. In formal interviews of experts or in more informal conversations on your topic, use the following listening techniques.

(1) Paraphrase.

Check your understanding of the points being made by paraphrasing and clarifying. This involves restating what you think you heard so the speaker can confirm or correct your interpretations: "In other words, what you are saying is . . ." or "Would this be an example of what you are talking about [give example]?" or "Are you using the term 'discrimination' with the connotation of conscious intent?"

(2) Ask follow-up questions for clarification.

In **8d(2)** on interviewing people, we suggest that you devise a list of specific, open-ended questions to keep the interview focused on the person's expertise while leaving the door open enough to permit him or her to go in a fruitful direction that you might not have anticipated. Careful listening will enable you to capitalize on this, as well as to focus on following up. As the expert answers the open-ended questions, follow up with more-specific questions in response to those answers: "You said a minute ago that the issue of class size may be more important in the long run than teacher development. Why do you say that?"

(3) Take notes.

Be sure to take notes as you gather information from another person. At first, having to write as well as listen may seem to get in the way of actually hearing what is being said. However, because the object is to optimize learning, it can make sense to employ a tool forcing you to think about what is being said so that you can write notes that make sense as well. (See **2c(3)**.)

2f. When conducting audience analysis, listen holistically.

For some purposes, listening is less about getting new information and knowledge, and more about gaining insight into a person. Listening for this latter purpose—to understand the whole person, in context, in the moment—is called holistic listening. Listening this way requires the open and receptive attitudes that characterize caring friends and helping professionals when establishing empathy is a major goal of communicating. A speaker might listen holistically when conducting audience analysis to get a general sense of how audience members see the world.

(1) Listen at multiple levels.

All utterances have a surface message. But there are other, less obvious, meanings that reveal how a person feels about the topic or the conversation. The full richness of meaning can be discovered by being alert to word choices, metaphors, and intensity of expression.

(2) Listen between the lines.

Another implication of holistic listening is that the full meaning of an utterance is embedded in the nonverbal cues that surround the words. We listen not just with our ears but with our eyes and hearts. You can observe when a person's vocal tones or body language are emphasizing or contradicting some of the words. Practice picking up on variations in emotional intensity, which can be highly revealing.

(3) Listen to the silences.

Sometimes, it's not the utterance that communicates. Form the habit of noticing what a speaker does *not* say. What topics are omitted or rushed through? When do long pauses occur? If a parent talks repeatedly about three children but never mentions the fourth, or a job applicant has a mysterious two-year gap in a résumé, or a salesperson talks about every feature of a product except price, these omissions may be significant.

2g. Avoid common listening pitfalls.

(1) Daydreaming, doodling, and disengaging

A comfortable seat, a soothing voice, too little sleep—a recipe for a snooze if you are not careful. Because good listening requires your active participation, do not put barriers in your own way. Restrain yourself and refocus if you find doodles appearing on your notebook.

It's easy for your mind to wander, in part because it takes a speaker longer to state an idea than for a listener to think the same thing. Listening experts recommend using that time differential constructively. Fill in your own examples. Think of questions to ask later. Stay mentally active in ways that connect to the speech topic. (See **2b**.)

(2) Allowing yourself to be distracted by superficial qualities of the speaker

You may notice that a speaker mispronounces a word, makes a grammatical error, sways back and forth, or has a vocal inflection that makes every statement sound like a question. Or, you may notice that another speaker has a charming accent, has a radio announcer voice, or looks wonderful in that shade of blue. In either case, letting yourself become obsessed with these traits hinders your listening to the message of the speech.

(3) Uncritically accepting a message

Don't automatically assume that if a speaker makes a statement it must be true. If something sounds wrong, it may be because it *is* wrong. Listeners share ethical responsibility for the meanings that come out of speeches. Passivity in listening abdicates this responsibility. Give ideas the scrutiny that respect for them requires. (See **2c**.)

(4) Prematurely or totally rejecting a message

Hear the speaker out. For instance, you may totally oppose capital punishment, but don't be quick to assume that this speaker is the same as all other proponents. Listen attentively, and you may hear a new argument or find an intriguing point you hadn't considered. (See **2c**.)

(5) Planning your response or rebuttal to a speech instead of listening to it

You can certainly be critical and analytical, but unless you are in a debate that requires on-the-spot refutation, don't divert your attention to the extent of composing your own messages. (See **2b**.)

(6) Failing to monitor your nonverbal behaviors as a listener

Even when you disagree or are confused, don't grimace or roll your eyes. For that matter, don't glaze over or look bored. As a matter of courtesy and respect, assume a supportive and responsive listening demeanor. (See **2c(1)**.)

Exercise 2. There are additional strategies you can use to improve your listening. Use your InfoTrac College Edition to perform a keyword search for *listening tips.*

Chapter 3

Speaking Ethics

Commit yourself to a set of ethical principles that will guide you as a public speaker.

This handbook serves primarily to help you plan and present public speeches that are effective—that is, that allow you to achieve your goals in speaking. Every speech has an additional dimension. Sometimes, a speaker succeeds in getting a point across or in persuading an audience but does so in a manner that is manipulative, exploitative, dishonest, or otherwise offensive. These cases raise questions about the ethical obligations of all speakers. Ethical questions are not about "What works?" but about "What is right?"

Fortunately, effective speaking and ethical speaking usually go together. The speaker who plays games with statistics or quotes authorities out of context frequently commits fallacies of reasoning in the process. The heavy-handed use of emotional appeals often boomerangs. Credibility suffers when listeners perceive an overly ingratiating style of speaking as insincere. There are no guarantees, though, that audiences will always respond best to those speakers who take the moral high ground; history is replete with examples of speakers who used all sorts of questionable tactics and were rewarded with great success. Ultimately, the question transcends the simple yes/no choice of "Can I get away with it?" and moves to the more complex realm of personal values, where each speaker has to decide what is ethically justifiable.

Your approach to the ethical choices involved in public speaking grows out of your more general philosophical and moral beliefs about such basic matters as how people should treat one another and what counts as honesty.

In one sense, ethical beliefs are so individual that they seem almost to be a matter of each person's own conscience. Yet our beliefs about right and wrong are highly influenced by other people. Professional groups such as doctors and lawyers have formalized codes of ethics. Other, less formal codes of ethical conduct come to us through family, religion, and culture.

3a. Be aware of the ethical implications of all human choices and the way these play out in public speaking.

If you are of a philosophical bent, you may delight in weighing the merits of the ethical systems set forth by Plato, Kant, Rawls, and Noddings. But if you are not, you can still be reflective about the pervasive and complex nature of the ethical decisions we make every day.

(1) Recognize that every action has an ethical dimension.

No decision a speaker makes is morally neutral. We speak because we believe that what we say will make a difference. And it does. The results of a speech can be as serious as persuading others to follow a dangerous course of action or as apparently harmless as wasting their time with an unprepared and unfocused message. Every time you speak, you exercise power and assume responsibility for the consequences of what you do or do not say.

(2) Recognize that ethical decisions are rarely clear-cut.

Often, the answer to questions about what works in public speaking is "It depends." Questions about what is the right or ethical course of action are just as complex. Ethics grow from our values, and values sometimes conflict. Classic communication dilemmas in everyday life deal with choices about whether to be honest (and hurt someone's feelings) or tactful (and be not quite truthful). Rarely are there black-and-white choices. The best we can do most of the time is to select the lighter shade of gray. As communicators, we are obligated to think hard about each case and to develop our judgment through experience and reflection. As time goes by, we should be more discerning about the nuances of situations and more skilled in using language and nonverbal communication in sensitive and responsible ways.

(3) Recognize that ethical decisions vary with context.

In a speech tournament, a debater might argue for legalized prostitution at 9:00 and argue against it at 10:30. In this context, it is understood that the rules of the game are to defend the assigned side of a topic as vigorously and skillfully as possible. This is considered no more unethical than the case of the football team that defends the north goal in the first and third quarters and just as vigorously defends the south goal in the second and fourth. However, if a candidate gets caught taking one position when speaking to voters in Oregon and then doing the opposite in Kansas, we judge that to be very unethical. This is because, as critical listeners in the political arena, we view such public speeches not as part of a game but as sincere statements of the speaker's true beliefs.

What you can pass off as your own words varies as well. A political leader is assumed to employ speechwriters who draft many of the speeches he or she gives. This is considered ethical because the demands on public servants make it impossible for them to personally prepare each speech they give. However, in an academic speech class, it is well understood that each person is expected to create and deliver his or her own speeches because the learning experience depends on acquiring a variety of skills and being assessed in them. To use your friend as a ghostwriter is clearly plagiarism in this context. (See **3d**.)

3b. Respect the integrity of your own core values.

As a public speaker, you are not simply a transmitter of messages; you also put yourself (your individual self) in contact with an audience. Though you may adapt and adjust and accommodate in order to meet your goals, you have an ethical obligation to be true to yourself. When you've finished a speech, regardless of how anyone else responds, you should always feel good about what you said and how you said it. Never be reluctant to speak from your heart, to express your passion and conviction on a topic.

3c. Respect the integrity of your audience.

An important tenet of many ethical systems is the recognition of each human being as a unique individual with free will and autonomy. Within this value system, those who have power over others do not have the right to use people as means to their selfish ends. Public speakers have a special kind of power. When audience members entrust you with their time and attention, you take on an obligation to treat them with fairness and concern. You have every right to pursue your own reasons for speaking, but not at the expense of your listeners' welfare. As an ethical speaker, you do not underestimate their intelligence or try to trick them into making decisions that endanger their health, safety, financial security, or other interests. And at the end of each speech, you should feel confident that the listeners are better off than before. Whether or not they agree with your points, you have given them a chance to consider ideas without coercion or manipulation so they can make rational decisions.

3d. Respect the integrity of ideas.

Because the "victim" of unethical behavior is not immediately obvious, speakers find the responsibility to honor the integrity of ideas to be the most difficult to understand, and thus the easiest to overlook. A commitment to this principle requires that you take a larger view of how each individual speech act either reinforces or abrades the fabric of society. To live and work together, people have to trust that, on the whole, communication proceeds honestly and reliably.

(1) Don't plagiarize.

Besides yourself and your audience, there are others, not present, to whom you have some ethical obligations. These are the people whose ideas and words you draw into the speech situation. Some individuals who would never dream of stealing another person's property seem to think it is somehow acceptable to steal a scholar's solution to a problem or to borrow a friend's outline for a speech. The ethics of public speaking generally proscribe using another's major ideas or exact words—or even the paraphrasing of them—without giving credit to the source. Plagiarism is a serious offense in academic institutions and in the world of publishing. Careers have been ruined when public leaders have been exposed as plagiarists.

To avoid even the appearance of unethical appropriation of speech content, form the habit of taking careful notes of the sources of all your ideas, statistics, and evidence. And when you hear a wonderful anecdote, story, or turn of phrase you might like to quote someday, make a note right then so you will remember to give credit to the source. (See **8e**.)

(2) Don't lie.

Nothing written here will stop the blatant lies of the pathological liar or the ill-intentioned person. For the majority of us, the issues surrounding honesty are much more subtle. Our courts require an oath to tell "the truth, the whole truth, and nothing but the truth," although testimony far short of that is not always deemed perjurious. And rarely do we live up to that standard in everyday interactions. For example, out of kindness, someone compliments a friend's new outfit even though it is not very attractive. Acting on the best information available, a presidential candidate promises there will be "no new taxes." A nurse tells a child that the shot "will only sting a little bit." You exaggerate a funny story to better entertain your listeners. The phrase "it depends" always crops up in conversations about what counts as a lie, a white lie, a fib, a prevarication, or tactful phrasing.

In public speaking, most people would consider that at least the following categories of behavior cross the line between honest and dishonest speech.

Making statements that are completely counterfactual
Here are two examples:

> I have no financial interest in this fitness center. I just care about your health. [when you receive a commission for every new member you sign up]

> I put my life on the line in the defense of this country. [when your military service consisted of clerical work in San Diego]

Playing word games to create a false impression
Sometimes, a speaker can use words with great precision of definition, being technically correct but totally misleading:

> One thing I learned in my many years of study in Berkeley . . . [when those many years of study consisted of reading books in your living room, not doing coursework at the University of California at Berkeley]

> In response to allegations of illegal drug use, let me say that I have never broken the laws of this country. [when the drug use was in another country]

Leaving out some part of "the whole truth" that, if known, would completely reverse the impact of the statement
Consider these examples:

> There are no convicted child molesters on the professional staff of this day care center. [but one of the five professional staff has been formally charged, and one of the nonprofessional staff has been convicted]

None of the studies in the dozens I reviewed show that smoking causes lung cancer. [but many show it is strongly linked to it]

(3) Don't oversimplify.

Another dimension of the integrity of ideas has to do with faithfulness to the facts and realities of your subject matter. Although we can hardly say that there is one "real truth" on any complex issue, we can say that some accounts are so shallow or oversimplified as to provide a basically false picture. Before you speak in public, thus contributing to and shaping the public discourse on a topic, you have an ethical obligation to do your homework, to look beneath the surface, to weigh evidence carefully, and to explore a variety of viewpoints.

3e. Understand that ethical decisions often involve weighing complex factors and competing goals.

As a speaker, you perform a delicate balancing act in many of the decisions you make. Be especially aware of the ethical impact of choices you make about language, emotional appeals, and persuasive strategies.

(1) Balance the value of using language in a lively and forceful manner against the risk of causing pain and offense.

We take issue with the old saying "Sticks and stones can break my bones, but words can never hurt me." No doubt it was born of bravado on some schoolyard where, as each of us can recall, serious emotional wounds are inflicted through verbal abuse. When occupying a public platform—and in a sense holding audience members hostage—speakers can cause similar pain by exposing some members to words they find demeaning, racist, sexist, or obscene. Some speakers routinely use violent and hateful language to make their points stronger. Language, especially in its cumulative effect, has the power to heal or to divide. In being respectful and responsible, a speaker does not have to rely on bland or wishy-washy phrasing. The wonderful richness of vocabulary, metaphor, and style provides many ways to be colorful, precise, and sensitive.

(2) Balance the importance of appealing to your audience at an emotional level against the risk of abusing emotional appeals.

For centuries, the mainstream rhetorical tradition has been that the speaker's first responsibility is to present a logically sound, well-documented argument.

33

If you adhere to this ideal, then you will not be tempted to substitute pseudo-logical emotional appeals for the logical foundation of your speech. Appeals to your listeners' feelings are legitimate ways to support and emphasize your points. We would not presume to set a precise ratio of emotional appeals to logical analysis. Nor would we judge any speaker who became a bit carried away now and then when presenting a deeply held belief. It seems, however, that a heavy reliance on appeals to needs, emotions, or values is highly suspect:

- when a need is created that listeners had not perceived before, this awareness of the need causes considerable pain or discomfort, and the action required in response to this need directly benefits the speaker
- when extreme emotional appeals are made to listeners at a time of great emotional susceptibility or are related to an area of their lives in which they are particularly vulnerable
- when emotional appeals are part of a sustained, systematic effort to make listeners feel more confused, dependent, insecure, or helpless rather than more independent, autonomous, and powerful
- when the basic logical argument underlying the emotional appeal would not be validated by dispassionate and informed observers—particularly if the speaker is unwilling to withstand such scrutiny

(3) Balance the right to use compelling persuasive appeals against the obligation to avoid simplistic persuasive techniques.

By definition, when you are persuading, you are not neutral. You have decided that one point of view is worth advocating. Using persuasive strategies as outlined in chapter 22 helps you succeed. But in your zeal to get across your point of view, you need to remember that a good speaker never short-changes the role of logical arguments supported by sound evidence. To use peripheral, edge-of-awareness methods to persuade someone to buy a certain brand of deodorant or to drive you to the airport may or may not be justified. However, to try to change other people's minds about important questions of fact, value, or policy on the basis of fuzzy thinking or irrelevant claims simply cannot be defended. The classic list of propaganda devices identified by a group of journalists some decades ago sets forth the techniques that unethical speakers can use to short-circuit an audience's rational processes.[1]

---

[1] Adapted from Alfred McClung Lee and Elizabeth Briant Lee, *The Art of Propaganda* (New York: Harcourt and Institute for Propaganda Analysis, 1939), 23–24.

Name-calling

By attaching a negative label to an idea or person, a speaker can provoke fear or hatred in an audience. For instance, highly charged words such as *sexist, terrorist,* and *unprofessional* can be used to short-circuit a listener's critical faculty. The speaker hopes this tide of emotion will gloss over the lack of substance in his or her position. (See **16f(1)**.)

Glittering generalities

At the other extreme is the speaker who generates a positive response to a concept or statement through the use of words or phrases that represent some abstract virtue. This technique attempts to convert listeners not on the merits of a position but because adoption of the position would be patriotic or good for motherhood and such.

Testimonials

Another way to generate positive emotions is to link a popular figure with some cause or product. Here, the speaker replaces sound argument with inappropriate extension of the person's credibility. Thus, an actor may be admired in his role as a doctor, but when he is used to endorse a headache remedy, he is way beyond his qualifications. In this case, the testimonial is based on a misleading impression.

"Just plain folks"

It is fine to build identification with an audience so that members are receptive to the ideas presented This process goes too far, though, when the speaker implies, "You should believe me, not because of the inherent validity of what I say, but because I'm just like you." Examples of the "we are all just plain folks here" technique include the politician whose entire platform is "I'm just a farm boy myself" and the speaker who discounts the theories and findings of educational psychologists on the grounds that "those of us who are parents know how kids really are." This device is often anti-intellectual in that it makes an unwarranted distinction between the "commonsense" notions of the audience and the "harebrained" reasoning of experts, academics, and opponents in general.

Card stacking

In this method, a speaker carefully uses only facts or examples that bolster her or his position, and the highly biased selection is passed off as representative. An opponent of hiring more police officers might stress accounts of police sexual misconduct and reports of pilferage of confiscated drugs and ask, "Do we want to spend money to put more of that kind of person in positions of authority?"

The bandwagon

This technique is useful to a speaker who wishes to discourage independent thinking. The "everyone is doing it" approach appeals to the need for security and plays on fears of being different or left out. Speakers frequently cite public opinion polls to support their positions. However, the fact that many people are in favor of some proposal does not necessarily make it right. A proposition should be sold on its merits, not on its popularity.

Transference

To make some unfamiliar thing more (or less) acceptable to an audience, many speakers will ascribe to it characteristics of something familiar. Often, there is no true relationship between the two. Consider the perennial local candidate whose last name is the same as that of a famous golf professional; although this candidate does not play the game, he always files with "Golf" as his nickname on the ballot. Similarly, characterizing video games as a "cancer spreading through our society" plays on the knowledge that probably every audience member has had firsthand or secondhand experience with that fearsome disease.

This list is far from comprehensive. Effective modern persuaders also use such techniques as snob appeal (the opposite of "just plain folks") and stand-out-from-the-crowd (the opposite of the bandwagon). Such persuasive appeals are questionable whenever they serve to:

- distract listeners from important issues
- cloud important distinctions
- introduce irrelevant factors in the decision-making process
- use emotional appeals inappropriately or excessively

Exercise 1. Here are some clichés about right and wrong that have come up again and again over the centuries. Relate each of these to problems a public speaker might face in trying to be ethical and fair.

1. What would the world be like if everyone did that?
2. Do unto others as you would have others do unto you.
3. Above all else, do no harm.
4. Can you look yourself in the mirror every morning?
5. The ends do not justify the means.

6. Two wrongs don't make a right.
7. Would you want your mother [favorite teacher/clergy member/most admired friend] to know that you did this?

Exercise 2. What can a listener reasonably expect from a public speaker? Write an "audience bill of rights" that you would like to see adopted.

Exercise 3. Evaluate these uses of emotional appeals according to the principles suggested in **3e(2).**

1. If you can pinch an inch of flesh at your midriff, you are disgustingly fat and should buy a membership in my health club.
2. We need a space-based defense system to defend our country from outside aggression.
3. The Lord came to me in a vision and said if I don't raise $8 million by April 1, He will call me home. Please send in your contributions.
4. I know how shocked you are by the death of your two classmates last week. They would certainly want you to write your congressman today demanding stricter penalties for drug pushers. You can show your love for them and save others from going through the pain you are experiencing.
5. You can make $50,000 a year in your spare time by becoming a distributor for our organization. But you must do exactly as I say. Put yourself in my hands, and I will make you rich.

Exercise 4. What are some additional consequences of cheating either in school or on the job? Use your InfoTrac College Edition to perform a search for *cheating*.

4a

Chapter 4

Overcoming Fear of Speaking

Understand, analyze, and accept your fear of speaking. Combine thorough preparation with relaxation and visualization techniques to increase your confidence.

4a. Put your fear of speaking into perspective.

Stage fright, communication apprehension, speech anxiety, reticence, shyness—these are among the most researched and analyzed variables in the literature on communication, precisely because the problem of feeling fearful about a public presentation is so widespread. Though all of this careful thought and research has not yielded any simple ways to eliminate the fear altogether, experts do offer some ways of thinking about this problem that can help you become more comfortable and confident when you speak in public.

(1) Accept some fear as normal.

Many speakers try to be completely calm in every speech situation. This is unrealistic. Whether they call it stage fright, shyness, or speech anxiety, all speakers feel some fear. One out of five people experiences rather serious fear, enough to adversely affect performance. One out of 20 suffers such serious fear that he or she is essentially unable to get through a public speech. For most of us, though, the fear can be managed and sometimes even turned to positive effect. People who perform in the public eye—actors, athletes, musicians . . . and speakers—have learned to function while concealing their fear. Despite their discomfort, they can use the rush of emotion to energize their performance.

The more speeches you give, the more confident you will become. You will recognize that fear is usually worst just prior to the speech and during the introduction. Once your speech is under way and the audience responds to you, negative emotions are often replaced by exhilaration.

(2) Analyze your fear as specifically as possible.

"I'm scared to death" is a common statement that describes the emotional intensity of stage fright. Although one survey found that people list the fear of public speaking ahead of the fear of death, few people really expect the experience to be fatal. But just what are we afraid of? An amorphous, ill-defined fear cannot be dealt with. Dealing logically with this fear requires examining its components so you can isolate a number of specific problems to be solved.

It is helpful to list your fears on paper. Be as specific as possible. If you write statements like "I'm afraid I'll make a fool of myself," ask yourself these follow-up questions: "How will I do that?" ("I'll forget my speech"); and "What will happen next?" ("The audience will think I'm dumb"). Use this format for your list:

> I am afraid that [specific event] will occur and then that [specific result] will follow.

When you have generated your list, you can classify the fears you have.

For items like "I'm afraid my visual aids won't be clear," the solution is simple. Check out the clarity of your visual aids with a few people, and if there is any problem, redesign them. As **4b** points out, many fears have roots in inadequate preparation. The mere act of writing the fears down makes them manageable and often points immediately to a solution.

Other fears on your list may relate to physical responses: "I'm afraid my hands will shake and my voice will crack." If many of your concerns fall into this category, pay special attention to the suggestions in **4c**.

A number of items on your list may relate to your failure to meet your own high standards. Recognize this fear as a positive motivation to do the best you can. Realize, too, though, that the power of suggestion is great and that dwelling on failure can cause it to happen. Use some of the visualization and verbalization techniques recommended in **4d** to create positive self-expectations.

If your fears are so pervasive you cannot even verbalize them, or if you list literally dozens, or if the consequences you dread are extreme ("I might collapse in the middle of the speech"), consider some of the more formal options mentioned in **4e**.

Finally, look at your list and decide which consequence is the one you are most afraid of. As with the college teacher who regularly lectures to a large student audience but quails at the thought of presenting a paper to twelve colleagues, for most of us the greatest fear is the fear of negative evaluation, particularly by peers or authority figures.

This fear of negative evaluation will translate into fear of your audience. As a group, they seem threatening and critical. Remind yourself that an audience is merely a group of individuals and that a speech is merely an enlarged conversation. If it would not be frightening to speak to any three or four of them, then it should not be frightening to speak to all of them together.

Of course, there are a few harsh, critical people in the world, but we have found that most listeners are charitable and supportive. They would just as soon hear a good speech, so they will, in effect, be rooting for you. In particular, they want you to appear confident. Recall how you felt when listening to very nervous speakers: Your discomfort and embarrassment were almost as great as theirs. This is testimony to the basic empathy of most audiences. Listeners will pick up on the speaker's emotional tone, so that, for instance, a tense speaker will create a tense audience. At the same time, you can actually feel an audience relax when a speaker who gets off to a shaky start hits his or her stride and the speech begins to roll.

If one technique in particular has helped people cope with stage fright, it is reconceptualizing the role of the audience, from "critic" to "recipient." A speaker must break out of the self-absorption of speech fright: "How do I look? Will they like me? Is my speech good enough?" Remind yourself that you are there not to perform but to share. Center your thoughts on hypothetical audience members who are sincere and responsive. What do you have to give these people? How will the ideas and information you offer enrich their lives?

All of this advice comes back to the importance of the conversational resource at the time of speaking. (See **1c(1)**.) Some recent research findings suggest that the best way to reduce communication apprehension is to change how you look at the public speaking event. It is not easy, but if you can think of yourself more as "talking with" the listeners and less as "performing for" them, you will feel much more comfortable.

4b. Build your confidence through thorough preparation and practice.

Why do sky divers think they can reach the ground in one piece? Preparation and practice allay their fears. Why do investors risk large sums of money? Preparation and practice have given them a clear view of the consequences. As we note elsewhere, the fact that good speakers make speech making look effortless does not mean that it is easy or uncomplicated. Their seeming lack of effort is based on extensive preparation over a period of time. The confidence they exude is also a result of preparation, not genes or fate or dumb luck. Nearly anyone can appear poised and confident giving a speech. The speaker who has prepared thoroughly can be as confident as the sky diver who has exhaustively checked all her gear or the investor who has studied innumerable projections.

If you feel uneasy about getting your speech started, perhaps your introduction needs more work. If you are fearful of losing the continuity of the speech, you may need to practice it aloud several more times to internalize the flow of ideas. If you find yourself becoming generally anxious, use this as a stimulus to go over your preparation yet again. Drill yourself on the particulars of your supporting material. Go over your outline a number of times. Whatever else you do, remember that time spent fretting about the outcome could better be used taking positive action to ensure a positive outcome.

As you prepare, follow the suggestions on practice sessions in chapter **25**. Avoid making last-minute changes in the speech, and avoid memorizing your speech and practicing it so much that the ideas become stale and your delivery mechanical.

4c. Cope with the physical effects of fear by using techniques of relaxation and tension release.

When we are fearful or anxious, our bodies react by tensing muscles to brace for attack and by releasing extra adrenaline to prepare us to fight or flee. However, these fight-or-flight responses, which are helpful when confronting a savage beast in the wild and were adaptive for our prehistoric ancestors, are not appropriate when the threat is psychological. When fear of speaking triggers our primitive sense of danger, we experience such symptoms as rapid heart rate, dizziness, butterflies in the stomach, trembling, perspiration, and dryness of the mouth. Muscular tension in the throat can cause a voice to quaver and sound strained and can even produce the unpredictable squawks of distant adolescence.

These physical symptoms will probably diminish with time as your successful experiences as a speaker make disaster appear less probable. But some degree of physical discomfort is likely to persist. Fortunately, you can master techniques to help you feel more comfortable.

When too much adrenaline makes you jumpy, physical activity usually helps to mitigate the effect. Of course, heavy exercise before a speech is impractical and overstimulating. But a brisk walk around the block or a little pacing in the hall can be enough to bring your body back to normal. If you have a few moments of privacy, light exercise will feel good—just a few knee bends, arm swings, and neck rolls. If you remain in sight of your audience before the speech, you may be able unobtrusively to clench and unclench your hands, but do not risk your credibility by going through any bizarre preparatory rituals. Once the speech begins, take advantage of the extra energy that the adrenaline provides to make your delivery more vigorous. Appropriate, dynamic gestures will help you discharge the nervous residue.

You can also handle symptoms of nervousness by learning relaxation techniques. Relaxation, like any other skill, is achieved through practice. Using any of a number of books or tapes on stress, tension, and relaxation, you can learn first to isolate the areas of your body that are tense and then to relax them. Try meditation, biofeedback, or self-hypnosis. Explore such methods as tightening and then relaxing certain muscle groups, breathing deeply, visualizing serene settings, or imagining sensations such as warmth or heaviness in parts of your body. There are great individual differences in people's responses to these techniques. Continue to experiment until you find one or more that are effective for you. After learning and practicing such techniques, you should be able to achieve relaxation, and even lower your pulse rate and blood pressure, before you speak.

Chemical aids to relaxation—alcohol, drugs, tranquilizers—are highly inadvisable. Most have side effects that impair your mental and physical performance during a speech, not to mention fabricating a false sense of security.

4d. Use positive self-suggestion to combat your anxiety.

(1) Visualize success.

Psychologists have discovered the tremendous power of visualization in influencing performance. When you experience fear, you are visualizing the most negative outcome for your speech. The more powerful your imagination, the more horrible and graphic are the disasters you can dream up. It is possible, however, to turn these fearful visions around. For example, tennis players, field goal kickers, and concert pianists, among others, have found it helpful to visualize what they are striving for.

When preparing a speech, do not let yourself think about failure. When you detect such thoughts in your mind, replace them with a positive scenario: "I will approach the lectern calmly, smile at the audience, and begin. My voice will sound strong and confident." Do not, however, set unrealistic standards of perfection. Build some contingencies into your fantasy: "If I forget a point, I'll look down at my notecard and concentrate on the main idea I am conveying." Run through these positive visualizations a few times a day before you speak. As you practice, picture the audience responding favorably to the speech. And just before you get up to speak, remind yourself of the general tone and image you wish to project: "When I get up there, I am going to communicate my sincerity and concern in a warm, natural, confident manner."

(2) Replace negative internal statements with positive ones.

One approach to reducing fears is based on a therapeutic technique called *cognitive restructuring.* In essence, it probes our mental commentaries, identifies the unrealistic or irrational statements that cause fear, and replaces them with more positive, logical, and realistic beliefs. We all have constant narrations running through our minds, voices chattering in the background. These commentaries are so familiar that we are barely conscious of them. With some introspection, you can bring them to the mental fore and examine the effect they have on your behavior. It is helpful to remember that these are not statements of fact but statements that you yourself have created and that you can choose to replace if they interfere with your efficient functioning. Once you become fully aware of the commentaries that govern your response to public speaking, you can work on replacing the unproductive beliefs with more positive ones. Table 4-1 gives some examples.

Your unproductive responses are habitual and will not change easily. At first, you will have to repeat the replacement sentences mechanically, over and over, as you might in learning a new formula or equation. Because the replacement sentences are so reasonable and logical, a large part of your mind will want to accept them. The reassuring nature of the words often helps you to become physically calmer, and this more comfortable sensation acts to reinforce the new beliefs.

Exercise 1. What false beliefs do you hold? Make your own version of Table 4-1, and create positive replacement statements to counter the beliefs.

TABLE 4-1   Replacement Statements

False Belief	Positive Replacement
My speech will be a failure unless everyone in the audience likes it.	I will be successful if most people present respond favorably.
A good speaker never says "uh" or "er."	A few nonfluencies aren't even noticed unless attention is called to them.
I'm going to go blank.	I've practiced several times, and I know the basic structure of this speech.
I can't handle this tension!	Even though I feel uncomfortable, I'm able to cope with tense situations.
I think I might faint!	Being the focus of attention will be fun, not frightening.
No one will be able to understand me because of my accent.	My listeners will want to hear what I have to say, not how I say it.
Someone will ask me a question that exposes my ignorance.	I'm not ignorant; I've researched this topic, and I'm prepared for any reasonable question.

4e. If none of the preceding suggestions works, seek assistance beyond this book.

Some fear of speaking is too deeply rooted to be remedied by the methods suggested here. If your fear of speaking is almost paralyzing, you may need help in coping with it. Research shows that even severe fear of speaking can usually be reduced to a manageable level when treated by a qualified professional. You do not need to commit yourself to a long-range course of therapy that fully explores all the causes of your anxiety. Training programs for speech fright may deal directly with the symptoms by adapting techniques used for overcoming phobias such as fear of spiders, flying, or close spaces.

Many colleges and universities offer special sections of speech classes for fearful students. Others offer ungraded workshops to supplement regular classes. These programs use systematic desensitization (a method that combines relaxation exercises and visualization), cognitive restructuring, skills training, or a combination of these and other methods. Psychologists and speech consultants also offer programs to help reduce fear of speaking. Such programs may be publicized under the names of stage fright, communication apprehension, speech anxiety, reticence, or shyness.

Exercise 2. Many articles containing practical tips for overcoming public speaking anxiety can be found by logging on to your InfoTrac College Edition and searching for *communication apprehension* or *stage fright*. Read an article under either term, and summarize the suggestions provided for controlling nervousness.

Part 2

Preparation

---

5 Planning
6 Topic Selection and Analysis
7 Audience Analysis
8 Research

Introduction

Some speakers pay little attention to the preliminary stages of preparing for a speech, subscribing to the misconception that "I know how to talk, so I must know how to give a speech." They think that the task will be easy, that sitting down a few minutes ahead of time to gather their thoughts will be enough. Others neglect the preliminary stages because they are fully aware of the difficulties they face and are impatient to get started—even before they know where they are going.

If you focus on the final *product* (a speech) rather than on the *process* (creativity), you experience a sense of urgency to produce something. When you are asked (or told) to give a speech, your immediate impulse may be to latch onto the first topic that enters your mind and start to practice expressing your ideas on the subject. After "sitting down" in this fashion, you may discover gaps in your knowledge that require a trip to the library. Once at the library, you may find it difficult to decide in which direction to press your research, especially if you are not sure of the audience you will be addressing. Later, back "sitting down," you may find that much of the information you have collected is not relevant to the purpose of your speech as it has evolved during this time.

At this point, you may wonder if the experienced speakers you have heard ever go through such wheel spinning. After all, they make speaking in public seem so effortless that surely their preparation also must be free of perspiration. Let us assure you that their performance, like that of expert athletes and musicians, reflects a mastery of skills and techniques built on careful planning and hard work. These experienced speakers save time and avoid duplicated and wasted effort by organizing their preparation. They understand that the creative process progresses unevenly and that if they persist through all its steps a creditable product will result.

Chapters **5–8** address the necessary preliminaries to the actual composition of your speech. Allot enough time for *planning*. The security of a sound master plan promotes effectiveness and increases your confidence as a speaker. Obviously, you cannot start to prepare a speech before you know *what* you are going to be talking about. Perhaps less obviously, you also need to know *why* you are going to speak. When you *select and analyze your topic,* the later steps of preparation will be easier because your topic will be more focused and your goals more concrete. Drafting a clear thesis statement and teasing out the questions implicit in that statement help direct your research and provide cues for organizing your information. When you envision the preparatory research for your speech, the tendency is to dwell on the amassing of data, examples, and arguments that deal with the topic itself. An important but frequently overlooked type of research is *audience analysis.* Through direct and indirect methods, you can obtain information about their characteristics and attitudes that will help you plan your speech. Finally, knowing *research* techniques and sources gives you access to a wide information base.

Chapter 5

Planning

Have a schedule to structure the preparation of your speech. Allow time to progress through the phases of creativity.

Preparing a substantial public speech is not a mechanical act like prepping the outside of your house for a new coat of paint. It is a creative act in which you bring into being something that has never existed before and that no one but you would have designed in exactly this form. Taken this way, speech preparation is much more like painting a picture or writing a short story. A perspective that involves creativity has implications for how you choose to manage your time.

5a. To design a unique message, allow time for the four phases of creativity.

It has been proposed that there are four phases to the creative process: preparation, incubation, illumination, and refinement.[1] For speakers, the preparation phase includes the gathering of materials, the analysis of the topic and audience, and the first stabs at putting the parts together. Incubation is a phase marked by frustration, and even despair, when the problems seem insoluble and the speech is set aside. During this phase, your unconscious mind and your peripheral awareness work on the problems. Suddenly, in a

---

[1]Based on Catherine Patrick, *What Is Creative Thinking?* (New York: Philosophical Library, 1955), 1–48.

moment of illumination, the pieces fit together, or there is a dawning awareness that grows in intensity. Illumination may occur while you are working on the project, but it is just as likely to occur when you are driving down the freeway, taking a shower, or even sleeping. Exhilaration and relief accompany this phase. You work eagerly and fluidly, accomplishing more in a few hours than you have in several days. Then the time comes for refinement. After the creative spurt, there follows a comparatively long period of checking details, fine-tuning, and polishing. Like the preparation phase, this phase is largely cognitive and requires concentration and discipline. Many creative products have never been shared with the world because the creator gave up during the refinement phase. Other fine ideas have failed to be appreciated because the speaker presented them directly after the illumination phase, without spending the needed time on refinement.

This delineation of the four-phase creative process is provided to stress the importance of allocating time for *each* phase. The rest of this chapter supplies guidance for optimizing your planning so that none of the creative phases is slighted.

5b. Make a realistic timetable for your speech preparation.

At one university, a group of public speaking instructors informally survey their students at the end of each term, asking what advice they would pass on to the next group of students. Consistently and overwhelmingly, the surveyed students' response is, "Start early." They all regret underestimating the time necessary to prepare a speech that reflected what they knew they could do. To know what is "early" enough for you, you need to spend the time to make a realistic timetable.

When professionals plan major projects—whether it is organizing a sales convention, designing a recycling campaign, or tooling up to manufacture a new product—they use a number of structured time management techniques. Without getting into the intricacies of PERT systems or Gantt charts, there are a few valuable principles that you can adapt.

(1) List the tasks you will need to complete to prepare the speech, and estimate the time needed for each.

Be sure that you include intellectual tasks such as analyzing your topic, and not just physical tasks like going to the library or making visual aids. For each task, jot down the most optimistic and least optimistic estimate of the time needed. Mentally run through some of the bleaker scenarios. What if all the periodicals you need are checked out of the library the first time you go? What if your phone rings a dozen times on the afternoon you set aside for working on the outline? Remember that certain parts of the creative process cannot be rushed. When setting a timetable for preparing your speech, always provide extra time to allow for emergencies. Speech research and rehearsal can go on when you have a headache or when you are in an emotional funk, but the creative aspects of speech organization require physical and psychological alertness.

Invest time right at the beginning to gather whatever information you need on schedules and availability of resources so that you can come up with an honest estimate of the time you will need for each task.

(2) Determine which tasks depend on the prior completion of other tasks.

This is what professional project managers call *determining the critical path*. It is not enough to schedule three hours for speech practice and call that "planning." Those three hours must occur after the speech outline is completed. The outline cannot be completed until you have articulated your speech purpose and goals, and so on. When you lay out the entire project in this linear fashion and add up the time estimates for each task, you will see if it is possible to reach your goals. Often, you will realize that the only way to succeed is to move the starting date up (usually to today!). Perhaps your speech is three weeks away, and you plan to work on it the week before. You determine that the bulk of your work can probably be done then, but you find that certain preliminary steps must be taken *now*.

To take this further, suppose your speech is due in three weeks, and the critical path adds up to five weeks. If your plans are unrealistic, it is better to discover this now than two days before the speech. In rare cases, the speech can be rescheduled for a later time, but more frequently, you must scale down your plans. Perhaps you will have to conduct two or three telephone interviews instead of eight personal ones. Perhaps you will have to go ahead with the best statistics you can find locally rather than wait for the materials that are being mailed from Washington. Perhaps you will have to substitute hand-drawn transparencies for the professional slides that take several days to process.

Ultimately, what's most important is that you decide at the outset on a schedule you can meet. Otherwise, you will end up skipping the final and crucial steps of practice and refinement altogether.

(3) Set intermediate deadlines for the major stages of preparation and practice.

In Figure 5-1, speech planning and practice is divided into four stages: initial decisions and analysis, research, development of speech materials, and practice. For each stage, the central tasks are contained in a box with a solid border. The related but less time-bound tasks are surrounded by a broken border. Generally, time flows downward and to the right in this chart. The figure also shows the transitions between stages where deadlines fall naturally. That is, the central tasks of one stage cannot really be started until the central tasks of the previous stage are completed. At some point, you must make preliminary decisions regarding a narrowed and focused topic, purpose, and thesis, and then get into your serious research. And, at some point, you must stop gathering material and put the speech together. If you do not have a speech outline soon enough, you cannot begin the first stage of practice. There is no point in scheduling your feedback practice sessions so late that you cannot take advantage of the feedback.

Sometimes, however, you must briefly retrace your steps. For instance, important new evidence may present itself, or a feedback session may show that more visual aids are needed. Such movement should be minimal, and under almost no circumstances should you be returning to tasks "way back." We feel very strongly that you should not be making any substantive changes to the speech at the last minute. During the final practice sessions, you should have complete mastery of the organization and basic content so your consciousness can center on refinement of phrasing, delivery, and timing, and on attainment of the desired audience response.

5c. Make your speech preparation an oral and collaborative process.

Because a speech is delivered orally, it should be composed orally. And because the meaning of a speech is dependent on the interaction between speaker and listeners, it should be created collaboratively. Keep the "speech as conversation" theme foremost even during those parts of preparation that require you to draw on your skills as a writer or performer.

Although you cannot practice "the speech" until your basic outline exists, one form of oral preparation begins with your first idea. This is the ongoing talk suggested by the large, dotted section in the Practice column of Figure 5-1. Talk to yourself about your topic. Talk to other people. Try out your

FIGURE 5-1 Speech Planning and Practice

Initial decisions and analysis	Research	Development of speech materials	Practice
			Ongoing talk
	Preliminary research Do background reading Locate resources		
		Jot down possible points Develop rough working outline	
	Main research effort Investigate articles and books Conduct interviews		
		Develop full-sentence outline of points to be covered Add supporting materials and attention factors to outline Prepare introduction, conclusion, and transitions	
	Continuing research Check details Locate a few specific facts/statistics Watch daily paper/newscasts for latest applications		
		Prepare visual aids and handouts Prepare speech notes Make minor revisions to content and style	
Select topic Narrow topic Clarify purpose Frame thesis statement Analyze topic Analyze audience			Developmental practice sessions Feedback practice sessions Refinement practice sessions

ideas and words, seeing if they make sense. You are not, however, practicing your speech in front of other people. Work your ideas into conversations over lunch and chats with colleagues and friends. You do not need a reaction to every idea from each individual you talk to. After talking to a number of people, you will find that you have begun to word the speech.

No person speaks in a single voice. Even when you sit alone at your desk preparing your speech, the ideas and intonations of your collaborators influence you. This is natural and should be used to your advantage.

If you are fortunate, you may be able to add continuity to this oral and collaborative process by structuring it to embrace a more formal method for obtaining feedback and support. (See **25.**)

5d. To present a speech that achieves the flavor of enhanced conversation, focus on different resources at different phases of preparation.

The first chapter of this handbook established that most speakers already have at their disposal substantial resources as conversationalists, writers, and performers. During the planning and practice stages of a speech, these are deployed in different ratios at different times to achieve a successful final presentation. Each of the resources is always present, or at least should be, throughout the process, but emphasis and attention shift according to the phase of the process. Figure 5-1 illustrates these changing priorities. Generally, during the preparation stage, writing skills come to the fore. *This does not mean that you write out your speech!* Rather, it means that your conscious competence is directed toward issues of selecting points, arranging them, choosing your support, and thinking of apt illustrations. You give attention to transitions between sections and begin to refine the language of the speech.

Once "the speech" exists in some form, you move into a practice phase, in which the importance of performative elements increases. Through oral practice, you can experiment with vocal and physical dynamics to emphasize certain points and to create certain effects. Here, you also introduce visual aids, props, and movements to begin to see how the entire presentation will come together to fully engage your audience.

If these resources are fully explored during preparation and practice, the writer and performer will recede during the actual speech, and the conversationalist will come forth. We use the term *enhanced conversation* to describe the general tone that is effective for almost all speech situations. You will seem conversational and natural, and your conscious attention will be centered on the give-and-take with the audience. Because of the time spent drawing on the writer's resources during preparation and on the performer's resources during practice, however, the conversation will be greatly enhanced over what would likely occur spontaneously. Your thought is more focused, your language is more graceful, your voice is more expressive, and your physical energy is more directed than in everyday talk—but naturally so. That is because the enhancements were internalized during the conscious competence work of preparation and practice and are revealed as unconscious competence during presentation. The nature of these changes is detailed in various chapters of the handbook. (See **17**, **24**, **26**, and **27**.)

5e. Avoid these planning pitfalls.

The errors that speakers make in their planning are fairly predictable, reflecting common human tendencies such as procrastination. Being alert to the pitfalls listed next will go a long way toward preventing you from accidentally sabotaging your efforts. Your topic, whatever it is, deserves the best development, and your audience deserves the fruits of that development.

(1) No time for incubation

Remember that the creative process cannot be forced. Be sure to schedule your preparation to give yourself time for reflection before settling down to the job of composing your speech. The best ideas come to you when you live with your topic for a while and let your unconscious and conscious minds interact.

(2) No margin for error

If you overrate your efficiency, you may cut your preparation time so close that even minor interruptions endanger the success of your presentation. And if a major catastrophe occurs, you may not be able to fulfill your commitments at all. Put together a schedule that gives you some breathing room.

(3) "Writer's" block

Although we stress the ways that speech preparation differs from writing, this pitfall is much like the paralysis that many writers face. As authors, we know all about the tendency to do a little more research, a little more thinking about it, a little more desk straightening, and even a little more floor scrubbing if that is what it takes to avoid the awful moment of having to confront a blank sheet of paper. For your speech to succeed, you must stop getting ready to create and start to create—well before the final deadline.

(4) "Speaker's" block

Do not put off working orally until the last moment. Unless you are one of the world's great speakers, the first time you give any particular speech aloud will not showcase its strengths. Make sure this is not in front of an audience by starting talking early in the process.

Chapter 6

Topic Selection and Analysis

Select an interesting and manageable topic, and determine what response you hope to evoke with the topic. To provide an even sharper focus for your preparation, distill your entire message into a concise thesis statement.

Do not settle on the first topic that occurs to you. Consider a number of different topics and examine their various facets. When you have chosen a promising one, narrow it down and crystallize your reasons for speaking about that subject.

6a. Select a speech topic.

As a speaker, you have varying degrees of freedom in topic choice, according to the situation. At one pole is the office manager who is told to give an oral report on the effectiveness of the current secretarial assignment system. At the other is the respected speaker who is given carte blanche to speak on a topic "you feel is important" or the student who is told, "Friday morning you will speak third and persuade us to do something, anything."

Most speaking situations fall between these extremes. You may be asked to welcome delegates to a conference or to speak to the Rotary Club about the economy. In these cases, you still have to select a theme for your talk. Even when the general topic is set, you need to home in on an approach that will fit you, the audience, and the situation.

(1) Draw the topic from your own experience, expertise, and interests.

You bring a body of knowledge to the speech situation. Perhaps this is why you have been asked to speak about your experiences in the Peace Corps [or stock market or Blue Angels]. Or your background may be the springboard for discovering a topic or a slant on a topic that can be developed into a compelling and substantial speech. You should ask yourself a number of questions to help you do this.

In answering the questions that follow, do not stop to evaluate every answer as you write it down. You want to generate a list of possible topics by brainstorming. With this technique, you do not let your internal censor dismiss any idea as not good enough for a speech topic. The principle behind brainstorming is that even an unworkable idea may trigger a good one, and a group of mediocre ideas may combine to make a great one. Therefore, you should not judge any one idea until you have amassed a list of many. Answer these questions in as many different ways as you can think of, even if some seem silly. Later, you will select your best topic in terms of audience and occasion.

What unusual experiences have you had?

Consider places you have traveled, jobs you have held, and events in which you have become enmeshed. Perhaps you have ridden in a hot air balloon or worked in the inner city or been a hostage in a bank robbery. Obviously, these are stories worth telling in the right context. However, do not overlook aspects of your experience that you take for granted but that might be interesting to others. If you are one of seven children or have always been self-employed or grew up speaking one language at home and another at school, you can increase your audience's understanding of events unfamiliar to them by sharing your experiences with them.

What special knowledge or expertise do you have?

Each of us has developed mastery in certain areas. How do you make your living? If your work in the real estate field has provided you with a good income, you can be certain that there will be an audience eager to hear about your techniques. Yet, a job need not be high paying or prestigious to generate speech topics. People like to know how things work. They are often quite interested in hearing about procedures, even ones that are considered mundane by the persons performing them. Jokes aside, how is your baggage routed from one airport to another? What goes on backstage at a concert?

Or, instead of talking about the mechanics of your work, you can build a speech around the people you meet in that context. If you enjoy observing people and have a flair for describing their behavior, you could become an informal anthropologist and social psychologist. You can give special insights into human nature or some aspect of our culture through topics like these: dog owners as seen through the eyes of a letter carrier, the curious tribal customs of the used car lot, and patterns of interactions in a dentist's waiting room.

Your course of study in school has increased your knowledge in areas that perhaps are obscure to your potential audience. Think, too, about the talents, hobbies, and skills you have developed. Could you build a speech around rewiring your house, playing a musical instrument as relaxation therapy, preparing gourmet meals for backpacking, or describing the British class structure as conveyed through mystery novels? You may have researched in depth topics that appeal to you: Woody Allen movies, holographic technology, varieties of beer, Sudanese history, religious cults, and so on.

What strong opinions and beliefs do you hold?

Suppose you are at a party and suddenly find yourself arguing fervently about gun control. The conversation up to this point had dealt with a number of equally controversial subjects, but your contributions were not so impassioned. What topics stir you up in this way? These issues, which probably touch on your core values (see **20c**) frequently make good speech topics. You will be less self-conscious if you are speaking from a sense of deep conviction. And the audience will be more generous in spirit, even when they are in opposition, if they see that you are speaking from the heart.

Besides those issues that can provoke you into heated debate, there are others that fascinate you intellectually. Do you have a pet theory about why the nuclear family has declined, why relationships fail, what makes a good manager, or whether there is other sentient life in the universe? Explaining the basis of your beliefs can make an excellent speech.

What would you like to know more about?

Perhaps, ever since signing the note for your most recent business loan, you have been curious about the workings of the Federal Reserve System. After reading about shifting alliances in central Europe, you might have become interested in the roots of the breakup of the Soviet Union. Coming out of the movie theater after seeing the most recent space adventure, you might have resolved to go to the library and look up information on the International Space Station. Use the occasion of giving a speech as an opportunity to research some topic that has piqued your curiosity.

(2) Select a topic appropriate to the audience and occasion.

By brainstorming answers to the questions in **6a(1),** you have created a possible subject list of great variety. To choose the one topic on which you will speak, you next need to think about the audience and the occasion. (See also **7.**) Two more questions you can ask yourself at this point are:

- What are *these* people's expectations? [audience]
- What are these people's expectations *now?* [occasion]

Knowing who the audience is and why its members are gathered together can help you rule out a number of topics. A speech on the fluctuating silver market could be interesting, but not to a seventh-grade class. Japanese architecture would probably not be the best subject for a speech given to the American Medical Association. Selling a product, promoting a candidate, or proselytizing for a faith would be out of place in a eulogy.

When you have removed the inappropriate subjects from your list, you then need to find the *most* appropriate of the remainder. Empathy is your best tool. Imagine sitting on those hard chairs in the boardroom or classroom. What would you sit still to hear?

(3) Select a topic that is both timely and timeless.

You may still have more than one possible topic on your list even after going through the processes in **6a(1)** and **6a(2).** Other things being equal, the best topics are those that are both timely and timeless. Certain issues have always been and always will be part of human discourse. The rights of the individual versus the rights of the group and the need for security versus the need for adventure were being discussed 1,000 years ago, 100 years ago, and this past year; they will continue to be discussed by our descendants. When you tie a contemporary event to one of these enduring human dialogues, you link the timely and the timeless.

Neither one of these conditions by itself is an indication that the topic will be a good one. Consider the criterion of timeliness. If an event has been front-page news for two weeks, a speech on that topic may be timely. But unless you can tell your audience what it all means in more universal terms, you probably will give them little that they do not already know. You have wasted their time. The reverse is true as well: Your audience can miss or fail to be interested in the profundity of your topic if you do not tie it into the fabric of their current existence. A profound, timeless topic should have a timely application. A timely speech should point out the timeless implication of the subject.

TABLE 6-1	Timely and Timeless Topics	
Timely (but Potentially Trivial)	Timeless (but Potentially Diffuse)	Timely and Timeless
There was a major confrontation last week when the Ku Klux Klan held a rally downtown.	Freedom of assembly must be protected for everyone.	Last week's confrontation over the Ku Klux Klan rally raised important questions about what restrictions, if any, should be placed on freedom of assembly.
I took a trip to Quebec.	Travel helps people understand diversity of human cultures.	My trip to Quebec helped me to understand my own culture by contrasting it to another.
Our company has adopted a new profit-sharing plan.	The best management philosophy is one that treats the employees like partners.	Our new profit-sharing plan will benefit the employees directly and reflect an enlightened philosophy of management.

Table 6-1 shows how topics that are too narrowly contemporary or too broadly universal may be altered to meet these criteria. Notice the different kinds of speeches to which the timely/timeless standard can apply.

Exercise 1. Suppose that each of the following topics is of great interest to you and that you are qualified to speak about them:

1. The Martial Arts
2. Mediation Before Litigation
3. Problems of our Social Security System
4. The Way Television Commercials Are Made
5. Western Misconceptions About Islam

Which would be best for each of the following audiences? Select more than one if you wish, but justify your answers.

a. A speech class in which the assignment is to support a thesis with factual and statistical evidence from several different sources
b. A community service club luncheon
c. A neighborhood youth group
d. A current events study group
e. A keynote address at a business conference

Exercise 2. Explain how each of the topics could be developed to reflect both timely and timeless concerns.

6b. Narrow your topic.

An old public speaking joke goes as follows:

A: I'm giving a speech at the annual banquet tonight.
B: What are you going to talk about?
A: Oh, about 15 minutes.

Speaker A's answer is not wholly facetious. It acknowledges the important principle that the selection of a topic is not complete until that topic has been narrowed to accommodate the constraints of time.

The main advantage of limiting a topic is to ensure depth of analysis. To avoid superficiality, you have to keep one eye on the clock while preparing your speech. To get into a topic, to get under the surface, you have to limit yourself to the number of points that can be adequately developed in the time available. You can expedite your research and preparation by narrowing your topic from the beginning. Thus, instead of looking up all the books and articles about higher education, you can focus on those related to the financing of community colleges, or to pass/fail grading, or to coed dormitories, as the narrowed topic warrants.

(1) Determine the number of ideas you can cover in the time allotted.

The average speaker utters 100–150 words per minute. If you speak very rapidly or very slowly, you may fall outside this range. Chances are, though, that your rate of speaking is somewhere near 125 words per minute. If you want to check your rate, see **26a(2).**

A typical journalistic paragraph of simple sentences runs about 125 words. Thus, a very general rule of thumb is that an average speaker speaks about one short paragraph per minute. If your material is highly technical or interspersed with statistics, dialogue, and dramatic pauses, or if you speak slowly, you had better allot two minutes per paragraph. This system, though rough, allows you to do some realistic narrowing of your topic.

For instance, if you plan on speaking informatively for 8–10 minutes on the U.S. criminal justice system, you need to set aside at least 1–2 minutes for the introduction and 1 minute for the conclusion. This leaves 6–7 minutes for the body of your speech. If you plan to talk about the history of the criminal justice system, the causes of crime, the way crime statistics are calculated, the workings of the probation department, and the difficulties of recruiting police officers, you can spend about 1–1½ minutes on each sub-

TABLE 6-2	Time Allotment of Speech Elements
Speech Part	**Minutes**
Introduction	
Welcome audience	1
Tell anecdote about Uncle Bob	1
State topic and preview main points	1
First main point	
Explain and define	1
Subpoint	2
Subpoint	2
Second main point, etc.	
	—
	—
	—
Conclusion	
	2
	20

ject. But can you do the subjects justice? By narrowing the topic to one of these areas, you can develop two subpoints for 3 minutes each or three subpoints for 2 minutes each—a more realistic plan.

The same principle can be applied to longer speeches, business presentations, and lectures. A 20-minute speech can be thought of as twenty short, simple paragraphs or ten longer, more developed paragraphs. Table 6-2 shows how this speech might be broken down.

Exercise 3. A speech has 2,900 words. Roughly how long would it take for the average person to deliver it?

(2) Select a few main ideas based on thorough analysis of the audience, the occasion, and your own strengths as a speaker.

In the preceding section, knowing that the criminal justice speech should be cut to one or two main points does not tell you *which* one or two to select. Consider the following questions, which can help you develop your ability to narrow a topic effectively.

Which aspects of your topic are best covered in the public, oral mode?

Is it wise to spend five minutes reading a list of numbers? Probably that data should be handed out for further study and the *meaning* of the key numbers discussed instead.

Also ask yourself: Is this an important topic to discuss in a public speech? A speech should not be used to transmit routine information, to discuss specialized problems of a small portion of the audience, or, of course, to indulge the speaker's ego.

Which aspects of your topic are best suited to this audience and occasion?

Let audience analysis direct the emphasis of your speech. Select those points that relate most directly to the needs, attitudes, knowledge, and expectations of your listeners. (See **7**.)

Which aspects of your topic can you present most effectively?

Select those points on which you have the most knowledge and in which you have the most interest. Do you excel at explaining complex material? At making abstract ideas personal? Are you better with human interest stories than statistics, or vice versa? Select those points that best fit your speaking personality.

Exercise 4. Select a speech on the Sample Speeches Web site. Suppose that you were allotted one third the time needed to give that speech. How would you limit the topic?

Exercise 5. Look at the outline on comic books in **10b**. If you were to present that speech to avid comic collectors, how would you limit the topic? Look at the outline on women in the labor force in **11b**. How would you limit that topic if you were given 15 minutes to speak to a high school social studies class?

6c. Clarify the purpose of your speech.

Each speech has a general purpose, a specific purpose, and a set of desired outcomes.

(1) Identify the general purpose of your speech.

What is your intention? Are you trying to change people's minds? To teach them something? To entertain them?

For instance, if you decide on "Jazz" as your topic and then narrow that topic further to "Jazz Saxophone Players," there are several possible speeches you might give. Do you want to explain the harmonic theories of Ornette Coleman to your audience? Or do you want to convince them that Sonny Criss has not been given the attention he is due? Or perhaps you want to inspire your audience by telling of the comebacks of Stan Getz and Art Pepper after they overcame drug problems.

The general purpose of a speech can be classified in one of three ways:

Inform: A speech designed to explain, instruct, define, clarify, demonstrate, or teach

Persuade: A speech designed to influence, convince, motivate, sell, preach, or stimulate action

Evoke: A speech designed to entertain, inspire, celebrate, commemorate, or bond, or to help listeners relive

The speech to evoke is often called the "speech to entertain," but we feel that this label unfortunately has come to connote snappy patter and one-liners, which is too narrow a definition. An evocative speech elicits a certain feeling or emotional response. The emotion or feeling can be one of fun, escape, and diversion—entertainment, if you will—but it can also be solemn and serious, as in a eulogy, in which a sense of community and an appreciation of individual worth may be evoked.

You will quickly discover that no speech has only one purpose. Most have a combination, but with one purpose usually dominant. For instance, a classroom lecture is used primarily to teach, but at the same time it can be used to shape attitudes. The purpose of a campaign speech is to drum up support for the candidate, but the speech can also entertain. An excellent sermon might do all three: inform, persuade, and evoke.

Exercise 6. Describe how each of the following topics could be made into a

    a. Speech to inform
    b. Speech to persuade
    c. Speech to evoke

Topics:
    Trains
    Natural Childbirth
    Investing in Gold
    Men's Fashions

(2) Determine the specific purpose of your speech.

Knowing which of the three purposes—to inform, persuade, or evoke—is predominant in your speech will help you in the next step: deciding what you really want to accomplish with your topic. In phrasing this purpose, isolate your central reason for speaking. You will have many incidental goals, but you cannot select and organize your materials without a very clear set of priorities. Be both specific and realistic about the purpose you set for yourself. Do you want to teach your listeners all about chess in a 10-minute speech, or do you simply want to give them the basic principles of the game? Do you want them to buy your company's telecommunications system or merely to agree to let you demonstrate it to a group of managers? Do not go any further until you can complete this sentence:

> If there is one goal I want to achieve in this speech, it is to . . .

At this point, your topic should have a clear focus:

Not:	My specific purpose is to inform the audience about politics.
But:	My specific purpose is to inform the audience about the role of the two-party system in American politics.

Not:	My specific purpose is to persuade the audience against drunken driving.
But:	My specific purpose is to persuade the audience of the need for stiffer penalties for those convicted of drunken driving.

(3) Specify the desired outcomes you seek from your listeners.

Once your goal is phrased in the terms of what *you* want to do, turn it around and phrase it in terms of what you want your *audience* to do:

> If there is one action I want my listeners to take after my speech, it is to . . .

In other words, if your speech is a success, what will your audience do? This is called the *primary audience outcome.*

Not:	My desired outcome is to sell this product.
But:	My desired outcome is to have you buy this product.

Not:	My desired outcome is to explain photosynthesis.
But:	My desired outcome is to have you understand the workings of photosynthesis.

After you have identified the single most important audience outcome that you are looking for, you can clarify your speech goals even further. Implicit in every general goal statement are many contributing subgoals that may also be phrased in terms of concrete audience behaviors. If your overall goal is to persuade members to take up the guitar, you want them first to *decide* that this is a good idea, second to *purchase* a guitar, third to *sign up* for lessons, and last to *continue* to practice.

Notice the significance of the verbs in each case. The emphasis is on the behavior you want the audience to adopt. This sort of goal analysis has proved effective in recent years in both education and business. In the schools, teachers have learned to phrase their previously fuzzy goals as concrete behavioral objectives, thereby enhancing both teaching and learning. In the business world, the management-by-objectives movement has helped employers and employees analyze tasks and set definite goals and deadlines.

The same procedures will help you plan your speech. Break the primary audience outcome into components, paying particular attention to using phrasing with verbs that describe overt actions rather than general states of mind.

"I want my audience to *appreciate* art" is fine for a primary audience outcome, but you must go further and ask yourself how you will know if you have succeeded. What, exactly, are people doing when they are appreciating art? If you think about the specific behaviors or operations that contribute to appreciating art, you will come up with a list like this:

- *Go* to galleries.
- *Read* books on art.
- *Create* pieces of art themselves.

Observe how speech purposes and outcomes can be crystallized for each type of speech:

General purpose: To inform.
Specific purpose: To inform the audience of the steps of a successful job interview.
Primary audience outcome: I want my audience to become familiar with the steps of a successful job interview.
Contributing audience outcomes: I want my audience to:
- *distinguish* between the job interview and other types of interviews.
- *understand* what the interviewer expects.
- be able to *list* the four phases of the typical employment interview.
- *recognize* the importance of appearance and body language.

General purpose: To persuade.
Specific purpose: To convince the audience that changes in individual behaviors are needed to protect our environment.
Primary audience outcome: I want my audience to commit themselves actively to environmental concerns.

Contributing audience outcomes: I want my audience to:
- *use* public transportation when possible.
- *minimize* the use of nonbiodegradable materials.
- *recycle* paper, glass, aluminum, and steel.
- *make* their dwellings energy efficient.
- *support* environmentally oriented political candidates and *contribute* money and time to environmental causes.

General purpose: To evoke.

Specific purpose: To celebrate the successful conclusion of a complex project and honor the individuals responsible for the success.

Primary audience outcome: I want my audience to experience a sense of community with all those who participated in the PowerCom software development project.

Contributing audience outcomes: I want my audience to:
- *recognize* the contribution and achievement of each group: engineers, designers, writers, testers, trainers, and support staff.
- *feel* pride in their individual contribution.
- *relive* some of the intermediate successes.
- *identify* with each other by laughing at "in jokes" that only someone involved in this project would understand.
- *share* in the warmth felt for Annette, the "spark plug" of the development group.

Note: The specific outcomes do not necessarily have to echo the language of the speech purpose. Sometimes, for instance, it is essential to inform the audience about specific points before they can be persuaded or to lighten a primarily informative speech with some entertainment. As a rule, though, the majority of the audience outcomes should be compatible with the general purpose of the speech.

Exercise 7. Look at all of the speeches on the Sample Speeches Web site. Identify them by their type—informative, persuasive, or evocative. State the one-sentence specific purpose you think each speaker had.

Exercise 8. List at least four contributing audience outcomes that might be developed for each of the following primary outcomes. Use specific, concrete verbs to describe the behaviors.

1. I want my audience to learn about genetic engineering.
2. I want to have my audience experience the thrills of a trip to the Galápagos.
3. I want my audience to drive more safely.

6d. Develop a clear thesis statement to guide your analysis of the topic.

(1) Frame a thesis statement as a single declarative sentence that states the essence of your speech content.

Many management consultants talk about the necessity of an organization's coming up with a short mission statement to focus the energy of its staff, giving them something concrete against which to gauge the appropriateness of any contemplated action. In a similar vein, your topic analysis needs a thesis statement that gives you something concrete against which to test ideas. In contrast to your "purpose" and "outcomes," your thesis sentence states your topic as a proposition to be proved or a theme to be developed. This sentence, sometimes referred to as the *central idea,* gives your speech this focus. It helps you make the transition from thinking about where you want to end up (your goal) to how to get there.

A thesis statement should not merely announce your topic. It should capsulize what you plan to say about the topic. The rationale for insisting on the complete sentence is the clarity of thought that comes when you must delineate both what you are talking about (the subject of the sentence) and what you are saying about it (the predicate of the sentence). A thesis statement whose single declarative sentence is "Today I will talk about roses" makes *you* the subject and makes the fact that you *are talking* the predicate—hardly the essence of your speech content. However, "Roses are beautiful" makes the topic (roses) serve as subject and the point being made about it (they are beautiful) the predicate. See **11b** for further discussion of the role of propositional phrasing in testing the relevance and completeness of ideas.

Be sure that the thesis statement includes enough information to differentiate your approach from other possibilities.

Informative Speech

Not: My speech is on gangs.
Or even: Young people find gangs attractive.
But: There are a number of sociological and developmental reasons for gangs being attractive to youths.

Evocative Speech

Not: We are here to dedicate the new hospital wing.
Or even: The opening of this wing is a great day for O'Connor Hospital and the community.

69

But:	This new surgical wing reflects the efforts of many dedicated fund-raisers and increases the quality and quantity of medical care available in our community.

Persuasive Speech

Not:	Something must be done about tuberculosis.
Or even:	Drug-resistant TB is on the increase and should be combated.
But:	The threat of a resurgence of TB requires a major governmental program of education, research, and treatment.

(2) Analyze your topic by breaking your thesis statement into a list of questions to be answered.

When chemists analyze a substance, they identify its components. As a speaker, you go through a similar process when you break up a topic to find all the subtopics within it. In persuasive speeches, this takes the form of a fairly structured issue analysis. (See **22b**.) Informative and evocative speeches require analysis as well. By committing yourself to developing a thesis, you take on an obligation to discover and answer a set of questions. These questions are the ones your listeners will be asking themselves before they accept your thesis. Thus, they are the ones you should identify before proceeding with your research.

Do not be restricted by the wording of your thesis. In analyzing the grammatical structure of a sentence, you probably learned to fill in the understood subjects and predicates. "Pick up that book and then let go" has to be seen as "(You) pick up that book and then (you) let go (of it)."

Consider this thesis for a persuasive speech:

Like other industrialized nations, the United States has a castelike social system based on race, sex, and age.

Embedded in this thesis are six questions your audience will be asking as they listen:

- Does the United States have a castelike system?
- Is the stratification based on race?
- Is the stratification based on sex?
- Is the stratification based on age?
- Is the United States an industrialized nation?
- Are these characteristics shared by other industrialized nations?

For a speech about comic books, you might develop the following thesis sentence:

> With their scope, history, and influence, comic books are an interesting component of American popular culture.

For this informative speech, four questions present themselves:

- What is the scope of comic book themes?
- What is the history of the comic book?
- What influence have comic books had?
- Are comic books an interesting component of American popular culture?

Even in an evocative speech at a retirement dinner, you might capsulize your message into this thesis sentence:

> Because of Braulio Fuentes' contributions to our organization and his personal qualities, we will miss him but wish him well in his retirement years.

As you think about developing this talk, you will identify four questions you ought to investigate:

- Exactly what contributions has he made?
- What personal qualities do we value in him?
- In what ways will he be missed?
- What specific good wishes do we have for his retirement?

To answer these, you can look into Mr. Fuentes' history with your organization. Ask those who work with him what they will miss most, and find out if he plans to travel, raise rare orchids, or start a consulting firm.

The answers to these questions will not necessarily be the main points of your speech, and you might not develop your ideas in this order. However, the analysis serves to direct your research and prevents you from any glaring oversights.

Exercise 9. Read one or more of the speeches on the Sample Speeches Web site, and formulate a single declarative sentence that best sums up the content. You may find the actual sentence in the speech itself, or you may, in the case of an implicit thesis, have to draft a sentence of your own.

Exercise 10. Evaluate the following as thesis statements for a speech. If they are not effective, rewrite them.

1. What shall we do about the problems of the cities?
2. Cambodia—its history, its people, its problems—will be the topic I will cover today.
3. The need for mandatory drug testing for athletes!
4. Taxpayers should not have to subsidize art that is pornographic or unpatriotic.
5. How to make a Caesar salad.
6. There are three causes of congressional gridlock.

Exercise 11. Look at the thesis statement in each of the speeches on the Sample Speeches Web site. Identify the questions implicit in each. Do the speakers address each issue?

Exercise 12. Identify the questions embedded in each of these thesis statements:

1. Grading on the curve is inaccurate, unfair, and elitist.
2. A cruise is an educational way to relax, make friends, and see the world.
3. Because the property tax is essentially regressive, it is an uncertain and inequitable source of revenue for the city.

6e. If necessary, select a speech title.

Although every speech needs a thesis and a purpose, not every speech needs a title. A title is necessary when there is to be advance publicity, when there is a printed program, and, usually, when the speaker is going to be formally introduced. Unless there is a definite deadline to announce your title, you can defer selecting one until after the speech is composed.

A title can take any grammatical form. It can be a declarative sentence, a question, phrase, or fragment:

> "Freedom of Speech Is in Jeopardy"
> "Is Free Speech Really Free?"
> "Threats to Free Speech"
> "Free Speech: An Endangered Species"

Note: Do not confuse the thesis statement with the speech title. The thesis statement is a declarative sentence essential for the organizing and composing of the speech. The title is not.

An effective title should pique interest in your subject and make the audience eager to listen. Sometimes, a metaphor, quotation, or allusion that is central to the speech can be part of the title:

"Who Will Be David to This Modern Goliath?"
"Social Security: A House of Cards"
"With Malice Toward All"
"Feeding Problems, Starving Opportunities"[1]
"From Little Rock to a Hard Place"[2]
"Relaxing at High Speed"[3]
"Mending the Body by Lending an Ear"[4]

In an effort to be clever or profound, do not devise a title that will totally mystify your audience, like:

"Babaloo!"

or

"The Heraclitus of Sycamore High"

Nor should you select a title that promises more than you can deliver. That is false advertising. Do not announce:

"How to Double Your Income While Working Two Days a Week"

and then give a speech on how to make one's first investment in income property. Likewise, a title such as:

"Digging Up Dirt at the White House"

might lead your audience to think that your speech has more titillating content than your recollections of work as a gardener in the White House Rose Garden. This may sell tabloids at the supermarket, but it is not considered good speaking technique.

Keep the title concise. Avoid the sort of windy title favored by 18th-century novelists:

"The Fortunes and Misfortunes of the Famous Moll Flanders & c. Who was Born in Newgate, and during a Life of continu'd Variety for Threescore Years, besides her Childhood, was Twelve Year a Whore, five times a Wife (whereof once to her own Brother), Twelve Year a Thief, Eight Year a Transported Felon in Virginia, at last grew Rich, liv'd Honest, and died a Penitent, Written from her own Memorandums . . . by Daniel Defoe."

---

[1]Richard J. Mohoney, *Vital Speeches of the Day* 60, no. 8 (1 Feb. 1994): 236–37.

[2]Malcolm S. Forbes, Jr., *Vital Speeches of the Day* 60, no. 11 (15 March 1994): 336–38.

[3]Jeff Davidson, *Vital Speeches of the Day* 68, no. 3 (15 Nov. 2001): 87–91.

[4]Carol Koehler, *Vital Speeches of the Day* 64, no. 17 (15 June 1998): 543–44.

and perpetuated by academics:

> "A Quasi-experimental Investigation of Latency of Response, Self-disclosure and Turn Taking in Same Sex Dyads: Etiology, Manifestations and Implication."

In short, do not give your speech in your title.

Exercise 13. Evaluate the titles of the speeches on the Sample Speeches Web site. Are they effective?

Exercise 14. Select titles for the speeches outlined in **10b** and **11b**.

Exercise 15. Find the lettered examples that match each of these categories:

1. General topic
2. Narrowed topic
3. General purpose
4. Specific purpose
5. Primary audience outcome
6. Contributing audience outcome
7. Thesis statement
8. Analysis question
9. Title

a. Have more lives been saved when a CPR-trained person has been present?
b. To convince the audience that, the greater the number of people who know CPR, the better the chance of more lives being saved every day
c. Encourage friends to take a class in CPR
d. Cardiopulmonary resuscitation (CPR)
e. I want my audience to actively work toward increasing the number of people who know CPR.
f. Learn CPR and make the world a safer place
g. As many people as possible should learn CPR to increase the probability that a person trained in this life-saving technique will be available in the event of a heart attack or similar medical emergency.
h. To persuade
i. The value of learning CPR

Chapter 7

Audience Analysis

Base your speech preparation on thorough audience analysis.

A speech is not an intention in the mind of a speaker, nor is it a text that exists in a vacuum. Speakers do not give speeches *to* audiences; they jointly create meaning *with* audiences. The ultimate outcome of any speech situation is a product of what the speaker actually says and how the listeners process and interpret what is said. Audience analysis therefore is much more than a step in planning a speech. It involves the constant awareness of those who are the "coauthors" of your speech—your listeners.

You speak to a particular group of people because you want a certain response from them. If you do not know the composition of that group, you cannot make intelligent decisions about what to include, what to emphasize, and how best to arrange and present your ideas. Research your audience thoroughly. Their age, sex, attitudes, and expectations are all relevant to your planning.

The composition of audiences varies. The members of one may have many similarities; the majority of another, little in common. Within a given audience, the degree of homogeneity or heterogeneity can differ for each of the characteristics discussed in this chapter. For instance, an audience can be fairly homogeneous in terms of sex—predominantly female, say—and heterogeneous in its composition of people who agree or disagree with your position.

We approach each of these characteristics as a discrete factor and describe the techniques to be used with various kinds of homogeneous audiences. *You* have to "mix and match" these techniques as you uncover the actual composition of your potential audience.

Later in the process of preparing your speech, you can use the information to adapt your materials to the audience.

7a. Develop an understanding of your audience by seeking information through as many channels as possible.

When you ask an audience to listen to your ideas, you are asking them to come partway into your experience. It is your obligation, in turn, to go partway into theirs. You and your listeners probably belong to some common, broad speech community, or you would not be interacting. Yet every person is also a member of multiple discourse communities that are tied to specific cultural heritages, geographical locations, occupational groups, and so on. Each of these communities has its own code of conduct and specialized vocabulary. By observing and reflecting on your audience from different perspectives, you can discover what communication links are already present between you—and what gaps need to be bridged.

The following are valuable sources of information about your audience. But it's important not to limit yourself to any one of them:

(1) Use direct observation.

This is the most reliable source of information about an audience. The easiest audience to analyze is a group of which you are a member. You know what will interest them, convince them, or make them laugh. With an unknown audience, if you have enough lead time, try to observe them functioning either as a group or as an audience. Observing a group's business meeting or their response to another speaker can tell you a great deal about them.

(2) Do systematic data collection.

One excellent way to become informed about your audience is to ask them about themselves. Politicians and advertisers spend millions on public opinion and market surveys. Such research reveals who their audiences are and how they think. Do not discount even a simple form of data gathering, such as distributing a three- or four-item questionnaire at a meeting before the one at which you will speak. You might arouse interest and curiosity while you gain information.

(3) Conduct selected interviews/focus groups.

When you cannot get information on the whole audience, arrange to talk to one or two members of the group. If that is not possible, talk to someone who shares characteristics with your potential listeners. For a speech to a group of teenagers, talking to one teenager—even if she or he will not be a member of that audience—can provide you with useful information. The same applies to interviewing someone who manages a department at IBM other than the one to which you will speak. Similarly, you will benefit from conversing with your friend Renea, active in the local chapter of the National Organization for Women, at whose regional conference you will speak.

In these interviews, try to find out not just *what* people think but also *how* they think. Ask open-ended questions and encourage respondents to expand on their answers by framing follow-up questions in a nonargumentative tone. Ask them for examples and anecdotes. Listen also to the language they use to address your topic. You can gain insight into what is most meaningful to people by tuning in to the words they choose and the metaphors they use. (See **17e**.)

(4) Talk with the contact person.

The person who asked you to speak has certain expectations about the interaction between you and the audience; otherwise, you would not have been invited. Ask this contact person to elaborate on his or her perceptions of the audience. Do not be reluctant to ask as many specific questions as occur to you. After all, both you and the contact person have a stake in the success of your speech.

(5) Use intelligent inference and empathy.

When you do not have any specific information about an audience, draw on your general knowledge of human behavior and groups. What are reasonable assumptions about an audience at a Fourth of July block party or at an open seminar on investment strategies? These need not be obscure; certain intelligent inferences can easily be made about the audience at a National Rifle Association conference.

Do not use only your reasoning powers; let empathy round out the image. Get outside yourself and adopt your listeners' frames of reference.

Even if you cannot relate to the specific details, try to recall a situation in your life in which the same underlying emotion was present. With all the big issues you face as a city councilperson, it can be hard to see why the neighborhood homeowners' group to which you will speak is so upset about changing one-way streets to two-way streets. Stop and remember those times when you perceived something in *your* neighborhood as a threat to property values and the security of your family. It may not always be relevant to ask, "When have I been in this situation?" But you can usually ask, "When have I felt this kind of feeling?"

7b. Analyze the demographic characteristics of your audience as an aid to predicting their orientation.

There is no such thing as an average audience. A speaker would be more than a little surprised to stand before a group of listeners whose composition followed exactly the distribution of the most recent census with regard to age, sex, race, socioeconomic status, and religion. Obtaining each audience's vital statistics enables you to make certain general predictions about their responses. Some pertinent questions might be:

- What is the average age of the audience members?
- What is the age range?
- What is the sexual breakdown of the audience?
- What racial and ethnic groups are represented, in about what proportions?
- What is the socioeconomic composition of the group?
- What occupations are represented?
- What religious groups are represented?
- What is the political orientation of the group?
- How homogeneous (similar) or heterogeneous (diverse) are the audience members for each of the above characteristics?

Obviously, these demographic characteristics are not all equally important for any given speech. Knowledge of the religious configuration of your audience will be important in preparing a speech on abortion, as will knowledge of the age distribution for a speech on Social Security reform. But, religion and age might have no bearing whatsoever on another topic. Despite differences in relative importance to a particular topic, each demographic characteristic should be noted, if only to give you a general picture. It is disconcerting to face a roomful of ethnically diverse teenagers if you had expected middle-aged professionals of northern European descent.

Holding an image of your audience in mind as you prepare and practice your speech will affect dozens of minor decisions not related to your overall strategy. Simply on the basis of your general cultural awareness, you will adapt your language usage, humor, and style of delivery to what you know about your audience. In addition, chapters **22** and **23** will help you plan more specific adaptations.

Caveat: Very few generalizations can be made on the basis of demographic factors. The studies from which data are drawn are often flawed. Also, social change occurs so rapidly that by the time this research is reported the situation has changed. And by the time the findings have reached the average layperson through synthesis or summaries, even more time has elapsed. Social science research, even when carefully controlled and well designed, tells us how one group *on average* differs from another group *on average*. For example, with respect to almost any trait you might select, the differences among individual women and among individual men are far greater than the differences between the average man and the average woman.

Still, it would be naive to assert that because people are individuals group data tell us nothing. If you know that an audience is all female or all over 65 or all Asian American, you know more than if you had no information about the audience at all. Demographic data let you make some *probability statements*. That is, you can say that many people in an audience *are likely to* respond in a certain way; you cannot say that any individual in that audience definitely *will* respond in a given way.

Understanding the limitations of such analysis, you should be aware of various demographic characteristics that may affect your audience's response—including the following.

(1) Age/generation

Maxims like "You're as young as you feel" and "Age is a state of mind" tell us to be careful when we make assumptions based on chronological age. Most of us have been exposed to octogenarians who routinely question authority and are open to new experiences, and to 18-year-olds who have already ossified their thought patterns. Despite these exceptions, some generalizations can be justified. Current theory holds that psychological development does not stop at the threshold of adulthood but continues through life in fairly predictable stages. Works by Erikson and Sheehy offer insight into the most common crises and value realignments of people in their twenties, thirties, forties, and so on.[1] (For our purposes, "younger" refers generally to people

---

[1]See, for example, Erik Erikson, *Identity and the Life Cycle* (New York: Norton, 1980), and Gail Sheehy, *Passages: Predictable Crises of Adult Life* (New York: Dutton, 1976).

going through adolescence, formal education, or the early phases of establishing career directions and of confirming life goals; "older" covers most everyone else.)

- Younger people tend to be idealistic. They respond positively to arguments based on change and innovation. They are impatient about social change and want to see results in the near future.
- Younger people are strongly affected by the values of their peers.
- Younger people like a speech to be organized in a fluid, narrative fashion. They prefer a rapid, exciting tempo and a delivery employing several media or channels of communication.
- Older people are more conservative. They are responsive to appeals to traditional values. They tend to have a stake in the status quo and to be reluctant to risk major changes. They are more patient in waiting for results.
- Older people prefer a linear, highly structured speech organization, with clear previews, transitions, and summaries. They are most comfortable with a slow, deliberate delivery.

In addition to thinking about the life stage of your audience, you can infer from the members' ages certain specific experiences they have had, based on their generational identity. For instance, it's not merely that your audience members at the turn of the century are 50 years old that is important. Unlike other 50-year-olds of the past and future, they were children during the post–World War II era of prosperity, students during the idealistic 1960s, disillusioned young adults during the Watergate era, and so on. This is a different audience from one of 50-year-olds in the mid-1970s, who were adolescents during the Great Depression and who came of age during World War II. Think about what current events have inspired and traumatized the particular audience you are addressing. What movies, TV shows, songs, and sports figures were central to their lives? What generational stereotypes might they have become weary of?

(2) Sex/gender

Sex is the demographic category that relates to biological maleness or femaleness. *Gender* refers to the socialized roles we have learned as appropriate for our sex. There may be a very few experiences that are directly linked to sex; a speech on breast-feeding or circumcision might take the actual male-female composition of an audience into account. Far more commonly, however, gender issues enter into audience analysis. The issue is not how many males and females are present, but how audience members of either sex think about masculinity and femininity. These gender expectations are highly culture bound and change rapidly in contemporary life.

Traditionally, women were socialized to be nurturant, sensitive, compassionate, and emotional. So, in the past, appeals to home, family, and the safety of loved ones usually were effective with women. Traditionally, men were socialized to be dominant, aggressive, ambitious, and unemotional (except when it came to sports). So, a speech to a predominantly male group used appeals to power, success, competitive values, and logic.

In recent decades, many more women and men have become more aware of how sex role socialization has limited their avenues of expression and growth. They are experimenting with new roles and divisions of labor in both public and private life. And men and women undergoing this process bridle when presented with stereotypical assumptions about social roles and power relationships.

As a speaker, you are well advised to avoid statements that may offend a sizable portion of your audience. Women, especially as they become aware of past oppression, are naturally sensitive to slights to their dignity and their role as autonomous adults. Many object to being referred to as "girls," "gals," or "ladies," or to overly cute designations such as "distaff side" or "the fairer sex"—all of which tends to trivialize their status. Many women believe that references to their clothes and appearance, however complimentary and well meant, focus on them as sex objects or decorative accessories. To be on the safe side with any audience, avoid such comments as:

I was chatting at dinner with your lovely vice president, Professor Ruhly. Now why didn't they have teachers like that when I was in school?

To Mr. Davis's left, the charming young lady in the pretty blue dress is our regional sales manager, Linda.

Also avoid examples suggesting that everyone fits into traditional roles:

Tomorrow morning as your wife serves you breakfast, ask her about the prices she finds at the grocery store. [In some households, men cook breakfast and shop for groceries.]

If you had a son about to take over your business, wouldn't you tell him . . . [Why not a daughter?]

Especially if you are female, do not perpetuate the myth of female incompetence in ways that may offend other women:

> Now, about the direction of market trends. [giggle] I'm not very good with figures, but I'm sure you men can make some sense out of these charts.

(3) Race/ethnicity

As with women and men, the differences between ethnic groups are not innate. The differences that do exist result from variations in socialization and experience. In our own home state of California, we daily encounter newcomers who migrated here voluntarily to be with their families or to enhance their opportunities, or who came involuntarily as refugees. Conversations with such diverse members of our communities encourage those of us who have been in the United States longer to remember why our ancestors came: some seeking opportunity, some escaping economic hardship or political and religious oppression, some involuntarily as slaves.

This expanding ethnic and cultural diversity can be seen as either a problem or an interesting opportunity. In the past, when there were three or four predominant ethnic groups in an area, it might have been a reasonable goal to become somewhat expert on the cultural values and symbols of those groups. Today, when dozens of cultures are part of a single community or organization, this approach to audience analysis becomes overwhelming.

To further complicate the challenge, it is not just that audiences are multicultural groups, but also that they are composed of individuals who are themselves multicultural persons. It is increasingly rare to find someone whose heritage is monocultural in any real sense. One person may have one European parent and one South American parent, and have lived on four continents. Another individual may be part of an ethnic group that has largely been oppressed but may personally have had a very privileged upper-middle-class lifestyle and education. A third-generation Korean American will share most of the cultural experiences of other native-born U.S. citizens but will have some experiences that may derive from having a Korean name or features that are related to by some as "Asian."

Because people's experiences, not their traits, shape them as listeners, there are no prescriptions for how to relate to predominantly white, African American, Native American, Latino/Latina, Hispanic, or Asian American audiences. Instead, you need to familiarize yourself as much as possible with the experiences of each group. The common experience of nonwhite racial groups and most other ethnic minorities in the United States has included discrimination and oppression. Members of these groups, like women, are justifiably sensitive to any communication that reduces their status or reflects old stereotypes. Forms of address, both collective and individual, are very important. Never refer to people by first names, diminutives, or nicknames unless invited to do so. And never address white males by titles such as "mister," "doctor," or "colonel" while addressing anyone else more casually. Find out what group designations your audience prefers, and respect their wishes.

Beyond showing sensitivity to the relationships between members of dominant and nondominant cultural groups, a speaker can also demonstrate an appreciation of cultural diversity. People of any ethnic group can tend to look at things from the standpoint of the group's own history and culture. Taking the time to investigate other cultural views can open up a number of refreshingly different avenues to good communication. Making the effort to pronounce unfamiliar names and phrases correctly, and avoiding the most stereotypical cultural generalizations, shows your goodwill and openness.

This kind of investigation is worthwhile only if it is put to appropriate use. The superficial approach, equivalent to the politician who is filmed eating his way through every ethnic restaurant in his constituency, results in a speech that rings false. The focus should be on the factors that influence communication: What constitutes a credible image? What level of eye contact is appropriate? How much controversy or intensity becomes discomforting?

7c. Try to understand what is meaningful to your audience.

Because speakers are not transmitting information, but rather are jointly constructing meanings with listeners, no part of audience analysis is as important as learning *how a particular group of people makes meaning.* The demographic data you collect can be useful, but only if treated within the context of this complex process. We know that a person's age, race, and sex all contribute to her or his interpretation of the world. But so, too, do religion, social class, educational level, economic status, sexual orientation, health, physical ability, and many other factors. As the incredible diversity and constantly changing profile of U.S. society have made clear, no formula can tell a speaker how each of these variables relates to a particular topic, let alone how they all interact. In a sense, as a speaker, you have been freed from the unrealistic goal of making predictions based on static traits of your listeners. Instead, your task is to thoughtfully consider how they engage in a constant process of constructing, and reconstructing, the world. Table 7-1 lists ways to relate to an audience.

This third and most useful way of understanding audiences requires both empathy and intellect. From this perspective, you can begin to grasp how

TABLE 7-1	Relating to an Audience
Level of Understanding	Analysis
Being oblivious to the audience (poor understanding)	Here is how I see this issue. You should see it the same way.
Adapting to the audience's traits (better understanding)	Because you are male, you are probably competitive and would respond to statements about being a winner. Because you are older, you may be conservative and would be skeptical about sudden change.
Understanding and respecting how the audience interprets the topic (best understanding)	Because of your experiences (which may or may not be linked to your demographic traits), you have this set of values and this way of defining yourself. I can see how your worldview makes sense to you, and here is how my position overlaps and resonates with what is most meaningful to you.

different people can observe the same events but interpret them "logically" to come to opposite conclusions. (See **16a**.) In this sort of audience analysis, you are trying to glimpse what some describe as *core values* (or *worldviews, personal construct systems, frames of reference, informal theories,* or *master narratives*). (See **20c**.) What do your listeners draw on to organize their experience and make sense of it?

There are two sources of such information. You can learn about cultural and group differences by reading, traveling, and exposing yourself to literature and art forms that shake up your own category systems. You can also learn by listening openly to and participating in dialogues with the people you want to understand. Many times, people can tell you explicitly about their beliefs and attitudes, but often, the processes by which they make meaning are taken for granted and are difficult for them to articulate. You may not get the insights you want through questionnaires or traditional interviews, so you need to rely on extended observation and careful attention to the ways their talk reveals their values, priorities, and conflicts. (See **17e**.)

7d. Determine the audience's attitudes toward your topic.

You could spread every possible reaction a person might have to the thesis of your speech across a continuum that ranges from extreme disagreement to extreme agreement. Much social science research is based on asking people to clarify their attitudes on scales like this one:

Strongly disagree	Moderately disagree	Slightly disagree	Neither agree nor disagree	Slightly agree	Moderately agree	Strongly agree

If your goal is to bring about some specific act, your listeners' responses will range across these categories:

Opposed to action	Uninclined to act	Ready to act	Taking action

If the majority of your audience falls to the left on either continuum, that audience should be considered *unfavorable,* and if it falls to the right, it is *favorable.* If in the middle, it is *neutral.*

Most speakers agree that knowing the audience's predisposition toward the topic is the single most important bit of information in planning their speech strategy. If your speech deals with a controversial topic, it is crucial that you interview people who differ from you in terms of attitude and experience. Listen carefully and respectfully to their accounts of the world. At the information-gathering stage, your goal is not to plan a strategy for changing them, but rather to try to see how their views and yours might be connected. This means letting go of your predispositions and judgments about people who disagree with you. Once you determine whether your audience is favorable, neutral, or unfavorable, you can follow the specific suggestions offered in chapter **22.** Although attitudes toward your topic are most obviously relevant to persuasive speaking, they can influence the speech to inform or evoke as well.

7e. Anticipate your audience's expectations by gathering details about the specific speech situation.

We have stressed the importance of knowing your purpose in speaking, but what is your audience's purpose in listening? Why are they sitting there giving you their valuable time? Perhaps they are required to as part of a class or job assignment. Maybe they are present voluntarily but for a reason unrelated to you or your topic—for example, they enjoy the social contacts of an organization and tolerate a speech as part of the meeting. Or perhaps, if you are fortunate, they are there because of an interest in what you have to say. In any audience, you will find combinations of these and other motivations. Knowing the predominant audience expectation is vital to the preparation of your speech. An excellent speech can fail miserably if the audience expected a different sort of talk altogether.

This is not to say that you must be bound by the audience's expectations. You can lead them to a new mind-set, but to do that, you need to discover what they know and expect to begin with. Start with these questions about your listeners and the occasion.

(1) What do they know about your topic?

Overestimating or underestimating the sophistication of your audience can be disastrous. No one likes to be "talked down to" or to waste time listening to what she or he already knows. It is equally frustrating for an audience to try to follow a technical or complicated talk that assumes a background and vocabulary they do not have. In both cases, your listeners will first become irritated and then tune out. People listen best and learn best when exposed to information that is just beyond their current level of comprehension. Then they are neither bored nor overwhelmed. But make no blanket assumptions about that level; rather, use the techniques of audience analysis to find it.

(2) What do they think about you?

Learn what your audience has heard, read, or assumed about you. If they believe you are an unquestioned expert, a misguided fanatic, or the funniest speaker their program chair has ever met, it will surely influence how they listen to you. You want to build on their positive expectations and overcome their negative ones. Knowing what your credibility is prior to the speech helps you decide how much you need to bolster it during the speech. (See **19a**.)

(3) What is the history of your audience as a group?

Audiences come in many different forms, with varied levels of group cohesion. An example of an audience with a low level of group cohesion is the people who show up after reading about your speech in the "coming events" section of the newspaper. Most audiences, though, have some common history, which may range from a long association in a business or club to a few weeks together in a classroom. Learn all you can about this collective history. What projects have they undertaken? What social events have they shared? What problems do they face? What have they accomplished as a group? What other speakers have they heard? You may find possible connections to your speech topic.

(4) What is the program surrounding your speech?

To understand an audience's expectations of you, it is essential to learn your speech's place in the context of their immediate situation. Whether you are part of a three-day professional conference or a high school assembly, familiarize yourself with the agenda and where you fit into it. Did your listeners just arrive from home, or have they been sitting in session since eight this morning? How long a speech do they expect? Have they had a cocktail hour or eaten a big meal? The overly relaxed or sated audience can be a challenge to a speaker, but so can the thirsty or hungry one. Have they just listened to a long treasurer's report, endless head table introductions, or a stand-up comedian? Is your speech the main event, or are they anticipating the election of officers, the juggling act, or the speaker to follow?

You obviously cannot control all these conditions, but this makes it all the more important to get answers to as many of your questions as possible beforehand. Then you can direct your time to preparing a speech ideally suited to the occasion.

Exercise 1. Suppose you are the contact person for a speaker who will talk about defense spending. Prepare an audience profile at least two paragraphs in length that summarizes the most relevant demographic and attitudinal data. If you are enrolled in a speech class, use the class as the audience you will describe. Otherwise, describe a group you know well, such as your department at work or an organization you belong to.

Chapter 8

Research

Research your topic. Use a strategy that enables you to gather information effectively from a broad range of sources.

Suppose that you have been asked to give a talk on your life history. Easy to do, you think; who knows you better than you? Simply a matter of spinning off tales as they come to you: "And then, in the summer of '96—or was it '95? . . ." But start again with a different supposition: A professional biographer has become interested in your life and wants to include it in her lecture tour repertoire. She will interview you and find out what happened in the summer of '96—or was it '95?—and then also interview your parents, siblings, children, professors, friends, and colleagues, and pore over files in the library. Granting that you and the biographer have equal speaking skills, which speech will give the audience more accurate information and analysis? Which will have a more balanced perspective? This facetious example is put forward to demonstrate that there really is not a speech topic, no matter how close to your heart, that can not benefit from research.

8a. Have a research strategy.

Plan a research strategy that optimizes your effort for the time allotted. This requires you to reflect upon your topic and the situation before dashing off to research it. How much time do you have? What facts are you compelled to look up based on the nature of your topic? What themes require investigation?

What are the objectives of your research? Other questions center on where you will get your information. What can be best found in the library? Which research can be done with a computer, using CD-ROM or connecting to online services and the Internet? Whom can you approach to discuss your topic?

(1) Fit your research to the time allotted.

Your approach to research can vary widely according to the time you have to prepare and the nature of your topic. Chapter 5 advises having a realistic timetable for preparation. With one day's notice, you cannot make an exhaustive study of the literature, but you can draw from general references like encyclopedias, whether at the library, on CD-ROM, or online. With more time, a broader effort is possible, starting with the information gleaned from general resources and using that as a guide as you progress through other, more specific sources.

(2) Approach your topic so that you progress from the general to the specific.

Start with an investigation of the "big picture." You do not want to commit yourself prematurely to only one avenue of research; you may miss signs of other paths important to your topic. As you move further into your research, you can get more specific. Now, knowing not only what you can afford to ignore but also whether other areas unexpectedly become pertinent, you have enough general understanding to be able to follow those trails effectively.

As the planning chart in chapter 5 indicates, a round of preliminary or exploratory research precedes a speaker's main research effort. With a topic about which you know very little, you have to do some general research anyway before you can develop your topic analysis. For a familiar topic, you need this preliminary research to crystallize in your mind the focus of your analysis as well.

There are two basic sources to tap for research: other people and recorded information. Unless you are fortunate enough to have unlimited access to an expert, it is usually best to start with the recorded information, saving the use of human resources for later when you know how best to take advantage of their expertise. Here, too, is where the general references become your initial and primary resource.

One of the most useful talents in the early stages of research is the ability to skim. Even if you have unlimited time to prepare, it makes little sense to grab the books and articles whose authors' names begin with *A* and read them from start to finish, then go on to the *B*'s, and so on. Before checking any books out from the library (or buying them, for that matter), look through a number of them quickly. Because you will not have time to read everything, try to get a feel for the most important approaches and theories. To do this, look at the tables of contents, skim the first and last chapters of the book, or read the first and last paragraphs of the chapter or article. Jot down the names of the key scholars and public figures who are frequently cited, as well as recurring concepts and studies. But do not feel obligated to read every single sentence.

You need to develop a similar technique as you search online—the ability to skim-"surf." Especially on the Web, it is easy to be seduced by a long set of links that are fun and interesting but that have absolutely nothing to do with what you are researching.

As you begin, look for summary or state-of-the-art articles and books that synthesize current thinking on your subject. Pieces that trace the history of your topic are also useful. Often, these sources are readily identifiable by their titles:

> "What Is a Working Woman?" [H. H. Stipp, *American Demographics*]
> "The Lasting Changes Brought by Women Workers" [*Business Week*]
> *Women in the American Economy* [Juanita M. Kreps, Prentice-Hall]
> "Women and the Workforce" [Alice Kessler, *The Reader's Companion to American History,* via Web search]

Skimming several sources and reading a few general ones will give you a good overview of your topic. You can then further narrow your topic and focus the remainder of your research.

(3) Develop a lexicon of the terminology peculiar to your topic.

Beginning to study a new topic is almost like learning a new language. As you start exploring your topic, make a list of key terms that come up. In researching women in the labor force, for example, you will find that you need to understand the distinctions made between *equal opportunity, affirmative action,* and *comparable worth.* You will notice that certain phrases such as *glass ceiling, queen bee syndrome,* and *pink-collar workers* have been coined by earlier writers and are widely used in the discourse on this topic. Familiarity with the language of your topic is essential as you continue your research, because you need to identify key words as you search through the literature.

(4) Use your analysis questions to direct your research.

When you've made one pass through for background research, but before you launch your main research effort, go back and analyze your topic. Consider whether you want to narrow your topic, adjust your speech objectives, or fine-tune the wording of your thesis statement. Carefully follow the suggestions in **6d(2)** to list what your audience will want to know. These questions become the basis of your research objectives.

Suppose that your thesis is this:

> Since the beginning of the Industrial Revolution, women in the United States have been exploited as a cheap and expendable source of labor.

Your audience will want to hear the answers to questions like these: Are women a cheap source of labor? Are women an expendable source of labor? Can the labor practices appropriately be labeled as exploitation? Has the treatment of women been rather consistent since the Industrial Revolution? Clearly, then, your list of research objectives will include goals like these: Find out how women's salaries compare with those of men who do the same job. Find specific examples of women having been treated as an expendable source of labor. Find an expert definition of *exploitation*. Find out how women's work changed at the time of the Industrial Revolution. And so on. Like a shopping list that you take to the store, this set of questions can provide focus and direction. Armed with this list of research objectives, you are ready to make the best use of your research time and to ask for the help you need.

8b. Use the library.

The first library appeared in the United States 300 years ago, and the first free public library appeared 200 years ago. For all these decades, libraries have existed to provide clarification to those who wish to know more about some topic. Even the smallest library usually has a connection to a larger system through which it can order what you need. In addition to the standard lending libraries, there are specialized libraries or collections that have a particular theme as a focus. And, of course, colleges and universities have at least one library on campus. It is not by chance that we start our discussion of where to go for research with the library. Even with the advent of the Internet, it is still the place to find the widest number of choices of research tools (including access to the Internet) and the place to find professional researchers primed to give you direction and help.

If your library gives tours of the facility, be sure that you go on one.

(1) Talk to a librarian.

Librarians are service-oriented information specialists and, contrary to the image presented in popular culture, are not there merely to shush people who forget to whisper. They are there to help you find the materials you need. Do not hesitate to ask them questions. They welcome the challenge of trying to understand your requirements and direct you to the answers you seek—whether you have questions about key terms, general resources for a particular topic, the best databases, and more.

(2) Use library resources to locate books and articles on your topic.

In addition to the librarian, important library resources include the book catalogue, periodical indexes and databases, and special dictionaries and encyclopedias.

The book catalogue

In most libraries, the book catalogue is a computer database. These database systems let you search for entries in a number of ways. For instance, you may choose to search by some combination of subject, author, and title. Or you can focus on topics as they are grouped in the Dewey decimal system or the Library of Congress classifications. Or you can search by keywords or *descriptors*—words or short phrases that the database uses to identify entries on related topics. (In our hypothetical example of women in the labor force, some keywords might be *labor market, women, wages & salaries,* and *sex discrimination.*) Or, in some cases, you may make a *free text search,* in which the computer does not limit itself to defined descriptors, but rather looks for words and combinations of words that you have chosen within the titles and content summaries of the books in the database. The lexicon you developed in **8a(3)** will be extremely helpful in both keyword and free text searches.

In libraries without computers, the book catalogue is the card catalogue—banks of drawers containing small cards that cite each book in at least three ways: by author, by title, and by variations of its subject. The subject cards are generally equivalent to the keywords of the computer database.

Special collections may have separate catalogues; check with the librarian to see which catalogues you have access to.

Periodical indexes and databases

You can locate magazine, journal, and newspaper articles on your topic using the periodical indexes and databases available at the library. This may entail perusing bound volumes, scanning a microfilm reader, or searching a computer database. Some of the indexes and databases are general in their coverage; others can be quite specific to a field or area of interest. Whether it be criminal justice, religion, engineering, business, music, tax law, or any one of a multitude of topics, there is a very good chance that a specialized index or database exists for it. Once again, do not hesitate to approach the librarian to ask for guidance in finding these sources.

There also are indexes for many major newspapers. The size of the library and its proximity to a major city are usually the factors determining the availability of such indexes.

Special dictionaries, encyclopedias, and similar resources

Special dictionaries and encyclopedias are useful tools, especially for clarifying terms and concepts as they are used in fields in which you may have little knowledge. Many such reference works cover world history, finance, law, medicine, science, philosophy, music, literature, and other subjects of significance.

Depending on its size, the library may have many other sources of information available, including filmstrips, microforms, records, compact discs, cassettes, film, and videotapes.

8c. Use electronic information retrieval.

There are a number of ways for you to retrieve information electronically. You can use an institutional search service that provides access to databases at remote sites. You can use a computer terminal at the library that provides access to databases on site. You can use a personal computer to dial up an online service you subscribe to. You can use a computer to hook up to an Internet service provider. These choices run from the highly structured (the institutional search service) to the highly unstructured (the Internet).

LEXIS-NEXIS, DIALOG, BRS (Bibliographic Retrieval Service), and Wilson OmniFile are services that provide information retrieval. The database you use can depend on your topic and on the system to which your search service subscribes. A service can have hundreds of databases to choose from; each of the databases can cover hundreds of thousands of articles and papers. You can gain access to one of these systems in a number of ways. Many public libraries subscribe to at least one service. College and university libraries are likely to have a search service, usually available only to students, staff, and faculty. Many companies have access to at least one of the major systems.

InfoTrac College Edition is an electronic virtual library that is available 24 hours a day via an Internet connection. It consists of full-length articles collected from hundreds of scholarly and popular periodicals, a range that embraces such diverse publications as *Time, Philological Quarterly, Journal of Soil and Water Conservation, Executive Female,* and *Arab Studies Quarterly,* to name but a small sample. Figure 8-1 shows a search conducted on InfoTrac College Edition using the keywords *comparable worth* and *equal pay.*

Online services accessible by personal computer offer information in a variety of areas, from an online edition of an encyclopedia or newsmagazine, to stock market performance, to government statistics, to news on sports and entertainment.

Seeking out information may be more esoteric on the Internet, where you can use such things as Gopher servers and the World Wide Web to track down what you are looking for. There are a number of ways you gain access to the Internet and, once there, a number of ways you move around in it. In fact, its combination of flexibility and arcane global structure can make it a daunting prospect for casual users. Tools for finding information include newsreaders to gain access to Usenet newsgroups or email discussion groups, search engines and metasearch engines to perform keyword searches on the Web (e.g., Google, Northern Light), subject directories consisting of links organized by subject (e.g., INFOMINE, the Librarian's Index to the Internet), and directed query engines that gain access to the databases of the "deep Web" not available through standard search engines (e.g., CompletePlanet, Invisible-web.net).

You can lessen the grief if you approach the available search engines and directories with a search technique that maximizes focus and minimizes ambiguity. Use Boolean operators ("this AND that," "this OR that," "this NOT that"), if the search engine allows, to keep from being overwhelmed by tens of thousands of "hits." For example, if you search for "Finland" in hopes of finding some information on Finnish exports in 1996, you may have to wade through Web sites extolling Grandmother Kovanen's cookie recipes, Bob and Diane's trip to Helsinki, and so on, before finding anything useful. Many engines permit users to specify that one word in the search should be near another and use other tools (such as wildcards and required terms) to be as precise as possible at the beginning.

FIGURE 8-1   A Search Using InfoTrac College Edition

Typing the keywords *comparable worth* and *equal pay* with the Boolean "OR" results in 32 hits.

Selecting "View" shows the list of results.

From the list, you may select the articles that best fit your research needs.

An excellent place to find information on the various search engines and strategies for using them is the Librarians' Index to the Internet (www.lii.org). See especially its "Searching the Internet" directory, which has links to tutorials for researching using search engines and subject directories, and comparisons of search engine capabilities.

For the most efficient use of any of these electronic resources, you must create a concise research strategy by narrowing your topic after considering different avenues of approach. (See **8a**.) Then you can decide what are the most likely categories, keywords, and search texts to identify information related to your topic. Coming prepared to do a search will help you avoid going down blind alleys and investigating topics before discovering their lack of relevance.

Caveat: Scrutinize Web-based materials with special caution. Although *any* information you gather in the course of research should be subjected to tests of credibility and reliability as described in **15d** and in chapter **19**, the wide-open nature of the World Wide Web invites a particularly critical eye. In contrast to the various review processes applied to getting ideas into print or onto film, all it takes to mount a Web site is the software and a server. Many Web sites are the equivalent of an opinion forcefully stated at a party: The authority resides in the volume, not the merit.

8d. Seek information directly from other people.

Research is more than delving into piles of books, papers, and printouts, and viewing screen after screen. You are surrounded by potential sources of information in the form of other people—either as individuals or as members of informal or formal information networks. These sources can complement and supplement your library and electronic research. But they are not a substitute for it. No matter how compelling any single narrative, you do not want to be completely seduced away from those piles of book, papers, and printouts. The speech you give must still be *your synthesis* of ideas and facts from many sources—not merely a report of someone else's ideas.

(1) Locate human resources.

Human resources are all around you—at home, at school and work, and in the community.

Acquaintances, family, and coworkers

As you start developing ideas on your topic, begin to talk about them with the people you come in contact with every day. You may encounter surprising sources of expertise. Your tennis partner may turn out to know quite a bit about computers, or your dentist may have gone to China last summer. On many topics, what these people can offer you is not so much expertise as a lay perspective that you will not find in any book. What are your closest friends' most amazing computer foul-ups? Have any of your acquaintances ever found someone worth dating in a singles bar? What do they think is the most urgent economic problem the country faces? (You might turn this into an informal survey, or even go a step further and develop a brief questionnaire.)

Note, though, that this is only the beginning. Do not stop your research at this point, but use these contacts as a springboard to other, more specialized resources.

Experts

In every community are people with specialized expertise in your topic. They can make a significant contribution to your research in that they often can tell you of unpublished data, local applications, or local examples of your subject, or they can direct you to obscure sources.

Educators. At whatever level—high school, trade school, college, or university—educators are usually very approachable experts. Dissemination of information is their business. If you do not already have a specific person in mind after your research to this point, call the appropriate department or school. They will direct you to someone knowledgeable.

Public officials and agencies. People elected to public office consider it one of their duties to make information available to their constituents. Most have staffs whose job it is to locate and send out government documents, copies of bills pending, and so on. In addition, scores of public agencies are staffed by experts who are ready to help you. If you do not know where to start, call the main switchboard of the local or regional government and outline the direction of your research. The operator can tell you the department with which to begin.

Independent agencies and special interest groups. Groups such as the American Cancer Society, Planned Parenthood, and the National Hot Rod Association can be excellent sources of information. Be aware, however, that such groups often represent a limited perspective. Talk to a spokesperson from, say, the

National Rifle Association or the Sierra Club, but weigh the information you receive against the standard of objectivity you have developed (it is hoped) through previous research. When possible, interview experts with differing orientations toward your subject, especially if the subject is controversial.

A useful resource for making contact with such groups is the *Encyclopedia of Associations,* available at the library. This encyclopedia contains descriptions of the groups and information on how to get in touch with them. Many of the groups listed have a toll-free telephone number that you can call.

Potpourri. Judges, athletes, businesspeople, police officers, doctors, merchants, accountants can all be experts. If you do not know a person in the particular field, see if you have a one-step link to one through a colleague or friend. Failing that, be alert to people mentioned in the newspapers. Chances are, if they have interviewed once, they will be willing to answer other questions. If you have no contacts in a monolithic organization, start with the public relations officer. However, when you know to whom you want to talk, there is no harm in calling that person's office and explaining your request. Maybe you will not get an appointment with the mayor, the chief of police, or the football coach, but you may be able to meet with a top aide or assistant.

Look also for experts who may have credentials of a less formal sort. A homeless person, for instance, is an expert on certain dimensions of homelessness. In short, do not skip a potential source of useful information and possibly a fresh viewpoint by limiting your definition of *expert.*

Along with the local community, there is also the electronic community accessible by computer. You can tap into an enormous pool of talent here. The newsgroups and conferences available online can introduce you to knowledgeable human resources at a national, and even global, level. Thousands of forums exist, covering just about every area of interest you could think of, and probably many that you would never think of—from Celtic music, to calculus, to corporate law, and from bicycling, to boycotts, to Barbie. In these groups and on message boards, people carry on extended dialogue on many issues. Questions are asked and answered, challenged and rebutted. Join in by asking your own questions, and engage in the multifaceted discussion that can result.

Before asking a specific question, check to see if it is one that has come up many times before. Questions of this sort, along with their answers, are usually posted in a Frequently Asked Questions (FAQ) file. If there is such a posting in your area of interest, read it first—you may find many answers immediately, and you may also find answers to questions that you had not yet thought to ask.

(2) Conduct interviews.

As with all aspects of public speaking, in interviewing, preparation is just as important as the process itself.

Preparing for the interview

Do not go into an interview cold. Analyze who the person is, and ask yourself in what ways she or he can best contribute to your research. If the person has written an article or book on the subject, read it. You should devise a list of questions that are specific enough that you will not be wasting this person's time by asking for information you could have gotten out of the encyclopedia. You want to prepare open-ended questions rather than yes/no questions or simple factual queries, but at the same time, you do not want to be so vague that you give the person no starting place. For instance, you are studying the history and present condition of women in the labor force, and you are directing your questions to the chair of the County Commission on the Status of Women:

Not:	How many women are there in the workforce in this county? [You could have looked up the figure before.]
Not:	What are the problems working women encounter? [This is too vague.]
But:	I've read that in this county the average woman's salary is 32 percent less than the average man's. To what do you attribute this?

During the interview

Spend the first few minutes establishing rapport and setting a context for the interview. Explain who you are, why you need the information, and how far you have gotten. Also, confirm your understanding of the time available. This may be a recapitulation of your initial phone call or letter. If you wish to tape the interview, ask permission at this point, but be ready with a notepad in case you do not get it. At any rate, you ought to take notes even if you do tape. Notes can help you keep track of potential questions and needed clarifications as you go along. They also provide a written record to assist you in finding important points when you later go over the tape.

When you begin to ask questions, be sure to let the expert do most of the talking. (See the suggestions on listening in **2c**.) Do not interrupt, disagree, or offer your own opinions. Be supportive verbally and nonverbally: Nod, smile, and express interest and concern with your posture and facial expressions. Encourage the person with short, noninterruptive comments such as "mm-hmmm," "I see," "That's interesting," and "Then what happened?"

Also, use questions to summarize and direct the interview: "So far you've talked about four problems working women face—unequal pay, lack of training, sexual harassment, and inadequate child care. Are there others?"

Allow for a closing phase for the interview. Respect the interviewee's time limit, and if you are approaching it, stop—even if you have gone through only half of your questions. Summarize your perspective of the interview. Often, it is productive to ask if the person would like to make a wrap-up statement. In some cases, you can ask, "What's the question I haven't asked that you wish I had?" And, of course, thank him or her.

8e. Maintain a complete record of your sources.

Form the habit of identifying the source for every piece of information you use and of recording complete bibliographic information for each source. Think about the battering your credibility will take if you are questioned about a bit of evidence and your only reply is "I found this in my research but I don't remember exactly where" or "Somebody told me this but I don't remember who." With electronic catalogues your task often will be easier—you may be able to print out the bibliographic information for each of your potential sources or perhaps download it onto a diskette. In other situations, you will need to record it yourself. Writing down volume numbers of journals, or the cities of publication of books, or the telephone numbers of interviewees—details that you will never mention in your speech—may seem unnecessary, but routinely recording all such information will help you retrieve sources if you need to check them again. And if you later develop your speech into a written report or article, your research notes will be priceless.

Because you are recording all the details about your sources anyway, we recommend that you master one of the standard formats for citing references. Then, if you need to append a reference list to an outline or decide to produce a handout for your audience, the sources of your research will be appropriately laid out. Three of the most popular formats are found in *The Chicago Manual of Style,* the *MLA Style Manual and Guide to Scholarly Publishing,* and the *Publication Manual of the American Psychological Association.* Individual variations notwithstanding, they all require an alphabetical listing that includes author, title, date, and publication details. In addition to the conventions for citing books, articles, chapters, and abstracts, there are correct ways to cite interviews, personal correspondence, TV shows, Web sites, and email.

8f. Capture the information and ideas in discrete units to facilitate retrieval and organization.

In the process of doing your research, you want to gather and record your information and ideas in a way that makes it as easy as possible to find things later on and to work with them creatively. The ability to photocopy whole chapters of books or to download pages and pages of text from the Web does not make it any easier to review the information you have. Smaller, more manageable units will promote creative flexibility as you arrange and re-arrange, structure and restructure your thoughts and data.

We talk about "notecards" in this section, but the important thing is not the media or the cardstock but the activity—and if you use an outlining tool or idea development software on a computer, these suggestions are as pertinent. That said, traditional 4″ × 6″ notecards are easy to manipulate and don't require a power source nearby.

(1) Notecards from print and electronic sources

As you read the book or article, jot down each discrete idea or bit of information on a separate card, being sure you add the identifying code and page number. Use only one side of each card. There are three kinds of data you might record: direct quotations or citations (see Figure 8-2), paraphrased ideas (see Figure 8-3), and references for later use (see Figure 8-4). Do not neglect to do this for materials obtained online. Even if you have a printout, it is valuable to go through the process of paraphrasing or quoting so that you isolate and internalize the key points that drew you to that source in the first place.

If you decide now or later that the table mentioned in Figure 8-4 is valuable, you may want to photocopy it rather than tediously transcribe it by hand If you photocopy lists, diagrams, tables, and other technical material, immediately head the sheet as you would a notecard.

For each source, select a one- or two-word identification code that refers to that source and no other. Usually, the author's last name is sufficient: "Berch." If there is another book by Berch among your references, you may need to use "Berch, 1982" and "Berch, 2000." Or, if there are two sources from that author and year, you could use "Berch, *Endless Day*" and "Berch, *Work and Worth*." Or, of course, if you have different authors with the same last name, then "Berch, B." and "Berch, F."

If you copy entire articles or chapters, be sure to make a bibliography card for each. Many people find it helpful to photocopy the title page and copyright page of the book or periodical.

FIGURE 8-2   Direct Quotations or Citations

Berch, p. 50.

On protective labor legislation for women (early 1900's):
"The ideology of protection seems only to have
reinforced the difficulties working women faced.
It left women isolated from the trade union
movement. It pushed women out of the industrial
sector of the economy, which was covered by
legislation, into the service and clerical field,
reinforcing existing tendencies toward occupational
segregation. And with all that protection by the
state, women still barely earned a living wage."

FIGURE 8-3   Paraphrased Ideas

Berch, p. 148

Cites research that shows no
discernable differences in aptitudes
of the sexes in 14 "key skills."
Shows that women surpass men
in 6 skill areas (e.g. observation)
and men surpass women in 2
areas (e.g. grip).

FIGURE 8-4   References for Later Use

Buck, p. 164

Table on "Women's Union Leadership."
For 17 unions it lists the % of women
in the membership and the % of women
in the leadership.
In all but one union women are
underrepresented in the leadership
(80% members / 7% leaders in one case!)

(2) Notecards from interviews and surveys

The suggestions in **8f(1)** relate to printed information but are easily adapted to information acquired through interviews and surveys. Make a bibliography card for each interview, citing the person interviewed, his or her qualifications, the date of the interview, and his or her telephone number or address. As you listen to the tape or review your notes, transcribe the information on cards.

(3) Grouping your cards

When you have gathered many notecards, you may want to stack them under cover cards with titles such as "History," "Causes," and "Solutions." Or you may decide to put these keywords in the upper-right corner. As you will see in part 3 on organization, this grouping of ideas and naming of categories usually occurs later in the process of preparing your speech.

Part 3

Organization

Introduction

Of the four phases of the creative process (described in **5a**), most speech training emphasizes the first and last—preparation and refinement—because these are logical, rule-bound processes. Incubation and illumination—the middle two phases—are rarely mentioned because they do not lend themselves to systemization. These middle steps touch the emotions. The process of creating a poem, story, painting, symphony, or speech can produce intense feelings of discouragement and excitement. After you have analyzed your audience and topic, and have thoroughly researched your subject, you discover that actually composing the speech is not always straightforward and systematic. Even with adequate preparation, you can find yourself pacing the floor, staring into space, and filling your wastebasket with false starts. Rest assured that you are not the only one to whom this happens.

In writing this book, we did not sit down at the computer, type the title *The Speaker's Handbook,* and then proceed unerringly through to the last page. The naming and arranging of categories took hours: Should practice be dealt with as an aspect of preparation? Can style be separated from content?

Does the motivated sequence fit under patterns of organization or under motivational appeals? Even when we had settled on a general outline, we altered the details of that outline again and again as the actual writing progressed. At times, the topics seemed so interconnected that we felt we were trying to untangle a skein of yarn rescued from a marauding cat. Would it ever come out in one straight line?

This frustration is an inherent part of the creative process. When you have read only one article on a topic, it is easy to write a summary of it. But when you have researched and analyzed a topic fully, you begin to suffer from information overload. First, you are overwhelmed by the amount of information; second, you see so many connections among the facets of the topic that you have trouble dividing it. This frustration is a sign that you have gone beyond the "book report" stage and are imposing your own creative structure on the topic. In effect, you are saving your audience from the agony of information overload by experiencing it yourself and then struggling until you have drawn something clear and meaningful out of the morass.

The analysis and synthesis of information have appropriately been called *invention*. *Analysis* is the taking apart of a topic, a process that follows specified rules. *Synthesis* is the remolding of the parts into a new whole—truly creating or inventing an interpretation that did not exist before. There are no set rules for synthesis. Although many people can collect the same information and divide a topic into certain logical parts, no two people will prepare the same speech. The synthesis that you create reflects your own personality, values, and approach to life.

Chapters 9–14 suggest ways to organize and structure your material to provide a unified speech. Given the many ideas you encounter in your research, it is necessary to *transform them into points* that best reflect your purpose in speaking. A set of parallel, clearly stated, mutually exclusive main points will be easy for you and your audience to remember. There are several effective ways to *arrange these points*. The speech *outline* is not simply an arbitrary and tiresome exercise imposed by teachers; a complete outline gives you a logical blueprint for your speech. Also important are the *transitions* that form the bridges between the parts of the speech. After you structure the body of your speech, you want to devise an *introduction* to lead your listeners into your topic and a *conclusion* to wrap it up for them. (See the Speech Structure Flowchart.)

SPEECH STRUCTURE
FLOWCHART

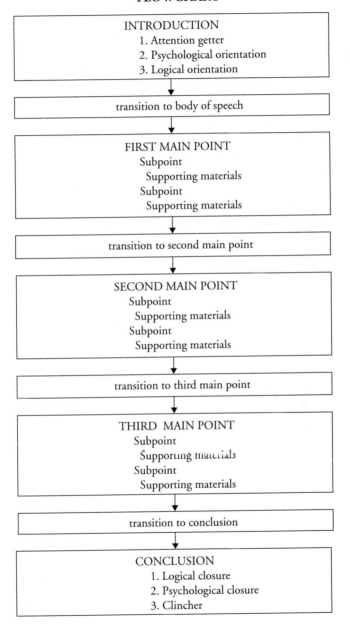

INTRODUCTION
1. Attention getter
2. Psychological orientation
3. Logical orientation

transition to body of speech

FIRST MAIN POINT
Subpoint
    Supporting materials
Subpoint
    Supporting materials

transition to second main point

SECOND MAIN POINT
Subpoint
    Supporting materials
Subpoint
    Supporting materials

transition to third main point

THIRD MAIN POINT
Subpoint
    Supporting materials
Subpoint
    Supporting materials

transition to conclusion

CONCLUSION
1. Logical closure
2. Psychological closure
3. Clincher

Chapter 9

Transforming Ideas Into Speech Points

Look for logical groupings of ideas that could be developed as points of your speech.

You may have lots of good ideas, but you need a procedure to assess which are important and where you want to go with them. The act of sifting through all your ideas on your speech topic and coming up with a satisfactory pattern, a coherent synthesis, is a demanding, multistep process that cannot be given short shrift. In essence, the process of organizing entails four stages:

1. Generating many ideas
2. Grouping them into clusters
3. Labeling each cluster
4. Reworking, adjusting, and culling the ideas until you have two to five major groupings that cover the most important ideas and that can be developed in your allotted time

9a. Assemble all the possible ideas and information that could go into your speech.

When you begin to prepare a speech, do not limit yourself. Jot down every item you might possibly cover in your speech, whether drawn from your research or from ideas that have been percolating. Follow the techniques of brainstorming; go for quantity rather than quality at this point. Do not judge or dismiss any idea, but instead write them all down. There is no need yet to impose any order on what you are writing. Work quickly, and do not worry if some ideas are variations on the same theme or if others are wildly divergent. You cannot start the process of organizing until you have some raw material to organize.

9b. Use a variety of organizational tools to identify potential points and examine their relationships.

Look back over the brainstorming list you made, and consider how you might cluster the entries. Are there any that stand out as possible main points? Are there any that seem obviously to fit together? Are there any that fall naturally under others?

There is no one correct way to group these ideas. Almost certainly, some ideas will be omitted altogether, and others will have to be forced a bit to fit into any category. You may notice points you grouped together that are not all of equal importance. Sometimes, one or more of the ideas from your brainstorming list will serve as a category around which to group lesser points. Other times, you will group several minor ideas first and then devise a superordinate heading.

You can use a number of different techniques to begin your organization, choosing one or a combination that suits how you work best, whether visually or textually.

(1) Create a rudimentary, working outline.

Perhaps the most traditional technique of speech organization is to arrange ideas in the hierarchical, indented outline format. At this stage of development, however, you do not want to be constrained by the requirements of the formal full-sentence outline. (See **11a** and **11b**.) The full-sentence outline has a very important role in ensuring that you properly elaborate your points and subpoints, but a less rigid form, the *topic outline,* is more useful at this point. Examples of both types of outlines are shown in **11b**, on the topic "The History of Working Women in the United States."

Because you are likely to experiment with several alternative groupings of ideas, don't spend time on phrasing or format. Just try to fit ideas under one another, nesting them in various ways until you discover the pattern that seems to make the most sense.

If this is a comfortable method for you, you will have a head start on developing the full-sentence outline. However, even this loose form of outlining may be premature if it blocks your thought processes. There are other, more spatially oriented ways to marshal your thoughts, which we describe next.

(2) Use concept mapping.

Concept mapping is a visual method of showing how your ideas relate to each other. In its most basic form, you quickly draw a simple diagram made of labeled circles and squares, connecting them with lines.

Starting with your central idea—your topic—you write it in a box or circle in the center of a sheet of paper. Thinking about the points from your brainstorming list, you jot some major ones around the topic, leaving enough room to add more subpoints. Your ideas will start to cluster around certain points; as you write each new one down, draw a line to connect it to its related point. This doesn't have to be done hierarchically, however. Subpoints might come to you before a broader point does. You can redraw as new relationships become clear.

There are a variety of styles for doing this, under the names of *clustering, mindmapping, branching,* and *ballooning.* Figure 9-1 shows a simple concept map, one that could have been part of the organizational process that led to the comic book outline in **10b.**

(3) Manipulate movable components.

This manipulation can be similar to concept mapping in that you organize things spatially, or it can be similar to outlining in that you put things together in linear form. It depends on the components you use. For example, you can jot your ideas on Post-it notes and stick them to a wall or desktop. You can cluster them according to themes, moving items from group to group until you are happy with the total grouping. Or, if you prefer to look at things more linearly, you can use the Post-its to make a rudimentary outline on whatever surface you're using, complete with indentation of subpoints.

Another possibility is to start with your research notecards and supplement them with cards on which you've written your own thoughts. In **8f,** we suggest grouping the research notecards under subject cover cards. You can write ideas, transitions, and syntheses on additional cards and plug them in where you think they fit. As with the Post-it notes, you can easily change the organization to experiment with a variety of approaches to your subject.

FIGURE 9-1   Simple Concept Map

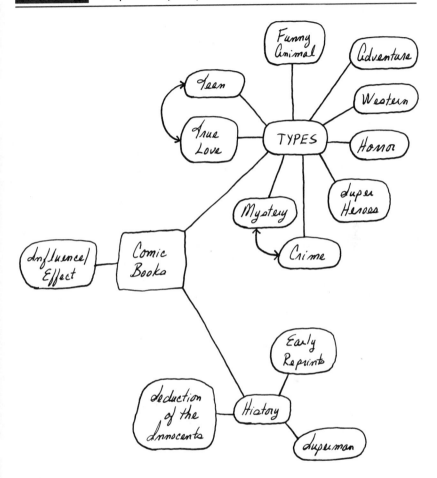

These two paper-based approaches can also be duplicated on a computer, using the simple outlining facility of word processing software or specialized idea development software.

To get the full benefit of each of these techniques, do not lock in too quickly to any one pattern. Leave yourself enough freedom to move things around until they click.

As a result of this process, you will have a set of potential points for your speech. The next step is to choose the points that are most suitable for your purpose and that work best together.

9c. Choose main points that, taken together, correspond exactly to your thesis statement.

To decide which main points to include in your speech, first look at your thesis statement. Follow the steps discussed in **6d** to identify the essential questions you must answer. For persuasive speeches that develop propositions of fact, value, or policy, consult **22b** for information on how to identify the essential questions with more precision. Once you know what a complete development of your topic requires, use the thesis statement as a standard against which to test your main points. Ask yourself:

- Is there any part of my thesis that is not developed in the speech?
- Is there any main idea of the speech that is not reflected in the thesis?

Look at the following thesis and the main points selected to develop it:

Thesis statement: The jojoba plant is an effective energy source capable of eliminating U.S. dependence on foreign oil.

    I. The jojoba plant is a virtually untapped source of energy.
    II. Energy can be produced from the jojoba plant efficiently and safely.
    III. Given an adequate educational program, the public would come to accept jojoba plant energy.

Obviously, something is missing. Either the thesis should be changed by deleting the last phrase or another main point should be added establishing the ability of jojoba plant energy to eliminate U.S. dependence on foreign oil.

Here is another set of main points developed from the same thesis:

Thesis statement: The jojoba plant is an effective energy source capable of eliminating U.S. dependence on foreign oil.

    I. The jojoba plant is a safe, efficient, marketable source of energy.
    II. The jojoba plant could create sufficient energy to eliminate U.S. dependence on foreign oil.
    III. The jojoba plant can be used as a source of protein.

In this case, the final main point has nothing to do with the thesis. This idea might be mentioned in passing as a part of the introduction or conclusion, but it should not be a main point unless the thesis statement is broadened to include the jojoba's value as a food source.

The following set of main points corresponds exactly to the thesis statement; nothing essential is missing, and nothing superfluous is included:

Thesis statement: The jojoba plant is an effective energy source capable of eliminating U.S. dependence on foreign oil.

    I. The jojoba plant is a virtually untapped source of energy.

    II. The jojoba plant is a safe, efficient, and marketable source of energy.

    III. The jojoba plant could create sufficient energy to eliminate U.S. dependence on foreign oil.

When appropriate, you may adjust your thesis to reflect the refinement of thinking that has resulted from the organizing process.

Exercise 1. Do the following sets of main points correspond to their thesis statement? If not, rewrite the outline and/or thesis so that the correspondence is exact.

Thesis: Cats make better pets than dogs.

    I. Cats are neater than dogs.

    II. Cats are more independent than dogs.

    III. Cats have an interesting life history in mythology and literature.

    IV. Cats are loyal and affectionate.

Thesis: A four-day work week would be beneficial to our company.

    I. Employees will enjoy longer weekends.

    II. Employees will miss rush hour traffic jams.

    III. Employees can share child care more equitably.

Thesis: Skateboarders are discriminated against wherever they ride.

    I. Public facilities have "No Skateboarding" signs.

    II. Skateboarders are needlessly harassed by property owners.

    III. Skateboarding is a difficult sport that encourages agility and physical fitness.

9d. Select main points that are mutually exclusive.

It is no accident that *main* points are so labeled. As explained in **9c** they are those few ideas that are central and indispensable to the development of the thesis.

Main points should be mutually exclusive for maximum clarity. That is, each category should exclude the ideas that are subsumed by any other category. Put more simply, this rule is a version of the maxim "A place for everything and everything in its place." The challenge for the speaker lies in finding a scheme in which each idea fits in just *one* place.

Sometimes, when you are grouping ideas under potential main points, you will find that many fit into two or more categories. When this overlapping occurs, you know that you have not yet found an effective system for classifying your ideas. Settling on a single organizational pattern is essential. If you do not know where an idea fits, your audience certainly will not. If you were unsure of your pattern, the result might be an outline like this:

Topic: Great Films
  I. Drama
    A. *One Flew Over the Cuckoo's Nest* (1975)
    B. *The Adventures of Robin Hood* (1938)
    C. *The Wild Bunch* (1969)
 II. Comedy
    A. *Annie Hall* (1977)
    B. *Singin' in the Rain* (1952)
    C. *The Producers* (1968)
III. Black and White
    A. *Raging Bull* (1980)
    B. *The General* (1927)
    C. *Stagecoach* (1939)

A quick look shows that the topic was not completely thought through before the speaker began to lay out the structure of the speech. Apparently, the speaker was unable to decide whether the discussion on film should be framed along lines defined by dramatic category or by color or the lack of it. Whether a movie was shot on color or black-and-white stock does not have any intrinsic relationship to the subject (being more a matter of the history of the technology). Thus, having the three main points be "Drama," "Comedy," and "Black and White" presents a problem: These three main points are not distinct categories.

Ideally, with a system of mutually exclusive main points, you will know how to classify any film and list it under one point only. If we put the sample outline to the test, however, we encounter uncertainty. *Raging Bull,* for instance, is a drama, but there it is under "Black and White," not "Drama." If we take a film not yet listed, like *Bringing Up Baby,* a black-and-white comedy from 1938, the uncertainty continues. There is no basis to exclude it from either the "Comedy" or the "Black and White" categories. So, although each main point taken alone seems a plausible way to classify some movies, the three main points taken together do not constitute a sensible way to look at the topic. It is like trying to add fractions to decimals.

114

Here is another example of an outline on the same topic:

Topic: Great Films
  I. Black and White
    A. Drama
        1. *Stagecoach* (1939)
        2. *Touch of Evil* (1958)
        3. *The Manchurian Candidate* (1962)
        4. *Raging Bull* (1980)
    B. Comedy
        1. *The General* (1927)
        2. *Bringing Up Baby* (1938)
        3. *Some Like It Hot* (1959)
        4. *A Hard Day's Night* (1964)
  II. Color
    A. Drama
        1. *The Adventures of Robin Hood* (1938)
        2. *Rear Window* (1954)
        3. *The Wild Bunch* (1969)
        4. *One Flew Over the Cuckoo's Nest* (1975)
    B. Comedy
        1. *Singin' in the Rain* (1952)
        2. *The Producers* (1968)
        3. *Annie Hall* (1977)
        4. *Tootsie* (1982)

Here, the topic is divided into main points along a single dimension: color, or lack of it. These main points are each broken down into two categories that are then repeated for each main point.

This same topic could be divided many other ways. For instance, the main points might also form along chronology:

  I. 1920s
    A. Drama
        1. *Greed* (1924)
        2. *Sunrise* (1927)
    B. Comedy
        1. *The Gold Rush* (1925)
        2. *The General* (1927)
  II. 1930s
    A. Drama
        1. *All Quiet on the Western Front* (1930)
        2. *The Adventures of Robin Hood* (1938)
    B. Comedy
        1. *It Happened One Night* (1934)
        2. *Bringing Up Baby* (1938)

Still other classification systems might include by language, by director, and by genre.

What is most important is that you choose *one* classification scheme for your main points that gives you a rule by which to include each item under one and only one main point.

Note: There will often be a few cases that fall in several categories or that are difficult to classify. For a general audience, it is usually best to narrow your topic to exclude these unusual cases, discussing them in the question-and-answer period if necessary. Be sure in laying out your categories to use such language as "westerns, in general, can be classified as . . ." or "with a few exceptions. . . ."

For a technical topic with a sophisticated audience, you might discuss the borderline cases in your introduction, conclusion, or transitions, or create a catchall category:

Theories of Language Development
 I. Chomsky's linguistic competence theory
 II. Skinner's behavioral theory
 III. Other theories

9e. Have at least two, but not more than five, main points in the average speech.

Although this rule sounds arbitrary, it is not as restrictive as you might think. As a speaker, you should be able to cluster your ideas around a few main themes. If every thought is treated as a main point, you will have no opportunity to *develop* any of them. With many random subpoints, you never extract meaning from an unorganized barrage of information. And if you have only one main point, you basically have a topic and no organization to speak of.

Understand, too, that your audience will not be able to remember more than a few main points.

9f. Express main points and subpoints to reflect coordinate and subordinate relationships.

Ideas of equal importance or of parallel logical function are called *coordinate points*. Points of lesser significance that support, explain, or contribute steps of logical development to other ideas are called *subordinate points*.

The relative importance of main and other points must be very clear in your own mind. Every point in the speech is subordinate, coordinate, or superordinate to every other.

If you were to classify methods of transporting goods, you might come up with:

Transportation of Goods
  Trains
  Trucks
  Airplanes
  Ships

In this example, each mode of transportation (trains, trucks, airplanes, ships) bears a coordinate relationship to the others and a subordinate relationship to the larger, or superordinate, category "Transportation of Goods." Each mode of transportation, in turn, may have more specific divisions:

Types of Trucks
  Tractors
  Vans
  Dumps
  Tankers
  Flatbeds

Here, each type of truck bears a subordinate relationship to the larger category "Types of Trucks" and a coordinate relationship to each other type.

Logical relationships are similarly shown through subordination and coordination, as in this example:

Trucks are an efficient means of transporting goods.
  [because]
  They have a wide network of destinations.
  [because]
  They have a great versatility of design.
  [and because]
  They are relatively cheap to operate.

It is evident that the reasons are subordinate to the points they establish.

(1) Subordinate points and subpoints should fit inside, or support, a larger idea.

Sometimes, ideas slip in that are "too big" for the points they are supposed to be supporting. Consider the following example from a speech on the role of aircraft carriers in World War II, and think about the fit of these points.

117

    I. Aircraft carriers were instrumental in winning the war in the Pacific.
       A. The successful use of aircraft carriers at the battles of the Coral Sea and Midway blunted the Japanese drive across the Pacific.
       B. Planes launched from aircraft carriers were able to inflict damage to enemy bases out of the range of land-based aircraft.
       C. Antisubmarine warfare was the major use of aircraft carriers in the Atlantic.

In this case, Subpoint C is not related to the major idea, nor is it subordinate in importance. The use of aircraft carriers in the Atlantic does not fit under their use in the Pacific. The two ideas bear a coordinate relationship, and the statement in Subpoint C should probably be Main Point II.

(2) Coordinate points and subpoints should be of equal importance.

Another problem occurs when an idea is "too small" to fit with the others at its level. In the following outline, the main points are not coordinate:

    I. Aircraft carriers were instrumental in winning the war in the Pacific.
       A. The successful use of aircraft carriers at the battles of the Coral Sea and Midway blunted the Japanese drive across the Pacific.
       B. A number of new aircraft carriers were named after carriers sunk earlier in the war.
       C. Planes launched from aircraft carriers were able to inflict damage to enemy bases out of the range of land-based aircraft.

Subpoint B jars when compared to the other two subpoints. There may have been some initial benefit from the confusion that such naming caused among the intelligence services of the Japanese, but it was hardly "instrumental."

    If you have one main idea that seems much less important than the other(s), omit it altogether, or create another main point so that this less important idea can become a subpoint, and mention the idea only as part of the introduction or conclusion. You might also occasionally consider a catchall main point, such as "There are several other factors . . ."

(3) Each subpoint should directly relate to the point it supports.

Do not group unrelated subpoints, as was done here:

    I. Aircraft carriers were instrumental in winning the war in the Pacific.
       A. The successful use of aircraft carriers at the battles of the Coral Sea and Midway blunted the Japanese drive across the Pacific.

B. The F4F fighter was redesigned to have folding wings so that aircraft carriers could carry more planes.
C. Planes launched from aircraft carriers were able to inflict damage to enemy bases out of the range of land-based aircraft.

Subpoint B is interesting and probably appropriate as a subpoint somewhere in this speech, perhaps supporting a superordinate point dealing with steps taken to make the carrier force more efficient. Clearly, though, Subpoint B has no *direct* relationship to the point about the war in the Pacific.

Chapter 10

Arranging Points

When you arrange your points, consider the traditional patterns of speech organization, and select or create the one that is best suited to your topic and purpose.

Once the main ideas of a speech are selected, you need to arrange them in the order that will maximize effectiveness. In some cases, the decision is virtually made for you. For an argument to seem logical to an audience, the premises must be unfolded in a certain order, as explained in **16g**. Debate speeches or closing arguments to juries, for example, have such strict requirements that they almost always unfold according to stock patterns, as shown in **22a**. Many ceremonial or special occasion speeches are so stylized that they follow a formula. (See **23**.) We can expect a commencement speaker to begin by congratulating the graduates and their parents, and then to enunciate a challenge for the future. And we can anticipate that at a retirement dinner the speaker will begin by summarizing the honoree's achievements and subsequently will speculate humorously about the honoree's coming leisure time. For the usual informative or persuasive speech, though, there is no given pattern. You, as a speaker, must select the best arrangement of ideas.

10a. Arrange main points in a pattern that arises inherently from the subject matter or from the requirements of the thesis statement.

There are several traditional patterns of speech arrangement: chronological, spatial, cause-effect, problem-solution, and topical.

(1) Use the chronological pattern to order ideas in a time sequence.

Probably the most ancient form of extended discourse is the narrative unfolding of a story. A time-ordered format still undergirds many contemporary speeches. *Historical* development is the most common chronological pattern. If you were giving a speech on the course of European music from 1600 to 1900, you might arrange it this way:

    I. The Baroque period (1600–1750)
   II. The Classical period (1720–1810)
  III. The Romantic period (1800–1900)

Also look at the outline on women workers in **11b.**

Another chronological pattern divides a topic into *past-present-future.* In a speech on automobile propulsion, you might arrange your ideas in this manner:

    I. In the days of cheap oil, auto engines did not need to be energy efficient.
   II. Today, redesigned engines provide increased efficiency.
  III. We can look forward to new technologies that may even replace fossil fuel–burning engines altogether.

A third way to look at a subject chronologically is to analyze a process *step-by-step.* The topic "How to Keep Fit Through Aerobic Exercise" could generate this outline:

    I. Determine the resting and working heart rate for your age.
   II. Begin each session with stretching exercises and low-level cardiovascular warm-up.
  III. Through vigorous exercise maintain your working heart rate for 30 to 40 minutes.
  IV. Allow at least 10 minutes for cool-down and stretching exercises.

(2) Use the spatial pattern to arrange points by location.

The spatial pattern is often based on geography. This can encompass the globe or the two blocks around your house:

  Topic: Crime
    I. Crime on the Eastern Seaboard
   II. Crime in the Midwest
  III. Crime on the Pacific Coast

Other geographical arrangements might divide this topic into "Crime in Europe [Asia, Latin America]" or "Crime in Manhattan [Brooklyn, the Bronx]."

Geography need not refer just to areas on a map but can show up as other ways of dividing the world spatially:

Topic: Crime
  I. Rural crime
 II. Urban crime
III. Suburban crime

The spatial pattern might also be applied to much smaller areas, such as the floor plan of a house or the arrangement of a library. The following example of a spatial pattern describes a very small area indeed:

Topic: An Aircraft Instrument Panel
  I. Instruments needed to maintain controlled flight are on the left side of the panel.
     A. Compass
     B. Altimeter
     C. Artificial horizon
     D. Turn and bank indicator
     E. Air speed indicator
 II. Instruments providing information on the operating condition of the aircraft are on the right side.
     A. Tachometer
     B. Manifold pressure gauge
     C. Oil temperature gauge
     D. Oil pressure gauge
     E. Fuel gauge

(3) Use the cause-effect pattern to move from a discussion of the origins of a condition to the ways it manifests itself.

This pattern is used to show that events that occur in sequence are, in fact, causally related. A cause-effect structure is well suited to a speech in which the goal is to achieve either understanding or agreement rather than overt action, as here:

  I. There has been a sharp increase in housing costs over the past generation.
     [as a result]
 II. It is extremely difficult for a one-income family to purchase a house.

Occasionally, the pattern may be reversed to an effect-cause sequence:

I. It is extremely difficult for a one-income family to purchase a house.
   [this is because]
II. There has been a sharp increase in housing costs over the past
    generation.

Of course, when using the cause-effect pattern, you must be sure that the causal relationship you propose is a valid one. (See **16d**.)

(4) Use the problem-solution pattern to examine the symptoms of a problem and then suggest a remedy.

This pattern is used in persuasive speeches that advocate a new policy or a specific course of action, as in the following:

I. The current system of financing health care in the United States is
   inadequate.
   [to remedy this]
II. A system of national health insurance would provide medical care to all
    citizens.

On rare occasions, a speaker might choose to use a solution-problem pattern:

I. A system of national health care insurance would provide adequate
   medical care to all citizens.
   [this is necessary because]
II. The current system of financing health care in the United States is
    inadequate.

The psychological and stylistic weaknesses of this pattern should be evident Most audiences will resist accepting a program of change before hearing the justification for that change.

(5) Use the topical pattern to divide a speech into elements that have no pattern exclusive of their relationship to the topic itself.

This is the most frequently used speech pattern. It is also the most difficult in that you cannot rely on a predetermined structure, but rather must understand the range and limitations of the subject itself in order to select an effective pattern. Some topics obviously fit a time or space sequence; many subjects, however, do not lend themselves readily to any of the arrangements discussed so far. In these cases, you need to generate an original system for structuring the speech. Because a pattern intrinsic to one subject will not work with another, the application of any topical pattern you select will be unique to that one speech.

Often, the best structure for a speech involves listing the components of a whole or listing reasons that add up to the thesis. The following is an example of a topical pattern that lists reasons for a conclusion:

Thesis statement: Capital punishment should be abolished.

   I. Capital punishment does not deter crime.
  II. Capital punishment is ultimately more costly than life imprisonment.
 III. The risk of executing an innocent person is morally unacceptable.

Sometimes, topical patterns may combine aspects of other organizational patterns. For instance, a *cause* leads to an *effect,* which is seen as a *problem* that therefore requires a *solution.* Here's an example:

   I. Children watch a great deal of television.
    [therefore]
  II. Children are not developing skills in reading and creative play.
    [and this is a problem; so, to remedy it]
 III. Parents should limit children's viewing time.

Other topics easily suggest their own arrangements, such as grouping the pros and cons on a controversial issue or answering questions that have been laid out checklist style by some expert on your subject.

When you are building a speech that supports a controversial thesis, as in most persuasive speeches, arranging your main points is more complex than merely choosing a pattern. Your speech will consist of an *argument* for your thesis, and the main points may be parts of that argument or may be a series of smaller arguments that add up to your overall conclusion. You have important decisions to make about how best to lead your audience through your reasoning pattern. For an unfavorable audience (see **7d**), this requires spelling out every step of the process. Besides these logical considerations, you also may need to think about the psychological impact you are attempting to create. These more advanced organizational patterns are discussed in chapters **15** and **22**.

Note: Sometimes, two or more organizational patterns will seem to fit your topic equally well. In this case, try to understand your audience's frame of reference to determine which sequence will be clearest and most persuasive to them. Suppose, for instance, you are giving an informative speech on a vegetable processing plant. You could arrange the speech chronologically—from when the produce arrives to when the cartons of packaged food are shipped out. Or you could arrange the speech spatially, leading the audience through the front offices and around the floor of the plant. For an audience familiar with food processing, either sequence might be fine. For an uninformed audience, though, the spatial arrangement, which might start out in the quality control section, could be confusing. The chronological pattern, starting with the vegetables arriving from the fields, would be preferable.

Exercise 1. By generating separate sets of main points, show how each of these topics could be presented in three different organizational patterns.

> Smoking and Lung Cancer
> National Parks
> Racial Discrimination in the United States
> Fundamentalism in Christianity and Islam
> Oriental Cooking

10b. Group subpoints according to a pattern, but do not feel compelled to echo the pattern of the main points.

After your main ideas are set, look at the subpoints under each. These, too, need to be arranged in some effective order—topical, chronological, whatever. You do not have to repeat the pattern used for the main points; you can choose the format that makes the most sense for each set of subpoints. Notice the different arrangements in the detailed outline that follows:

> Thesis statement: With their scope, history, and influence, comic books are an interesting component of American popular culture.
>
> I. Comic books are not merely "comic," but rather explore a range of subject matter.
>   A. Funny animal comics and kid comics are parables and parodies of the human condition.
>   1. Elmer Fudd and Bugs: Tradition versus the pioneering spirit.
>   2. Barks's ducks: Epic adventure and human foibles.
>   3. Harvey's rich kids: Capitalism with a human face.
>   B. True-love and teen comics present a hackneyed, boring, and sometimes disturbing picture of male/female relationships.
>   1. True-love girl meets, loses, gets, marries boy (and vows never to be so stupid as to put her needs above his again).

Topical

2. Teen comic girl fights other girls for the favors of a jerk male like Archie, who her father thinks is a twerp.

3. True-love and teen comics foster the "us versus them" view of the male/female world.

C. Western and adventure comics concentrate on the triumph of good over evil.

1. Western cattle barons learn that six-gun-slinging saviors arise naturally from oppressed common folk.

2. Adventure stories pit virtuous types against the blind malice of uncaring nature.

D. Horror and mystery comics investigate ethics and morality while titillating and scaring readers.

1. Eternal punishment for an unethical choice is a recurring theme of horror comics.

2. The tempting hedonism of wrongdoers is graphically displayed in mystery comics—until the ironic twist of fate on the last page.

E. Superhero comics manifest the unspoken and sometimes frightening fantasies and aspirations of the American people.

1. Superman is the supremely powerful spokesman and policeman for the American definition of the "right way."

2. The jackbooted hero, Blackhawk, was created in World War II to fight totalitarian fire with fire.

3. Mar-Vell personifies the desire for total knowledge and the wisdom needed to use it.

4. Spider-Man is the embodiment of the perennial underdog triumphant.

II. Comic books started as anthologies of another medium but soon grew into a separate art form developing along a path of its own.

A. Early comic books were mostly reprints of Sunday newspaper comic strip sections.

1. "Foxy Granpa" was reprinted in a number of comic books just after the turn of the century.

2. The following decades saw strips like "Mutt & Jeff," "Little Orphan Annie," and "Moon Mullins" reprinted.

3. Reprint books in the thirties included such titles as "Tarzan" in *Tip Top Comics* and "Terry and the Pirates" in *Popular Comics*.

B. By 1938, the majority of comic books contained original work, and, with the appearance of Superman, the golden age of comics began.

1. *Detective Comics* was the first single-theme, all-original comic.

2. Superman, the first costumed superhero, was featured in *Action* no. 1.

3. More than 150 titles were in print by the end of 1941.

C. During the decade after the war, comic books for the most part went into a slump.

1. With the Axis powers defeated and the Cold War not yet focused,

Topical (vertical label)

Chronological (vertical label)

the perceived need for superheroes lessened, and the sales of their books slacked off.

2. Many horror, mystery, superhero, adventure, true-love, and teen comics fell before the wave of censorship following the publication of *Seduction of the Innocent.*

3. Funny animal comics and kid comics retrenched behind the strongest series.

D. By the late fifties, comic books had started to recover, overcoming their tarnished image.

1. In creating the Comics Code Authority, publishers hoped to reassure worried parents and legislators.

2. The silver age of comics began with the reintroduction of long-idle golden age characters.

E. In the early sixties the trend toward emphasizing characterization, motivation, and involvement with issues initiated a new and still-developing era in superhero comics, the effects of which were eventually felt in the other comic genres.

1. The Fantastic Four, Spider-Man, and the Hulk were the first fallible and self-questioning superheroes.

2. Comic books became accepted by a wider, more literate audience.

3. Concern with ethical and even political questions became more evident, even in kid comics and funny animal comics.

III. Comic books have an effect beyond their entertainment value.

A. Comic books are a unique and vigorous art form.

1. Comic books have developed exciting and innovative methods for transcending the static nature of the panel format (series of distinct pictures across and down the page) to produce a sense of motion and drama.

2. The art of comics is not confined to the work within a single panel, but also touches the arrangement of panels on a page. [as a result]

B. Comic books can be seen to influence other media.

1. Many filmmakers' use of split screens and quick cuts demonstrates a stylistic adaptation of the comic panel format.

2. Camp and pop art drew heavily on comic book themes and styles. [and as a result]

C. Comic books are in demand with collectors.

1. Some issues of rare comics can bring prices in the thousands of dollars.

2. Every year there are many large conventions around the United States where comics can be bought, sold, and traded.

*The left margin labels:* Chronological *(beside D and E)* and **Cause - Effect** *(beside A, B, and C)*

Exercise 2. Use your InfoTrac College Edition to analyze speech organization: perform a PowerTrac search for the journal *Vital Speeches*. Select two speeches to review, and identify the main points in them.

127

Chapter 11

Outlining

Use a formal outline as an organizational tool.

The speech outline is an indispensable tool of speech organization. A clear outline helps you keep track of the points you want to cover; using one also increases the chances that your audience will retain the gist of your message. The act of outlining—laying your ideas out on paper—forces you to select the points that support your thesis and to demonstrate how they fit together. Until you have something concrete in front of you, how can you say you truly know what you are going to talk about? As the planning and practice chart in chapter 5 illustrates, you must develop a logical outline of your points and supporting materials before you can finalize the oral version of your speech.

Only through this outline development can you avoid falling into one of these familiar traps: either overestimating your preparedness or underestimating it. In the first case, you might say, "I've researched this subject so much that I've got it down cold." But until you give the speech—or begin writing down your ideas—how can you be sure? In the second case, you might say, "I'll never understand this topic, even though I've spent weeks in the library!" An outlining session could surprise you by making evident your unconscious understanding of the subject. In short, the written outline gives you some distance from the thoughts that are spinning around in your mind. Freezing these ideas on paper makes them accessible for you or others to evaluate. A teacher, colleague, or peer group can tell you if the connections you make are clear and compelling.

It is important that you understand the concept of outlining that appears in this chapter. Some outline formats include the introduction and conclusion as main points of the speech. We do not recommend this. Rather, outlining as used here refers to the ordering of the *basic* ideas in the body of the speech. Also, do not confuse the formal speech outline with informal research notes (see **8f**), preliminary organizational tools (see **9b**), or speaking notes (see **25c**). Although any of these may take an outline form, the *outline* referred to in the following sections is a detailed, logical plan of the speech.

Also, this outline is not an essay, nor is it the speech itself. Do not make the mistake of having your outline transform itself into a manuscript speech. (See **24**.)

It is essential to begin laying out your formal outline at the correct point in the planning process. Because full-sentence outlines are so much like actual writing, they must not be used too early in the process (thus producing writer's block) or too late (thus resulting in a speech delivered in a written rather than an oral style). Oral composition and oral practice should surround this one excursion into writing.

11a. Use the conventional outline format.

By following certain rules of outlining, you will be able to visualize the relationships among the ideas of your speech.

(1) Follow a consistent set of symbols.

It is conventional to use roman numerals to label the main ideas of the speech and to alternate between letters and numbers for each successive level of subordination, in this manner:

I. Main point
   A. First level of subordination
      1. Second level of subordination
         a. Third level of subordination
            (1) Fourth level of subordination
               (a) Fifth level of subordination

Do not skip levels. If your speech has only main points and one level of subpoints, use I, II, III and A, B, C. If your outline includes a second level of subordination, use 1, 2, 3. Do not indulge in idiosyncratic systems of labeling levels such as:

> 1—Dogs
>   *Hunters
> a: Spaniels
>   b—Retrievers

Dashes, colons, and inversions of the standard progression may make sense to you. It would be to your benefit, however, to get into the habit of using the universally accepted format. Not only is this format simple (though still allowing you to go to a fifth level of subordination), but most people find it familiar and easy to understand because of its widespread use.

(2) Show the logical relationship of ideas through proper indentation.

Each subordinate idea should be indented several spaces to align with the first word—not the labeling numeral or letter—of the point it supports. This makes the relationship among ideas visually obvious.

Wrong:

> I. Bagpipes are not solely a Scottish instrument.
>   A. Bagpipes originated in Asia Minor.
>   B. There are various forms of bagpipes in Ireland and Spain, for
> example.
>   1. Spanish bagpipes are similar in construction to Scottish pipes,
> with the sizes of the parts different.
>   2. Uilleann bagpipes in Ireland differ from Scottish pipes in that the
> piper uses bellows under the arm to keep the bag full rather than blowing
> into the bag.

Wrong:

> I.   Bagpipes are not solely a Scottish instrument.
> A. Bagpipes originated in Asia Minor.
> B. There are various forms of bagpipes in Ireland and Spain, for
> example.
> 1.   Spanish bagpipes are similar in construction to Scottish pipes, with the
> sizes of the parts different.
> 2.   Uilleann bagpipes in Ireland differ from Scottish pipes in that the piper
> uses bellows under the arm to keep the bag full rather than blowing into
> the bag.

Right:
I. Bagpipes are not solely a Scottish instrument.
  A. Bagpipes originated in Asia Minor.
  B. There are various forms of bagpipes in Ireland and Spain, for example.
    1. Spanish bagpipes are similar in construction to Scottish pipes, with the sizes of the parts different.
    2. Uilleann bagpipes in Ireland differ from Scottish pipes in that the piper uses bellows under the arm to keep the bag full rather than blowing into the bag.

Note how in the last example your eye was directed down the levels of subordination. Your outline should not look like a piece of prose. Your outline exists only to illuminate and clarify the structure of your ideas.

(3) As a general rule, develop each level of subordination with two or more parts.

English teachers are fond of saying, "Never have a 1 without a 2 or an A without a B." Generally, this is good advice. The concept of dividing an idea into parts—subordination—becomes nonsensical if a major point is "divided" into only one subpoint. Categories are useful because they encompass several related things. Suppose you outline a main point of your speech as follows:

I. Redwood City is the best California city in which to live.
  A. It has the best climate.
II. ....

If Redwood City's climate is your only example, you are in trouble. A good climate is hardly enough to justify the conclusion you have drawn. Thus, you are guilty of hasty generalization. To avoid this fallacy, outline your speech following the rule of having *at least* two supporting points at each level of subordination. It is far better to develop a few points fully than to cover many points superficially. The rule "No 1 without a 2 and no A without a B" is a good one to ensure depth of analysis.

(4) Have each symbol designate one point only, and be sure every point has a symbol.

Do not combine two or more ideas in any point of your outline. Give each separate idea its own logical heading. By the same token, your outline should not contain any free-floating words or phrases. Every idea should be firmly anchored to a symbol in the hierarchy of points.

WRONG:

Causes
- A. Both economic and sociological factors contribute significantly to urban decay.
- B. Political factors are of minor importance.

RIGHT:

    I. Urban decay has a number of causes.   **Free-floating header made into a main point**
        A. Economic factors are the major cause.
        B. Sociological factors are also significant.   **Old Point A split into two points**
        C. Political factors are relatively minor.

Exercise 1. Outline one of the speeches on the Sample Speeches Web site. How many levels of subordination does the speaker use? Are there cases of a 1 without a 2, or an A without a B?

11b. Use a full-sentence outline to ensure coherent development of your speech.

The thesis statement (see **6d**), the main points, and at least the first level of subpoints should be stated as declarative sentences. The declarative sentence is, in effect, a proposition. As such, it can be proved or disproved, accepted or rejected.

Look at the following sentence:

    I. Secondhand smoke harms nonsmokers.

If this sentence were presented to you on a true/false test, you could, with adequate knowledge, answer one way or the other. It is the black-or-white condition of the declarative sentence that makes it such a useful tool.

But what would you do if you encountered these items on a true/false test?

    I. Nonsmokers' rights

or:

    I. What is the effect of secondhand smoke on nonsmokers?

Obviously, an answer of true or false to either of these examples is impossible. It would be equally absurd if a stranger approached you and asked, "Do you agree with me about the growth of the welfare state?" Your inevitable retort would be, "Well, what *do* you think about the growth of the welfare state?"

Far too many speeches are constructed around just such vague phrases, questions, and uncompleted ideas. Listeners can identify the speaker's general topic but cannot always recognize the specific points the speaker is trying to make. Consider these examples:

Wrong: I. What are the causes of crime?
Right: I. Crime is caused by a combination of sociological and psychological factors.

Wrong: I. The history of the feminist movement in the United States
Right: I. U.S. feminism can be divided into four historical periods.

Wrong: I. Buying a house will have tax advantages. You will also build equity. House ownership is fun and fosters pride.
Right: I. House ownership builds equity, provides tax benefits, and gives pleasure.
or
            I. There are both economic and emotional benefits to owning a house.

Besides rendering the speech more coherent for your audience, the use of declarative sentences in your outline makes you more conscious of the exact points you want to make and forces you to frame them explicitly. As you begin to research any topic, you will find scores of interesting details and perspectives. How do you decide which ones to include in your speech and which ones to leave out? Once the thesis and main points are stated in propositional form, they will provide a basis against which you can test all other speech content.

The following outlines deal with a topic, "The History of Working Women in the United States," that could fill—and has filled—many volumes. Observe how the use of a thesis sentence and full-sentence main and secondary points in the first outline provides a basis for the speaker to decide what to include.

Full-Sentence Outline

Thesis statement: Since the beginning of the Industrial Revolution, women in the United States have been exploited as a cheap and expendable source of labor.

I. In preindustrial colonial settings, the boundaries between men's and women's spheres were indistinct.
   A. Colonial women ran self-sufficient domestic factories.
      1. Women produced the major source of artificial light, candles.
      2. Clothing and bedding were manufactured.
      3. The making of soap was a major contribution.
   B. The rigors of frontier life decreed a more equal division of labor between women and men than found on the rapidly industrializing Eastern Seaboard.
      1. Men and women shared long hours of joint farmwork.
      2. Women were often left alone for long periods to run the farm.
II. Between the Revolution and the Civil War, increased industrialization led to increased exploitation of women workers.
   A. Factories undercut home production.
   B. When the western migration caused shortages of male workers, women became a cheap source of labor for the factories.
      1. The percentage of women in the workforce increased.
      2. Women, in 1829, earned one quarter of what men did.
   C. Women workers' efforts to improve their lot were not successful.
      1. The first women's strike was in 1824, but poor organization made it and others ineffective.
      2. Associations of women workers failed because of the women's isolation and inexperience.
III. In spite of increasing unionization between the Civil War and World War II, women's position in the workforce remained inferior.
   A. Women were an unwelcome minority in trade organizations.
      1. Male union leaders did not believe in equal pay for equal work.
      2. Women were barred from union offices, men said, because "no conveniences were available."
   B. Attempts by women before 1900 to organize among themselves met with failure.
      1. Women's unions were not taken seriously.
      2. Women workers were usually too impoverished to strike successfully.
   C. Important gains by women workers in the first decades of the 20th century yielded little net improvement.
      1. Women's situation had improved in some areas.
         a. Unionization of the garment industry was successful.

       b. New job classifications were opened to women during World War I.

    2. Women workers still had neither security nor equality.

       a. Men got their jobs back after the war.

       b. Women received one half of comparable men's pay.

IV. During World War II and after, women were used as a dispensable and secondary source of labor.

  A. Traditional views of femininity were conveniently set aside according to economic needs.

    1. Three million women were recruited to replace our fighting men.

    2. "Rosie the Riveter" became a mythic ideal.

  B. After the war, labor, government, and industry cooperated to push women out of their new jobs.

    1. Although most women wanted to keep working, by 1946 four million were gone from the workforce.

    2. When plants began to rehire men, women's seniority was often ignored.

    3. With the unions' tacit approval, many jobs held by women during the war were reclassified as men's jobs.

    4. Many of the laid-off women were denied unemployment insurance.

    5. Articles and pamphlets exhorted women to return to their "primary role."

       a. Women were needed to provide a haven for returning men.

       b. Women were needed to nurture the nuclear family.

Here is a *topic outline* on the same subject.

Topic Outline

Topic: The History of Working Women in the United States

  I. Preindustrial

    A. Colonial women

      1. Soap

      2. Clothing

    B. Frontier women

      1. Indian attacks

      2. Farmwork

  II. Increased industrialization to Civil War

    A. Women in factories

      1. Smaller hands suited to weaving

      2. One dollar per week, less lodging

    B. First union attempts

       1. 1824
       2. Lady Shoe Binders, Lynn, Massachusetts
 III. Post–Civil War to pre–World War II
    A. Growth
       1. 225,922 in 1850
       2. 323,370 in 1870
    B. Conflicts
       1. Male union leaders
       2. Strikes
    C. The struggle for suffrage
       1. Elizabeth Cady Stanton
       2. Susan B. Anthony
    D. World War I
       1. New jobs
       2. Department of Labor Women's Bureau
 IV. World War II era
    A. Rosie the Riveter
       1. Three million women
       2. Patriotic appeals
    B. Women in the military
       1. WASPS
       2. Army nurses
    C. The feminine mystique
       1. Home as haven
       2. Rise of suburbia

At first glance, the topic outline seems to be a coherent, tidy arrangement of points. All the main points appear to relate to the topic, and all the subpoints appear to relate to the main points. But can you form a sharp image of what the speaker is saying about working women in the United States? For example, the first main point of the speech is "Preindustrial." Preindustrial what? The preindustrial *era,* presumably. Yet "preindustrial" is so broad that it could include the first humans to appear in America, thousands of years ago. In fact, this point will probably deal with the work that women did between the first European colonization and the advent of the Industrial Revolution, but it ought to be phrased to leave no doubt.

This is only half the job, though. No matter how refined, a subject still needs a predicate. Although a speaker can delimit a subject with precision, using sufficient modifiers and qualifiers, it still may not be clear what she or he means to say *about* that subject. Even if the speaker refines Point I of the topic outline to describe a specific group of women in a specific era (e.g., "Colonial life for women, 1620–1783"), you cannot pinpoint what idea is being developed: That there were many working women? That their lives were hard? That they participated in all spheres of work? As these questions are raised and answered, the speaker transforms a loose phrase into a full sentence. If it turns into something like Main Point I in the full-sentence outline, the speaker will probably decide that stories about Indian attacks, however interesting, do not belong in this speech.

Exercise 2. As we did for Main Point I, compare the remaining main points of the two outlines, and specify which subpoints are extraneous and which need to be modified.

The use of a full-sentence outline is important in informative and evocative speeches, as well as in argumentative and persuasive speeches. In a speech to evoke or to inform, you do not literally *prove* a thesis or its main points, but you do have an obligation to cover topics fully. Using sentences rather than phrases will focus your speech development and provide you with clearer criteria for deciding which points to include and which to leave out. Full-sentence outlines are not extra work, but rather are a needed tool to demonstrate logical relationships in the speech. Once you think these issues through, you can proceed to a more spontaneous and fluid oral form of expression, confident that the underlying structure of your speech is sound.

11c. Phrase the main points of the outline in a way that directly forecasts the subpoints to be developed.

It is not enough to have an outline with full sentences as main points. The sentences must logically encompass the main ideas of the speech. Suppose a speech outline has the following as a main point:

I. Many people are unaware of the origins of the paper they use every day.

If this is *really* the main idea being developed in this section of the speech, the subpoints should look something like this:

A. Ursula is utterly unaware of the origin of paper.
B. Clint is clueless about where paper comes from.
C. Ned never thought about paper for a minute.
D. . . . and so on . . .

Obviously, the speaker does not intend to spend this whole portion of the speech exposing the ignorance of the general public. More likely, she or he will talk about where paper comes from. And the main point should reflect this. The phrase "many people are unaware" does not have to be jettisoned altogether, but it can become merely a transitional lead-in, not an essential component of what is to follow.

Because the main points of a speech can be thought of as subthesis statements, the tests that were introduced in **6d** can be applied to their phrasing. Recall that a thesis statement was required to answer two simple questions about the speech: "What's it about?" and "What about it?" Each main point should be cast so that it answers these same questions about the section of the speech that is being covered.

	Wrong:
Subthesis sentence:	I first would like to take a few minutes to discuss the origin of paper.
What's it about?	A speaker talking for a few minutes.
What about it?	The topic being talked about is the origin of paper.

	Wrong:
Subthesis sentence:	Another interesting point is the origin of paper.
What's it about?	The origin of paper.
What about it?	It is interesting.

	Right:
Subthesis sentence:	The origins of paper can be traced to the use of papyrus in ancient Egypt.
What's it about?	The origin of paper.
What about it?	It can be traced to papyrus in ancient Egypt.

Do not include in the outline transitional phrases that might be part of your oral presentation. They make for pseudosentences. Also, do not include your supporting evidence in the phrasing of a main point.

	Wrong:
Subthesis sentence:	A study done by Dr. Wilson showed that in three major companies in our area 148 people were diagnosed with carpal tunnel syndrome last year.
What's it about?	A researcher did a study.
What about it?	The study found that carpal tunnel syndrome affected 148 people at three companies.

	Right:
Subthesis sentence:	Carpal tunnel syndrome is one of the most common forms of repetitive strain injuries.
What's it about?	Carpal tunnel syndrome.
What about it?	It is a very common form of repetitive strain injury.

It is highly unlikely that this one study is a *main* point of a speech. Keep statistics, testimony, and examples at the subordinate levels. Your main points should express the more general ideas of the speech; these are supported by evidence or data.

11d. Phrase main points and subpoints in clear, effective, and parallel language.

Once you have framed your main ideas so that they are logically and grammatically complete, take time to recast your points in language that highlights them for your audience. In this final phase of refining the outline, you move from one aspect of composition—organizing points logically—to another—sometimes called "writing for the ear." This step forms the bridge from completing the outline as a blueprint to beginning to imagine the oral performance that will ultimately occur. Of course, you will not be reading or memorizing your full-sentence outline, and you may never state the points as they are written out. But you want to phrase the key ideas so that they stand out from the overall flow of your presentation. When you express your main points in parallel language—that is, when you present them in sentences that repeat a certain syntactic structure or a particular grammatical form—you make them more easily identifiable. This augments the techniques of signposts, previews, and reviews covered in chapter **12**, all of which you use to make your organization clear to your listeners.

Ideas that are phrased in concise, colorful, parallel language are more likely to be remembered by both speaker and listeners. (See also **17**.) Look at the following main points from a speech on higher education with the thesis "a college education offers you many opportunities for improvement."

Wordy and Unparallel

I. The skills you will learn in college will add to the probability of your earning more money, not only in your first job, but throughout your entire lifetime.

II. Through higher education, one can also gain a perspective on many aspects of life, to enrich the nonworking hours and provide for a more creative use of leisure time.

III. While they are in college, most students have a variety of social and interpersonal experiences and make new friends through extracurricular activities and informal exchanges.

These are declarative sentences, as they ought to be, and they do show three separate, important arguments in favor of the thesis that a college education is valuable. The points, though, are too wordy and redundant to stand out clearly from the general flow of the speech.

Here, they are made considerably more concise without sacrificing their basic meaning:

More Concise

I. Your earning power will be increased by a college education.

II. One can prepare for a richer use of leisure time by attending college.

III. In college, students meet new friends and enjoy worthwhile social experiences.

Still, these main points can be made more memorable and effective. The sentences lack parallelism: One is in the passive voice, and two are in the active voice; one is in the second person, and two are in the third person; one is plural, and two are singular. Listeners are not as quick to see the relationships between points when the perspective and the focus keep changing. Whenever possible, strive for grammatical consistency of structure, person, number, and voice:

Concise and Parallel

I. A college education will enhance your earning power.

II. A college education will enrich your use of leisure time.

III. A college education will expose you to new people and social experiences.

Exercise 3. Rephrase the following main points so that they are concise and parallel.

Thesis: The United Nations is essential to world peace and harmony.

I. The United Nations serves the useful function of providing all countries with a place where they might air their grievances or propose courses of action they consider desirable.

140

II. It would be better if all countries could articulate their hopes for the future and use the United Nations to direct their energies toward a common goal.

III. With the world "getting smaller," everybody is beginning to realize that we are all one big, human family and that we need the United Nations to help us keep in touch with other "family members."

Thesis: Advertisers use a variety of techniques to influence consumers.

I. Tone and mood can be established through color.
II. Many advertisers use symbols effectively to attain their goals.
III. You can manipulate shapes for visual impact.

Chapter 12

Transitions

Transitions should link points to provide unity and express relationships among ideas.

Transitional sentences, phrases, and words serve as bridges between points. They also signal to listeners how two ideas are related. The connective words can completely change the impact of a message. Observe the not-so-subtle differences in these three sentences:

> He plays the piano, *and* I invited him to my party.
> He plays the piano, *so* I invited him to my party.
> He plays the piano, *but* I invited him to my party.

Clear and evocative transitions are more important in speaking than in writing because the spoken message is ephemeral. (See **17a.**) In this book, for example, we show you the relationships among ideas by indenting, capitalizing, and using different punctuation and typefaces. As a speaker, however, you do not have access to these devices. You need to use verbal signposting techniques to show how your points relate. You can keep your listeners informed about the overall structure of your speech by the generous use of phrases like these:

> My next major point is . . .
> The third cause of inflation is . . .
> To show you what I mean, let me tell you three stories.
> In summarizing this entire argument . . .
> The final point we should consider is . . .
> What, then, is the solution to this three-part problem I have outlined?

Do not worry about using too many signposts. Your audience will appreciate them.

12a. Select transitions that reflect the logical relationships among ideas.

The transitions you choose should illuminate the basic organizational structure of the speech. Without even seeing their content, you can tell what pattern these speeches follow:

Thesis: ....

   I say that for three reasons. First,
  I. ....
   This situation is also due to
  II. ....
   Last of all, we can attribute the problem to
  III. ....

or

Thesis: ....

   Initially,
  I. ....
   Next,
  II. ....
   Finally,
  III. ....

The transitions alone tell you that you are hearing an effect-to-cause speech in the first case and a chronologically arranged speech in the second.

  Points can be related in a number of ways. Crystallizing these relationships and expressing them through appropriate transitional phrases will enhance your clarity. Try to use a variety of transitions instead of linking all your ideas with "OK, now let's look at . . ." or "First of all . . . , second of all . . . ," and so on. Table 12-1 lists common transitional words that can be used to tie main points to one another, main points to subpoints, subpoints to one another, supporting evidence to arguments, and introductions and conclusions to the body of the speech. Transitions are needed in all these places.

143

TABLE 12-1	Transitional Words That Signal Relationship
Relationship	Transitional Words
Chronological	First, second, third Next, then After Following
Cause-effect	So, since, thus Therefore, hence Consequently, as a result Due to Because
Part-to-whole	One such Another The first (second, third) of these For instance, for example Illustrative of this A case in point Let me give you an example
Equality	Similarly, additionally Another Of equal importance Also, moreover
Opposition	But, though, however On the other hand Conversely, on the contrary Yet In spite of Nonetheless, nevertheless

Notice how Carnegie Foundation president Ernest L. Boyer uses simple transitional words and phrases in his speech on the importance of preserving the arts in education.[1] He states at the end of his introduction that lifelong learning in the arts is crucial for several reasons. Then, after developing his first point, he says:

> *Besides* expressing feelings and insights words cannot convey, the arts are necessary to extend the child's ways of knowing and bring creativity to the classroom.

---

[1]Ernest L. Boyer, "Lifelong Learning in the Arts," *Vital Speeches of the Day* 61, no. 1 (15 Oct. 1994): 15–18. (Emphasis added in extracts.)

After a few paragraphs of development, he uses a combination summary and preview to bridge to his third point:

> The arts extend language. They encourage creativity and give children new ways of knowing. *But we also need the arts* to help students integrate learning and discover the connectedness of things.

And he introduces his fourth point with this transition:

> *Further, the arts, while essential for all, have special meaning* for children who are socially insecure, emotionally distressed, or physically restricted.

Notice that the italicized words and phrases serve to tie the parts of the speech together and provide a sense of unity to Boyer's speech.

12b. Make use of internal previews and summaries.

The importance of previews in speech introductions and of summaries in conclusions is emphasized elsewhere. (See **13** and **14**.) Sometimes, transitions between main points should take the form of internal summaries or internal previews that pull together two or three main points.

Internal Preview

Once your résumé is prepared, the next step in job seeking is to prepare a list of specific job openings. The three best sources here are newspaper listings, your campus placement service, and word-of-mouth recommendations. We will examine the pros and cons of each of these.

Internal Summary

Because the problems in our department were affecting morale, and because we had found they were caused by poor communication, we instituted an unusual training program. Let me tell you about it.

Internal Summary and Preview

I've told you why we need to reduce our dependence on the automobile, and I hope I've convinced you that a light rail system is the best alternative for our city. Now, you're probably asking two questions: "What will it cost?" and "How will it work?" I want to answer both these questions. First, the question of cost.

Caveat: Do not forecast the end of your speech prematurely by bluntly saying "In summary" anywhere but in the conclusion. (See **14d**.) Carefully qualify your internal summaries by using phrases like "So, to summarize this first idea . . ." or "Let me review the points so far."

Exercise 1. Write transitions to connect the main points of the comic book outline in **10b** and the working women outline in **11b**.

Exercise 2. Identify the transitional sentences, phrases, and words in one or more of the speeches on the Sample Speeches Web site.

Chapter 13

Introductions

Use an introduction to establish a relationship with your audience and to orient them to your topic.

Once you have outlined the body of the speech according to the organizational techniques described in the previous chapters, you are ready to compose an introduction that will prepare your listeners to deal with you and your topic. Both speaker and audience need a period of adjustment before getting to the meat of the speech. You know from experience as an audience member how long it takes to get used to a speaker's appearance, mannerisms, and style of talking. If you are feeling self-conscious during this part of the speech, it is probably appropriate. Chances are, the audience is paying more attention to you personally than to your ideas. Your task is to shift attention from you to the topic.

This chapter identifies and explains the important features of an introduction that will propel you through the potentially uncomfortable moments and into the body of your speech.

13a. Project confidence and preparedness when the attention shifts to you.

It is important to realize that your speech really starts before you utter the first word and that that first word is crucial to the success of the speech. The moment the attention shifts to you—whether you are sitting at the head table or in the first row of seats, or standing to the side of the boardroom—you need to begin to develop a rapport and prepare your audience to listen to you. For the most part, they want to like you and want to listen, and there is some tension as a result. Because you know how important these initial moments are, you will have planned your first few sentences very carefully. Your listeners will relax when they see that you know what you are doing, that you are obviously in control.

Perhaps you have witnessed speakers who start talking halfway up from their seats, continue talking while walking to the podium, and then notice the audience. When you become the center of attention, stand up and, if necessary, move confidently to the position from which you will speak; then pause to engage audience members. Look at them and acknowledge nonverbally the fact that you and they are together.

13b. Frame your opening sentences carefully to engage your audience's attention.

Even experienced speakers who do not worry beforehand about the exact wording of the body of their speeches tend to plan and prepare their introductions carefully. Because you will be preoccupied with all the things that are going on at the beginning of your speech, you don't want to risk leaving your opening sentences to the inspiration of the moment. You need strong basic material that will carry the speech forward.

Start with a sentence that leaves no doubt that you are beginning. Avoid false starts and apologetic or tentative phrases: "Is the mike on?" or "Well, here goes nothing" or "Let's see, where shall I start?" Tone is almost as important as content here. Your immediate purpose is to command the attention of your audience. (See **18a.**) Techniques such as suspense, novelty, humor, and conflict are effective, and you will probably use them throughout your speech; they are almost mandatory in your introduction.

You can begin the attention-getting phase of your introduction by telling a joke, relating a story, citing an apt quotation, making a startling statement, or asking a provocative question. Be imaginative, and even a little dramatic; but do not go too far. An attention getter should emerge logically from your topic and have at least a reasonable connection to it. Avoid contrived and gimmicky openings such as flicking off the room lights and asking, "Are you in the dark about . . . ?" Your attention getter also should be consistent with your personality and the situation. What is perfectly normal for someone else may seem unnatural for you. Adopting an unnatural style is doubly troublesome; not only will you be uncomfortable, but your audience will sense that you are not being yourself.

With this in mind, consider the following possible attention getters for the comic book speech in **10b**. A humorous or light way of introducing the topic may suit you best:

> Did you ever want to leap a tall building in a single bound? I did. Did you ever want to be more powerful than a locomotive? I did. Did you ever want to be faster than a speeding bullet? I did. As you can tell, I was warped early by the influence of comic books.

Or perhaps you are more comfortable with a dramatic attention getter:

> On a May afternoon in Washington, Frank Salacuse and John Snyder wrapped up their negotiations and shook hands. Both were happy with the result. Snyder walked away with $17,500, and Salacuse's syndicate now had a mint copy of *Marvel Comics,* no. 1, a comic book with the 1939 price of 10 cents on its cover.

A straightforward conversational approach to the topic can still get attention:

> In the 10 years I've been collecting comic books, I've learned that they are more than escape or entertainment. As I read the 13,000 comics in my collection, their contribution to popular culture becomes clearer and clearer.

As this third example illustrates, attention getters need not be unduly catchy or clever. However, it is essential that you begin your speech with a few well-planned sentences that say, in effect, "I know where I'm going and I want you to come with me—it will be worth your while."

Exercise 1. Do all the Sample Speeches on the Web site have clear attention-getting steps? What devices are used?

Exercise 2. Write an engaging attention getter for the speech on working women in **11b**.

13c. Provide a psychological orientation.

Attention, once gained, must be transformed into interest. Before you can ask your audience to concentrate on the substance of your message, you need to orient them psychologically. This orientation has two parts: establishing a good relationship with your listeners and interesting them in what you have to say.

(1) Establish a relationship with your audience.

Speakers can seem remote and aloof, cut off from the audience by role and status. Use your introduction to create a personal bond with your listeners. You can do this with references to everyday, common occurrences. If your audience can visualize your going to the dentist, seeing a movie, losing your keys, or playing with your kids, they will be more conscious of you as a human being and not merely as a dispenser of information.

In addition to establishing a relationship that is warm and friendly, you want the introduction to set a tone of collaboration with your audience. For the most part, people learn better when they are active than when they are passive, and they are more committed to decisions in which they have participated. You can therefore appreciate that a collaborative tone will aid you in achieving your speech goals. Here are some ways to create a sense of dialogue even in a speech that is primarily a monologue:

- Acknowledge your audience's expertise: "As managers, you could give me a dozen examples of what I've just said."
- Admit your own fallibility: "One issue I'm still struggling with is . . ."
- Ask for their help: "I hope that during the discussion period later you'll share some of the solutions you've found to these problems."

In general, the idea you are trying to project is this: "Although I'm doing the talking now, I'm here to learn from you as well as instruct you. I hope to influence your thinking, but I'm willing to have you influence mine."

Caveat: Some speakers are so intent on seeming human that they become gratingly humble. They lose credibility altogether with such comments as "I'm a little nervous being up here," "Now, where are my notes?" and "I'm not really the one who is qualified to be telling you this."

When deciding how to build a positive relationship with your audience, you should ask two questions:

- What relationship do I have with these people now?
- What relationship do I need to have in order to accomplish my speech purpose?

In effect, you are conducting one of the phases of audience analysis described in **7e.** The answers to these questions will help you decide which combination of the following techniques to use in your introduction to build rapport with your listeners.

Establish credibility.

The judgments audience members make about you as a person influence the judgments they make about your topic. To gain respect and credibility, a speaker should be perceived as being competent, concerned, trustworthy, and dynamic. (See **19.**) For instance, the chairperson's glowing introduction may leave no doubt about your expertise on law enforcement, but to meet your goal of persuading these students to consider careers as police officers, you need to establish your concern for them. Or you may be speaking to a group of friends who like and trust you but wonder what you really know about nuclear energy. In this case, you can use the introduction to bolster your credibility in the area of competence.

Establish common ground.

You can emphasize similar background, experience, interests, and goals to show what you and your audience share. Observe how William A. Dimma builds a sense of common ground in his introduction to a speech sponsored by York University in Toronto:

> For over the past twenty-three years I've been associated with York as a part-time student, an alumnus, a professor, an academic administrator, a longtime governor, the father of a student and, as of last Saturday evening, the father of a graduate with a bright new B.F.A. degree.[1]

Refer to the setting or occasion.

One way to demonstrate your personal connection to the immediate speaking situation is to refer directly to the time and place. Jeanne Wakatsuki Houston, coauthor of *Farewell to Manzanar,* began a college commencement speech this way:

> Many years ago—forty-three to be exact—when I stood on the ground where De Anza College now stands, I looked out onto lush orchards, fragrant with blossoms in springtime and laded with plump fruit in summer. I viewed the acres of foliage carpeting the earth with green—patches of beans, tomatoes,

---

[1]*Vital Speeches of the Day* 56, no. 9 (1990): 283.

and squash, and long furrows of strawberries glistening red under their leafy canopies.

In those days, I knew this area well, for I had spent several summers picking those berries at a large strawberry ranch called Esperanza, located not far from here. *Esperanza,* the Spanish word for "hope," was farmed by Japanese families. . . . [After briefly recounting her family's experience as part of the U.S. government's internment of Japanese Americans in World War II, she continued:] Why do I tell you this? I tell you this because when I picked those berries I never dreamed I would be speaking at a college that someday would rise up within view of where I knelt in the dirt. It was beyond my imagination. But here I am sharing with you some thoughts and insights I have accrued since those days in the strawberry fields more than forty years ago.[2]

Flatter your audience.

Everyone likes to be complimented, as long as it is personalized and not too heavy-handed. Audience members who perceive that you like and admire them are likely to reciprocate.

In a speech presented at a workshop for teachers, one of the authors used this approach:

> Those of you who gave up your Saturday morning to be here are not a typical group of teachers. Study after study reveals that the teachers who show up voluntarily to in-service workshops on teaching skills are the very best teachers. Just look around you. The ones who most need this workshop aren't here today, are they? But a brush-up is always helpful. "A" teachers want to learn to be "A+" teachers. And maybe together we can find some ways to reach those "C−" teachers who didn't come.

Refer to the person who introduced you or to some other person present.

One good way to build a relationship with a group is to demonstrate that you relate successfully to one of its popular members:

> Thank you, Jack, for that very flattering introduction. You know, it's said of some speakers "this person needs no introduction." I'm not one of those. I need all the introduction I can get. Recognizing that, Jack was kind enough not to mention that he's had to bail me out, both figuratively and literally, many times in the fifteen years we've known each other.

---

[2]Jeanne Wakatsuki Houston, "A Tapestry of Hope: America's Strength Was, Is, and Will Be Its Diversity," *San Jose Mercury News,* 19 June 1994: 1C, 4C.

Use humor.

A sense of humor is a good basis for a relationship, both at the interpersonal level and on a larger scale. Show your audience that you and they laugh at the same things. However, this is a particularly perilous technique; see **18c** for cautions about its use.

In a business communications course, Ellen Watrous started her speech on historical cost accounting versus replacement cost accounting in this fashion:

> A French balloonist once floated across the English Channel and landed in a field of wheat. He spotted an Englishman and said, "Excuse me, sir. Can you tell me where I am?" The Englishman replied, "Certainly. You are in a basket in a field of wheat." "You must be an accountant," said the balloonist. "Amazing," said the Englishman. "How did you know?" "Easy," replied the balloonist. "Your information is typical: totally accurate but absolutely useless."

(2) Motivate your audience toward your topic.

This motivational step is one of those most often overlooked in speech making, but it is *the* pivotal step of the introduction. Your speech, in spite of your enthusiasm for your topic, can be derailed by your audience's "what's-it-to-me?" attitude. This attitude is not limited to the hostile audience; it is characteristic of nearly all audiences. You need to reassure your listeners that there are good reasons for them to be warming seats, that your topic—whether it be of an informative, persuasive, or evocative nature—has a link with their own experiences and is thereby worthy of their attention. Ellen Watrous's speech on accounting was presented to a class of undergraduate students in various fields of business. She went on to say:

> Everyone here destined to work for business enterprises is in the same basket with the lost balloonist. In fact, many of you will become the balloonist. You will be the person who makes investment and credit decisions through which business enterprises obtain financing, accumulating capital for production and marketing of goods and services. And you will depend on information provided by financial statements to make those investment and credit decisions which will inevitably affect your working lives. Yet financial accounting suffers from the same malady that the Englishman in our story suffers. That is, accounting fails to provide relevant information about the effects of inflation and price changes on the financial statements of business enterprises.

Sometimes, a two-step link is necessary—not every speech topic can be sold to your audience on the grounds that it will make them rich, save them time, help them succeed, or make them popular. When you cannot make a direct link to a basic need, motivating your audience depends on a step-by-step exposure of connections that lead from your topic to some core value. For instance, at the outset of your speech, your listeners may not be immediately stimulated by your topic of "African Firewalking." They may not care about foreign cultures as such, but you can make a two-step link. First, you can explain firewalking so that your audience understands its place in African culture. Second, you can show the audience that the world is changing and that they will need to understand diverse cultures (like African culture) so that they can learn how to deal productively with people coming from backgrounds that differ from their own.

Understanding the information in chapters **18** ("Attention and Interest") and **20** ("Motivational Appeals") will be especially useful.

Exercise 3. Analyze how psychological orientation is provided in each speech in the Sample Speeches on the Web. What steps, if any, do the speakers take to establish a relationship? To motivate the audience?

Exercise 4. Suppose you are speaking to the following audiences on the topics indicated. How will you go about building a positive relationship? How will you motivate them to listen further?

 a. A civic organization of businesspeople about the need for reducing the dependence on private automobiles for daily commuting
 b. A group of firefighters about public speaking
 c. A college speech class about kinds of running shoes

13d. Provide a logical orientation.

Now that your audience is *motivated* to listen, you must be sure they are *prepared* to listen. In the logical orientation, you show your listeners how you will approach and develop your topic—in effect, giving them an intellectual road map.

"Logical" is used here, in its broadest sense, in contrast to "psychological" as used in the previous section. The emphasis has shifted from an orientation generated by consideration of the audience to one that grows from your subject. The essence of logic is part-whole relationships. In this phase of your introduction, you show the larger whole into which your speech fits and the way you have partitioned your topic.

(1) Establish a context for your speech.

Give your audience a perspective on your topic by using one or more of the following approaches.

Fit your topic into a familiar framework.
Consider this statement:

> San Jose is located fifty miles south of Oakland and fifty-four miles southeast of San Francisco, about thirty miles inland from the Pacific Ocean.

Here, the unknown is linked to the known in a geographical sense. You can also relate your topic to some schema, chart, organizational structure, or process with which your audience is already familiar. In this case, your listeners presumably know where the Pacific Ocean and San Francisco are, so they can start to think about San Jose.

In the next example, the speaker places the object of discussion in its relationship to a known organic structure:

> As you know, the federal government is divided into three branches: the legislative, the judicial, and the executive. When we think of the legislative branch, we think of the Congress. However, there are several other parts of this branch. Today I want to describe to you the workings of the Speech Writing Division of the Legislative Reference Service, part of the Library of Congress.

The speaker can also connect an unfamiliar topic to the familiar by using an analogy:

> When the traffic lights break down on a busy corner, you see a traffic cop standing in the middle of the intersection, blowing a whistle and telling impatient motorists where to go. In effect, that is what I do as crisis manager at the Metacom Corporation.

Place your topic historically.
Another way to provide perspective on your topic is to describe its historical context. It helps listeners to learn about the events that led up to the situation as it stands at the time of your speech. One of the most famous speeches by an American, Abraham Lincoln's "Gettysburg Address," used this simple form of introduction:

Fourscore and seven years ago our fathers brought forth on this continent a new nation, conceived in liberty and dedicated to the proposition that all men are created equal. Now we are engaged in a great civil war, testing whether that nation or any nation so conceived and so dedicated can long endure. We are met on a great battlefield of that war. We have come to dedicate a portion of that field, as a final resting place for those who here gave their lives that that nation might live. It is altogether fitting and proper that we should do this.

On far less momentous occasions, whenever an audience needs to be briefed or reminded about the background that forms the context for a particular speech, a historical recounting can be effective:

Last June, following the series of gang-related incidents in the Ravensbrook and Southside neighborhoods, our mayor appointed a special task force to explore the scope and causes of increasing gang violence in our city and to make recommendations to the city council. Throughout the summer, eleven of us on that task force held a series of briefings by experts and scholars. Then, between September and January, we held eight "town hall" meetings throughout the community. To complete our data analysis, we also conducted over one hundred interviews. Tonight's meeting is the first open hearing on the preliminary draft of our recommendations. I am now going to present and explain those recommendations; our purpose is to get your reactions and suggestions to these ideas before we finalize our draft to submit to the council next month.

You might also want to place your topic in a broader historical context. For example, in the introduction of a speech dealing with some aspect of the French Revolution, mention can be made of what was happening in America, the rest of Europe, or the Far East at that time in history, thereby providing the listeners with the larger picture.

Caveat: We are talking here about a brief historical recapitulation. In many speeches, however, a fairly extended narration of past events is important; in such cases, history becomes a main point of the speech. Look at your thesis sentence and see what it dictates. It might state: "Past injustices require us to provide compensatory educational experiences for minorities." This would demand a main point dealing with the history of the minorities in question.

Place your topic conceptually.

Just as you can place your topic in time or space, so can you locate it in the world of ideas. By showing your listeners how your speech fits in with certain familiar theories, concepts, and definitions, you help them prepare to listen. For example:

> You're familiar with the law of supply and demand as it relates to goods and services. Let me review this basic market mechanism with you, because I want to ask you to apply these same essential principles to our system of information exchange.

Provide new definitions and concepts.

If you use unfamiliar terms and concepts in your speech, or use familiar terms in unfamiliar ways, prepare your audience. Related to this, if you use a term or phrase that has been co-opted as a slogan or rallying cry by some group, with all the attendant distortion of meaning, be sure early on to define exactly how you plan to use it.

Here is how you might introduce an unfamiliar term:

> *Operations Support Systems* for a telecommunications service provider are software applications that deal with four broad areas: billing and customer care, provisioning, planning and engineering, and network management.

Here is how you might define a familiar term used in an unfamiliar way:

> Often, when people speak of a system of restitution for criminals, they refer to a program in which prisoners contribute wages to a collective pool of some sort. The restitution system I will be talking about involves direct compensation from individual criminals to their victims.

In introducing her topic, Carol W. Kinsley, executive director of the Community Service Learning Center, took care to clarify her topic:

> Here is a definition: Community Service Learning is an educational process . . . that involves students in service experiences with two firm anchors: First, their service is *directly* related to academic subject matter; and second, it involves them in making positive contributions to individuals and community institutions.[3]

(2) Orient the audience to your approach to the topic.

The second step in a logical orientation—once you have shown how your speech fits into some larger context—is to preview the structure of your

---

[3]Carol W. Kinsley, "What Is Community Service Learning?" *Vital Speeches of the Day* 61, no. 2 (1994): 40–42.

speech. If you have given your listeners a framework on which to attach your points as your speech unfolds, their comprehension of your topic and thesis is made that much easier.

Reassuring your audience of what you are going to cover will reduce anxiety and internal counterarguing. Suppose you declare, "I will discuss the background of the problem and discuss my solutions to it, and then I will answer those objections most often raised against my position." Hearing this, your audience will be more patient, not raising those arguments in their minds to block out your position before you have stated it.

In most introductions, you will explicitly state one or more of the following: your topic, thesis, title, or purpose—for example, "I would like to persuade you to change your vote on this bond issue." The circumstances that would make this strategically *not* the thing to do are discussed in chapter **22** on persuasive strategies. At times, you also want to tell what you are *not* talking about—essentially explaining to your audience how you have narrowed your topic.

Here is an example, derived from the comic book outline in **10b**, of a speaker spelling out what the speech will not cover:

> I am not going to tell you which comic books are currently the best investment. Nor am I going to explain how to treat and store comic books so that the acid in the paper won't turn them into yellow confetti. I *am,* however, going to tell you some things about comic books that will help you better understand their place in American popular culture.

You must also decide whether to give an exact preview of the points you are going to cover or merely a much more general overview of your topic. Explicit previews are useful in the majority of speeches and absolutely essential for speeches with fairly technical or complex topics. The speaker gives his or her listeners a reassuring road map to carry through the speech, one that they can refer to if they start to get lost. When should you not use an explicit preview? If your speech is built around a dramatic sequence, you should not ruin the effect by giving the climax away in a preview. Rather, summarize your ideas in the conclusion. In addition, when each point builds on the audience's understanding of the previous points, a detailed preview might do more harm than good. Finally, very short, simple speeches rarely need previewing.

Exercise 5. What methods are used by the speakers in the Sample Speeches on the Web to provide logical orientation? Would any of these speeches be more effective if they did or did not include a specific preview?

Exercise 6. Write a logical orientation for either the comic book outline in **10b** or the outline on working women in the labor force in **11b**. Include a specific preview of the main points. Then rewrite it, substituting a more general preview that paraphrases and capsulizes the main points. Under what circumstances would each form be most effective?

13e. Make your introduction as compact as possible by combining or omitting steps when appropriate.

Generally, the introduction should take up 10–15 percent of your speaking time. If your introduction includes all the steps given in this chapter as discrete units, it might be longer than the speech itself. If you progress mechanically through these steps, your introduction will be choppy, disjointed, and overlong. Organize the introduction in a natural narrative style, keeping in mind the *functions* of getting attention and providing psychological and logical orientation. Whenever possible, select material that fulfills several of the functions of an introduction.

In addition to combining parts of the introduction, it is often appropriate to omit steps altogether. A presidential speech can begin, "My fellow Americans, tonight I want to talk about the serious problem of international terrorism." Attention, credibility, and motivation to listen are assumed.

When attention is already riveted on you—as when you are about to announce the long-awaited results of a competition—a lengthy opening story is out of place, and maybe even hazardous to your health. Likewise, if you are a minister speaking to your own congregation or a candidate addressing a rally of your campaign workers, you certainly do not need to waste time building a relationship. And with a group of angry property owners gathered to protest a tax increase, it serves no real purpose to tell them how important the topic is. Finally, a study group that meets regularly to hear lectures on a certain topic needs very little logical orientation; rather, you can jump quite directly into the substance of your speech.

Examine your audience, the occasion, and your speech purpose to see what aspects of an introduction can be combined, handled with a passing sentence or indirect reference, or omitted altogether. Just be sure that, by the time you begin your first main point, you can answer all these questions in the affirmative:

- Are they listening?
- Do they want to keep listening to me?
- Do they want to know more about this topic?

- Do they understand where I'm coming from?
- Do they understand where I'm going?

Exercise 7. Examine each of the speeches in the Sample Speeches on the Web. Are all of the steps of an introduction present in each? What steps are omitted? Do you think the omissions are justified? What functions are combined?

13f. Avoid common introduction pitfalls.

1. *Don't* begin with "Before I start, I'd like to say. . . ." You have already started. (See **13a**.)
2. *Don't* begin with an apology like "I'm not really prepared" or "I don't know much about this, but. . . ." (See **13b**.)
3. *Don't* read your introduction. Or, if you have memorized it, be sure it does not sound mechanical. This is a time when you should maximize eye contact and keep your inflection natural and conversational. (See **26c**.)
4. *Don't* be dramatic to the point of assuming a whole new identity or persona. Leave that to the cabaret impersonators, and give *your* speech as *yourself*. (See **13b** and **17c**.)
5. *Don't* use an attention getter that has no real link to your topic. Avoid the temptation to stretch a point so you can start with an unrelated joke you think is hilarious. Similarly, firing a starter's pistol in the air at the beginning of a speech on "How to Get a Running Start on Your Competition" will do more to distract than attract your audience. (See **13b**.)
6. *Don't* make your introduction seem disproportionately long. (See **13e**.)
7. *Don't* use stock phrases like "Unaccustomed as I am to public speaking" or overworked apocryphal stories. Ask a friend to give an honest critique of your trove of expressions and anecdotes. (See **17d**.)
8. *Don't* name-drop to build your credibility. You do not want your audience to think that you are simply gratifying your ego. (See **19c**.)
9. *Don't* startle your audience by bursting out of a yogalike trance into an explosion of oral energy. This is a favorite of high school orators. Engage your audience before you start. (See **13a**.)
10. *Don't* start with a long quotation that leaves your audience wondering where the quotation ends and your words begin.

Exercise 8. Use your InfoTrac College Edition to analyze speech introductions. Perform a PowerTrac search for the journal *Vital Speeches,* and select several speeches to review. Do the speakers fall into any introduction pitfalls? If so, how would you change the introduction?

Chapter 14

Conclusions

Use a conclusion to provide logical and psychological closure.

Many speakers make the mistake of not leaving sufficient time for a proper conclusion. It is not enough to finish developing your last main point and then mumble, "I guess that's all I wanted to say." Just as you led your audience into your topic step-by-step in the introduction, so must you lead them out again in a conclusion, tying all the threads together and leaving the audience with a sense of completeness or closure. Like the introduction, the conclusion should be precisely planned, almost to the point of memorization. Social scientists tell us that people are most likely to remember what they hear last, so you should choose your words carefully.

14a. Provide logical closure.

Although you have already demonstrated the interconnectedness of your points and ideas in the body of the speech by the use of transitions and internal previews and summaries, you still need to tie it all together for your audience at the end.

(1) Summarize the main ideas of the speech.

In all but the shortest of speeches, you are well advised to include a fairly explicit restatement of your thesis and main ideas. There are sometimes good reasons not to state your thesis and main points in your introduction. These do not apply to the conclusion. For instance, at the end of your speech, even an unfavorable audience may as well be informed that your intent has been to persuade them. The argument or dramatic sequence you did not want to reveal at first has now been unfolded, and it will be helpful to recapitulate.

In a technical or argumentative speech, it can be particularly useful to restate your thesis and main points exactly. For instance:

> So, in this speech, I have shown you why conjugal visits should be allowed in prisons. First, I explained the system of conjugal visits that has been adopted successfully in some penal institutions. Second, I noted that conjugal visits contribute directly to the morale and rehabilitation of prisoners. Finally, I documented that the visitation system is beneficial to society as a whole.

If this kind of summary seems too mechanical, you can paraphrase rather than restate exactly, summing up the content, but not in the identical words:

> Today, I have tried to give you some sense of how conjugal visits have worked elsewhere and of the benefits they would bring to prisoners and to society as a whole.

Only in a short, one-point speech can you safely omit a summary. Otherwise, there is no reason not to summarize—you have nothing to lose and only clarity to gain.

(2) Reestablish the connection of your topic to a larger context.

There can be an integration of the parts of a speech that goes beyond mere summary. In some cases, a conclusion serves to pull together several ideas into a pattern that has been implicit all along. This can be true for either inductive or deductive lines of reasoning, when the final relationship among points needs to be spelled out. (See **16.**) In other cases, you might want to build on the points you established to highlight broader implications or ramifications of your topic. There may not be time to address these topics in your speech, but you want to at least raise them for your audience to think about.

In the introduction, you drew your speech topic out of some broader context. After developing your ideas, you may want to show how they tie back to the original larger picture. For instance, a speech on the training of teachers may have such a format, as shown graphically in Figure 14-1.

FIGURE 14-1   Relationship of the Introduction, Body, and Conclusion to the Larger Picture

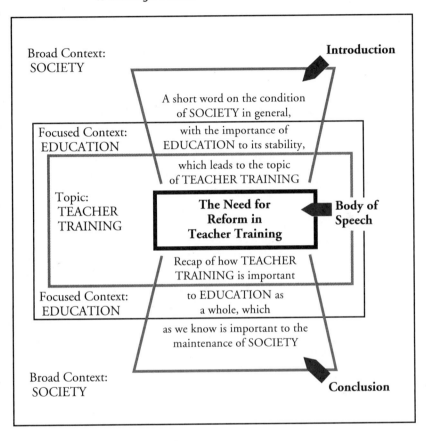

If you have introduced new definitions and concepts, or familiar definitions and concepts in unfamiliar ways, use the conclusion to reinforce your use of them.

Exercise 1. How do the speeches in the Sample Speeches on the Web provide logical closure? Do you approve of the speakers' decisions to summarize explicitly, generally, or not at all?

Exercise 2. Write a logical wrap-up for either the comic book outline in **10b** or the outline on working women in **11b**.

14b. Provide psychological closure.

Making your main points fit together logically for your audience is not enough. Members should walk away psychologically satisfied with your speech—you need to have touched them. When you plan your conclusion, think not only about what you want your listeners to understand and agree with but also about how you want them to feel at the end of the speech.

(1) Remind the audience how the topic affects their lives.

In the introduction, you make the topic personal to your audience. During the speech itself, you implicitly sustain that orientation by making your examples and manner of speaking appropriately personal. At the end, you bring the topic home again and show your listeners why it should be of more than academic interest to them—why they have a stake in what you have described.

In the financial accounting speech referred to in **13b**, the speaker moved away from the audience's immediate concerns right after the introduction. The body of the speech consisted of a rather technical comparison of historical cost accounting and replacement cost accounting. However, in the conclusion, the speaker returned the spotlight to her listeners:

> Whether you work for a large organization or have your own small business, whether you keep your own books or deal with a cadre of accountants, these two systems will affect you. Understanding the basic logic of each is necessary if you are to make sound decisions.

(2) Make an appeal.

Part of the psychological wrap-up of a speech can be a direct appeal to your audience, especially in a speech to persuade. Ask them directly to behave in a certain way (through adoption, deterrence, discontinuance, or continuance; see **22a**), or ask them to change their attitudes. Robert Kennedy, in a speech to the Democratic legislative dinner shortly after the Watts riots of 1967, ended this way:

> For us as Democrats the responsibility is clear. We must reject the counsel of those willing to pass laws against violence while refusing to help eliminate rats . . .
>
> We must offer that leadership—in every legislature and school board and city hall—which dares to speak out *before* it tests the shifting wind of popu-

lar anger and confusion; that leadership which prefers facts to illusions, actions to sullen withdrawal, sacrifice and effort to indulgence and ease.[1]

An appeal can be strengthened by a statement of your own intent: "I plan to give blood tomorrow morning, and I hope to see you down there."

In some speeches, the appeal makes the most sense if it is partitioned. You might make one appeal for long-range action and another for immediate action. Or you might make one appeal telling people what they can do individually and another telling them what they can do collectively. With a large and diverse audience, you might direct different appeals to segments of the audience, as Peter M. Gearhart did in wrapping up his speech on the future of the legal profession:

> In closing, I have separate messages for lawyers and the general public.
>
> For lawyers, my message is this. Our challenge is not public relations, it is human relations. Our challenge is not too much commercialism, it is too little attention to making legal markets work better. Our challenge is not to protect the mystery of the legal profession, it is to *project* its humility. . . .
>
> Ultimately, my message is not to fight change, but to capture change, to make it work *for* the public in the context of professionalism. It will be good for the public, and I think that it will make practicing law more fun.
>
> To the nonlawyers, I add this: We lawyers are here to serve. Call on the best that is in us. You can, and should, expect a legal system that works for you. It is your legal system; ultimately, we are going to put you in control of it. It is precisely because what we do is so central to the American experience, so central to protecting individuality while building the American community, that your expectations should be high. When we fail to meet these expectations, we will try to do better. But *watch us* do better. We have a lot of good still to do.[2]

Exercise 3. What do the speeches in the Sample Speeches on the Web do to provide psychological closure? Are they effective?

14c. End your speech with a clincher.

It is as important to plan your last sentence as it is your first. Every speech needs a sentence that leaves no doubt that the speech is finished. Speakers who have not prepared this clincher tend to keep summarizing while trying

---

[1]*Congressional Record,* 6 Aug. 1967.

[2]Peter N. Gearhart, "The Future of the Legal Profession," *Vital Speeches of the Day* 60, no. 11 (1994): 347–352.

to devise a good exit line. As a result, many of them taper off in dismay and defeat with such frail endings as:

> I guess that's all I wanted to say.
> Oops! My time is up. I'd better stop now.
> Well, I'd like to say more, but I ought to take questions.

Other speakers do not taper off; they simply stop short, leaving the audience to decide whether the blank air is a pause or the real ending.

One type of effective clincher for a speech ties back to the attention getter used in the introduction. This involves answering definitively the provocative question you asked initially or reintroducing your opening joke or story and taking it one step further—or twisting it in the light of your thesis:

> Frank Salacuse's syndicate spent $17,500 for its comic book, but all *you* need is a pocketful of change and transportation to the nearest newsstand or grocery store to rediscover a unique facet of Americana.

Also consider clinching your speech with a proverb, aphorism, quotation, or snatch of poetry. Martin Luther King, Jr., ended his historic "I Have a Dream" speech by evoking the words of an old spiritual: "Free at last, free at last, thank God Almighty, we are free at last."

Do not use "thank you" as a substitute for a clincher. It is customary to thank your audience, not after a classroom speech or a business presentation, but only when you have been honored by a special invitation to speak. In this case, "thank you" can be the transition from the other parts of your conclusion into your clincher:

> And so, for all these reasons, I hope you agree that government regulation must be checked.
>
> Thank you for inviting me to be here and for your kind attention. As you seek solutions to the complex problems of your industry, I hope that you will remember the words of Thomas Jefferson: "The price of liberty is eternal vigilance."

The delivery of your clincher is as important as its content. Do not mumble your final sentence in a throwaway voice or spend the last few speaking moments gathering up your notes and slinking away. Be familiar enough with your clincher that you can deliver it while maintaining eye contact with your listeners. When you finish, lower your gaze briefly and then reestablish eye contact to indicate willingness to answer questions or to acknowledge applause. Inevitably, just as in the beginning, you will be self-conscious at this point. You will feel the focus changing from your message back to you. Remind yourself to project a confident image here so that you do not undo the effect of your clincher.

Exercise 4. Evaluate the last few sentences of each speech in the Sample Speeches on the Web. Does the final sentence of each successfully serve the functions of a clincher?

Exercise 5. Write a clincher for either the outline on comic books in **10b** or the outline on working women in **11b.**

14d. Avoid common conclusion pitfalls.

Here are some common conclusion pitfalls to avoid:

1. *Don't* end with an apology: "I guess I've rambled on long enough," or "I don't know if I've made this clear," "I'm not usually this hyper; it must be the coffee."
2. *Don't* trail off. Do your audience the courtesy of wrapping things up and using a clincher. (See **14c.**)
3. *Don't* introduce a whole new point in your conclusion. The body of your speech is the place for that. (See **9c.**)
4. *Don't* read your conclusion. Or, if you have memorized it, be sure it does not sound mechanical. Practice moving into your conclusion naturally so that you maintain eye contact and keep your vocal presentation natural and conversational. (See **24d.**)
5. *Don't* make the conclusion disproportionately long. It is a summary and ending.
6. *Don't* end in a style or mood that is at odds with the tenor of the rest of the speech. You do your listeners a disservice if you have kept them laughing up to the very end only to hit them with a stark recitation of doom. (See **17c.**)
7. *Don't* use the phrases "in conclusion" or "in summary" in any part of the speech other than the actual conclusion. You will lose part of your audience while they reorient themselves to the fact that the speech is continuing when they thought it was winding down. (See **12b.**)

Part 4

Development

Introduction

In talking about the power of words, VerLynn Sprague, the father of one of the authors, customarily gave this rebuttal to an old cliché:

> It's been said that a picture is worth a thousand words. Well, I'm not sure how true that is. Some pictures are worth a million words. It depends on the words. Let me choose the words for you: the Twenty-Third Psalm, the Lord's Prayer, the Preamble to the Constitution, the introduction to the Declaration of Independence, the "Gettysburg Address," and Shakespeare's Sonnet 18. A person would be hard-pressed to find a picture that means as much to me as those thousand words do.

The next nine chapters deal with words and pictures, and the pictures we draw with words. Of all the choices you make as a speaker, by far the most important is your choice of the message you will send.

Too often, people think of a speaking assignment as a burden, a block of time to be filled. Approach it more positively! Here is a chance to share something you really believe in. Have you ever thought about the potential power a public speaker has? Look at just one dimension of that power—the amount of time you control as a speaker. If you give an eight-minute speech in a class, that does not seem like much—until you consider that with an audience of 30 people you have been granted 4 hours of human time and attention. If you give a 2-hour training workshop to a dozen coworkers, that is 24 human hours—one full day. Or, if you deliver a one-hour keynote address to 150 people at a conference, you have consumed 150 human hours—*almost a week*. This view of the speaking situation dramatizes your tremendous opportunity and responsibility.

Being entrusted with these precious hours of human time should motivate you to prepare extensively. You do not want to waste your listeners' time by underestimating their intelligence, stating the obvious, boring them, or taking twice as long as necessary to make a point. Remember, you are not doing all this work for an eight-minute result; you are getting set for four hours of potential influence.

It probably took VerLynn Sprague at least an hour to select and count the thousand words that would best illustrate his point about their power. He knew his ratio of preparation time to speaking time was going to be 60 to 1, but he felt it was worth it to formulate material that was original, effective, and memorable.

We believe that a speaker, to show good faith with an audience, has an ethical obligation to respect their interests, as well as his or her own. Of course, the speaker has a purpose in speaking, but the power of the platform should not be abused. If you are skilled, you can use personal charisma, emotional appeals, and loaded language to have an almost hypnotic effect on listeners. We cannot say that these techniques are ineffective, but we do deem them unethical.

A good speech should never substitute emotion for reason. When you presume to command people's time and attention, you owe it to them to know what you are talking about. Your message should be logical, factual, and coherent. Only after developing the sound rational base should you move on to making the message personal and palatable.

Chapters **15–23** guide you through the concepts pertinent to the development of your speech. The first six chapters introduce the concepts, and the remaining three suggest ways to weave them into strategic tapestries and adapt them to specialized situations.

Selecting the proper *supporting materials* provides proof of and amplification for your ideas. Familiarity with basic principles of *reasoning* helps you establish logical patterns of thought and avoid fallacies. The relationship of *language* and thought influences speech development, which is not complete until ideas are cast in a clear, effective oral *style*. There is a psychological and interpersonal component to speech; it comes into play through sparking listeners' *attention and interest,* through establishing your *credibility* with them, through making *motivational appeals* to their needs and values, and through evoking their delight. "Strategy" may bring to mind battlefield moves by generals or game plans by football coaches, but in speech it carries none of the combative or manipulative and tricky connotations of these images. A speech strategy is only this: a master plan for combining your content with other elements of speaking to meet a certain goal. Depending on the nature of that goal, you can formulate effective *informative strategies* or *persuasive strategies.* And once you master the skills and perspective associated with these elements, you can apply them as you *adapt* your message in light of your speaking context.

Chapter 15

Supporting Materials

Clarify and justify each of your points with a variety of supporting materials. Be sure these materials meet the tests for sound evidence and are smoothly integrated into the speech.

When you have set up the basic structure of your speech, you then turn to selecting the materials—whether gleaned from research or from your thought processes—that will make up its real building blocks. This process is analogous to "fleshing out" a skeletal drawing of a figure or to adding the siding to the frame of a building. These supporting materials are crucial to the success of your speech. They are the "stuff" it is made of. They probably determine whether your listeners characterize your utterances as valid or invalid, interesting or boring.

You can select the forms of support only in reference to a basic structure. It is impossible to judge the appropriateness of supporting materials unless you are very clear about what you are supporting. We are appalled to hear speakers say things like, "My first point is the Chicago example, and my next point is the study done by the Harvard sociologist." Example of what? Study proving or explaining what principle? It is extremely important, as we stress in chapters **6** (on topic selection and analysis) and **9** (on transforming ideas), that you measure every component of your speech against a logical outline. If your point is that crime is on the increase, then the story of a single crime, however graphic and compelling, should not be the basis for your development. To *support* that point, you need comparative data—examples collected from at least two periods of time to establish a trend.

Supporting materials may take the form of clarification or of proof. Often, especially in speeches to inform or evoke, these materials amplify, clarify, or expand on ideas. In other cases, materials are used to bolster controversial claims for which a speaker seeks acceptance. Although the possibility of ever actually *proving* a point completely could be questioned on philosophical grounds, we speak of supporting materials as proof because they can serve to justify an idea, adding to the probability of its acceptance. Frequently, a single piece of support, such as a statistic, functions as both clarification and proof of a point. Some kinds of support, though, like hypothetical examples or definitions, can be used only as amplification; they never serve to prove anything. For a fuller discussion of methods for clarifying ideas, refer to chapter **21** (on informative strategies). For further advice on proving controversial claims, see chapter **22** (Persuasive Strategies).

Select the support for your ideas first on the basis of relevance, then soundness, and then interest value. Avoid the rut some speakers fall into when they use mostly examples, or mostly testimony, or mostly explanation. Form the habit of using a variety of the following methods to develop your speech.

15a. Define unfamiliar words and concepts.

We all have listened to speakers who used so many unfamiliar terms that they might as well have been speaking in a foreign language. Or we may have had a hazy notion of the speaker's meaning but craved reassurance: "regressive taxes" *(poor people pay more—no—less?),* "left-brain function" *(is that the logical side?),* "deglaze the pan" *(something like sauté, probably).*

There are many methods of definition you can use to save your audience from this kind of experience. Select one or more of the following, depending on which type best suits your situation.

(1) Logical definition

Logical definition, also known as genus-species or dictionary definition, has two steps. It first places the concept to be defined into a category; then it explains the characteristics that distinguish that concept from all other members of the category. For example:

	ANTHROPOLOGY is a	
Step 1	formal field of academic study that studies the human species	[not a religion or a political system or a health food]
Step 2	as a whole to develop a comprehensive understanding of human nature and history.	[which differentiates it from physics, sociology, biology, psychology]

173

Some speakers make the mistake of skipping Step 1. Listening to a description of the *Spitfire* as being "more effective, certainly, than the *Boulton Paul Defiant* and faster and more agile than its predecessors and contemporaries" will not be enlightening if the listener is not told that the *Spitfire* is in the category "WWII British fighter aircraft." Note that the category is fairly specific. It provides a better focus than the less specific category "airplane," which can bring to mind images of everything from the *Wright Flyer* to a Boeing 767.

(2) Etymological and historical definitions

One way to clarify a word's meaning is to explain how the word was derived, either as linked to some historical event or as drawn from root words in an older culture:

Etymological

Anthropology is drawn from the Greek *anthropos,* meaning "human being," and *ology,* meaning "the study of."

Historical

In 1880, Charles G. Boycott, an English land agent in Ireland, refused to reduce rents. In response, his tenants refused to pay them. The word *boycott* has entered the language to mean the act of refusing to engage in social or economic interaction with some entity, either to coerce or to express disapproval.

(3) Operational definition

One way to explain a term is to tell how the object or concept referred to works or operates. Such operational definitions may simply indicate the steps that make up a process:

The *mean* is what you get when you add up all the scores and divide by the number of scores.

Logging on to the computer consists of specifying the system, giving your user ID number, and designating the form your data will take.

Social scientists use operational definitions to explain how conceptual terms are measured:

A *physically active person* will be defined as someone who spends at least six hours a week participating in a vigorous form of exercise.

A *good supervisor* will be defined as a person receiving a score of 25 or higher on the supervisor rating index.

Returning to the anthropology example, you might define the field by telling what an anthropologist does:

> An *anthropologist* makes systematic observations about past or present human behavior and then synthesizes these observations into generalizations about human nature and history.

(4) Definition by negation or opposition

Socrates said, "Nobody knows what justice is, but everyone knows what injustice is." In many cases, the best way to clarify a term is to explain what it is not. Abstract notions such as fairness, clarity, and power can sometimes be better defined by describing actions that are unfair, relationships that are unclear, or people who are powerless.

Reference to opposites can be used to explain concrete terms, too:

> Hypoglycemia is something like the opposite of diabetes.

> Anthropologists do not amass specialized data on a whim—digging for bones because they need the exercise or living among the natives because the indigenous fish are delicious.

This sort of definition can be powerful and intriguing. For a well-rounded picture, however, negation is best combined with other forms of definition.

(5) Definition by authority

This method of defining is useful for controversial or vague terms for which a choice must be made among plausible alternatives. The arbiter of meaning becomes the person with the most credibility or the most power (see also **15d**):

> I don't know what *you* mean by "a little late," but the boss says anything over 15 minutes goes on your record.

> Free speech cannot be suppressed unless a "clear and present danger" exists. The Supreme Court has defined it thus: "No danger flowing from speech can be deemed clear and present, unless the incidence of the evil apprehended is so imminent that it may befall before there is opportunity for full discussion. If there be time to expose through discussion the falsehood and fallacies, to avert the evil by the processes of education, the remedy to be applied is more speech, not enforced silence. Only an emergency can justify repression."

In the anthropology speech, you could cite the renowned Margaret Mead:

> She characterizes anthropology as a latecomer and an uncommitted discipline that spans several fields: "It does not fall, with relentless traditionalism, into any category of science or of humanities or of social science. . . . It is in this very anomalousness that I believe anthropology can make a unique contribution to a liberal education."[1]

(6) Definition by example

Among the many supporting roles played by examples (see **15b**), definition by example is a common and effective means to make terms concrete. The speaker explains something by pointing at it, verbally or literally:

> When I talk about a charismatic leader, I mean someone like John Kennedy, or Martin Luther King, Jr., or Adolf Hitler.

> The weapon used in kendo is a bamboo practice sword called a *shinai.* Here is one [hefts *shinai*].

> There are two basic ways to cause the strings of the guitar to vibrate: strumming, which sounds like this [strums], and picking, which sounds like this [picks].

> Anthropology includes such works and studies as L. S. B. Leakey's archeological research in the Olduvai Gorge, Margaret Mead's description of sex roles of the Tchambuli society, Noam Chomsky's treatise on transformation linguistics, and Konrad Lorenz's arguments for the innateness of human aggression.

Note that the examples chosen to define *anthropology* were familiar and diverse, representing four distinct areas of anthropological research.

Exercise 1. Define each of these terms using two different methods:

1. Cross training
2. Love
3. Collective bargaining
4. A tachometer
5. Sibling rivalry

---

[1]Margaret Mead, "Anthropology and Education for the Future," *Readings in Anthropology,* 3rd ed., ed. Jesse D. Jennings and E. Adamson Hoebel (New York: McGraw-Hill, 1972), 3–6.

15b. Make frequent use of examples.

Few words perk up an audience better than "Now let me give you an example." Beyond the universal appeal of a good story, examples provide audience members with a chance to check their perceptions of a speaker's message. When concepts are linked to actual cases, the listeners can see if their images coincide with those of the speaker. As a speaker, you need to make decisions about whether to use real examples or hypothetical ones and about how brief or how extended these examples should be.

(1) Use factual examples to illustrate and document your points.

A *fact* is an assertion that is universally accepted. Sometimes, it is directly verifiable, as in "Sandra Day O'Connor is a justice of the Supreme Court." Even if you were not at the swearing-in, there is enough corroborative evidence from many sources to satisfy you that this is a factual statement. "The earth is 93 million miles from the sun" is another assertion accepted as a fact although it is not *directly* verifiable through any of the five senses. But we do accept it, because we have constructed theoretical frameworks based on consistent results of observation and can make predictions of near-absolute certainty. Knowing the speed of light in Einsteinian space/time, we can calculate the distance of the earth from the sun using instruments that extend the senses.

When you use such examples for explanation, it is essential that you imbue them with clarity, relevance, and variety. When you use examples to prove a point, though, specific logical tests must be met. This is the essence of inductive reasoning as discussed in **16b**.

Are sufficient examples given?
To establish the point that high schools in your county are failing to teach basic literacy skills, it would hardly suffice to tell about a few functionally illiterate graduates you know personally. The more examples you give, the less likely your listeners are to dismiss the phenomenon as the product of chance.

Are the examples representative?
Even if you gave a dozen examples of local graduates who were functionally illiterate, the conclusion would be suspect if all the cases were from one remedial class in one school. To be credible, examples should represent a cross section of students in the county.

Are negative instances accounted for?

Your conclusion about the failure of the schools might be countered by someone citing the example of her niece who was a National Merit Scholar or pointing out that test scores at Arbor Estates High School were above the national average. When you reason by example, you must look into and account for dramatic negative examples. Perhaps the niece has an IQ of 175. Maybe Arbor Estates High School has a cadre of charismatic English teachers. Your obligation, if you wish to carry your point, is to show how these examples are atypical and why they should be excluded from a consideration of the general status of most students in most schools in the county.

(2) Use hypothetical examples for clarification, speculation, and adaptation to the immediate situation.

Sometimes, when no factual example quite suits your purpose, or when you are speculating about the future, you might give a brief or extended hypothetical example. Here are two illustrations of *extended hypothetical* examples:

> How should you develop an investment portfolio? Well, let's imagine that you have a monthly household income of $4,000 and that your expenses run to about $2,800. Let me show you how to calculate what portion of the remainder should go into fairly liquid low-risk areas like the money markets or short-term T-bills and what portion can go into higher-risk areas like commodities.

> Picture a young woman—let's call her Katie—heading toward her car after working overtime. Because she's so tired, she doesn't hear the footsteps behind her until she's some distance from the building. Katie quickens her pace . . .

Hypothetical examples do not have to be extended ones. Here is a speech segment that uses three *brief hypothetical* examples in quick succession:

> What would happen if this tax law were to pass? Well, Miguel over there couldn't deduct his business lunches. Audrey wouldn't be able to depreciate her buildings. You, Tom, with kids about to start college . . .

Obviously, hypothetical examples cannot *prove* anything. They are useful for clarification because they can be tailored to fit the subject exactly. As the previous example demonstrates, hypothetical examples allow you to bring the members of your audience into your speech. When you design your examples, follow the suggestions in **18a**.

Be aware that the examples you pick reflect a set of assumptions about the world. Be sensitive to racist or sexist implications of your illustrations.

Are all the bosses men, and all the secretaries women; do all the laborers have Polish names, and are all the drunks Irish? If your examples imply that you see the world in terms of these inaccurate stereotypes, some audience members will be offended. We live in a pluralistic and rapidly changing society, so you should mix up the names, sexes, races, and roles to reflect that diversity.

(3) Determine the appropriate amount of detail to include in your examples.

Examples in a speech can be kept brief when you can safely assume that the audience already accepts them. This means that you can point quickly to several familiar examples. To clarify an idea, you might say, "The employee benefits manager handles all of the forms of reward that are not wages—medical insurance, dental insurance, bonuses, profit-sharing plans, company scholarships, for example." To prove a proposition, you could also point to familiar and accepted cases: "In the early campaigns in Virginia, the generals of the Confederacy repeatedly demonstrated superior tactics. Think, for example, of Jackson's Valley Campaign, or Lee and the Seven Days' Battles and Second Bull Run." But, obviously, these *brief factual* examples will not be effective with listeners who have never heard of profit sharing or who know nothing of the Civil War. In such cases, more detail will be needed.

When a succession of quick references will not illuminate a point for your listeners, develop the example into an illustration, as in this *extended factual* example:

> Let's look at one example of the tactical superiority of Confederate generals: Lee's Campaign of Second Bull Run. With daring and skill, Lee kept his opponent, Pope, off balance. Lee first sent Jackson around to capture the Union base of supplies 20 miles to Pope's rear. When Pope predictably went after Jackson, Jackson eluded him. During this time, Lee moved his army to put it into a position where, when Pope did finally find and attack Jackson, Lee was able to make a devastatingly decisive flank attack.

Though these scenarios take time to develop, they create vivid images that might make the point with more emphasis than would shorter examples.

When you use examples, you must decide how long or short to make each one. This is an area of unconscious incompetence for many speakers. (See **1d.**) Some use only such brief references that we are left mystified by their cryptic allusions to "what happened in New Jersey" or the "Browne affair." Others tell every detail of every case. For instance, we end up knowing not only that the software product works but also the color of the CD-ROM package, the thickness of the plastic wrapping, the cleanliness of the monitor screen, the length of time spent waiting at the checkout counter, the name of the salesperson, and on and on.

Be conscious of the choices you make. Select the appropriate degree of elaboration for each example based on audience familiarity with the incident, on the effect you want to create, and on an understanding of the best use of the time allotted to you. Ideally, a speech blends several short examples with a few extended ones. Properly selected, these show the audience both the breadth of your subject and some in-depth aspects of it.

Exercise 2. Look at three of the speeches on the Sample Speeches Web site. How many examples are used in each? Label each as brief or extended, and as factual or hypothetical. Evaluate the variety of any examples used to establish an inductive line of argument.

Exercise 3. Select one of these topics:

Teenage Suicide
Media Impact on Elections
Organ Transplants

Now develop an example in each of the following categories, and briefly explain in what sort of speech situation it would be most appropriate.

a. Brief factual
b. Extended factual
c. Brief hypothetical
d. Extended hypothetical

Exercise 4. Select one of the three topics in Exercise 3, and develop an inductive argument that meets the tests in **15b(1).**

15c. Use statistical evidence to quantify, clarify, and prove your points.

When examples are systematically collected and classified, they are reported as statistics. In the case of the literacy topic discussed in **15b(1)**, it would not be feasible to discuss, by name, all the students who illustrate your point. It would simply take too much time to give enough examples to show the seriousness of the problem. This is when you turn to statistical evidence. By examining test scores, conducting follow-up studies of graduates, or interviewing teachers, you could clarify and support your speech with material like this:

> Fifty-eight percent of the seniors in our county high schools did not reach the basic proficiency level on the state reading exams.

> One third of our graduates who went to college failed freshman English.

> Teachers report that one out of four students has trouble comprehending material written at the seventh-grade level.

(1) Check the accuracy of statistical evidence by applying the tests of *who, why, when,* and *how.*

Who collected the data?

Investigate the qualifications and competence of the researchers. Was the work done by a professional pollster or the host of a call-in radio show? A graduate student or a noted scholar? An advertising agency or a government task force?

Why were the data collected?

The motivation behind collecting certain information can make the data suspect. Statistics from research done by a political candidate's staff, purporting to show massive support for the candidate, may better reflect a need to demoralize the opposition than a need to show a true picture to the public. Most people have more confidence in inquiries rooted in a desire to advance knowledge. Although not totally free of bias, independent pollsters, investigative journalists, scientists, and academics tend to be more objective than persons committed to selling a product or promoting a cause.

When were the data collected?

Be sure your evidence is up-to-date. Attitudes change as swiftly as prices, and some data are obsolete by the time they are published. If you are dealing with a continuously active subject, like the economy, it won't hurt to consult an expert about a source for the most recent data.

How were the data collected?

Find out as much as you can about the design of the research and the details of its execution. If a certain statistical finding supports a key point of your speech, do not settle for a one-paragraph reference from *Psychology Today*. Track it back to the *Journal of Social and Experimental Psychology* and learn more about the original study.

First, compare definitions. You may find the title of the study promising, but a closer reading could show that the investigator defines "part-time workers" or "effective leadership" in ways that do not apply to your speech.

Next, check how the cases were chosen. Subjects and examples should have been selected randomly or through some other logical and unbiased system.

Finally, evaluate the method of data collection—observation, experiment, or survey conducted by phone, mail, or personal interview. If possible, look at the actual instrument used. Are there leading questions or unrealistic forced choices in the interviews and questionnaires? Even if you are not an expert, you can spot bias introduced into the research method—for example, through the phrasing of directions or the way the findings are analyzed and presented.

(2) Avoid misleading statistics.

We know that language is ambiguous, but we tend to believe that numbers make straightforward statements; there is no mystery in 2 + 2 = 4. However, numbers *can* be just as ambiguous, with statistical pitfalls to trap the unwary.

The fallacy of the average

A critic once said, with tongue in cheek, that a person could stand with one foot on a block of ice and one foot in a fire, and be *statistically* comfortable. Although the average can be a useful tool for analysis, it sometimes gives a picture absurdly at odds with reality.

Less absurd, but just as misleading, might be the report that the Smurge Company has an average of 6 computer scanners per department when, in fact, the marketing department has 40 scanners, and most other departments have one or none. As this demonstrates, calculating the arithmetic *mean* is not appropriate when one or two extreme cases skew the distribution. The *median* (the number or score that falls at the midpoint of the range of numbers or scores) or the *mode* (the most frequently occurring score or number) can be more meaningful averages to use in this example, although they, too, can be abused. See Figure 15-1 for a graphic representation of the scanner distribution in the Smurge Company. In this case, although the *mean* is 6, the *median* is 2 (scores of 0 and 1 below it, scores of 3 and 40 above it), and the *mode* is 1 (the largest number of departments—three—have this score).

The fallacy of the unknown base

When a speaker uses percentages and proportions, he or she can imply that a large population has been sampled. In fact, data are sometimes reported in this manner to give credence to unscientific or skimpy evidence: "Two out of

| **FIGURE** 15-1 | Distribution of Scanners at the Smurge Company |

Dept.	*Number of Scanners*
Marketing	□□
Development	□□□
Finance	□□
Administration	□
QA	□
Cust. Support	□
Production
Facilities

Mode — Median

Number of Departments

3
2
1

0 1 2 3 ... 40

Scanners per Department

three mechanics recommend this synthetic oil." Most listeners would see this as shorthand for "We polled 300 mechanics around the country, and 200 of them recommended this synthetic oil." How valid would this recommendation seem if it came to light that in reality only *three* were polled?

Similarly, "80 percent of the crimes in this county were committed by teenagers" seems to point to a serious problem. It certainly has more impact than "We had five burglaries this year, and four were committed by teenagers." But four instances do not make a crime wave, and 80 percent is not necessarily an epidemic.

The fallacy of the atypical or arbitrary time frame

Recently, an executive of a computer circuit board company told us that sales in February were double those of the previous month. These data could be misleading unless you know that January is always the worst month in the yearly cycle of the computer industry. If the executive had compared February and November, the month in the cycle in which the pre-Christmas home computer and videogame buying frenzy reaches its peak, then the picture would have been quite different. A more valid example to demonstrate company growth would have compared February with February of the previous year.

By choosing longer or shorter time frames, this executive could give varying spins on the company's health. If he chose November-December-January, with its sharply downward trend, he might convince employees that this is

183

no time to talk about raises. Or he might reassure stockholders by reporting a gradual but steadily upward trend revealed by the figures from the last five Novembers.

(3) Make your numbers and statistics clear and meaningful to your listeners.

The stereotypical dry, plodding speech is one that is overloaded with statistics. After a short while, the audience becomes overloaded, too, and starts to build a mental dike against the numbers flowing over them. When you do use statistics, round them off. Say "about fifteen hundred" instead of "one thousand four hundred eighty-nine point six." Use comparisons to make the numbers more understandable:

> For the amount of money they propose to spend on this weapons system, we could provide educational grants in aid to all the needy students in the eleven western states, or triple the government funding for cancer research, or upgrade the highway system in this state and its three neighbors.

> The immensity of time taxes our ability to perceive it. The universe came into existence 15 billion years ago; our distant mammal ancestors watched the dinosaurs die out 65 million years ago; our closer ancestors came down from the trees 20 million years ago; recorded history began a scant 7,000 years ago. Think of this in terms of a cosmic calendar: The Big Bang set off the celebration on January 1. It wasn't until late on December 30 that mammals began to supplant the giant reptiles, and not until 7 p.m. on December 31 did protohumans start feeling more at home on the ground than in the trees. And recorded history did not begin until three seconds before midnight on that same day.

Avoid overused comparisons. Too many dollar bills have been laid end to end and too many large objects have been improbably dumped onto football fields or placed next to the Empire State Building. Furthermore, audiences are no longer shocked to consider the "five people in this room" who will suffer some fate, or the dire toll of outside events that will be racked up "by the end of this speech" or "by the time I finish this sentence."

Exercise 5. What additional information would you need to have before accepting the following statistical evidence?

1. Studies show that over two thirds of the total meaning a person communicates is conveyed nonverbally.

2. Of people who chew gum, four out of five surveyed prefer sugarless gum.
3. Researchers have found that the average social drinker has eight serious hangovers a year.
4. Dozens of cases of police harassment have been brought to my attention during my opponent's term of office.

15d. Draw on testimony from authorities.

Often, we call on statements from other people to get our point across. Testimony can be viewed as an outward extension of the speaker's own fact-finding. When we do not have the opportunity to verify something through our own senses, we rely on the observations of others. For instance, even if you have never been arrested or never been a public safety officer, you can give a credible speech on the penal system by making judicious use of testimony.

It might be effective to recite the events of a typical day in prison or to deliver the comments of an inmate on the surroundings. You can draw on the authority of experts or eyewitnesses:

> Remembering his five years of incarceration, Mike Carson said, "Every day was the same. We sat in our cells doing nothing but waiting for our hour of exercise or our chance to eat the same lousy food."

> Based on her study of prison conditions, noted criminologist Sarah Jackson reports, "Only a few inmates have the opportunity to attend classes or to hold a job that will teach them a useful skill."

Testimony may be cited directly or paraphrased. You might use a direct quotation in the following manner:

> According to a report of the Second Circuit Court of Appeals: "Beginning immediately after the state's recapture of Attica on the morning of September 13, and continuing until at least September 16, guards, state troopers, and correctional personnel had engaged in cruel and inhuman abuse of numerous inmates. Injured prisoners, some on stretchers, were struck, prodded, or beaten. Others were forced to strip and run naked through gauntlets of guards armed with clubs . . . spat upon or burned with matches . . . poked in the genitals or arms with sticks."[2]

---

[2]Jessica Mitford, *Kind and Usual Punishment: The Prison Business* (New York: Knopf, 1973), 265–66.

Or you might paraphrase the statement:

> A report of the Second Circuit Court of Appeals catalogs the cruel and inhuman abuse following the Attica riots. When the state regained control, guards and prison personnel subjected the prisoners to harsh physical punishments.

(1) Evaluate the credibility of the authorities you cite when you use testimony as proof.

You do not have to research a controversial topic for very long before you find that there are seemingly authoritative quotations to support every side of an issue. It is easy to find citations that say almost anything; it is much more difficult to select those that provide legitimate support for your points. Test the credibility of the authorities you quote by asking these questions.

Does the authority have access to the necessary information?

A person does not have to be famous to be an authority. The eyewitness to an accident can tell you authoritatively what happened in the intersection. Your neighbor does not have to be an expert China watcher to report on a trip taken to that country. The farther removed someone is from the source, however, the less trustworthy that person's information. A quotation from the accident eyewitness is preferable to a quotation from an acquaintance recounting what the eyewitness said.

Ambiguous descriptions can be misleading. "My brother works for the government, and he says there's a massive conspiracy to cover up the cost overruns in the Defense Department" or "It is the opinion of a noted psychologist that the murderer is definitely insane" is testimony that loses its effect when we learn that the brother is a postal clerk and the psychologist has only read the newspaper accounts of the trial. When you use an authority, be sure that the person had firsthand experience, direct observation, or personal access to relevant facts and files.

Is the authority qualified to interpret data?

As stated previously, anyone can credibly describe what she or he saw. It is when a person starts making interpretations, forming opinions and conclusions, and proposing recommendations that the standards of credibility become stricter. People earn the right to be considered experts either by holding specific credentials—such as a law degree, Ph.D., or Realtor's license—or by establishing a record of success and experience.

Is the person acknowledged as an expert on this subject?

When the Washington Redskins football team executed a play suggested by then-President Nixon, we saw a peculiar variation of the practice of presenting a sports figure in commercials as an authority on nutrition or automotive engineering. President Nixon's acknowledged expertise in the field of foreign policy did not make him a credible football authority. There are other cases in which an expert's opinions have subtly stretched beyond the range of his or her expertise. A tax attorney may be presented as an expert on constitutional law, a social psychologist may express an opinion on the causes of schizophrenia, or a well-known chemist may receive national attention for her or his views on the efficacy of vitamin C. The opinions they express may or may not be valid, but their expertise in a related field makes them, at best, only slightly more credible than an informed layperson.

Is the authority figure free of bias and self-interest?

It is not very surprising when the chair of the Democratic National Committee characterizes the party platform as a blueprint for justice and prosperity, or when a network spokesperson describes a new television show as an incisive and intelligent portrayal of the human condition. Nor is it very persuasive. We give much more credence to the opinion of a political analyst or a television critic who appears to have no personal stake—ideological or financial—in the response to the opinion. What would be surprising, and highly persuasive as well, is reluctant testimony. If you can find testimony from a person speaking *against* his or her interests, presumably because of honesty or as a duty to a larger concept, then it certainly will be an effective addition to your presentation: "Even the National Committee chair admitted that the platform is fuzzy on foreign policy."

(2) Take care, when editing quotations, to retain key points without distorting their meaning.

Shortening quotations to highlight the basic thrust of the message is perfectly acceptable. What is unacceptable is editing a person's statements to such a degree that they appear to support positions other than or even opposite those espoused in the actual quotations. There is the old joke about the movie critic who wrote that "the wretchedness of the acting in this film is nothing short of amazing!" only to find later that an advertisement for the movie quoted him as saying "this film . . . is amazing!"

Do not edit a quotation so radically that it loses all substance. Virtually content-free quotations are sometimes deliberately used to confuse listeners or to overwhelm them with an apparent preponderance of evidence. A common example of this is the recitation of the conclusion reached by an authority without including any of the reasoning that led to the conclusion: "About the job-retraining program, the mayor has said that it 'is a disappointment.' The president of the Chamber of Commerce stated that it 'has not fulfilled our expectations.' The chair of the Council of Unions labeled it 'a failure.'" The people cited may be authorities on the subject, but their reservations may result from an analysis that is not at all pertinent to the speaker's point. For instance, they all may be complaining of inadequate funding rather than attacking the concept of the program. It is impossible to tell from these cryptic quotations. It is also possible that these experts could be wrong. Listeners need to hear more about *why* they drew the conclusions they did.

15e. Weave supporting materials smoothly into the speech, and cite your sources.

When you have chosen appropriate definitions, facts, examples, statistics, and testimony, you still have to marshal these supporting materials and present them effectively. You want to emphasize the quality of your materials, make them clear and understandable, and organize them appropriately in relation to the points they support.

(1) Cite the sources of your supporting materials.

By giving credit for your supporting materials, you build your own credibility, by showing the range of your research. You are also providing information your listeners are almost certain to want. Very few audiences will settle for "studies show . . ." or "one researcher found . . ." or "a friend once told me . . ." To evaluate these statements, listeners need to know more about where the information came from.

This does not mean that you are required to present regulation footnotes in oral form, citing volume and page numbers. Nor do you need to recite an authority's complete biography or necessarily explain a study's design intricacies. Although you should know the *who, why, when,* and *how* of every bit of data you use, you will probably mention only a couple of these in introducing the evidence.

How do you decide which to include? You can follow two basic approaches. The first one encompasses those questions you predict your audience will have. Put yourself in the listeners' place and adopt a skeptical outlook: What would you question about the data? A hostile audience might want to know whether your expert was objective; a group of social scientists might question whether the opinion poll you cite was scientifically conducted. The second approach involves stressing what is most compelling and impressive. If you have a 30-year-old quotation from a Supreme Court justice but think the sentiment expressed is timeless, stress the *who* and not the *when*. What is the best feature of the evidence—its recency, the large size of the sample, or the prestige of the journal in which it appeared?

(2) Use a variety of lead-ins for stylistic effectiveness.

Do not get into the habit of introducing all your illustrations, statistics, and so on with the same phrase: "Some figures about this are . . . some figures about that are . . ." Be prepared enough that you can employ a number of lead-ins for each kind of supporting material. There are many possibilities:

> To support this idea . . .
> This point is verified by . . .
> _____ put it well, I think, when she said . . .
> In the words of _____ . . .
> What causes this situation? One answer to that question was offered by _____ when he wrote last year . . .
> Let me tell you about a survey taken in the early eighties by a Brandeis psychologist . . .
> There are several examples of this. Let me share just two . . .
> I was immediately struck by the similarity to an experience I/he/_____ once had . . .

However you decide to introduce a quotation, do not say "quote, unquote" or wiggle pairs of fingers in the air to approximate quotation marks. A subtle change in your voice or posture is enough to indicate to your listeners the boundaries of a direct quotation.

Exercise 6. Compare the use of supporting materials in the speeches on the Sample Speeches Web site. Note the presence of explanation, definition, examples, statistics, and testimony in each.

1. Does every speech use a variety of methods?
2. What are the two favored forms of supporting material in each speech?

Chapter 16

Reasoning

Use sound reasoning to develop your speech. Avoid logical fallacies.

Reasoning is the process by which we come to understand something previously unknown, through analyzing and integrating those things we already know. Your goal in a public speech is to share your insights with your listeners by "thinking" out loud, retracing for them the steps that led you to your conclusions. If you have not fully reasoned out your conclusions, or if you have made gross logical missteps in reaching them, the chance of those conclusions being accepted by an audience becomes exceedingly slim. Any remotely intelligent group of listeners will not be moved by hearing *what* you think; they want to know *why* you think it. Consequently, the reasoning that should be the foundation of every speech can also be seen as "the giving of *good* reasons."

People reason every time they make links between ideas. We speak in grammatical sentences (at least most of the time) even if we do not know the formal parts of speech or rules of grammar. By the same token, speakers and listeners reason competently a great deal of the time, or else they would not have survived to adulthood. When people disagree, it is not because one of them does not know the rules of formal or everyday logic. Rather, it is because they disagree about the facts and evidence, or about the interpretation of them. Making sure that your supporting material is valid was covered in chapter 15. Without getting into the intricacies of formal logic, this chapter addresses how to make sure your interpretation of the evidence is valid *and comes across as valid.*

To develop a logical line of thought and test its validity, you need to understand a little more about how reasoning functions to link key points of a speech together. You also need to become familiar with standard patterns of reasoning and with a few of the common fallacies. Only then can you decide how best to use reasoning in putting your speech together.

There are four patterns of reasoning discussed in this chapter: inductive reasoning, deductive reasoning, causal reasoning, and reasoning by analogy. They are not analyzed here in depth as logical forms separate from one another, because most complex reasoning involves a combination of methods. For instance, a causal connection might be established either inductively or deductively. Or perhaps a literal analogy might be used to justify a statement that becomes, in turn, the major premise of a deductive argument. As you read the remainder of this chapter, do not expect to master the intricacies of logical reasoning. Look instead to incorporate into your thinking a general sense of four very common patterns that you can use to structure speech material in a rational way.

16a. Identify each point in your preliminary speech outline where reasoning is needed to provide an essential link.

Every speech involves synthesizing data, explaining ideas, and clustering points. For some topics, developing the points then becomes a matter of merely "unpacking" the clusters. If your point is that there were three causes of the Spanish Inquisition, then you need to list and explain those. In many cases—in all persuasive speeches and some sections of evocative and informative speeches—a far more challenging task confronts the speaker. You must develop lines of argument through reasoning. For instance, if you have a cluster of ideas gathered around the point "reasons for allowing fetal tissue research," simply listing and explaining those reasons will not suffice. You will be informing the audience of what your reasons are or perhaps of what some experts say. But you will not convince them that your list of reasons warrants their acceptance unless you explain why you (and the experts you cite) come to the conclusion you do. This *conclusion* can also be called a *claim*. Claims are any statements that you need to substantiate because they are not taken for granted by your listeners. Your thesis sentence is a claim, your main points are claims that support that claim, and even some of your subordinate points have to be reasoned through before they become acceptable.

Some of the statements that make up your speech outline may not be controversial (e.g., "poverty is bad") or may be obvious (e.g., "most people would prefer not to pay higher taxes"). But many other points will need to be supported. The supporting materials, evidence, or data discussed in chapter 15 bolster your point—at least you think so, or you would not have put those data and that claim together. However, the challenge of reasoning is to show how the data and claim are linked.

(1) Recognize that evidence does not necessarily lead to a certain claim.

Suppose you have a conclusion or claim that you want your listeners to accept, and you have some evidence or data that you believe support that claim. Clearly, everyone who confronts the same facts and figures does not automatically come to the same conclusion that you do. What links the data to the claim, or *warrants* its acceptance, is the process of reasoning. For example, suppose two different people are confronted with the fact that more people go to the doctor in countries with national health care programs than in countries with privately funded health care. Person A concludes that this is an argument in support of adopting national health care in the United States. Person B concludes that it is an argument against national health care.

As Figure 16-1 shows, there is no connection between evidence and claim except through the reasoning link that you provide.

FIGURE 16-1   Reasoning Links Evidence and Claim

(2) Recognize that, in linking evidence to claims, people look for patterns of regularity that fit with what they have observed in the world.

In the health care example, Person A is drawing on a pattern observed in the past—namely, that people who cannot afford a service they need will seek out that service when it becomes affordable. This is perfectly reasonable and logical; we all can think of plenty of commonsense examples.

Person B is also being logical and reasonable in linking the evidence of increased medical visits to the claim that national health care would be undesirable. This person is drawing on another observed pattern of human behavior—that people who see a resource as free and unlimited may use it inappropriately and wastefully. There is also plenty of support for this view.

The issue here is not what the facts *are*, but what the facts *mean*. For our purposes, the significance of these opposing views is to show that there are many sensible ways to interpret the same piece of evidence. A speaker who uses evidence to support a claim cannot simply present the evidence and hope it speaks for itself. The speaker must explain the relevance of the evidence and justify the link to a particular claim.

The orientation toward communication taken in this book is that speakers do not merely transmit information to listeners. Rather, speakers and listeners create meanings together. Therefore, for any complex and controversial topic, you need to show your audience why your evidence is meaningful and help them build the argument with you. This is done by spelling out your interpretation of the data and showing how this interpretation fits one of the common patterns of reasoning familiar to your listeners.

Exercise 1. For each of these claims, list at least three pieces of evidence you could use to support it. To find the supporting evidence, log on to your InfoTrac College Edition, and perform a search for articles that contain information on the subjects, using the keywords provided.

1. Smoking should be banned in all indoor public places. [keywords *smoking ban*]
2. Bicycles are a good choice for beating urban traffic. [keywords *bicycle, congestion*]
3. Drivers over the age of seventy should have to take a road test every year to renew their driver's license. [keywords *elderly drivers, safety*]

After you have listed the evidence, explain how each piece of evidence supports the point.

Exercise 2. Show how the evidence presented here can be linked to the two different claims. What logical pattern is drawn upon in each case?

Example A

Evidence: The form of government in the United States has existed for over two hundred years.
Therefore
Claim 1: We should maintain our present form of government.
Because
Link or reasoning:

or

Therefore
Claim 2: We should change our present form of government.
Because
Link or reasoning:

Example B

Evidence: Deaths from firearms have increased in the past few years.
Therefore
Claim 1: We need even stronger gun control laws than the ones we have.
Because
Link or reasoning:

or

Therefore
Claim 2: We should get rid of gun control laws.
Because
Link or reasoning:

16b. Use an inductive pattern of reasoning when your argument consists of combining a series of observations that lead to a probable conclusion.

The simplest and most common kind of reasoning is induction. Dozens of times a day, we draw inferences that go beyond what we observe directly. Induction assumes an orderly universe. We could not function unless we trusted regularities in events, unless we believed that much of what has happened before will happen again. We step in front of oncoming traffic because we believe from previous experience that the cars will obey the traffic signals. After several sleepless nights, we stop drinking coffee at bedtime. Figure 16-2 depicts the process of inductive reasoning.

FIGURE 16-2   Inductive Reasoning Draws Inferences from Observations

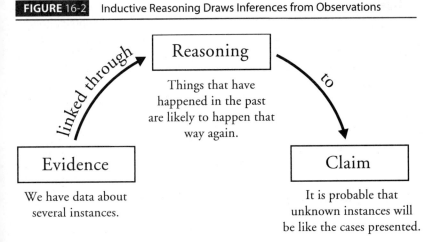

Reasoning

Things that have happened in the past are likely to happen that way again.

linked through

to

Evidence

We have data about several instances.

Claim

It is probable that unknown instances will be like the cases presented.

---

(1) Look before you "leap": Be sure the instances on which you base your inferences are sufficient and representative.

Inductive reasoning consists of collecting enough instances to establish a pattern. Remember the logical tests in **15b(1)**. A typical line of inductive thought can be portrayed as follows:

Orchid$_1$ has no fragrance.
Orchid$_2$ has no fragrance.
Orchid$_3$ has no fragrance.
....
,,...................................
....
Orchid$_n$ has no fragrance.
Therefore, it is probable that all orchids have no fragrance.

The extent to which you can generalize from such observations is linked to the extent of your sampling. If you smelled only the orchids in one corner of one hothouse, you would be less able to make a general conclusion than if you had smelled orchids in different hothouses throughout the country.

By far the greatest problem in this kind of reasoning is determining the value of *n*. Obviously, you want to test several cases before drawing a conclusion, but how many are enough? This is the issue of "enoughness." If you drive five Hupmobiles and they all have mechanical difficulties, is that enough to say that Hupmobiles are bad cars? If a researcher finds that 132 out of 150 soap opera fans surveyed do housework while listening, is that enough to justify a conclusion about that group? At best, you can say, "It is likely that Hupmobiles are lemons," and "Soap opera fans probably do housework while listening." The conclusions drawn from induction are always *probable* rather than *absolute*. The only way you could say that *all* Hupmobiles are lemons would be to test every one. This would be counting, not reasoning. Reasoning, as you will recall, is defined as drawing conclusions about the unknown.

Be cautious in drawing inferences from limited data. How many cases did you examine? Were they selected fairly? Are the contrary instances accounted for? (See **15b** and **16f**.)

(2) Recognize the degree of probability of your claim.

An inductive conclusion can fall anywhere along this continuum:

Possible	Probable	Almost
		certain

The degree of certainty depends on the methods used in making our observations and on the number of observations made. A conclusion like "The last two times I've gone to that restaurant the service has been lousy—I'll bet they've changed management" would fall far to the left. Two observations is a very small number, and there are many other viable explanations for the poor service. At the other end of the continuum is a statement like "Birth control pills prevent fertilization." This conclusion is based on a great many observations collected systematically. We can say we are 99 percent sure it is true, but we still lack complete certainty.

How strong must this probability be before you can consider the conclusion of an inductive argument to be valid? A 51 percent probability, or 75 percent, or 99 percent? Unlike deductive reasoning, for which there are agreed-upon tests of validity, the test of an induction varies in every case. There is no mathematical or logical answer to the question. The issue of enoughness is more a psychological question of individual perception, as is explained next.

Would you leap off a 20-foot wall for $1,000? Many would say yes. It is *possible* that you could be killed, but it is probable that you would escape with no worse than a sprained ankle or broken leg. Would you jump from the roof of a three-story building for $1,000? Most people would say no. It is *possible* that you would be unharmed, but not very probable. In both cases, you set the acceptable level of probability by weighing potential risks against potential gains. In flipping a coin, you have a 50 percent probability of getting heads (or tails)—good enough for a dollar bet, but would you bet your life on a coin toss? When you choose to ride in a car, the probability is tens of thousands to one that you will arrive safely, and the gain of speedy transportation outweighs the minimal risk.

(3) Demonstrate the cost/reward analysis that led you to accept or reject the probable claim.

When induction is used in a public speech, the speaker's task is to convince the audience members that the conclusion arrived at is probable enough to warrant their acceptance. The so-called inductive leap is based on an apt image. You lead the listeners to a certain point with your data and then ask them to jump across an imaginary chasm to the conclusion you see. Here, as in the preceding examples, the level of enoughness is contingent on the risks and benefits perceived.

Suppose you know of a new drug rehabilitation program that has been found to be quite effective in pilot studies in three different communities. In urging its adoption in your city, your line of reasoning might go like this:

> The program worked in Community A.
> The program worked in Community B.
> The program worked in Community C.
> Therefore, it is probable that the program is effective and will work here.

Because these other cases were not studied totally systematically (e.g., with control groups, random sampling, and follow-up studies) and because there are only three cases in your sample, you cannot state your conclusion at a high level of probability. You must recognize that the drug rehabilitation program could fail in your community. Imagine that it were possible to assign concrete levels of probability and that both proponents and skeptics of the program agreed that there was about a 75 percent chance of its success. A member of your audience might well ask, "Why should we spend $650,000 for just a three-out-of-four chance we might help a bunch of junkies?" You cannot change the 75 percent odds, but you can influence your audience's assessment of the costs and rewards. Tell them how the program, if it works, will benefit the whole community: It will decrease crime, put former addicts back into the workforce, and lower the temptations for adolescent drug use. Also minimize the costs: "I know $650,000 sounds like a lot, but it's only 85¢ per citizen." When the listeners reassess the costs and rewards, and see them as you do, the 75 percent odds may look more attractive.

Consider another example, in which the conclusion's probability is very high:

Nuclear power plant A has had no accidents.
Nuclear power plant B has had no accidents. .
Nuclear power plant C has had no accidents.

....

Nuclear power plant *n* has had no accidents.
Therefore, it is probable that nuclear power plants are safe.

Suppose the conclusion could be granted a 95 percent level of probability. Even so, you or someone else might not feel the evidence is sufficient to make the inductive leap. In explaining this to the audience, you would minimize the rewards—most of the energy we would get can be obtained through other sources—and maximize the risks by describing just how awful a nuclear accident would be. Your argument is: "I'm not willing to subject my family to a 5-out-of-100 chance of this sort of destruction just to have a few extra electronic luxuries."

In the case of the drug program, a low probability met the test of enoughness for the speaker. In the case of the nuclear power plant, even 95 percent was not enough. The difference lies in the perception of risk and reward. No level of enoughness is too high or too low—no inductive argument is innately logical or illogical. The validity is negotiated between you and your audience.

16c. Use a deductive pattern of reasoning when your argument demonstrates how the relationships among established premises lead to a necessary conclusion.

Unlike induction, in which the emphasis is on collecting observable data, *deduction* consists of manipulating verbal statements, or premises, according to formal rules. Deduction, then, involves not bringing new data into play, but rather rearranging what you already know. If this is the case, how can we learn anything new through the process of deduction if we are dealing with the known? Bits of data are useless until we can assign meaning to them by discovering how they fit together. From this are derived scientific breakthroughs, brainteasers, gossip, and the English murder mystery. In the obligatory denouement of the last-named, the detective patiently explains to a roomful of suspects the meaning of the details known but not assimilated by the reader:

Everyone who had a motive appeared to have an alibi at the time of the murder. Because people cannot be in two places at once, I deduced that the time of the murder must have been earlier than we thought. Remember the maid who discovered the body in the bedroom, saying it was as cold as ice? But the bedroom was quite warm from the fire in the fireplace. A corpse is not as cold as ice unless it has been stored in a very cold place for hours and only later returned to the bedroom. And then there were the cobwebs almost imperceptible against the corpse's silver hair. What place in this manor is both cold and cobwebby? The wine cellar. Only Peters, the butler, had a key to the wine cellar!

Having the clues is not enough; it takes a supersleuth to find the perfect pattern. Figure 16-3 depicts the process of deductive reasoning.

In our everyday lives, we have that "Aha!" experience when we suddenly discover the pattern underlying separate facts. Just as you are falling asleep, you might sit up abruptly and exclaim: "Wait a minute! My sweetie claimed to be at the library all evening but in our late night phone call mentioned having to drive around the broken power lines on High Street. I heard on the late news that those lines went down just tonight. But High Street is nowhere near the library. It's over by Club Danz Tilyadrop."

This kind of reasoning is quite different from induction, which involves gathering data. In deduction, facts that are already known are put together in a way that reveals their implications. In this case, the implications are as follows:

If you were at the library, you couldn't have known about the power lines.
You did know about the power lines.
You were not at the library. (You dirty . . .)

FIGURE 16-3   Deductive Reasoning Finds the Patterns in What You Already Know

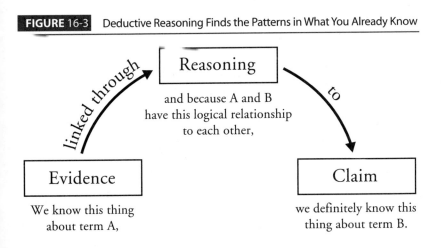

linked through

Reasoning

and because A and B
have this logical relationship
to each other,

to

Evidence

We know this thing
about term A,

Claim

we definitely know this
thing about term B.

(1) In a formal deductive syllogism, there are only two terms, and the major premise sets up an absolute relationship.

Because the correctness of deduction lies in whether it adheres to certain rules, experts in deductive reasoning learn complex symbolic formulas by which they test arguments. For the purpose of this book, we need only touch on the basic concept of deduction: If we know certain things about how two terms (concepts, events, characteristics) are related, we can discover other relationships that are logically entailed or implicated:

> Term A is related in a known way to Term B.
> We know certain things about B.
> Therefore, we can draw certain conclusions about Term A.

To use deductive reasoning in a speech, you need to transpose this into a series of steps:

> Step 1: Establish that a relationship exists between two terms.
> Step 2: Establish the actual condition/status of one of the terms.
> Step 3: Show how a conclusion about the other term necessarily follows.

Step 1 in deduction—establishing the *major premise*—takes many forms. It always involves an absolute relationship between two terms. Here are examples of four common relationships. One term may be an intrinsic characteristic of the other:

> All ducks have webbed feet.
>
> Conflict is inherent in the collective bargaining model.

One term may be a category that includes the other:

> All Volkswagens are motor vehicles.
>
> The Food Stamp program is part of the social welfare system.

One term may be inevitably linked to the other:

> If you heat water to 212 degrees at sea level, then it will boil.
>
> If corporate taxes are cut, then investment will increase.

The two terms may be the opposite of or exclude each other:

> Either that fabric is natural or it is synthetic.
>
> Unless we crack down on drunken drivers, fatalities will rise.

When you have established one of these basic major premises, you have set up a formula that will serve as the linking device at the top of your arc of reasoning. When you move to Step 2, you establish something about one of the two terms—in what logicians call the *minor premise*. A piece of evidence like "Daffy is a duck" might mean many things, or nothing, in some lines of argument. But in the context of the first major premise illustrated earlier, it is the minor premise, and the resulting, relevant implication is that Daffy has webbed feet.

Feed in the data you have, follow the rules of deductive logic, and certain conclusions are inevitably entailed:

> This blouse is made of a synthetic fiber, *so it is not made of a natural fiber.*

> We did not crack down on drunken drivers, *so traffic fatalities must have increased.*

The beauty of deduction lies in its certainty. If your listeners accept the premises, they *must* accept the conclusion.

This seems so attractive that you might wonder why a speaker would use any other method. Why waste energy on the probable conclusions of induction, with their floating points of enoughness that allow audiences to capriciously—yet legitimately—reject a 95-percent-certain conclusion? Why not stick with deduction, in which the rules are clear and the conclusions have to be accepted? The problem with deduction is that, in order for its conclusion to be absolute, its premises must be absolute. Unfortunately, most absolute statements of relationships are either untrue or trivial. Who really cares if ducks have webbed feet or really needs to reason about it? The things we do have to reason about, and tend to give speeches about, are complex issues of public policy, human behavior, and social values. In these domains, we rarely find acceptable statements that "*all X is Y,*" or "if *X*, then *Y always* follows," or "either *X* or *Y* and *no other alternative.*" The requirement of having an all-or-nothing beginning premise is so restrictive that true, formal deductive reasoning is rather rare. In speaking (if not in logic class), it is acceptable to use a slightly less rigorous form of deduction.

(2) When using a modified deductive form of reasoning, make it clear that probable premises can lead only to probable conclusions.

In the if-then statement about tax cuts, does a reduction on corporate taxes absolutely *have* to result in increased investment? A more honest syllogism would be:

It is highly probable that a cut in corporate taxes will increase investment.
Congress is almost certain to cut taxes.
Therefore, it is highly probable that investment will increase.

But now we have lost the tidy inevitability of deduction. No longer do the rules of logic force our listeners to accept our conclusion. We are back to the same kinds of problems we face in induction—persuading the audience to weigh the probabilities as we do. Our appeal to them would be:

If you grant this premise as probable,
and
if you grant this other premise as probable,
then it is logical to grant this conclusion as probable.

When you look at deduction this way, you can, as a speaker, take some liberties not available to the logician. You may build a deductively structured argument with premises that are not absolute, recognizing, of course, that the conclusions you derive will not be absolute, either. Each point needs to be supported sufficiently to persuade a member of the audience to say, "I'll grant that point; it's reasonable; it's probable." Thus, the degree of probability of any conclusion is a product of the degree of probability granted to each premise. (If quantification of probabilities were possible, it might look like this: Major premise that is 80 percent probable × minor premise that is 75 percent probable = conclusion that is 60 percent probable.)

The form of a deductive argument is still an elegant way to justify a conclusion, even when it has been modified to lose the clean force of a true syllogism. In its diluted but more realistic form, it provides an effective structure for part of a speech, or for the entire speech. When the conclusion you want your audience to reach can be arrived at through many logical channels, seriously consider arranging your points in a deductive format.

(3) As a general rule, explicitly lay out all the premises of a deductive argument.

One of the real advantages of structuring ideas deductively is that you must state the relationships among the concepts with which you are dealing. When you clearly state the major premise on which your argument rests, you call to your listeners' minds certain values, assumptions, and even logical truisms. The audience can then apply these concepts when you move on to specific cases in developing your minor premise. In the following logical arguments, notice how the major premise serves in each case to direct the listeners' awareness to a statement that the speaker might otherwise have left implicit.

Anyone who has been elected to high office has had to make a number of political compromises along the way.
Candidate J has served as governor and U.S. senator.
Therefore, Candidate J has made a number of political compromises.

A person denied access to the benefits of society will either become embittered or turn to crime.
Many members of ethnic minorities who are denied access have not committed crimes.
Therefore, many are embittered.

It has always been the goal of our social welfare system to help recipients become self-sufficient.
Certain current programs encourage dependency and discourage initiative.
Therefore, these programs should be changed.

A good friend is a person who helps you reach your potential.
Several people in this organization have helped me strive toward my potential.
Therefore, as I say good-bye, I feel like I am leaving a number of good friends.

Sometimes, speakers have so internalized a point of view that they leave out parts of their argument they see as obvious. When this is done intentionally for persuasive effect, because the speaker and listeners share common values, these economical lines of argument (called *enthymemes*) can be powerful. (See **22c**.) But these are rare exceptions. On controversial topics with diverse audiences, neglecting to lay out all parts of the argument is dangerous. In excellent speeches, speakers take the time to articulate and justify their premises. Consider the previous examples. The first point of each argument might have been omitted or tossed in as an aside rather than developed. By the same token, in saying, "Of course Thompson should be hired, he has the most experience" or "We couldn't possibly pass this bill, it endangers the free enterprise system," you are assuming that your audience accepts your assumption that "the person with the most experience should be hired," or that "anything that endangers the free enterprise system is undesirable." If they do not accept those assumptions, all your efforts to prove Thompson's experience or the bill's effects are wasted. If they do agree, you will not have lost much time by reiterating those points. Listeners will be more likely to remember your specifics if they have a logical framework for them.

Like the detective with the clues, your task is not merely to list the facts, but to demonstrate how they fit together and what they ultimately mean. Often, the conclusion of the speech is the place to weave together the threads of a deductive argument:

So, I've shown that it is our goal to reach full employment and that the only available paths are through direct provision of public sector jobs or through indirect stimulation of private sector jobs. Because I went on to give you several reasons for rejecting the public sector alternative, there is only one conclusion left. To create full employment, the private sector must be stimulated.

Exercise 3. Here are some conclusions that could have been reached either inductively or deductively. Briefly lay out an inductive and a deductive argument that leads to each.

1. Natural childbirth is best for parents and infant.
2. More states should institute regulations protecting computer users from workplace conditions that can cause carpal tunnel syndrome and other repetitive strain injuries.
3. The Academy Awards are rarely given to the best films.

Exercise 4. What costs or risks would you need to minimize and what benefits would you need to maximize in order to establish a high probability of acceptance for these conclusions?

1. This new treatment for herpes should be marketed.
2. Every school bus should be equipped with seat belts.
3. We should hire only college graduates for our sales department.
4. You should cut animal fat out of your diet.

Exercise 5. What unstated assumption or absolute statement of relationship underlies each of these arguments?

1. She must be doing a good job. She hasn't been fired.
2. You should buy a condominium. It's cheaper than a house.
3. Well, it's not a win for labor, so I guess management wins.
4. I thought he had some self-respect, but now I learn he's on welfare.

Exercise 6. Identify the basic reasoning pattern in each speech on the Sample Speeches Web site. Are they inductive or deductive? Can you lay out the underlying argument in three or four sentences?

16d. Use causal reasoning to demonstrate that one event results from another.

Causal reasoning is the backbone of all speeches that deal with policy and problem solving. In most cases, if a person says, "I don't favor your policy (or program, or solution)," what that person is really saying is, "I disagree with you that *X* causes *Y*." This means that you must carefully scrutinize the relationship between two events to satisfy yourself that it is causal. Then you must provide your listeners with information indicating how thoroughly you tested this relationship. Figure 16-4 depicts the causal reasoning process.

Of course, in a problem-solving or policy speech, there is rarely one lone cause. To assert that there is would be a gross oversimplification jeopardizing the acceptance of your conclusions. Still, it helps to understand the rigorous tests you have to apply to a statement if you are to assert a pure causal relationship in it—that is, "one cause leads inevitably to one effect."

(1) Test the validity of the causal relationships you claim.

A causal relationship is stronger than mere correlation or coexistence or coincidence. Two events may occur together or in sequence without one causing the other. For instance, morning sickness and weight gain often occur together, but neither causes the other; they are the result of a third condition, pregnancy. To be sure that the relationship is a causal one, apply these tests.

Do the alleged cause and alleged effect occur together?

To prove that a causal relationship exists, at least two formal comparisons must be made, as with a control group and experimental group. Otherwise, mere coincidence or correlation cannot be ruled out. It is not enough to show that the alleged cause is present with the alleged effect; you must also show that, in the absence of the alleged cause, the alleged effect does not appear:

FIGURE 16-4   Causal Reasoning Links Cause and Effect

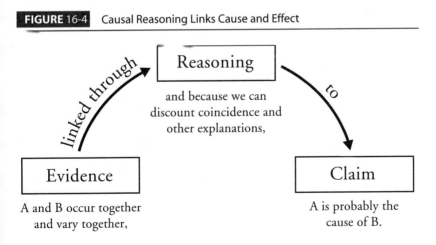

If a rash appears every time you eat tomatoes, and never appears when you haven't eaten tomatoes, this is strong evidence that tomatoes cause the rash.

There are three groups of arthritis sufferers, matched in all important characteristics such as age, sex, diet, and general health. Group A receives the drug Painaway, Group B receives a placebo, and Group C receives no treatment. Members of Group A experience dramatic relief, and there is no change in the condition of members of Group B and Group C. This supports the claim that Painaway causes a reduction in arthritis symptoms.

To prove a causal relationship, you must show both concurrent presence and concurrent absence. Technically, all that is needed to *disprove* a suggested causal relationship is to point to a case in which the alleged cause was present without the alleged effect, or vice versa. So, if you found that your rash occurred occasionally when you had not eaten tomatoes, or if you had once eaten tomatoes and not gotten the rash, a pure causal relationship does not exist. For example:

Classical economic theory suggests that raising tariffs reduces imports. Yet, when we increased the tariff on Argentine beef, imports remained constant.

For years, I believed the other teachers who said students would read the book only if they were given weekly quizzes. Then, one semester, I dropped the quizzes and found that students were as well prepared each week as before.

Do the alleged cause and the alleged effect vary together?

Another test of causation is to determine whether the magnitude of change in the cause matches that in the effect:

If one bite of tomato gives you a small rash, and consuming many tomatoes gives you a big rash, this is one more bit of evidence to suggest that tomatoes cause your rash.

High school graduates, on average, earn more than high school dropouts. People with some college education earn more than high school grads, but less than college graduates. People with advanced degrees, taken as a group, have the highest incomes. Though you can think of individual exceptions, research on groups of people shows that each increment of formal education is accompanied by an equivalent increase in earning power.

(2) Do not oversimplify causal relationships.

In the worlds of physics and chemistry, there are some clear, straightforward causal relationships:

An action results in an equal and opposite reaction.

Adding silver nitrate solution ($AgNO_3$) to sodium chloride (NaCl) will cause silver chloride (AgCl) to precipitate.

This type of relationship between cause (*C*) and effect (*E*) could be represented as:

$$C \rightarrow E$$

However, in the areas of politics, psychology, medicine, economics, and the like, more complex patterns usually exist.

Some effects have multiple causes.

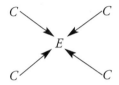

If smoking were the single cause of lung cancer, then every smoker would have lung cancer, and every victim of lung cancer would be a smoker. Obviously, this is not the case. Yet research does show smoking to be one causal factor contributing to lung cancer. The simple tests outlined in **16d(1)** cannot be applied to cases of multiple causation. If you speak of issues like poverty, crime, divorce, and economic recession as though they had a single direct cause, you will justifiably lose credibility with your audience.

Some causes are also effects, and some effects are also causes in a long causal chain.

When we designate a cause of a certain event, we can look at the immediate cause or a more distant factor. A doctor might say that the cause of a particular death was a cerebral hemorrhage. What, though, was the cause of that? Perhaps a fractured skull, which was caused by going through a windshield, which was caused by the impact of a car with a tree, which was caused by excessive drinking, which was caused by worry over being unemployed, and so on:

$$C \rightarrow (E/C) \rightarrow (E/C) \rightarrow (E/C) \rightarrow E$$

In a speech, you need to discuss enough of these links to give a realistic picture and to demonstrate to your listeners that you understand the complexity of the process—without going so far back in the chain as to be absurd.

It is sometimes important to point out the cyclical nature of certain causal chains. For example, ignorance about a particular group may lead to prejudice, which in turn results in lack of contact with that group, which perpetuates ignorance. This sort of analysis is far more interesting than positing a single cause of racial disharmony.

Some effects result from a one-time cause, and some from ongoing causes.

Effects that are labeled undesirable can be dealt with in two ways, either by treating the effect directly, or by blocking the cause that produces the effect. To decide which strategy makes the most sense in a given context, you need to determine whether the cause is one-time or ongoing.

Picture a neighborhood with bare dirt for landscaping, busted windows, broken furniture in the yards, and residents in need of medical care. You are concerned about these symptoms and want to take some action. If you find that a tornado whipped through the area, you may push for emergency relief, intervention by the Army Corps of Engineers to clear wreckage, and loans to rebuild. However, if you learn that the area is depressed and that poverty is chronic, you may choose to advocate organizing retraining programs, launching campaigns to attract businesses to the community, and setting up health clinics. A mistake in evaluation, whereby the effect of an ongoing cause is treated as if it resulted from a one-time cause, will lead to the eventual reappearance of that effect.

Attempting to remedy problems through minor adjustments in laws and institutions when the real causes lie in basic attitudes and values is the worst kind of oversimplification. Nearly as bad is the tendency to advocate "education" as the answer to all social ills. Better to lay out a two-phase solution, with short-range steps to deal with the symptoms complemented by a long-range attack on the underlying causes.

(3) Explain your causal claims fully and fairly.

Pure, simple causal arguments like those scientific truths cited in **16d(2)** deal with absolute relationships. In this sense, they are like the deductive arguments in **16c.** Like deductive major premises, however, valid but nontrivial examples of absolute relationships are rare. More common are lines of reasoning that lead to probable causal claims, like the following:

> X was present in these cases, and Y occurred.
> X was absent in these cases, and Y did not occur.
> Changes in the amount of X have often led to corresponding changes
>   in the amount of $Y.$
> Therefore, it is probable that X causes $Y.$

Probable to what degree? To the degree that your examples are sufficient and representative, and that conflicting examples are minimized or explained. With this sort of causal argument, follow the advice in **16b.** Do not overstate your claim. Say, "This is a major cause," and not "This is *the* cause." Say, "There is strong evidence of a causal link between . . ." and so on.

The establishment of a probable causal claim requires the same sort of risk/benefit analysis as does inductive reasoning. If it is highly likely that eating red meat causes cardiovascular disease, what are the risks of ignoring this link? What are the benefits of accepting it?

Also, whenever possible, explain the way the causal connection operates. Otherwise, even if you demonstrate perfect correlation between two factors, you may succeed in establishing only that one is a sign, signal, or symptom of the other. Causal reasoning tells more than *what* is connected; it tells *why* things are connected. Whenever applicable in your speech, include a brief explanation of *how* the cause leads to the effect. Cite expert testimony if possible or useful. The more explicit your analysis of causation, the less likely your audience is to dismiss your causal claim as mere coincidence.

Exercise 7. Explain two ways you might *disprove* each of the following causal assertions, using principles from **16d(1):**

  1. Supreme Court rulings on arrest procedures have allowed criminals to go free.
  2. Unfair laws have caused discrimination against women.
  3. Strokes are caused by stress.
  4. Lack of educational expenditure has produced an inferior generation of college students.

Exercise 8. Explain how each of the causal statements in Exercise 7 might reflect one or more of the kinds of oversimplification referred to in **16d(2).**

Exercise 9. Identify at least one instance of causal reasoning in each speech on the Sample Speeches Web site. Are the causal links valid?

16e. Use reasoning by analogy to draw conclusions about unknown events, based on what you know about similar events.

When we reason by analogy, we compare two things that can be placed in the same category. In the process, we assume that, because we know that A and B have a number of characteristics in common, we can conclude that those

FIGURE 16-5   Analogy Compares Two Things in the Same Category

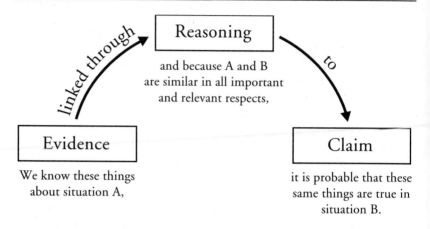

Reasoning

and because A and B
are similar in all important
and relevant respects,

linked through

to

Evidence

We know these things
about situation A,

Claim

it is probable that these
same things are true in
situation B.

things we do not know about B are highly likely to resemble their counterparts that we do know about in A. Figure 16-5 depicts the process of reasoning by analogy.

Reasoning by analogy is a natural and powerful way to make links. People
intuitively look to similar examples when they want to understand something.
Suppose the president's foreign policy advisors are trying to decide whether to
intervene in a foreign country's internal struggles, or a judge is pondering
whether to admit expert testimony on battered wife syndrome, or you are
wondering whether to take the freeway or back streets to work. In all these
cases, from the most cosmic policy issues to the most mundane everyday decisions, people ask themselves, "What is this like that I already know about?"

That we draw so readily on analogy to make our own decisions impels
speakers and advocates naturally to turn to it when they want to make a case
for a certain interpretation. The attraction of analogy lies in its naturalness;
listeners are accustomed to thinking about logical links in analogous terms.

Like the other forms of reasoning we have explored, analogies can be
used to support contradictory claims. Some of the president's advisors will
argue that the foreign country is just like Somalia, and so intervention will be
fruitless. Others will insist that it is more like Panama and that vital matters
of principle are at stake. One lawyer will tell the judge that the case at hand
is like one in which such evidence was admitted. Opposing counsel will
insist that it is more like another one in which expert testimony of this sort
was excluded. One member of your carpool will claim that today is like other
Mondays, when traffic is light on the freeway. Another will point out that on

other rainy days like today there are often accidents that slow things down on the freeway.

Although reasoning by analogy is so innate—or *because* it is—you need to approach it with a careful eye on the analogies you use.

(1) Be sure that when you reason by analogy the two cases are similar in all relevant and important respects.

Here is the sort of unconscious analogy we all use everyday. Does it meet the test?

> Alternately sulking and throwing tantrums was effective in manipulating my father. Therefore, these same tactics should be effective with my boss, Fred.

There are certain similarities between the father and the boss: Both are authority figures, both are male, both are older, both have trouble dealing with emotions. It is also easy to point out differences: the father is tall, and Fred is short; the father drives foreign cars, and Fred drives a pickup. No cases are identical, and simply pointing out differences does not discredit an analogy automatically. Do they differ in relevant and important ways? In this instance, yes. The relationship with the father is a personal one; the one with Fred is professional. In one case, a child and a parent are relating; in the other, two adults are doing so. Major personality differences between the father and Fred may exist. These stated differences are probably important enough to lead the person to reject the conclusion that sulking and throwing tantrums are effective ways of dealing with the boss.

When comparing cases from different geopolitical areas, be especially aware of cultural differences. The identical institutional changes might be adopted in Scandinavia or Syria or Sri Lanka with radically different effects. Even within a national culture, microcultural differences exist. A university faculty will not respond to management practices the same way a business organization does. The innocent belief that "people are people" must be modified by our increasing awareness of the role played by gender, social class, race, sexual orientation, and numerous other factors in influencing people and shaping their experiences, even when living under externally similar conditions.

Reasoning by analogy should also be tempered by an awareness of the impact of history. Comparisons between the Vietnam War and the Gulf War were often made, yet the very experience of Vietnam irreversibly altered U.S. perceptions of foreign policy, military strategy, and media coverage. Any war following Vietnam will be different *because* of Vietnam.

(2) Do not confuse a literal analogy, which is a form of reasoning, with a figurative analogy, which is used only in a descriptive function.

Reasoning by analogy requires a comparison of two members of the same category. Figurative analogy compares the members of different categories:

> Convincing my boss, Fred, to adopt a new procedure takes as much persistence, luck, and timing as starting my 1972 Fiat on a January morning.

> Going to war in Vietnam was like tap-dancing on quicksand.

These analogies may have stylistic impact, but they cannot support a conclusion. The examples in **16e(1)**, however flawed in their logic, did make comparisons within the same categories—two human relationships or two wars. The examples in **16e(2)** compare a human relationship with a human-machine relationship, and a war with an athletic impossibility.

Exercise 10. Return to Exercise 1 and look at the ways you linked your evidence to the claims. Classify each line of reasoning as inductive, deductive, causal, or analogous.

Exercise 11. Identify at least three similarities and three differences between each of the following pairs of concepts. Now go back and think about how these enter into the way we reason by analogy. Write one argument for each topic in which the similarities are sufficiently relevant and important to justify the conclusion. List other lines of reasoning on each topic that would probably be discounted due to the differences you identified.

1. A football game and a war
2. A family and a group of employees
3. "Ethnic cleansing" in the Balkans and racial discrimination in the United States
4. The national debt and one's personal checking account

16f. Avoid common reasoning fallacies.

Some people commit reasoning fallacies knowingly, with dishonest intent. Others commit them due to a lack of practice or skill in doing their own thinking. The good public speaker wants to avoid the appearance of either. Once you have built your speech around sound, logical arguments, go through it to detect any constructions that even hint of sloppy thinking. One glaring fallacy in your speech will make all your other conclusions suspect. It is not necessary to learn all the fallacies—over one hundred have been categorized—but you should be familiar with the most common of them.

A bonus of learning about these fallacies is that you can improve your critical listening skills. Not only will you be able to construct a logically sound speech, but you also will be able to detect thoughtless, sloppy, or false lines of reasoning.

(1) Attacking the person rather than the argument (*ad hominem*)

This fallacy substitutes character assassination for solid refutation or persuasion:

> Anyone who advocates abortion on demand is a murderer anyway. It certainly wouldn't surprise me to find them taking kickbacks from the clinics that would receive government funds.

(2) Setting up a straw figure

This fallacy consists of creating a weak argument, attributing it to the opposing side, and then proceeding to demolish it. The false implication is that all the opponents' arguments are as flimsy as the "straw figure" and could be dismissed with equal ease if time permitted. A familiar example was the cry of "they'll plunder Social Security!" in every discussion of the Balanced Budget Amendment.

Opponents of affirmative action policies are sometimes heard to raise these objections:

> We can't hire people from underrepresented groups without regard for their qualifications. It's not right to hire a mathematician to teach English just because she's a woman.

This is misleading, because proponents of affirmative action do not advocate disregarding qualifications. The speaker has distorted matters with these extreme examples to avoid confronting the complexity of the issue.

(3) Extending an argument to absurd lengths (*reductio ad absurdum*)

This fallacy makes a potentially sound argument appear groundless by extending it to a point at which it can be ridiculed. Often, this extension goes beyond reasonable interpretation of the original point. In challenging current methods of criminal sentencing, a speaker might say:

> The average criminal is condemned to a bleak cell while top government wrongdoers lounge around in "country club" facilities. The logic is that the latter have already been punished considerably by loss of face, prestige, and professional standing. This seems to say that punishments should be harsher on those who have the least to lose. By this reasoning, the senator who commits murder might get off with a citation and public embarrassment, while an unemployed ghetto dweller who shoplifts should be put on bread and water, with regular sessions on the rack.

Pointing out these patently outrageous inequities does not constitute a legitimate attack on the basic concept that the impact of punishment on an offender can be one valid criterion for decisions about sentencing. This kind of fallacy relies on the humor of the cockeyed image it creates. Disarmed by a ludicrous example, listeners lose sight of the real issue.

(4) The slippery slope

This common fallacy consists of making the false assumption that taking the first step in any direction will inevitably lead to going to dangerous lengths in that direction. The image is of someone sliding down a slope without being able to stop.

> Domino effect: If one country in a region falls into ethnic conflict, all those around will fall.

> If you ever take just one drink, you will become an alcoholic.

> If we let the government ban the sale and possession of assault rifles, banning all firearms is next.

> If we let the government abandon support of the arts, artistic freedom will die.

(5) Circular reasoning

Circular reasoning assumes as one of its premises the very conclusion it sets out to establish. Most of us know the hopeless feeling of trying to deal logically with such dead-end arguments as "you can't get credit unless you have a good credit rating, and you can't have a good credit rating unless you have gotten credit." Often, circular reasoning results from granting absolute authority to some source, and thus being blinded to the fact that others might not attribute similar authority to it, as in this example:

> I know that God exists.
> It says so repeatedly in the Bible.
> And everything in the Bible is true because it's the inerrant word of God.

Other instances of circular reasoning come out of definitional word games:

> No sane person would consider suicide, because it's insane to want to take your own life.

> We need a court of equity to resolve labor-management disputes, because collective bargaining results in settlements that aren't equitable. What do I mean by an equitable settlement? I mean the kind of settlement that is arrived at by a court of equity.

(6) The semantic fallacy

The rich, connotative nature of words, which so enhances communication, can also abet fuzzy thinking. When midstream shifts of definition are obvious, they can be funny, as in "blackberries are red when they're green" or "not a single burglar was arrested this month; they must all have been married."

More subtle and dangerous shifts in definition can occur in various critical parts of an argument:

> The free enterprise system, which we all cherish, could not exist without competition. This bill to protect small businesses threatens our whole economic structure. There can be no true competition when one group is given special protection.

In the underlying value premise, the word *competition* is used in the general sense of a market mechanism. In claiming that the bill endangers competition, the speaker uses the term in a much narrower sense, as in "a specific contest between individuals." The semantic fallacy is especially difficult to identify and frustrating to respond to because the syllogistic form of the argument appears to be valid. The problem arises from the slight slippage of definition as a term is used with different meanings in different premises.

(7) False dichotomy

It is fallacious to base reasoning on an *either/or* statement when the two alternatives are not really mutually exclusive or when other alternatives exist. Many speeches set up artificial choices:

> Would you rather have a football program or a band and orchestra at our school?

This can be a false dichotomy. Through careful economic management and marshaling of resources, it may be possible to maintain both. Here's another example:

> Either we stand up to naked aggression, or we lose the confidence of our allies.

This basic premise so oversimplifies a complex issue that no conclusions can be drawn from it. Do not set up a deductive argument with a false dichotomy as its major premise.

(8) Faulty reversal of an if-then statement (affirming the consequent or denying the antecedent)

Another kind of deductive reasoning is based on an "if *X*, then *Y*" relationship. A common fallacy is to assume that because *Y* necessarily follows *X*, the reverse is also true: that *X* necessarily follows *Y*. Consider this statement:

> If I hear voices through the wall, then there is someone in the next room.
> I hear voices through the wall.
> Therefore, there is someone in the next room.

This is a valid statement. However, its validity in this form does not mean that its reverse will also be true. The following cannot be derived from the original if-then statement:

> I don't hear voices, so there must be no one in the next room.

This problem arises from lazy thinking, in which a person knows that two factors are associated but has not carefully analyzed which follows from the other—if, indeed, that sort of relationship exists at all.

Guilt by association is the most common manifestation of this fallacy:

> If a candidate agrees with all the principles of an organization, then he or
>   she will receive that organization's endorsement.
> The People's Counterinsurgency Brigade (PCB) endorsed Elizabeth Day.
> Therefore, she must agree with all their principles.

This is a fallacious conclusion because there is nothing in the first statement that requires an organization to endorse only those candidates who are in 100 percent agreement with its principles. It is entirely possible that Day's opponent shares no values with the PCB, and Day only one, so she receives the endorsement as the lesser of the evils. The conclusion that Day must agree with all PCB principles would be valid only if the original if-then statement were reversed, with total agreement necessarily following from endorsement. That relationship has not been established in this example.

Political candidates so fear this kind of faulty reasoning by voters that they often publicly repudiate the endorsement of extreme groups and their supporters. They cannot count on the electorate to recognize the difference between a group endorsing a candidate and a candidate endorsing a group.

(9) Hasty generalization

This fallacy entails making a premature inductive "leap." (See **16b.**) It is glorified in the pomp surrounding Groundhog Day, when data from an isolated event are blindly accepted as gospel in relation to a much wider range of events.

This statement has a faulty leap:

> The savings and loan scandal proved that every elected official has a price.

Time may not allow you, as a speaker, to include all the data that led you to some conclusion. It is especially important, then, to have the unused data at your fingertips so that you can respond to any accusations of hasty generalization that may come up.

(10) Confusing sequence with cause (*post hoc, ergo propter hoc*)

The Latin label for this fallacy translates as "after the event, therefore because of the event." It is natural to try to understand the world around us by looking for cause-effect patterns wherever possible. So strong is this motivation that we are frequently guilty of imitating Chanticleer the rooster, who firmly believed that it was his predawn crowing that caused the sun to rise each day.

A famous example of this fallacy is the "Tut Curse." Not long after he opened the tomb of the Pharaoh Tutankhamen in 1923, Lord Carnarvon died in Cairo from complications following an insect bite. At the moment of his death, Cairo was said to have experienced a power blackout, and this was interpreted by many to be a manifestation of an ancient curse. Thereafter, if anyone remotely connected to Egyptology died, it was attributed to the curse, no matter if the agent of this "curse" was heavy traffic or arteriosclerosis.

To avoid this fallacy, never assume causation based on time sequence alone. Test every causal hypothesis against the criteria in **16d**.

Exercise 12. Identify the fallacy or fallacies in each statement:

1. I'm surprised you health food nuts eat granola packaged in cellophane bags. Aren't you afraid the synthetic chemicals will poison the contents?
2. Anyone who drives a foreign car doesn't care about this country anyway.
3. You said you could prove the point by sheer logic. Well, I agree. The logic was pretty sheer.
4. It always rains on Easter. I remember it has for the last three years.
5. Well, either you support your country, or you are critical of the government. Which is it?
6. The jury system should be abolished. Last year a jury awarded $3 million to a woman who didn't like the nose job she got. The next month the doctor committed suicide.

Exercise 13. Examine the reasoning in the speeches on the Sample Speeches Web site. Do you find any fallacies in reasoning?

16g. Through organization and word choice, make it clear to your listeners exactly how your reasoning links your evidence to your claim.

It is not enough to have a speech that is well reasoned and free from fallacies. The reasoning process must be made clear to listeners. When speakers present only a cluster of evidence or a cluster of reasons for a claim, they are acting as if communication occurs through the simple transmission of messages. The perspective taken in this book is that communication consists of *making meaning together.* Therefore, as a speaker, you need to show listeners what makes your evidence meaningful to you.

(1) Organize points to show the logical relationships.

As explained in **16a,** controversial claims can be found at all levels of a speech. How overall patterns of reasoning come into play is determined by how you lay out the speech.

Sometimes, the thesis statement is supported by a line of reasoning, and each main point is part of the argument. For example:

> Thesis statement: Prayer should not be allowed in schools because it violates the doctrine of separation of church and state, which is a central tenet of U.S. society that must be preserved.

> I.   The doctrine of separation of church and state is a central tenet of U.S. society that must be preserved.
>   A. Why we have this doctrine
>   B. Why it must be preserved
> II. Prayer in the schools violates the doctrine of church and state. (Develop through testimony and examples.)
>   Therefore: In conclusion, (Restate thesis.)

In other cases, the thesis statement may be an "umbrella claim" that is supported by several separate and somewhat independent claims:

> Thesis: Preschool programs like Head Start are economically, socially, and morally justified.

The economic, social, and moral claims are separate main points where most of the reasoning of the speech will be found.

In still other cases, reasoning is necessary at very specific subpoint levels in the speech to justify important claims.

There is no one way to display your lines of reasoning in a speech outline, but it is very important that you phrase points to show the connections. Do not simply group "reasons." Show reasoning.

Wrong:

> I.   The United States cannot afford to have a middle-class tax cut.
>   A. A tax cut would lead to a deficit.
>   (Support by testimony and statistics.)

    B. The loss of revenue would hurt vital programs.
       (Support by testimony and statistics.)

Better:

I. The United States cannot afford to have a middle-class tax cut.
    A. To adjust for a tax cut, we would have to either cut spending or go into debt.
       (Briefly explain why these are the only alternatives.)
    B. It is not desirable to cut spending.
       (Support by testimony and statistics.)
    C. It is not desirable to go into debt.
       (Support by testimony and statistics.)

Wrong:

I. Having a longer school day does not improve learning.
    A. They tried it at Riverdale High School, and test scores were unchanged.
    B. They tried it at Glenbrook High School, and test scores actually went down.
    C. At Creekside High School, test scores have gone up even though their school day has not been lengthened.
    D. Braeburn High School shortened their school day, and test scores did not change.

Better:

I. Having a longer school day does not improve learning.
    A. In cases in which the school day was lengthened, test scores did not improve.
       1. Unchanged at Riverdale High
       2. Went down at Glenbrook
    B. In cases in which the school day was not lengthened, test scores were not lower.
       1. Improved at Creekside
       2. No change with shorter day at Braeburn

Summary transitional statement: If there were a causal relationship between the length of the school day and learning as measured by test scores, we would logically expect that scores would be higher where the school day is longer and lower where the school day is shorter. I have just demonstrated that this is not the case. Sometimes, the opposite is true. So you can see why I conclude that having a longer school day does not improve learning.

Remember the difference between points and support for the points. (See **11c** and the introduction to **15.**) Do not use sources in place of reasoning. In the first example that follows, a speaker attempts to support a causal claim by saying that experts have agreed with the claim. But the listeners do not know *why* these people came to the conclusion they did. In the second example, the reasoning behind the causal claim is explained, with experts used to back up specific points.

Wrong:

I. The use of sexist language perpetuates discrimination against women.
   A. Dr. Deborah Stone says sexist language causes problems.
   B. Professor Lydia Sorenson says sexist language is the root of many social problems.
   C. Linguist Chris Nupriya states that language affects behavior.

Better:

I. The use of sexist language perpetuates discrimination against women.
   A. Language shapes social perception.
      (Cite experts and studies.)
   B. Speech that leaves women out can lead to people overlooking them.
      (Cite experts and studies.)
   C. If people subconsciously exclude women from certain roles, they discriminate against women.
      (Cite experts and studies.)

(2) Use words, phrases, and transitional sentences that spell out what your evidence means and how the parts of your argument are linked.

In addition to setting up a speech structure that highlights your reasoning, you should give thought to selecting language that illuminates the logical linkages between your ideas. Never merely jump from one point to the next. Practice adding phrases that are specific cues to the kind of reasoning you are using.

For inductive reasoning
Show the strength of your examples.

> One case that supports my claim is . . .
> Another example that adds to this pattern is . . .
> These statistics illustrate a widespread . . .

These instances are just a sample of the . . .
Across many levels of income and many parts of the country, the same pattern holds true. For example . . .

Acknowledge the probable nature of your data by using qualifiers:

Many . . .
Most . . .
Virtually every study in the literature . . .
Evidence strongly indicates . . .
I can say with near certainty . . .
From these cases, I feel quite confident in concluding . . .

Demonstrate costs and rewards:

I'm willing to bet my tax dollars that this program will work . . .
I think these are good/bad odds because . . .
This is a gamble we can't afford to take . . .
The risks, though they do exist, seem minimal compared to the rewards . . .
Is it worth it to you to . . . ?

For deductive reasoning
State your premises:

I base this on a core value of mine that . . .
Underlying my position is one of the fundamental tenets of our constitutional form of government.
The argument for my claim rests on one basic assumption that I hope you will agree with. It is . . .
Either . . . or . . .
If . . . then . . .
Only when . . . can . . .
Anyone who . . .
To the extent that . . . , then to that extent . . .

Spell out your reasoning:

Because I've shown you X and Y, . . .
Therefore . . .
This entails . . .
From this it follows that . . .
What this means is that . . .

We have no choice but to conclude that . . .
Based on this, I reason that . . .
It seems logical to conclude that . . .

For causal reasoning
Show how the cause and effect are related in a predictable way:

In state after state where spending on education went up, crime went down.
Notice that as soon as that company closed down pollution was reduced.
This is no coincidence. When X occurs, then Y occurs.
For every unit of increase in X, notice that there is a proportional increase . . .

Qualify your causal claims if necessary:

There may be many causes, but the one I have identified is a major causal factor.
It is highly probable that smoking causes these health problems.
In the vast majority of cases, X causes Y.
At least in middle-class white families, where most of the research so far was conducted, there seems to be a strong causal link between watching violence on television and acting in antisocial ways.
Except in small family-owned companies where a different dynamic seems to be in effect, employee morale is greatly enhanced by offering a series of options for benefits.

Explain the mechanism of the cause:

The reason all these experts have concluded that X causes Y is that . . .
I've shown you all these cases in which being abused as a child seems to lead to being an abusive parent. Let me explain how that happens.

For reasoning by analogy
Stress the points of similarity:

In Ecuador, as in neighboring Colombia and Peru, . . .
In three cities of about the same size and makeup, the same pattern recurred.
For eight of the ten other universities in our conference, adding women's sports to the athletic program has led to more alumni support.
Likewise, . . .
Similarly, . . .
In a parallel case, . . .

Explain points of difference that your listeners may be concerned about:

> Although *Kully vs. California* was tried in district court, the principle still applies here because . . .
> Despite differences in size, our company can learn from this story because . . .
> I realize that some of these instances happened a long time ago, but I don't think human nature changes much in this respect.

Spell out the link:

> If it worked in New Jersey and Idaho and Georgia, it will work in the rest of the country.
> The analogy holds true. We can apply these solutions to our problems.
> The other groups who tried such proposals have been disappointed. Let's learn from their mistakes.
> Let's not wait too long on planning for earthquake safety. We put off dealing with flood control, and the results have been tragic.

As we stated in chapter **12,** transitional phrases are more important in speaking than in writing because listeners cannot look back at previous points. These cueing phrases play a crucial role in developing an oral argument. In an outline, claims are stated before their supporting reasons and evidence. This is an organizational artifact and should not obscure the fact that claims are reached only at the end of a line of reasoning. However, for purposes of signposting and keeping your audience informed about the direction you are taking, it is generally a good idea to first state the claim and then explain the reasons for it. Listeners may become lost as the steps of an argument unfold, though. By the time you reach the end of your reasoning, they may forget what claim you were trying to support. Therefore, it is also generally a good idea to restate the claim after you have presented the argument.

In the following example, the speaker's thesis is the claim that marijuana should not be legalized. Each main point is a separate claim supported by a different form of reasoning. Observe how at the end of each main point she recapitulates her reasoning to show how it led to her claim, which she then restates. These brief statements can make the difference between a speech that makes sense only to the speaker and one that makes sense to listeners.

I.   People are dangerous when they are under the influence of marijuana. (examples of accidents that were caused by people who were under the influence of marijuana)

Summary of Main Point I: These five tragic stories about innocent people who were killed by someone who was under the influence of marijuana provide us with one reason marijuana should remain illegal: People are dangerous when they use marijuana.

II. Marijuana is a highly addictive drug like cigarettes and alcohol. (testimony from doctors and other experts)

Summary of Main Point II: We all know how easy it is for some people to become addicted to nicotine and alcohol, and the problems that can result. Marijuana is very similar. It, too, can be addictive.

III. Smoking marijuana often causes people to use "harder" drugs. (statistics and testimony from drug users and doctors)

Summary of Main Point III: Therefore, even though many marijuana users do not go on to use harder drugs, many do. These experts claim that contact with the criminal element and experiences with "getting high" serve as significant causal factors in predicting subsequent usage of harder drugs.

IV. Marijuana use reduces intelligence.
   A. Reduced brain cells lower intelligence.
   B. Marijuana kills brain cells.

Summary of Main Point IV: Because anything that kills brain cells reduces intelligence, and because marijuana has been shown to kill brain cells, you can see that it follows logically that marijuana reduces intelligence.

Conclusion: (restatement of thesis, showing how the points are linked to it) I have shown that marijuana use puts innocent people in danger, is addictive, leads to use of hard drugs, and reduces intelligence. It seems logical that we should not legalize any practice that has these serious consequences.

Exercise 14. In the marijuana example just given, what kind of reasoning is being used in each of the four statements? Do you see any potential fallacies in the reasoning of the marijuana speech?

Chapter 17

Language and Style

Choose words and constructions that make your ideas clear and memorable. Respect the power of language.

Certain interpretations of classical rhetoric tended to treat language as an adornment to ideas—a sort of gift wrapping put on the package to make it appealing. Some modern communication models similarly suggest that an idea is first fully thought out before it is encoded for transmission. Current understandings of language grant it a much more central role in communication: Language is the essence of thought, not a mere vessel for it. We no longer believe that our ways of thinking are universally "programmed in"; rather, they develop as we interact, linguistically, with others. This means much more than learning to speak English instead of Cantonese. It means that if you had been born in a different time and place you would not only use language differently but also think differently. So, language reflects culture and shapes our society.

Because of the pervasive and largely unconscious power of language, we are leery of any treatments that relegate language to a single step late in the communicative process. In this handbook, we stress the importance of "talking ideas into being" throughout the entire process of speech preparation. Competent speakers are conscious of the ways they develop their ideas through language to achieve an effective speaking style.

Style is a word of many shadings. A "stylish" person is one who conforms to the latest fads and fashions. A "stylized" drawing is one in which the artist includes the least amount of detail needed for comprehension. "Style" is decorator colors—whatever that means—and it is tight jeans or loose jeans, depending on the year. Style is none of these things to a speaker.

In the context of speaking, style is simply your choice of words and the way you string them together. "Good" style involves choosing and combining those words so that your audience can easily understand and assimilate your content. Good style is clear, appropriate, vivid, and varied language.

17a. Understand how oral style is different from written style.

Speech is very much a slave to the fourth dimension—time. Words are uttered, and immediately the resonances and overtones start to fade. Listeners have but one contact with each word, and memory is the only instant replay. In contrast, a written essay exists as a time machine: It allows a reader to return to a place where the eye had been a few seconds or many years before. This quality of the written word has obvious implications regarding comprehension, and although oral style and written style use the same components, the styles are not interchangeable.

Naturalness is a theme that runs through this handbook. The natural-sounding speaker understands how oral style differs and talks *to* an audience rather than delivering what appears to be a ten-page quotation. Listeners expect to hear patterns that reflect the norms of conversation, if more refined. The ideal balance between the orality and literacy of a speech depends on the audience and occasion. (See **1c(4)**.) Sometimes, you will draw more heavily on the communicative resource of the writer. Other times, you can use the language and cadences of conversation.

There are some important ways in which oral style differs from written style. Even with the redundancy built into the language, a speaker is more likely to use repetition to ensure comprehension. In oral style, there is a greater frequency of signposting, internal summaries, and internal previews to make the organization clear. (See **12.**) Shorter sentences and words of fewer syllables are characteristic of oral style as well. And sentence fragments are acceptable, as are contractions. Even in a formal setting, a speech will still be more colloquial than an essay on the same topic. Table 17-1 lists some key differences between oral and written style.

It would be wrong to think that these qualities of oral style are limitations. To view orality as the mere lack of literacy, Walter Ong says, is equivalent to describing horses as automobiles without wheels. Appreciate the spoken word and take advantage of its unique features. The rhythm and meter of speech aid memory. The physical immediacy creates a bond between speakers and listeners. Attune your ear to the music of the spoken word, and use it

TABLE 17-1	Differences Between Written and Oral Style
Written Style	**Oral Style**
As mentioned above . . .	As I said a few minutes ago . . .
One cannot avoid individuals with this characteristic.	We can't avoid people like that.
A hypothetical case in point might be a situation where government . . .	Imagine this. Suppose Uncle Sam . . .
It is unlikely that such will result.	Well. Maybe.
Subjects were randomly assigned to either a control group or one of three experimental treatment groups, pretested for initial attitudes toward the topic, then posttested after each experimental group had received a persuasive message containing one of three levels of fear appeals.	Here's how we did our research. First, we randomly assigned the subjects to four groups. Next, we gave all four groups a pretest to see what attitudes they held toward the topic. Then, three of the groups heard persuasive messages. One had a high level of fear appeals, one a medium level, and one a low level. Last, we posttested the attitudes of all four groups, including the control group that received no message.

to your advantage as you phrase your ideas. Drawing on the resources of performance—part of every effective speech to some degree—involves a feel for the power of the spoken word.

Exercise 1. Rewrite these statements in a style more appropriate to oral communication.

1. After having removed the air filter, one can begin to investigate origins of the problem.
2. All clerical and administrative personnel will undergo semiannual performance appraisals designed to evaluate their competence and clarify objectives for the next appraisal period.

17b. Strive for clarity in your language.

We know that language does more than label objects, concepts, and actions. Words *are* acts. They do things, like promise or threaten; they can even serve to marry or excommunicate people. Because of this power, we sometimes make messages intentionally vague—perhaps to save face or build solidarity. For the most part, though, the clear transmission of information is to be valued over other ends. "Bear come. We go. Now!" may not be subtle or poetic, but it certainly conveyed an important image from one prehistoric human to another. Some modern speakers in love with their own verbiage should do so well! If you understand the priorities of communication, the first question you will ask yourself is, "Did my listeners get the picture?" When speaker and listeners end up with totally different mental images, something has gone awry. Perhaps the speaker has used words in nonstandard, idiosyncratic ways, or has chosen words so general that they evoke many different responses, or has buried the significant words in an avalanche of extraneous phrases.

To construct clear messages, you must do two things. First, invest some effort in clarifying your own thoughts. Know exactly, not approximately, what you want to get across. Second, consider who the receivers of your message are and what the words are likely to mean to them.

(1) Be precise.

To avoid fuzzy and ambiguous communication, you need to seek out the word that means precisely what you wish to convey and use it in a structure that illuminates, not obscures, its meaning.

Use the proper word.

Many words can denote the same object or idea; however, each may have a slightly different focus. Do not say a person was "indicted" for robbery if in fact you mean "arrested" (much less serious) or "convicted" (much more serious). Learn important distinctions and honor them.

Be careful around words that sound similar but have no similarity of meaning. *Allusion* means "a passing mention," and *illusion* means "a false perception." Some other troublesome near-homophones are *affect/effect, imminent/eminent, casual/causal,* and *aesthetic/ascetic.* Remember that oral language is simpler than written language. Avoid using a precise word when it may seem pretentious. Table 17-2 gives some examples.

Be sure you know what an unfamiliar word means before rushing to use it. Malaprops may be funny for the audience, but they are devastating for the speaker. Imagine the response to a speaker who means to say, "The answer I've reached is inescapable," but actually states, "The answer I've reached is inexplicable."

TABLE 17-2	The Simpler Oral Style
Pretentious	Better
I was appalled at the feculence that oozed from the typewriter of this so-called greatest living American novelist.	I was appalled at the filth that oozed from the typewriter of this so-called greatest living American novelist.
Then I butted heads with the misoneists of the planning commission.	Then I butted heads with the planning commission, which seems to have a pathological hatred of change.
Hear my obsecration!	Hear my supplication!

Keep your figurative language unmuddled.

In attempting to convey your picture vividly, do not confuse the issue by throwing discordant images together. (See **17d(2).**)

The wife of an official charged with taking a bribe accused the government of entrapment in this manner:

> The FBI has created the *illusion* of a crime. It's like raping Alice in Wonderland.

No doubt the speaker knew what she meant, but the rest of us were not so lucky. Wonderland is a crazy, illogical world where the powers-that-be are capricious—and that is a good image to accompany an accusation of entrapment. But used as it was, it only left her listeners deaf to the rest of her words while they tried to pick out the real meaning of the image.

(2) Use specific and concrete language.

The more specific and concrete your words, the less is left to your listeners' imaginations. When a speaker says, "NCAA academic standards for college athletes are ineffective," one listener may think, "Yes, they are racist"; another may think, "Yes, they are too low"; and still another may think, "Yes, they should be set by the faculty at each college." Yet all of these may be at odds with the intentions of the speaker, who perhaps feels that the standards are too high. Do not have your words name a broader category than they need to. Table 17-3 gives examples of specific, concrete language.

Minimize the use of abstract words such as *love, freedom, justice,* and *beauty*—words that have no tangible, physical referent. When you have no option but to use abstract words, supplement them with concrete examples to make them less cerebral and ethereal:

TABLE 17-3	Specific, Concrete Language	
Do Not Say	If You Really Mean	Or Even
We need to attract individuals.	We need to attract customers.	We need to attract grocery shoppers.
This will cause problems.	This will be expensive.	This will cost us $2,500 we don't have.
Our committee has studied it.	Our committee researched and discussed it.	Our committee read documents, heard testimony, and deliberated for several hours.

What is more important to me than peace? Freedom is more important to me than peace.

If I weren't able to travel where I wish, if I weren't able to worship as I please, meet to discuss grievances, read and write what I want, then I would struggle to regain all these things.

(3) Be economical in your language.

The bloated language of the bureaucracy, both civil and military, is a common target of ridicule in schools and the media. Unfortunately, all this attention has done little to slow the general acceptance, or at least tolerance, of wordy, euphemistic language. In the interest of clarity, you should express yourself with the fewest, most straightforward words that still effectively convey your meaning.

Sometimes, speakers use long words, extra words, and convoluted constructions for the untenable reasons listed in Table 17-4.

Most often, though, wordiness results from lack of discipline. Editing is not a simple process, and many people shy away from it. These speakers prefer a machine-gun style of word choice, spewing out redundancies while bracketing the target with approximate synonyms. The clear speaker is more like the sharpshooter who takes careful aim and makes every word count.

Wordy

Some individuals express their feeling that it is objectionable to eliminate and remove laws which serve to protect female members of the labor force. No one could really be in favor of doing away with protective laws for workers if the elimination of these laws would lead to the exploitation of the people no longer covered. The question I want to raise, however, is whether there is really any relevance to the sex of those workers who should be protected

231

TABLE 17-4   Motives for Bloated Language

	Uneconomical	Economical
To Hide Meaning, as with Doublespeak	We sustained losses through friendly fire.	We shelled our own troops.
To Avoid Responsibility, as with the Passive Voice	It has been determined that your services are no longer needed.	I have decided to fire you.
To Soften Unpleasant Messages, as with Euphemism	Jesse has gone on to his reward.	Jesse died.

from exploitation, since wages and working conditions ought to be equitable for all employees.

Economical

There are objections to wiping out laws protecting women workers. No one would condone exploitation. But what does sex have to do with it? Working conditions and hours that are harmful to women are harmful to men; wages that are unfair for women are unfair for men.

—Shirley Chisholm

17c. Use appropriate language.

There is no standard style to use in speaking. Different audiences and topics require different approaches. In the light of your audience analysis, you must make decisions about how formal to be, which part of your personality to project linguistically, and how deeply to descend into specialized language. Your age, status, and personality also determine what language is appropriate for you. Listeners have expectations about the vocabulary and stylistic level suitable for, say, a senior executive, that differ from those for a teenager or a poet-in-residence.

Language is not fixed. New words and phrases are always coming into our language, and others fading out. Meanings change, as do standards of appropriateness. A real presidential speech we heard as we worked on the third edition of this book sounded very much like the fanciful example we chose for the first edition of this text to illustrate unthinkable informality for a presidential address.

(1) Adapt the formality of your language to the occasion.

Just as you dress differently for formal and casual events, so should you tailor vocabulary and usage to fit the situation. Would it not be a little startling if the organizer of a PTA bake sale were to finish an announcement in the following fashion:

> This, then, is my plea to you: For the sake of our children, for the sake of our school, for the sake of our PTA, give of yourself for this culinary endeavor.

Equally inappropriate would be a CEO's annual address to stockholders that began:

> Well, folks, things look kinda grim, but don't get bummed out, we'll be OK if we just hang in there.

In general, the more formal the occasion,

> The more serious the tone
> The more subtle the humor
> The more elaborate the sentences
> The greater the number of figures of speech
> The greater the departure from everyday word choice

More formal occasions include debates, presentations of policy statements, and ceremonial speeches. Less formal occasions include business conferences, roasts, rallies, and after-dinner speeches. In short, the more formal the occasion, the less you can rely on the resource of conversation and the more you must put in the time to incorporate the resources of writing and performance.

(2) Be judicious in your use of jargon or slang.

Both jargon and slang can be used to create a bond with a specialized audience. At times, jargon can also allow you to get a point across more quickly. Slang, when called into play at opportune moments, can enrich the texture of your language. But the perils they introduce are substantial. You may confuse your audience with technical terms or sacrifice your credibility by using slang expressions that are offensive or out-of-date.

Notice how this excerpt from a talk on "Preventive Maintenance" is made understandable to a larger audience by substituting plain English in the second version:

Slang and Jargon Version

Let's look at how Jack could have benefited from a little PM. He burned a lot more number two than he needed to before he got around to running the rack on his Slam-bang. A maintenance schedule would have pointed out any problems long before the engine started smoking. Same thing with the front SQ drop-in. He wouldn't have cooked it if he had periodically checked and renewed the oil.

Plain-English Version

Let's look at how Jack could have benefited from a little preventive maintenance. He burned a lot more diesel fuel than he needed before he got around to adjusting the fuel injection system on his dump truck. A maintenance schedule would have pointed out any problems long before the engine started smoking. Same thing with the drive axle gears. They wouldn't have overheated and failed if he had periodically checked and renewed the oil.

(3) Avoid substandard usage.

Remember that the competence of the speaker as perceived by the audience has a large bearing on the credibility they ascribe to him or her. Although acceptable usage varies from place to place, there are many words and constructions that are rated substandard by consensus. The speaker who consistently uses *ain't* for *isn't* or who gets sloppy with noun-verb agreement will find that a large percentage of the audience does not give serious consideration to her or his points. Of course, you can sometimes break the rules for dramatic effect, like capping your opposition to a proposal with "Ain't *no* way!"

Where will you find a guide for what is standard? Expose yourself to models of literate and graceful usage by reading quality magazines and good literature, and by listening to respected public speakers and commentators. This exposure often leads to an intuitive recognition of correct usage. If you have never heard one of your language models say, "This here's the nexus of the problem," then you would be wise not to say "this here" yourself. Table 17-5 gives some more examples of standard versus substandard language.

Caveat: Not all nonstandard language is substandard. Sometimes, when people try to "standardize" the language others use, they are actually trying to change the content or to mold the identity of the speaker. Women should not have to talk like men. People of color should not have to talk like their compatriots of northern European descent. You will not feel comfortable or seem authentic if you abandon your own idiom. Strive to find a way to maintain

TABLE 17-5	Substandard and Standard English
Substandard	Standard
Ten items or less.	Ten items or fewer.
... said to my friend and I ...	... said to my friend and me ...
I could care less!	I couldn't care less!
A large amount of people attended the rally.	A large number of people attended the rally.
Where'd you put it at?	Where'd you put it?
He hits the ball good.	He hits the ball well.
They couldn't hardly see what happened.	They could hardly see what happened.
I would have went there myself.	I would have gone there myself.

your own cultural, ethnic, and individual identity while still speaking in a way that will not lead to social stigma.

(4) Use language that is respectful and inclusive.

Referring to a group or individuals by the name they prefer is a sign of respect. When changes are made, those changes are often symbolic of a new status or image. For those used to the word *Negro*, the transition to *black* in the 1960s caused some problems, yet now the term seems natural. In fact, it is the baseline that some defend in the transition to *African American*. Today, many adult females want to be called *women*, not *girls* or *ladies*. It is not possible to please everyone or to be on top of every trend. (Is it *Mexican American, Chicano, Hispanic,* or *Latina?* Is it *minority, Third World,* or *people of color?* Is it *handicapped, disabled,* or *physically challenged?* There are definite differences in the meanings of these words and preferences as to their use.) What you can do is make a reasonable effort to learn which reference people prefer. You can make a commitment to flexibility. Acknowledge that it is worth the temporary inconvenience of changing a language habit if that change is highly symbolic and important to the person involved.

A more complex stylistic issue involves the use of the generic *he/man/ mankind.* Now that attention has been focused on these images, no speaker or writer can feign innocence of their impact. You may not mean to exclude females by such usage, but you should be aware that many listeners—male and female—now find the generic terms jarring. If you want to avoid distracting, and possibly offending, many listeners, consider using *he or she* and replacing *man* with *humanity, people,* or *humankind.* Sometimes, in a series of singular examples, alternating pronouns between male and female can have the same effect. If you are worried about distracting the dwindling segment of an audience offended by the current preferred usage, you can avoid the issue altogether by using plural and collective nouns instead of pronouns and by replacing words like *chairperson* with *presiding officer* and *mail person* with *letter carrier.*

Exercise 2. Rewrite the following sentences so that they are clearer. Make them more concrete, economical, correct, and inclusive.

1. It's a very unique sort of thing how Karen just makes everybody feel sort of good. She's real notorious as the most respected girl on our whole staff of salesmen.
2. At this time I'd like to say that one point to consider is the fact that we were totally surrounded by smokers who caused us considerable irritation and distress and aggravation.
3. Plus, I personally feel that we also face a serious crisis of psychological morale. We need to get off our duffs and sit down and talk about this epidemic that has us running on only three cylinders.

17d. Use vivid, varied language.

You can keep your listeners attentive and interested by avoiding dull, stale, and predictable language. Your message may never get past their short-term memory if you do not infuse it with vigor and a sense of newness. Why settle for the common and trite? Energize your language by effective use of various verbal devices.

(1) Employ imagery.

When you describe something, put the senses and the imaginative capacities of your listeners to work:

Not:	The life of the long-haul trucker is rough. Aside from being worn down by the effort of driving, the trucker can get discouraged by the tedium.
But:	The long-haul trucker pulls to the side of the road. Throughout the day, the road has fought back through the springs and steering wheel. Even though the truck is stopped, his arms up to his elbows still throb to the rhythm of hitting four hundred miles of highway expansion joints. The harsh roar of the engine and the cacophonous flexing of the cab rivets leave him with an infuriating ringing of the ears. After a bor-

ing, wholesome dinner, the trucker slips into the cramped womb of the sleeper cab, hoping to sleep. In the morning, the cycle of noise, sweat, and stress starts anew.

(2) Use stylistic devices.

Enliven your language through the planned use of figures of speech and certain arrangements of words and phrases.

Simile and metaphor

You can add vigor to your speaking by using language that connects objects or ideas to vivid images. A *simile* makes a comparison between two things ordinarily dissimilar: "When she came in from shoveling off the walk, her hands were like ice." No one would mistake a hand for some ice, but in this case they share the characteristic of extremely low temperature. A *metaphor* creates a figurative equation that implies two unlike things are the same: "Her hands were ice cubes" or "We stand in horror as our money disappears down the gluttonous maw of the federal government." Making the government a shark forms a more compelling image than "We stand in horror as the federal government operates with fiscal irresponsibility."

Personification

One way to bring objects or ideas to life is to imbue them with human qualities. We know that no room is really "cheerful," that winds do not actually "whisper," and that, being legless, the economy cannot possibly "limp." Nevertheless, all of these images are potent because we find it easier to identify with reflections of our own behavior. Here's another example:

> Israel now faced the choice of either to be choked to death in her southern maritime approaches or to await the death blow from northern Sinai.
>
> —Abba Eban

Hyperbole

To emphasize a point, you may deliberately overstate it in a way that is clearly fanciful rather than misleading:

This paperwork will be the death of me.

I thought about nothing else for the next three days.

The governor has repeated this same promise to you a million times.

Repetitive language or structure

By repeating key words or phrases, you make your listeners feel that your points are snowballing to a certain conclusion. Use parallel structure to emphasize relationships.

Sometimes, a syntactic construction is repeated:

> How serious is the morale crisis? We have lost several key employees. What has caused the problem? Lack of clear upward and downward communication. How can we change things? By hiring an interpersonal and organizational communication trainer for a series of workshops.

Notice that no phrases are repeated, but the question-answer format creates a sense of momentum in this paragraph.

You can also use repetition to introduce consecutive paragraphs. For instance, a speaker can build a sense of urgency or dedication by repeating the phrase "We must act now to . . ." as each problem is presented.

Within a paragraph, you can achieve a similar effect by starting a series of sentences with the same words or by using a sentence as a connecting refrain.

> You see, I was born to a teenage mother, who was born to a teenage mother. I understand. I know abandonment, and people being mean to you, and saying you're nothing and nobody, and can never be anything. I understand. Jesse Jackson is my third name. I'm adopted. When I had no name, my grandmother gave me her name, my name was Jesse Burns 'til I was twelve. So I wouldn't have a blank space, she gave me a name. To hold me over. I understand when nobody knows your name. I understand when you have no name. I understand.
>
> —Jesse Jackson

Or you might end several sentences with the same words:

> What remains? Treaties have gone. The honor of nations has gone. Liberty has gone.
>
> —David Lloyd George

Additionally, for emphasis, you can repeat key words or phrases within a sentence:

> But, in a larger sense, we can not dedicate—we can not consecrate—we can not hallow this ground.
>
> —Abraham Lincoln

Alliteration and assonance

Use of these devices involves saying the same sound in a sustained sequence. (Sorry about that silly sentence.) Whether it is with consonants (*alliteration*) or vowels (*assonance*), this repetition can make an idea more memorable, or at least charge it with a sense of poetry.

At his brother's grave, Robert Green Ingersoll said the following:

> He who sleeps here, when dying . . . whispered with his latest breath: "I am better now." Let us believe, in spite of doubts and dogmas, and tears and fears, that these dear words are true of all the countless dead.

Antithesis

When you want to contrast two ideas, certain sentence structures serve to dramatize the differences. *Antithesis* uses forms like these:

Not . . . , but . . .
Not only . . . , but . . .
Never . . . , unless . . .

Consider these examples:

> We live in a society that emphasizes military expenditures over education. We spend millions teaching young people how to kill and be killed, but we won't spend money teaching them how to live and make a living.
> —Harry Edwards

> It was we, the people; not we, the white male citizens; nor yet we, the male citizens; but we, the whole people who formed the Union. And we formed it, not to give the blessings of liberty, but to secure them; not to the half of ourselves and the half of our posterity, but to the whole people—women as well as men.
> —Susan B. Anthony

Upon the receipt of the 2001 Nobel Peace Prize, Kofi Annan in his Nobel lecture combined antithesis, alliteration and assonance, and repetitive structure:

> Today's real borders are not between nations, but between powerful and powerless, free and fettered, privileged and humiliated.

(3) Use fresh language.

The power of figurative language lies in the images stimulated in the listener's mind. After too many repetitions, the original psychological impact is lost.

"Fresh as a daisy" once summoned a picture of a clean, bright, dew-studded blossom. At the first turn of the phrase "it went in one ear and out the other," its aptness produced pleasant surprise. Now both expressions are likely to be processed as just extra, empty words.

Certain fad words attract a cult following. *Bottom line, prioritize,* and *networking* become overnight sensations and are used to the exclusion of many good (and fresher) synonyms. Purge your language of such flatulent phrasing. Invest the time needed to select original combinations of words and phrases that capture the image, mood, or thought you want to get across.

(4) Vary the rhythm of your sentences.

Although oral style is characterized by simpler, shorter phrases with fewer different words, you are not compelled to homogenize your sentences into dullness. The "singsonginess" associated with doggerel can creep into a speech if you fail to pay attention to how you are stringing your sentences and phrases together. Be sparing in your use of parallelisms and repetition. Consider this plodding passage:

> The association's annual convention should be user supported. The convention is attended by a core of regulars. The average association member doesn't benefit from the convention. These average members shouldn't have to bear more than their fair share.

The choppiness of this tedious passage results from the sameness of sentence length and structure. Recasting the sentences will create a more fluid and graceful paragraph:

> The association's annual convention should be user supported. Who attends the convention? A core of regulars. The average association members, who don't benefit from the convention, shouldn't have to bear more than their fair share.

Exercise 3. Use at least two different stylistic devices to enliven each of these phrases:

1. A cold, rainy day
2. An unworkable policy
3. A delicate, intricate procedure
4. A very stern leader
5. A huge crowd

Exercise 4. Identify at least three different examples of imagery or stylistic devices in at least three speeches on the Sample Speeches Web site.

Exercise 5. Think of fresh ways to replace these overused phrases:

1. Like comparing apples and oranges
2. Caught between a rock and a hard place
3. Two steps forward and one step back
4. Always darkest before the dawn

17e. Synchronize your language with that of your listeners.

Language is not the sole possession of speakers. Our words are shared with our listeners, drawn from a common pool of possible utterances. As we emphasize, speech consists not of messages sent, but of meanings jointly constructed within the context of a discourse community. Among the many possible ways to talk about a topic, the most effective way is the one that overlaps and resonates with your listeners. When you use phrases and metaphors that are comfortable for your audience, you say, "I may not be exactly like you, but I am part of your discourse community." This creates a bond with listeners that goes beyond the literal definitions of the words you use and lays the foundation for more communication. This sort of bonding is particularly important with an unfavorable audience.

In the process of bonding, be careful not to parrot phrases you do not understand, mock anyone's accent, or seem to talk down to your listeners. As a speaker, you must be yourself. But you have many facets, and without being artificial, you can choose to bring into your speech those aspects of your own language that best match your audience.

People who like each other and agree with each other come to talk like each other. And people who talk like each other come to like each other better and to agree with each other more. This cyclical pattern reinforces itself; groups whose members spend time together pick up common phrases and sentence structures. Language can readily disclose the insiders and the outsiders. After a couple of minutes of small talk, for instance, you can tell if a new acquaintance is a true sports fan in the way you and your group define it, or if this person is a "guru" or a "wannabe" in your area of business expertise. With language being this potent an identifier, you want it to work *for* you.

Synchronizing your language with your listeners' involves close audience analysis. Listening to them and engaging in genuine dialogue will reveal the terms and categories that organize their reality. Every aspect of style can be subtly adjusted—level of formality, use of jargon or abbreviations, selection of figures of speech and metaphors. Matching words or phrases is important, not for its own sake, but rather because paying attention to the audience's words gives you clues about how they see the world. If you respect your listeners, you will almost subconsciously scan for terms that reveal that respect. If you do not understand them, there is the potential to get off on the wrong foot and truly offend them. For example, the board member of an orchestra who talks to the musicians about Beethoven's Ninth Symphony as a good "product" may alienate them irretrievably. Or the lack of understanding may not be as dramatic: Perhaps it is simply a feeling of not really connecting, though neither speaker nor listeners can explain why.

Exercise 6. Suppose you are going to speak on the topic of why a two-day strategic planning retreat is a good investment for an organization. You visit three different departments of the organization to which you will be making separate presentations. Based on the following observations, how would you characterize each audience, and how might you adapt your topic and your language to establish a tone that is in sync with theirs?

Group A makes use of these terms: *the real go-getters, on the fast track, it's a rat race every day, pressure cooker.*
Group B makes use of these terms: *dotting the i's and crossing the t's, getting your ducks in a row, doing your homework.*
Group C makes use of these terms: *our family here, the team, touching base, backing each other up.*

Chapter 18

Attention and Interest

Adapt your speech material so that it captures your listeners' attention and retains their interest.

Think back to your most recent walk through a department store. Did you notice every single display, each ten feet from the last and all competing for your attention? Or did you pass most without a flicker of interest, brought to a halt only by a few that drew you to them through color, or movement, or contrast, or an unusual juxtaposition of images?

Some attention factors are universal, and others are more idiosyncratic. Such things as sudden movement or bright colors will catch almost anyone's eye. But you might stop by snow tires while your friend looks at computer games. Or you might linger in the food department on a day you are hungry but rush by it on another day when your thoughts are on the fact that you have no luggage for the trip you wish to take.

Why is it that some things always catch our attention and others are noticed only by some people or only in some situations? And of the thousands of things that receive momentary notice, what causes a few to be chosen for closer scrutiny? As a public speaker, you can profit from giving some thought to questions like these. After all, when you give a speech or presentation, your words are competing for attention with every other sight and sound in the room and with every daydream or concern in the mind of each listener. The better you understand the psychology of attention, the more likely you will receive the compliment most sought for and appreciated by speakers: a sincere and simple "That was an interesting speech!"

18a. Engage your audience's attention by making extensive use of techniques that enliven your speech.

A common misconception is that, once you have grabbed your listeners' attention with a snappy introduction, this attention is yours until you relinquish it at the end of the speech. Unfortunately, it takes more than a clever opening to keep an audience listening. People are easily distracted, and unless reengaged, their thoughts may stray every half-minute or so. When composing a speech, take every opportunity to weave in materials and to phrase statements characterized by the following factors that have been identified as most likely to gain attention:

- *Activity or movement*—appropriate physical mobility of the speaker and a lively treatment of the content that creates a feeling of something happening
- *Reality*—reference to actual people, events, and places; being specific and concrete rather than abstract
- *Proximity*—reference to what is close at hand: people in the room, current events, local references, and so on
- *Familiarity*—the use of recognized examples, well-known phrases, and commonplace events
- *Novelty*—the opposite of the familiar: startling facts, odd turns of phrase, surprising images, and unusual combinations
- *Suspense*—stimulation of curiosity about what will happen next through puzzles or provocative questions
- *Conflict*—pros and cons, opposing viewpoints, competing schools of thought
- *Humor*—playful remarks, silly or exaggerated images, amusing plays on words, ironic twists of fate, entertaining stories, and the like
- *The vital*[1]—reference to something that is important to listeners, ranging from matters of survival to anything that saves them time, earns them money, or makes their life more pleasant

People are intrigued by things that are unusual, that spark their curiosity. Paradoxically, they also respond to well-known, everyday references. Most of all, as in the case of "the vital," people attend to material they see as connected to their own self-interest. Do not worry about using plenty of these techniques. Think of all the speeches you have heard labeled dull or boring.

---

[1]Bruce E. Gronbeck, Kathleen German, Douglas Ehninger, and Alan H. Monroe, *Principles of Speech Communication,* 12th brief ed. (New York: New York: HarperCollins, 1995), 145–49.

Did you ever hear a complaint that a lecture was too fascinating? The use of these techniques can be made second nature without much effort or time. Here are some examples:

Not: A college athlete might be having trouble in one of his classes.

But: Suppose Larry Linebacker can't tell the difference between Bizet and "The Bizarroes" in his music appreciation class. [humor, reality, familiarity]

Not: A number of technologies have made business communication faster and more efficient.

But: As I walked into my office about two hours ago, the red light on my phone was blinking. I picked up four voice mail messages, forwarding one to my colleague. I next jumped online to see if there were any email messages and found that our client in Atlanta had changed the specifications for the contract we are bidding on. I quickly generated computer graphics reflecting the new data and faxed them to Chris, who, as you all know, is making his presentation right about now. [activity, proximity, the vital]

Not: When time is short, a good executive takes action first and then worries about causes, procedure, and policy.

But: If I told you people in the fourth and fifth rows that that chandelier's going to fall in 10 seconds, what would you do? Darn right! You'd get out of the way! Later, we'd talk about why it happened, whose fault it was, and how to fix it. [proximity, novelty, suspense, reality]

Be guided by the following principles as you incorporate attention factors into your speech.

(1) Use materials that are concrete and close to home.

Examples are always more interesting when they are specific and real. Notice how these paragraphs from a speech by Senator Edward Kennedy create images in your mind—more tangible and believable than vague references to "the victims of our economic crisis:"

> I have listened and learned.
>
> I have listened to Kenny Dubois, a glassblower in Charleston, West Virginia, who has ten children to support, but has lost his job after thirty-five years, just three years short of qualifying for his pension.

I have listened to the Trachta family, who farm in Iowa and wonder whether they can pass the good life and the good earth on to their children.

I have listened to a grandmother in East Oakland, who no longer has a phone to call her grandchildren because she gave it up to pay the rent on her small apartment.

I have listened to . . .

Never say "a person" or "one" if you can give a name. Use well-known figures, members of the audience, or hypothetical characters. And give place names, brand names, dates, and details.

(2) Keep your audience involved.

If you have done a thorough audience analysis, you should have many references to the audience built into the speech and can make use of attention factors like proximity and familiarity. But there are always opportunities to adapt to your audience once you start your speech. Be willing to throw out what you have if you can replace it with something "closer to home." Here are some adaptations you might try.

Use the names of people in the audience.

Replace supporting material with items drawn from the audience's direct experience. Before giving a speech, you may have a chance to meet a few members of your audience. It is often effective to refer to them. Why say, "Suppose a businessperson wants to obtain a loan," when you could say, "Suppose Ms. Silver's [nodding toward a listener] hardware business is expanding so rapidly that she decides to take out a loan to enlarge her store?"

Refer to the person who introduced you and to other speakers on the program.

Listen to the comments of the person who introduces you and to the content of any speeches that precede yours. You might be able to return a compliment, engage in banter, or, best of all, forge an intellectual link between their speech ideas and one of yours. For instance, an alert member of a speech class might include something like this:

So now that we have examined the causes of stress, let us look at four ways of reducing it. The first of these is physical exercise. Nearly everyone can find an activity she or he likes. Hong was telling us about the joys of tennis. Similarly, aerobic dance is . . .

Refer to details in the immediate setting or from shared experience.
Do not use a hypothetical example of a point or process if you can draw on a more concrete example from something related to the group:

> And all of that expensive atom-smashing machinery was housed in a room not half the size of this one.

> Everyone in this class knows about *situational stress*. The five of us giving speeches today are especially aware of it.

Create an active rather than a passive role for your audience. Even though it is your show when you speak, you can still stimulate a sense of interaction with your listeners. Use audience participation techniques. Ask for shows of hands if pertinent, have listeners provide examples, and ask questions of them:

> How many people here had breakfast this morning? Ah, I see about half of you raised your hands. What did you have, sir? Bacon and eggs? Over there? Coffee and a donut. I hear juice and toast, yeast shake, Cheerios, and yogurt. Would anyone care to hazard an answer to this question: What percentage of elementary school students go to school with no breakfast at all?

When you do not want to relinquish control or when overt audience participation is impractical for some reason, you can still keep your audience mentally involved and active. Ask rhetorical questions, have your listeners visualize examples, and ask them for nonverbal feedback and respond to it:

> Are there any Monty Python freaks here? Great, I can see there are. Well, do you remember the sketch about the cheese shop?

> There is yet another problem with home repairs. I'll bet this has happened to everyone here.

> I have one colleague who always gives me feedback at the wrong time and place. Do you know people like that? Several of you are nodding. Isn't it frustrating?

> We can learn from our mistakes. Think of the last mistake you made. Take a minute to recall a big one. Do you have it in mind? Okay. Now I want you to think about how you felt.

An even less complicated technique to maintain attention is the liberal use of the word *you:*

You've probably seen . . .
Do you sometimes wonder . . .
In your morning paper . . .
Now, I'll bet you're saying to yourself . . .
You could undoubtedly give me a dozen more examples.
In your city here . . .

Be careful, however, not to overuse these techniques. In our experience, there have been a number of occasions (mostly banquets and awards) in which the presenter got so caught up in making oblique references to historical (and allegedly amusing) events with members of the organization's old guard that it became annoying even to longtime members.

(3) Keep the energy level of your speech up through variety and movement.

Change attracts attention. Sameness is dull. One visual aid may add interest to your speech, but a succession of visual aids can drag a speech down if they are not used judiciously. If your content or delivery becomes totally predictable, audience members' interest will start to wane.

Vary your forms of support—do not rely on only statistics or only testimony. Draw examples from many domains. Three political illustrations of one point are less interesting than a single political illustration combined with a sports example and one drawn from a popular film. Similarly, repetition of the same sentence constructions and overuse of a word or phrase should be avoided. (See **17d.**)

Whenever possible, give the speech a sense of movement. Create images of activity. Use verbs with vivid connotations, and stay in the active voice as much as possible. For instance, instead of saying, "Five new businesses can be seen downtown," say, "Drive down First Street and you will see five new businesses." If you need to point out the features of a piece of equipment, describe it in use, with "fingers flying over the keyboard" or "gears turning" or "shutters clicking" or even "electrons crackling."

In your delivery, too, remember the importance of vocal variety and physical movement. Who wants to listen to a deadpan speaker monotonously delivering a presentation while standing on a particularly adhesive spot on the floor? (See **26c** and **27.**)

(4) Use humor in appropriate situations.

Integrate humor into your speech. But make sure it is appropriate to your personality and to the situation.

248

Of the many factors of attention, humor is so powerful and at the same time so tricky that it deserves a careful look. An infusion of humor into any speech can ease tension, deflate opponents, enhance the speaker's image, and make points memorable. You need not consider yourself a humorous speaker or your speech a humorous talk to benefit from using this attention-getting technique.

Developing your use of humor is not a matter of collecting jokes and gags that have limited applicability. What is important is the ability to spot a potentially humorous idea in your speech and to craft it into a genuinely funny moment.

Draw humorous material from a variety of sources.

Look for the humor in your everyday experience. Most of us have days when one disaster follows on the heels of another, and there comes a point at which we have to accept the humor of the situation—or crack. "This will make a good story . . . someday" is an utterance that bears witness to the fine line between tragedy and humor. The boring, frustrating, and mundane aspects of life all have their humorous elements.

Take note of the everyday things that make you laugh: on your job, in your relationships, on television, and in the paper. Decide which of these humorous items have any bearing on potential speech topics. Some are merely amusing; others are both amusing and instructive. Jot them down, clip them out, and establish some sort of filing system so that you do not find yourself, six months later, saying, "Now, what was the funny phrase the judge used?"

Be selective when you draw on collected humor. You can definitely benefit from reading books *on* humor, but take care when using books *of* humor. Timeliness and original twists are so important to humor that the lag time involved in publishing renders stale much of the content of such books. Nevertheless, topically organized books of humor can sometimes yield just the gem you need. Better than joke books or magazine joke pages, though, are the works of genuine humorists. Read Mark Twain, Will Rogers, and Robert Benchley, and contemporary columnists, essayists, and commentators like Dave Barry, Molly Ivins, David Sedaris, Sandra Tsing Loh, and Sarah Vowell. They will introduce you to comic points of view that are more useful than jokes.

Exercise 1. Think over the spontaneous laughs you have had in the past few days in unstructured interpersonal interactions. Can you describe what your friends or acquaintances did that amused you? Do these people have uniquely funny approaches to life or ways of responding to events? Turn this around: Can you describe what you've done to amuse your friends and acquaintances?

18b. Convert attention to interest.

Prehistoric peoples quickly discovered that keeping a campfire burning continuously was easier than laboriously rubbing two sticks together to light a new fire for each individual task. You will be working altogether too hard as a speaker if you must constantly light new fires under your audience with a succession of attention getters. If, however, you can kindle a sustained *interest* in your topic, your job becomes easier. When audience members become more than merely attentive, but actually interested, they start to take a more active role. Pushing distractions aside, they put forth the effort to stay with you even through complicated lines of thought or technical material.

When you have gained attention, through the methods recommended in **18a**, you need to use those moments to demonstrate how and why your topic is worthy of your listeners' interest.

(1) Emphasize the link between your topic and the listeners' self-interest.

Most times, when people say, "So what?" they are really saying, "What's it to me?" Do not assume that the benefits of your particular approach are obvious; motivate your audience to listen by spelling out the rewards. Do careful audience analysis and tap into as many of your listeners' needs and values as possible. (See **20**.) Here are some examples:

> If you take the time to learn the basics of car maintenance, you'll no longer be at the mercy of a mechanic. You can shop around for the most economical and reliable car care, and have the added peace of mind of knowing that you'll be able to spot potentially dangerous conditions.

> I know that many of you work in the helping professions—as teachers, social workers, counselors, and nurses. Learning to read the subtle cues of body language will help you interpret messages your clients may be unable to transmit in words.

> You don't have to be a vegetarian or a gourmet cook to benefit from these menu ideas. By serving just a few meatless meals a week, you can save 30 to 100 dollars on your monthly grocery bill and also provide a healthier diet for your family.

(2) Incorporate some of the techniques of effective storytelling.

A reader will innocently open a book at bedtime to read a few pages before turning out the light. Dawn comes, and the bleary-eyed reader is still engrossed, even if the subject is not one that normally produces any interest or relates to a part of the reader's life. A well-constructed story, whether it deals with elves and hobbits or secret agents in the world of international intrigue, commands the interest of nearly everyone. The raconteur who can take the chaos of everyday experience and produce a compelling narration will never have trouble attracting an audience.

People are fascinated by human interest stories, as well as by hard news of matters that concern them directly. Notice how excellent feature articles and documentary films share many of the qualities of good fiction or drama. A speech, even if it is an annual report, can captivate an audience if it unfolds in a narrative fashion with suspense, conflict, intriguing characterizations, lively bits of dialogue, and a moment of climax leading to the denouement. Your speech need not promise to make your listeners rich or famous if it takes them outside their experience in an engaging way.

Exercise 2. Identify the attention-getting factor or factors in each example:

1. A good accountant can help you avoid paying extra taxes.
2. You've all heard the phrase "the bottom line."
3. Our own accounting department has developed some new techniques.
4. I was trembling when I went into the tax auditor's office. Could Melvin's ledgers save me or was I . . . ?

Exercise 3. Describe how you could use at least five of the attention getters from **18a** in a speech on each of these topics:

Electric and Hybrid Vehicles
Art Frauds and Forgeries
Federal Regulatory Agencies

Exercise 4. Identify at least four attention factors in each speech on the Sample Speeches Web site.

Exercise 5. Select one speech on the Sample Speeches Web site and discuss how the speaker transforms attention to interest.

18c. Avoid common attention pitfalls.

(1) Avoid inappropriate stories, humor, and other attention "grabbers."

Don't risk losing the goodwill of your audience by using questionable material. It is a safe bet that ethnic jokes, sick humor, and vulgarities will offend someone in every audience. Sensitive audience analysis should cause you to revise or eliminate stereotypical treatments of women, homosexuals, mothers-in-law, and senior citizens. Knowledge of your listeners will also help you make a judgment about the inclusion of a slightly risqué remark or politically loaded story. Insults or ridicule—unless stylized as in a "roast"—should be avoided unless you are very sure that the object of your putdown genuinely enjoys public teasing.

(2) Don't let a story or joke consume your entire speech.

It is easy to spend so much time getting attention there is no time left to deliver your substantive message. Every bit of supporting material in a speech has to make a direct contribution to the thesis. A string of unrelated jokes and stories or aimless clowning pulls the focus away from your topic. Constructing a transition that "huffs and puffs" to tie in an unrelated joke is a waste of time.

(3) Do not tell jokes unless you have mastered the techniques of joke telling.

Everyone can be funny, but not everyone can and should tell jokes. Telling a joke takes skill, and telling a long, complex joke with voices, intricate timing, and physical movement takes consummate skill.

If you do choose to use jokes, you should to do more precise planning than that necessary in the more conversational parts of your speech. To succeed, you need to draw on the writer's attention to word choice and the performer's sense of presence and voice. An excellent public speaker should not diminish his or her image of competence by bungling a joke in these all-too-familiar ways:

- Having an inadequate lead-in or setup.
- Fizzling midway through a climactic joke ("So anyway, this same thing happens four or five more times").
- Not committing yourself to actually telling the joke. This involves describing the nature of the joke and delivering the punch line, but never getting into the storytelling aspect.
- Overintroducing your humorous material, using tedious and empty lead-ins like "Now here's a real funny story my cousin told me. It really points out what I'm talking about, and you're going to love it."

(4) Be careful that audience participation does not cause you to lose control.

A half-hearted attempt to get listeners involved can result in awkward silences. At the other extreme, overly responsive audience members can turn a speech into a group discussion.

Chapter 19

Credibility

Establish your credibility, both before and during your speech, by projecting the qualities of competence, concern, trustworthiness, and dynamism.

Your content and delivery determine, to a great extent, whether your listeners believe what you say. However, there is an independent force at work that can doom even the most exquisitely wrought speech to failure. Beyond what you say and how you say it, your audience is influenced by who you are—or, more accurately, who they think you are. Your *credibility* is that combination of perceived qualities that makes listeners predisposed to believe you. For centuries, scholars have been fascinated by credibility—from classical discussions of *ethos* to contemporary investigations of concepts like *image, personality,* and *charisma.* What is it about some speakers that makes you want to accept what they say, while others make you want to reject what may be an identical message? Aristotle observed that audiences are most inclined to believe a person they see as having good sense, goodwill, and good character. Modern social scientists have tried to isolate the characteristics that distinguish the most credible speakers from others. Their lists include competence, dynamism, intention, personality, intelligence, authoritativeness, extroversion, trustworthiness, composure, and sociability.

You can enhance your credibility, and thus the chances of meeting your speech objective, by projecting these qualities. You can build up your image or reputation prior to the speech, and you can take steps to improve your credibility as you are speaking. The first step, though, is to assess your present image.

19a. Conduct an honest assessment of your speaking image.

The perfect speaker is seen as competent, concerned, trustworthy, and dynamic in discussing all topics with all audiences, but most of us fall short of this ideal. One speaker might seem warm, charming, and likable—but somehow have trouble being taken seriously on weighty issues. Another may have a demeanor that immediately inspires confidence—but suffer from seeming dull or distant or not human enough.

Before you can work on improving your credibility, you need to see where you stand now. Is your overall credibility high or low? Do people agree with you because of, or in spite of, your personality? Which components of credibility are strongest for you? Which need to be developed? If possible, have some friends or acquaintances help you with this appraisal. It is very hard to gauge how others see us.

The following diagnostic questions, fall into three areas: your *image prior* to the speech, your *content,* and your *delivery.* Suggestions for improving your credibility in each of these areas are provided in **19b, c,** and **d.**

(1) Are you perceived as *competent?*

Image: Do you have education, experience, or credentials to make you an expert on this topic? Does your audience know that?

Content: Have you researched broadly and deeply? Does your speech reflect this with well-documented, factual information?

Delivery: Does your delivery connote competence? Do you seem to be "on top of your information," well organized, and composed?

(2) Are you perceived as *concerned* about your audience's welfare?

Image: If you have a history of generosity or selflessness on relevant issues, is it known? (For example, have you sponsored a scholarship, or volunteered your time, or made a sacrifice of some sort?)

Content: Do you stress the audience's needs and goals throughout the speech?

Delivery: Is your delivery warm, unaffected, friendly, and responsive to the audience?

(3) Are you perceived as *trustworthy?*

Image: | Is your past record one of honesty and integrity?
Content: | Do you make a special effort to be fair in presenting evidence, acknowledging limitations of your data and opinions, and conceding those parts of opposing viewpoints that have validity?
Delivery: | Is your style of presentation sincere and honest, and not slick or manipulative?

(4) Are you perceived as *dynamic?*

Image: | Is your image one of an active, fairly aggressive person—a leader rather than a follower, a doer rather than an observer?
Content: | Does your speech have a sense of movement? Do the ideas build to a climax rather than dropping into a static heap? Is your language lively and colorful?
Delivery: | Is your delivery animated, energetic, and enthusiastic?

Exercise 1. Complete your image inventory. In a few sentences, describe your prior image as a speaker in your speech class or in a social or professional group you relate to regularly. Which is your strongest area: competence, concern, trustworthiness, or dynamism? Which is your weakest?

Exercise 2. Consider how your credibility varies from topic to topic. Name three topics on which you have already high credibility and three on which you would have to work very hard to establish credibility.

Exercise 3. Rate the last four U.S. presidents' credibility as high, medium, or low on competence, concern, trustworthiness, and dynamism. Discuss your choices and reasons.

Exercise 4. Name a public figure who you believe is competent, concerned, and trustworthy but whose image suffers due to a lack of dynamism. Can you think of a public figure for whom the opposite is true?

19b. Build your credibility prior to the speech.

(1) Provide the contact person with adequate information about your qualifications.

Do not be overly modest when asked for information for advance publicity. Send a résumé that lists your background and achievements. Include clippings, testimonials about your speaking, a list of your books and articles, and a photograph if appropriate.

(2) Help the person introducing you to set a favorable tone.

In addition to providing written information, be available to consult by phone or in person with whoever will introduce you. If there are aspects of your background you would like to have stressed for a particular speech, be sure to say so.

(3) Be aware of your image in all dealings with the group prior to the speech.

In a speech class, you know that you have a certain image. Based on daily classroom interactions, you can tell if you are considered serious, funny, prompt, lazy, cheerful, argumentative, intelligent, informed, and so on. These perceptions will affect the way your first speech is received. A similar situation exists if you are to speak in front of the service group you belong to or your professional association.

Speaking before an unfamiliar audience is different. Because these people have little to go on to form an impression, virtually all of your interactions with them will affect your credibility. Your friendliness, professionalism, and confidence in negotiating arrangements and even in making small talk prior to the speech will be very influential.

19c. Bolster your credibility through your speech content.

As you prepare your speech outline and select your supporting evidence and examples, think about ways to communicate your competence, concern, trustworthiness, and dynamism. The following suggestions are especially relevant in the opening minutes of the speech, when first impressions are being formed (see **13a**). But many credibility boosters can be woven in throughout the entire speech as well.

(1) Present your credentials.

The majority of inexperienced speakers find it difficult to "blow their own horn" and do not do as much credibility building as they should. Do not be reluctant to provide information about your qualifications to speak:

In my 15 years as a kindergarten teacher . . .

The most common error I see in the 20 to 30 loan applications I look at each week is . . .

I've had a special awareness of the barriers the physically handicapped face since 1991, when my brother Dave returned from the Gulf War.

Judgment and tact are important in deciding which qualifications to mention and how to work them into the speech. Our culture frowns on bragging and name-dropping, yet false humility is out of place. The too-humble speaker insults listeners by implying that if they knew anything at all they never would have invited the person to speak. However, you can include many statements of your qualifications without seeming boastful if you play it straight and present them matter-of-factly. Include only relevant qualifications. Do not talk about how many celebrities you know unless it relates to the topic, and do not expound on your financial success unless the speech is specifically about making money.

(2) Demonstrate a thorough understanding of your topic.

To communicate a sense of expertise, you must let listeners know you have done your homework. Mention the nature of your research when appropriate:

The seven judges I interviewed all agreed on one major weakness in our court system.

I read the minutes of all the committee hearings on this bill, and not one expert mentioned . . .

There is considerable disagreement on this point in the books and articles I read. Several scholars say . . .

Use concrete examples, statistics, and testimony. Be sure you have your details straight. One obvious error early in the speech can ruin your credibility.

Just imagine what it would have been like for the Union soldier crouching in the trenches around Richmond, his jacket zipped up tight in a futile battle against the cold and the wet.

The people listening to this would probably think, "If this speaker doesn't know that the zipper wasn't invented until long after the Civil War, I wonder what other information is all wrong?"

(3) Be sure your material is clearly organized.

A sense of competence depends on your being in command of the material and seeming to know where you are headed. Listeners will view you as uninformed rather than unorganized if you wander from topic to topic or if you must apologetically insert, "Oh, one thing I forgot to mention when I was discussing . . ."

(4) Make a special effort to present a balanced and objective analysis.

To demonstrate that you are fair, trustworthy, and of good character, go out of your way to acknowledge the limitations of your evidence and argument, if appropriate:

> Now, I know there are some problems with relying on surveys, but this one was carefully conducted. It seems safe to conclude that at least many, if not most, working mothers are dissatisfied with the quality of child care available to them.

> I'm not saying television is the only cause of these problems. I realize that's an oversimplification. But I do think that TV has had a pronounced effect on the imaginative thinking of the last two generations.

Also be sure to acknowledge the existence of opposing evidence and opinions:

> Some studies indicate that an alcoholic can return to social drinking, but . . .

> I recognize the contributions the administration has made to social welfare programs, but it has failed in so many other areas that I still maintain it is time for a change.

Acknowledge self-interest when it exists to prevent the audience from thinking you are trying to hide something from them.

> It's true I'm a Realtor and I stand to profit by having folks invest in real estate. But that's not my main reason for urging you to invest.

If they discover later that you are more partisan than you made it sound, your credibility will suffer.

(5) Explicitly express your concern and goodwill toward the audience.

Let them know that your speech is offered to serve their interests:

> I'd do anything to save your families the headaches and heartaches that go along with having a relative die without a will.

> Taking up cycling has added so much to my life that I'd love to see some of you share in that fun.

19d. Use your speech delivery to increase your credibility.

Too many expert and well-prepared speakers lose effectiveness because they cannot *transmit* these qualities to their audience. Dropping cards, reading in a shaky voice, fumbling with whatever is at hand—all suggest lack of competence. An unexpressive face and voice might be interpreted as disdainfulness and detract from perceived goodwill. Hesitancy and uncertainty are sometimes falsely seen as shiftiness or dishonesty. Listless, monotonous, colorless speaking is the very opposite of dynamism. To be seen as a believable source of information and opinion, continue to work on all aspects of delivery covered in chapters **26** and **27**.

Exercise 5. How does each speaker on the Sample Speeches Web site directly establish his or her credentials to speak? Which examples do you find effective? Are there any that strike you as heavy-handed or arrogant?

Exercise 6. Find an example of how each speaker on the Sample Speeches Web site explicitly establishes concern for the welfare of the audience.

Exercise 7. What sections of the speeches on the Sample Speeches Web site seem to present the speakers as fair, objective, honest people?

Chapter 20

Motivational Appeals

Motivate your listeners toward your speech purpose through appeals to their emotions, needs, and values. Be sure that these appeals supplement, but do not replace, the sound logic and evidence upon which you base your speech.

This book stresses the role of clear analysis in support of ideas, but it also emphasizes making those ideas meaningful to an audience. A good speaker is constantly aware of the humanness of the audience. To be human is to be rational, but it is more than that. Love sometimes overrules logic, reverence often transcends reason, and emotion frequently contradicts evidence. Understanding the humanity of your audience means reaching them as total persons—packaging your essentially logical case so that it touches the listeners' feelings, needs, and values.

20a. When developing the content of your speech, be conscious of the emotional impact you want to create or avoid.

Keep in mind that everything you say has the potential to trigger some sort of emotional response in your audience. Generally, you can strengthen your speech by selecting main points, supporting material, and language that can engage your listeners' feelings. Positive emotions—hope, joy, pride, love—are surefire motivators. Negative emotions like fear, envy, disgust, and contempt can also motivate; witness the popularity of roller coasters and horror films. The motivational effects of negative emotions are less predictable, however, and can sometimes boomerang. Moderate levels of fear appeal can enhance persuasion, but higher levels may work against the desired effect. Some presentations feature gory films of traffic accidents, vivid visual aids showing cancerous lung tissue, or detailed descriptions of the plight of a family whose breadwinner had no insurance. These can either cause the audience to tune out the unpleasantness or seem too extreme to be statistically plausible fates for the listener to worry about. When adding emotion to your speech, remember the old adage, "Although some is good, more is not always better."

Devoid of Emotion

A dose of 600 rems produces acute radiation illness. Japanese A-bomb victims experienced a variety of physical symptoms and usually died within two weeks of exposure.

Moderate Emotion

A dose of 600 rems or more produces acute radiation illness. Thousands of Japanese A-bomb victims died from this sickness within two weeks of the bomb explosions. Such exposure to radiation kills all actively dividing cells in the body: Hair falls out, skin is sloughed off in big ulcers, vomiting and diarrhea occur, and then, as the white blood cells and platelets die, victims expire of infection and/or massive hemorrhage.[1]

Excessive Emotion

The bomb has fallen, and you're unlucky enough not to have been killed immediately. There's nothing you can do except sit there dumbly, in your own vomit and excrement, while the omnipresent radiation kills off the process of life. With no cell growth, your skin becomes leprous and detaches from your body in great clumps; but you don't notice because your white blood cells have died and dark swelling has overtaken all of your body, immersing you in a pain that will not subside until a weakened artery in your brain bursts in a final geyser of black blood.

For any topic, there are these three levels. What you have to do early on is discern where your listeners draw the dividing lines. Try to include the optimal amount of emotional appeal—not so little that you fail to touch them, and not so much that you turn them off.

---

[1] Helen Caldicott, *Nuclear Madness* (Brookline, MA: Autumn Press, 1978), 29.

20b. Relate your speech to the needs of your listeners.

The best-known way of classifying human needs is the hierarchy devised by Abraham Maslow.[2] Figure 20-1 shows the hierarchy.

In this hierarchy, the lower-level needs have to be met or satisfied before an individual can become concerned with the needs on the next-higher level. For instance, on the topic of physical fitness, you could appeal to your audience at any of the following levels:

- The effect of exercise in reducing risk of cardiovascular disease appeals to the survival need.
- Security might be drawn in by mentioning how physically fit people are more likely to be able to resist or evade attackers.
- The need for belonging can be linked to becoming trim and attractive, as well as to making friends through physical activity.
- Esteem needs can be tied into the current popularity of fitness and the social desirability of an active image.
- Fitness can be related to the need for self-actualization—the highs of exercise, and the mental and physical challenge of reaching one's potential.

FIGURE 20-1   Maslow's Hierarchy of Needs

---

[2]Abraham Maslow, *Motivation and Personality,* 2nd ed. (New York: Harper & Row, 1970), 35–58.

The significance of Maslow's hierarchy to the speaker is apparent. You must analyze your audience well enough to determine which need is most salient. Listeners whose jobs are in danger and who are struggling to feed their families do not want to hear you contrast local economic programs in terms of the implications drawn from Keynesian theory. They want to know which one will create jobs. Being absorbed with their security needs, they are not likely to respond at the self-actualization level.

It is counterproductive to aim your emotional appeals too high and unethical to aim them too low. Suppose a speaker wants to convince colleagues to adopt a different software system from the one currently in use in that department. If the company is doing well and the colleagues are satisfactory employees, then it would be inappropriate to use a fear appeal with visions of the organization going out of business and people being tossed into the street if the new system is not adopted. The more ethical approach would be to build a case related to the colleagues' needs for efficiency, productivity, success, and prestige (esteem and self-actualization levels).

To be fair, you should respond to existing needs, and not foster an artificial sense of insecurity in your listeners. Speakers who abuse their influence in this way falsely assume that the most primitive needs are the strongest. We disagree. Altruism is an extremely effective motivator. In fact, we might place another pyramid beside Maslow's, illustrating our belief that every person has a basic need to *protect* others' survival, to *give* security, to *spread* love, to *build* esteem, and to *nurture* self-actualization. Appeals to the idealistic, caring sides of human nature can be at least as powerful as self-oriented appeals.

20c. Relate your speech to the values of your listeners.

Suppose, in a presentation, you use the argument "and this procedure will speed up your assembly line," but you are actually unveiling only a part of the following syllogism:

> Anything that speeds up your assembly line is good.
> This procedure will speed up your assembly line.
> Therefore, this procedure is good.

You assume that your listeners share increasing production speed as a value, and as a result, you do not feel it is necessary to clutter your talk with the other parts of the syllogism. As it turns out, however, these particular listeners are currently satisfied with the speed of production but are more concerned with the accuracy of assembly. A little audience analysis could have alerted you to the fact, and you might have worked from the following syllogism:

> Anything that improves accuracy is good.
> This procedure improves accuracy.
> Therefore, this procedure is good.

Both arguments are logically sound (and, we hope, both are true), but the second is psychologically more effective because its underlying premise reflects the dominant value of the listeners.

We hold a certain value if we believe that a particular thing is either good or bad, in the broadest sense of those terms. Specifically, we *evaluate* concepts, people, objects, events, or ideas every day as we label them just or unjust, wise or foolish, beautiful or ugly, and so on. Whereas emotions and needs are considered to be innate (and therefore consistent across cultures, societies, and individuals), *values* are judgments or choices made by individuals. Looking at two people in isolation, we could predict that they both fear certain things, and both have a need for status, simply on the basis of their humanness. But we could not so easily predict whether one hates homosexuals or the other is a passionate supporter of the free enterprise system.

(1) Incorporate appeals to the general values of the culture.

Although values are individually chosen, the choice is not often a totally conscious and rational one. Culture has a strong influence, shaping values through families, schools, media, and peers. Moreover, values are rarely formed in isolation; rather, they are organized and structured into related clusters. By knowing the culture of your listeners, the influences on them, and perhaps some of the other values they hold, you can make an educated guess as to how much particular values might shape their attitude toward your speech topic.

Look at one popular classification of contemporary American values.[3]

- A comfortable life (a prosperous life)
- An exciting life (a stimulating, active life)
- A sense of accomplishment (lasting contribution)
- A world at peace (free of war and conflict)
- A world of beauty (beauty of nature and the arts)

---

[3]Sandra J. Ball-Rokeach and Joel W. Grube, *The Great American Values Test: Influencing Behavior and Belief Through Television* (New York: Free Press, 1984), 90.

- Equality (brotherhood, equal opportunity for all)
- Family security (taking care of loved ones)
- Freedom (independence, free choice)
- Happiness (contentedness)
- Inner harmony (freedom from inner conflict)
- Mature love (sexual and spiritual intimacy)
- National security (protection from attack)
- Pleasure (an enjoyable, leisurely life)
- Salvation (saved, eternal life)
- Self-respect (self-esteem)
- Social recognition (respect, admiration)
- True friendship (close companionship)
- Wisdom (a mature understanding of life)

Sometimes, identifying values in your own culture can be extremely difficult. With the constant currents of change, predominant values and trends often do not become clarified until years later, much too late to do a speaker any good. However, there is always at least one writer or commentator who captures the essence of the changes while they are occurring. Your audience analysis will be enriched by awareness of the changes in mainstream values caused by economic and technical trends, counterculture movements, and liberation movements. Pay attention to editorial writers and news commentators, who can help you get a clearer picture of the "national mood." Be aware that many public opinion polls on specific issues like abortion, immigration, capital punishment, and energy policy contain questions specifically addressed to values.[4]

(2) Identify and relate to the core values of your audience.

If the members of a culture share common values, why do we not see lock-step agreement on every issue? Obviously, not all members of a culture give equal importance to the common values, nor is there a standard ranking of them. Values are very general, and any particular issue can touch on many values, on both the pro side and the con. Examples of this value conflict can become common around election time. Suppose there is a proposed bond issue to build an expensive fine arts complex. A person may be drawn toward approving the bond as a result of holding the values of a world of beauty and a sense of accomplishment. But the individual may also have reservations about taking on a greater tax burden because of a belief in the values of a

---

[4]One resource for poll information is the Inter-University Consortium for Political and Social Research (ICPSR) data bank in Ann Arbor, Michigan (www.icpsr.umich.edu).

comfortable, prosperous life and family security. The resolution of this conflict is a function of how this person has prioritized these values.

Because nearly every topic stirs up such value conflicts, a list of audience values will not be useful unless it is supplemented by some estimate of the relative ranking. As Figure 20-2 shows, one way to map this prioritizing is to imagine a series of concentric circles, with the deepest-held values at the core, and the degree of importance of the other values determining their distance from the center. The innermost circle contains *core values,* the ones so central to a person that to change one of them would amount to a basic alteration of that person's self-concept. The next band out from the center contains the *authority values,* the values that are influenced by and shared with

FIGURE 20-2 Ranking of Values

PERIPHERAL
VALUES

AUTHORITY
VALUES

CORE
VALUES

"Abortion
is wrong."

"Republican
candidates
are best."

"Content-free
commercials
are tacky."

groups and individuals most significant to the person. *Peripheral values* form the outer band.[5] These are the more-or-less incidental evaluations, easily made or changed.

Suppose that, over the course of several political campaigns, Rodney has developed a distaste for the kind of content-free commercials that are normally done. This value, though peripheral, can be strong enough to influence Rodney's voting behavior in contests in which, other things being equal, he has not taken a position. Other things are rarely equal, though. In a race between a Republican who uses content-free commercials and a non-Republican who does not, Rodney's values will come into conflict. Because his preference for Republican candidates is tied to an authority value, and so is closer to the core than a peripheral value like aesthetic dislike of content-free commercials, he will normally resolve this conflict in favor of the Republican. However, the non-Republican opponent supports a constitutional ban on abortion while the Republican views such an amendment as an unwarranted governmental imposition on individual rights. Rodney's opposition to abortion is one of his most deeply held moral principles. Again, he will experience conflict but will resolve it in favor of the core value over the authority value—to do otherwise would require a thorough rethinking and reevaluation of his ethical system.

Understanding this, you should try to make reasonable inferences about your listeners' core values and stress them in your speech or presentation. For example, suppose you have an educational innovation you want the local school system to adopt. In speaking to the school board, you might stress the values of practicality, efficiency, and local control of education. In speaking to the teachers, you might stress the more idealistic value of progress in education. Although your approach in these two cases is different, this does not mean you assume that teachers are impractical or that school board members care nothing about educational progress. The members of both groups probably hold each of these values. However, as a speaker, you make a decision to stress those values that are likely to be closer to the core in each audience.

(3) Forge strong, logical links between the issues of your speech and the values of the audience.

The *issues* of your speech are the questions that must be resolved in your listeners' minds before your speech purpose can be met. (See **6d.**) Decisions

---

[5]This approach to values is adapted from Milton Rokeach's method of classifying beliefs by their centrality: Rokeach, in collaboration with Richard Bonier and others, *Open and Closed Mind* (New York: Basic Books, 1960).

about what is worth knowing, what should be done, or what touches our spirit often depend on the prior acceptance of certain values. Not only do people differ in what values they hold and how they prioritize them, but they differ in how they perceive connections between particular values and particular issues. Even when listeners share almost identical values and priorities, it is possible for them to perceive links differently. Take two audience members who value creative freedom and efficiency, with efficiency being closer to the core. If your issue is the abolition of tenure, one listener might link that issue to creative freedom and be antagonistic to your speech goal, whereas the other might link it to efficiency and look upon your proposal favorably.

It is not enough, then, to know what values your listeners hold. You must try to discover which values they see as linked to your topic. Often, you need to spell out for them new issue-value links that are logical but perhaps not readily apparent. As you prepare a speech, draw out as many *valid* links to values as you can discover. One of the less obvious ones may be just the connection that strikes through to a core value. Table 20-1 gives some examples.

(4) Use motivational appeals to broaden your listeners' sense of history and community.

Understandably, when people first encounter an issue, they tend to analyze it from a perspective that is close to them in time and space. They ask, "How

TABLE 20-1	Issues and Value Links	
Issue	Obvious Value Links	Less Obvious, but Probably Valid, Value Links
Achieving equality for women and marginalized groups	Justice, fairness, compassion	Increased productivity, avoiding waste, patriotism (world image)
Buying laptop computer	Efficiency, speed, scientific advancement	Creativity, expressiveness, economy (in the long run)
Deregulating small business	Lack of government interference, pioneer spirit of small entrepreneur	Honesty, trust of fellow citizens, dislike of red tape and paperwork
Welcoming delegation of foreign businesspersons	International harmony, U.S. hospitality, pooling of information	Efficiency, progress, pragmatism

does this affect me and my immediate circle, now and in the near future?" In contrast to this impulse, a Native American proverb suggests that every decision should be evaluated in terms of its impact on the seventh generation in the future. John Donne's statement that no man is an island has been amended by contemporary thinkers to mean that, today, no person is even a peninsula. One of the most powerful ways that public speakers can use motivational appeals is to draw people outward and refocus their awareness on larger frames of reference.

This broader awareness is there and available to be tapped. When the U.S. public really saw and felt the suffering of Romanian orphans, there was an outpouring of financial support and a series of adoptions. Pictures of fish disfigured by discarded pop-top rings contributed to beverage companies' using a different system for opening soda and beer cans. As a speaker, you can create powerful word pictures to remind listeners of their interdependence with other people and creatures, and to transport them into the past and the future. You can use your words to show people the historical and cultural meanings of endangered objects and places. You can take listeners into the future and reveal the effects of our environmental policies or our national debt on unborn generations. Link your speech topic to your audience's values in ways that tie in to the broadest sense of community and situate the present in relation to the past and the future.

20d. Avoid excessive and inappropriate use of motivational appeals.

Throughout this chapter, we have promoted the effective use of appeals to the emotions, needs, and values of your listeners. We must end with a caution about the overuse and misuse of these appeals. A speech with too much emphasis on feelings can embarrass and offend the audience. If listeners perceive that the speaker is playing on their emotions to the exclusion of sense and logic, they can become infuriated. It is always a mistake to underestimate the intelligence of an audience. Aside from the issue of effectiveness (advertisers and politicians show us that many times these appeals can be effective), there is the question of ethics. (See **3.**)

Exercise 1. Which needs are appealed to in each of these examples?

1. Following the dress-for-success formula has helped countless people advance in their careers.
2. Every home should have an electronic alarm system.
3. Meditation will enhance your understanding of the universe.

4. Some of the marijuana available on the street is laced with deadly chemicals.
5. This shampoo makes your hair more touchable.

Exercise 2. Identify at least three appeals to needs in each speech on the Sample Speeches Web site.

Exercise 3. Of the 18 values in the Great American Values Test, which 3 or 4 would you designate as your core values?

a. Which do you think are most salient in the value system of the United States today?
b. Which values do you see as undergoing the greatest change in the past few years?

Exercise 4. Return to the items in Exercise 1. Rewrite each statement on the same general topic so that it relates to at least two of the values listed in **20c(1).**

Exercise 5. Analyze an audience you speak to regularly (speech class, professional association, study group) in terms of their probable responses to a speech on the problems of mental illness.

a. What needs could you appeal to?
b. What core values could you appeal to?
c. What authority values could you appeal to?
d. What new value-issue links could you forge?

Exercise 6. Log on to your InfoTrac College Edition and perform a search using the keywords *core values*. From the articles listed, pick two examples from the industries, groups, organizations, or communities and summarize and compare their core values.

Chapter 21

Informative Strategies

For informative speaking, plan a strategy based on an understanding of information processing. Use clear explanations to aid your audience's comprehension.

A large part of speaking is merely explanation—stating an idea and then restating it in a way that develops or expands upon the basic notion. Unfortunately, some explanations do more to confuse than to clarify. Usually, this occurs when the speaker has lost sight of which of the many details of a complex process or idea are the essential ones. It is a real challenge to select the most significant details and present them in the clearest order. How can you most economically create the mental picture that will aid your listeners' understanding?

According to an old saying, "Those who can, do; those who can't, teach." This seems to imply that it is much easier to teach another to do something than to do it yourself. In fact, we find the opposite is often true. That is, people can perform a task very competently but cannot describe to another what they have done. (Frankly, we find it much easier to give effective speeches than to write this book explaining the process.) However, a knowledge of the way people learn can make teaching both easier and more effective.

21a. Base your speech on an understanding of how people acquire, process, and retain information.

(1) Avoid information overload.

When you speak on a topic that you know a great deal about, there is a tendency to want to bring your audience up to your level immediately. When you give out too much information in too short a time, the result is information overload. The consequences of this condition—usually in this order—are anxiety, confusion, irritability, anger at the source, and finally, a complete tune-out. Do not engulf listeners with a tidal wave of facts or bury them under an avalanche of data. The job of the informative speaker is to manage a large mass of information and to deliver it to listeners at the right pace and in the right-sized chunks to be useful and meaningful. This means being selective. Your audience does not necessarily know what is important and what is not. You are the expert, and you must pick out the important points for them. Bear in mind the information-processing principle known as *seven, plus or minus two*. Research suggests that this is how many points the average person can comprehend at one time, so select just a handful of points to develop.

(2) Give listeners a framework for organizing the information.

Have you ever tried to put together a jigsaw puzzle without looking at the picture on the box? What you have is a jumble of unrelated pieces. Once you see the big picture, you have some idea of how things are supposed to fit together. This is the same principle that makes you want to look at a map before starting off on a trip or to skim the table of contents before diving into a text. Do not plunge directly into the specifics of the topic before giving your audience some sense of the whole.

(3) Move from the simple to the complex.

Even at the risk of temporary oversimplification, it is advisable first to lay out the most basic concepts and later to introduce qualifiers, exceptions, and interesting tangents. Think of each listener as the newcomer to town who first wants to learn the basic route from home to work, and only after mastering that wants to learn about shortcuts and scenic detours.

(4) Move from the familiar to the unfamiliar.

Any group can learn about any subject if you start where members are and move along at the proper rate. Teachers will attest that learning proceeds best when they are able to adjust the focus of their instruction to a point just beyond the current knowledge level of the group. If the instruction duplicates what the group already knows, the material will not be challenging. If the focus is two or three levels beyond them, group members will get discouraged.

This fourth principle, even more than the others, ties directly to audience analysis. A creative speaker thinks of examples and analogies that relate directly to the experiences of a particular group of listeners. Hearing references to familiar topics bolsters their confidence that they can understand the new material.

21b. Adhere to common principles of clear explanation.

(1) Use organizers.

Provide your listeners with cues as to how they should structure the information.

Signposts
One organizer is the *signpost*. Signposts, like their physical counterparts, point the way you are going and can serve as a reminder of where you've been:

> First, I'll show you how to make a simple white sauce, and then move on to three more elaborate sauces that start with the basic recipe.

> So, from this short description of one novel and three of her poems, you can see once again the two themes that permeate Sylvia Plath's work.

Enumeration
Numbering is an obvious organizational cue:

> The many steps in building an apartment complex can be grouped into these three phases:
> One: Finding attractive sites with the proper zoning.
> Two: Negotiating for the purchase of a piece of property.
> Three: Contracting with architects and builders.

Acronyms
An *acronym* is a word that is formed from the first letters of a series of words and that can be pronounced like a word. For instance, *radar* is an acronym formed from *RAdio Detecting And Ranging*. Other examples are *SETI,* for *Search for ExtraTerrestrial Intelligence,* and *GIGO,* for *Garbage In, Garbage Out.* An acronym can make a point more memorable, as in the following example:

When you want to show empathy through nonverbal cues, remember to SOFTEN your listening style:
[Writes on board]
Smile
Open posture
Facial expression
Touch
Eye contact
Nodding

Slogans, catchwords, and memorable phrases

Like acronyms, these types of cues give your listeners a framework for remembering your points:

> So, look at those files in your drawer that you haven't used in a year, and assess their real value. Keep in mind Peg Bracken's advice about leftover food: "When in doubt, throw it out."

> Try to do something decisive with each piece of mail as you open it. Apply the "Four D's": Drop the item, Delay the item, Delegate the item, or Do the item.

(2) Use emphasis cues.

Underline and highlight key points with phrases like "this is very important," "if you don't remember anything else . . ." and "here's what it all comes down to . . ."

You can also emphasize points by vocal or physical cues. When you want an idea to stand out, speak much louder, or occasionally much softer. Pause before and after the big idea. Step forward. Let your facial expression forecast the seriousness of a point.

(3) Use examples liberally.

When an audience is feeling confused, nothing reassures them like the appearance of a concrete example. You might begin with a simple, even whimsical, example:

> A "win-win" negotiation has occurred when both parties achieve their important goals without perceiving that they have had to make a major sacrifice. Phil and Dave are roommates, and they both think the other needs to do more around the apartment. After talking about it, they agreed that Dave

would do all the cooking and Phil would do all the cleaning. Each thinks he got off easy.

Next, you could move to a more complex and realistic example:

Or suppose that you have a used car for sale and your neighbor wants to buy it but does not have all the cash now. You offer to carry an interest-free note due in six months if your neighbor will take care of your pets and plants for three weeks while you are on vacation. You are happy because you will receive the asking price for your car and not have to worry about arranging for a housesitter. Your neighbor is happy because she can have the car now and does not have to pay finance charges on a loan.

Finally, you might give an example sophisticated, subtle, and complex enough for your audience to apply to situations they may actually encounter:

Now, let's see how these principles apply to a typical real estate negotiation. On this chart you will see the seller's prioritized needs and bargaining chips listed in Column 1 and the buyer's prioritized needs and bargaining chips in Column 2. Let's start with the original offer that was made . . .

Sometimes one example can be extended and elaborated on throughout an entire presentation to provide unity.

(4) Use analogies.

Continually compare the known to the unknown. You might start with a simple analogy:

A nuclear power plant is like a steam locomotive. The fireman shovels coal into the furnace, where the heat it gives off turns the water in the boiler into steam. The steam travels through pipes to pistons, where the energy is converted and carried by driving rods to the wheels, pulling long trains of cars down the rails. Substitute a nuclear pile for the coal, a turbine for the pistons, and an electrical generator for the drive wheels, and you have a nuclear power plant.

Then you could clarify the points of dissimilarity:

Of course, where in the locomotive you'd see a grimy engineer squinting at a pressure gauge with a pop-off valve, in the plant you'd see a large number of scientists and operators presiding over banks of sensors, controls, and computers, each with triple-redundancy safety telltales. The biggest difference, as we know, is that a lump of plutonium contains 240 million times the potential heat energy of a similarly sized lump of coal.

To reinforce points and reach more listeners, draw analogies from many areas: sports, movies, nature, history, other cultures, and so on.

(5) Use multiple channels and modes.

Your message will be clearer if you send it through several channels. As you describe a process with words, also use your hands, a visual aid, a chart, or a recording. Appeal to as many senses as possible to reinforce the message. A good rule to follow is this: If a point is very important or very difficult, always use at least one other channel besides the spoken word to get it across.

(6) Use repetition and redundancy.

People learn and remember what they hear repeatedly. If a principle is important, say it over again, in the same words or different words. Repeat it. Paraphrase it. Reinforce it. Refer back to it. Then mention it again.

Exercise 1. How many analogies and metaphors are used in this chapter? Do they help clarify things?

Exercise 2. How might you link the familiar and the unfamiliar when speaking to these groups?

a. A motorcycle club about nutrition
b. A group of engineering students about writing a résumé
c. Elementary school students about endangered species

Chapter 22

Persuasive Strategies

Plan a strategy based on sound logical analysis and an understanding of audience attitudes. Select and arrange your content for maximum persuasion.

What gives one person the right to try to change the attitudes or behavior of another? Some would say that you earn the right by having a noble end in mind. But what aspiring persuader would claim any other kind of goal? We maintain that *inquiry* is a prerequisite to *advocacy.* You earn a license to persuade by "doing your homework"—by researching the topic fully, thinking about it analytically, and examining the best evidence on both sides. Then and only then are you in a place to recommend your position to someone else. When you take on this challenge, you want to plan a unified persuasive effort according to some guiding principles. This requires an understanding of how and why people change their minds.

There are many theoretical frameworks for approaching persuasion—from Aristotle's *logos, pathos,* and *ethos;* through post–World War II models of social judgment theory and consistency theories; up to the contemporary cataloging of compliance-gaining strategies. An examination of these theories is out of place in a practical handbook, though we allude to several in the suggestions that follow.

Earlier, in the chapter on reasoning, we talked about the benefits of exposing your reasoning steps to your listeners, of showing how your data and your claims are linked. As it turns out, in the area of persuasion, this is not only the ethical road to take but also the practical one. Studies have shown that, when a person's attitude is the result of processing issue-relevant arguments, it is more predictive of his or her actual *behavior,* and it tends to last longer and to be more resistant to counterpersuasion.[1] What this boils down to is that it is less useful to say, "Do this [adopt/continue/avoid/stop] because Eddie Expert says it's the right thing to do and because everyone is doing it," and more useful to say, "Do this because my reasoned presentation of the relevant arguments shows that it is the right thing to do." So, if you have earned the right to be persuasive through careful analysis, and you've invested the effort to construct and deliver a persuasive message, why not do it right? Stress the argument and its merits. True, it is usually easier to plant a weak suggestion at the periphery of the listeners' awareness and hope it has influence without being scrutinized. But the well-developed and well-supported position will usually work better and last longer.

22a. Clarify the goals of your persuasion.

A strong grasp of purpose is especially important in persuasive speaking. When you try to change people, and not simply educate or inspire them, you are more likely to run into resistance. It helps to know exactly what your goals are—and what they are not. (See **6c.**) You want to aim for a realistic target.

Some authorities distinguish between persuasive speeches that seek to change actual behavior and those that merely try to influence beliefs and attitudes. Although an attitude is a predisposition to respond in a particular way, holding a certain attitude does not guarantee certain behaviors associated with the attitude. People may say they believe in recycling but never drum up the energy to separate their trash. Generally, if you want action, you should set your goals in terms of action and tell the audience what to *do,* not what to *think.* An exception is when you will be speaking to an unfavorable audience. (See **22c.**) Here, it is better to set a realistic goal of obtaining agreement with your views; you risk losing the audience if you ask for too much too soon. In any persuasive speech, then, ask yourself if you are *primarily* trying to change people's minds or *primarily* trying to change their actions.

It is also important in setting goals to think carefully about the nature and direction of the impact you seek. There is a tendency to characterize persuasion as "getting people to start doing something," such as buy a product or vote for a candidate. This persuasive goal, known as *adoption,* is only one of four. You might also try to persuade a person to stop doing something (*dis-*

---

[1] Richard E. Petty and John T. Cacioppo, *Communication and Persuasion: Central and Peripheral Routes to Attitude Change* (New York: Springer Verlag, 1986), 5.

continuance), to keep doing something (*continuance*), or to not start doing something (*deterrence*).[2]

On the general topic of physical fitness, for example, you could choose one of a number of persuasive tacks for your speech, such as persuading your audience to:

- *Adopt* an exercise program
- *Continue* eating healthful foods
- *Stop* eating junk foods
- *Avoid* taking up cigarette smoking

Technically, then, persuasion is not always geared toward change. The advocates of continuance or deterrence want "change" from what they fear is about to happen. These two persuasive goals make sense only if there is some jeopardy or pressure from the opposite direction. Exhorting an audience to *continue* breathing would not require much in the way of persuasion. The football coach asking the booster club to *continue* supporting the team knows that his audience has other demands on their time and money. If a speech admonished the audience to "avoid the instant gratification syndrome of credit cards," it would be relevant only in a Western culture, in which there is great pressure in the opposite direction.

22b. Base your persuasive efforts on sound analysis.

Inquiry precedes advocacy for both ethical and practical reasons. Before you can design a persuasive message that will achieve your goal, you need to analyze, or break down, the logical obligations you have taken on. In **6d**, this process was described as finding within your thesis statement the list of questions that absolutely must be answered. In **16a**, the process was discussed in terms of the kind of reasoning needed to provide a link between the evidence you have and the major claim(s) of your speech. Here, we pursue the analysis process more specifically from the direction of understanding the type of proposition you support and identifying the points at issue as you set out to prove your case.

(1) Identify whether your persuasive goal requires you to establish a proposition of fact, of value, or of policy.

The thesis of a speech and the claim of an argument are also described as propositions—in persuasion, the speaker *proposes* something to the audience.

---

[2]Wallace C. Fotheringham, *Perspectives on Persuasion* (Boston: Allyn & Bacon, 1966), 32.

There are three kinds of propositions: the proposition of fact, the proposition of value, and the proposition of policy. Discovering which kind of proposition lies at the heart of your speech is essential to identifying your obligations and planning your persuasive strategy.

Proposition of fact

It may seem that if something is a *fact* there is no need to use persuasion to establish it, but there are issues in the factual domain that cannot be verified directly. For instance, there either is or is not life on other planets. The question is one of fact, but because we lack the means to find out, we must argue from the data we have, drawing the most logical inferences therefrom. Here are some other examples:

> Lee Harvey Oswald did not act alone in the assassination of John F. Kennedy.
>
> More than two cups of coffee a day increases the chance of cancer of the pancreas.
>
> Converting to solar energy can save the average homeowner money.

Proposition of value

Persuasive speakers are often attempting to prove evaluative positions. Their goal is to judge the worth of something, to establish that it is good or bad, wise or foolish, just or unjust, ethical or unethical, beautiful or ugly, competent or incompetent. For example:

> It is wrong to try to avoid jury duty.
>
> The free enterprise system is the best economic model for the working class.
>
> Charlie Parker was the greatest sax player ever.

Proposition of policy

Most common and most complex among persuasive theses is the proposition of policy, which advocates a specific course of action. Here are some propositions of policy:

> The federal government should legalize marijuana for private use.
>
> You should vote for Dan Huboi for union president.
>
> You should send your children to private schools.

When you undertake to prove a thesis statement that is a proposition of policy, you must be very specific about what plan or program should be adopted by what specifically empowered group or agency. Otherwise, although your thesis includes *should* or *should not,* it is really a disguised proposition of value. "Tax loopholes should be closed," for example, is only another way of saying, "The present tax system is bad." To be a proposition of policy, it must read, "Congress should change the present tax structure to reduce oil depletion allowances, vacation home deductions, and home office deductions."

The thesis of a speech is a claim that, in turn, is supported by subclaims. (See **16a**.) By the same token, notice that the types of propositions are cumulative: The proposition of value assumes certain propositions of fact, and the proposition of policy takes its direction from a proposition of value. Or, proving that something *should/should not* be done depends on proving that something is *good/bad,* which, in turn, requires establishing that something else *is/is not* the case. For instance, to establish this proposition of policy:

> Our local government should/should not commence the aerial spraying of malathion to eradicate the Mediterranean fruit fly,

one has to prove at least this proposition of value:

> It is appropriate/inappropriate to risk some danger to human health in order to protect an important agricultural product.

To accept this proposition of value, three propositions of fact need to be established:

> The effect of malathion on human health is/is not minimal or nonexistent.
> Malathion is/is not effective in controlling the Mediterranean fruit fly.
> The fruit attacked by the fly is/is not important to the agricultural economy of the area.

Propositions of fact:	IS/IS NOT
Propositions of value:	GOOD/BAD
Propositions of policy:	SHOULD/SHOULD NOT

Exercise 1. Identify which of the following are propositions of fact, value, or policy:

1. The cost of maintaining the International Space Station will be astronomical.
2. Music on MTV is simplistic and tasteless.
3. Cats make better pets than dogs.
4. Children should learn a foreign language before fifth grade.

Exercise 2. Write a proposition of fact, value, and policy on each of these general topics:

Atheism
Nutrition
Women in the Military

(2) Use stock issues, when possible, to help you analyze your topic.

Drawing on preestablished, "stock" issues can save you time and effort in preparing a speech. For the standard argumentative problem-solving approach, there is no need to reinvent the wheel. Central to understanding stock issue analysis is the concept of burden of proof, drawn from the legal system and from formal debate. The individual or side that advocates change has specific responsibilities.

As an extreme example, consider all the burdens on the prosecutor in a murder case in Great Britain. In British law, *murder* is defined as:

<u>the unlawful killing</u> <u>of a reasonable creature</u>
    1   2
<u>who is in being</u> and <u>under the Queen's peace</u>
   3   4
<u>with malice aforethought, express or implied,</u>
       5
<u>the death following within a year and a day.</u>[3]
       6

We have underlined and numbered each of the six issues the prosecutor must prove. To fail on even one issue is to lose the case. That is, if the defense can show that any *one* of the conditions was not present—for instance, that there was no malice aforethought, or that the killing was not unlawful (as in self-defense), or that the victim survived a year and two days after the alleged act—then murder has not occurred. The burdens on the prosecutor are great, but they are publicly acknowledged and agreed to. For some kinds of speeches, well-defined lists of requirements, or stock issues, guide speakers. Propositions of policy lend themselves to formal argumentative analysis, and so referring to a list of stock issues can be helpful.

---

[3]F. T. Giles, *The Criminal Law: A Short Introduction* (Harmondsworth, England: Penguin Books, 1967), 197.

Stock debate issues

In a formal debate on a proposition of policy, the speaker advocating a change must provide the audience with satisfactory answers to the following questions:

- Is there a compelling need for change?
- Is that need inherent in the very structure of the present system?
- Will the proposed solution meet the need presented?
- Is the proposed solution workable and practical?
- Do the advantages of the proposed solution outweigh its disadvantages?

You do not have to be a debater to use these stock issues—they serve as helpful guidelines in analyzing any persuasive topic.

Stock issues against a change

The examples in the previous paragraph apply to persuasive speeches in which the primary objective is adoption. In a speech that argues against a policy—in which deterrence or discontinuance is the goal—this list of stock issues can be turned around. Because the burden of proof lies with the advocates of change, an opponent of change can succeed by establishing a negative answer to just one key issue.

Exercise 3. Which stock debate issue is being addressed in each of the following points?

1. Putting more money into the welfare program will not get at its underlying problems.
2. Adopting a voucher system for the financing of education will allow parents to choose the educational approach that is best for their children.
3. Violent crime has gotten out of control in our cities

22c. Adjust your speech content in light of your audience's attitude toward your topic and you.

Section **7d** asks you to analyze your listeners' possible reactions to your thesis. Based on surveys, observations, or inference, you can make some determination of their predisposition toward your topic. The following continuum classifies audiences according to that predisposition:

Types of Audiences

Unfavorable			Neutral	Favorable		
Strongly	Moderately	Slightly	Neither agree	Slightly	Moderately	Strongly
disagree	disagree	disagree	nor disagree	agree	agree	agree

Here are some suggestions on how to deal with such favorable, neutral, or unfavorable audiences.

(1) Favorable audience

A speaker facing a favorable audience is relieved of a number of burdens. In this situation, as a speaker, you rarely need to establish credibility. Your listeners, perceiving your position as identical to theirs, approve of you and your good taste already. Furthermore, a favorable audience will not raise internal counterarguments for you to deflect or defuse.

Being relieved of a few burdens, however, does not release you from all responsibility as an effective champion of your position. A poorly prepared speech can actually erode audience support. But if you accept the challenge of speaking to a favorable audience, you can solidify or strengthen their attitudes, or you can cause them to move from theoretical agreement to positive action.

Make use of emotional appeals to intensify your listeners' support.

The difference between intellectual agreement with and commitment to some purpose, and the difference between commitment and action are usually a function of emotional arousal. Out of the vast number of positions you might agree with, there is a much shorter list of issues that you really *care* about. These issues appeal to your most basic needs, touch on your core values, or have a personal effect on your life.

To get your speech topic on your listeners' list, make extensive use of appeals to basic values such as patriotism, humanitarianism, and progress; appeals to basic needs such as survival, security, and status; and appeals to basic emotions such as fear, pity, and love.

Here is one example of how a position can be intensified:

Logical Stem

It is only fair to allow groups with which we disagree to exercise their legal constitutional rights.

Emotional Intensifier

Where will it stop if we allow selective enforcement of the protection provided by the Bill of Rights? Today, the flag burners or skinheads may be
denied their rights as Americans; tomorrow, it may be any of us. [appeal to
fear, appeal to core value of civil liberties]

Look also at the examples in the appropriate sections of chapter **20.**

When listeners agree with you but are not taking action, they probably
do not feel personally involved with the subject. A major task in speaking to
a favorable audience is the creation of that personal involvement in two ways.
First, be very specific about how their lives are affected, and then show them
that their actions can make a difference:

> Your 10-dollar check can feed a Sudanese refugee family for a week.

> If you can take that extra second to switch off the lights as you leave the
> room, you can save yourself 50 dollars a year.

For most audiences, emotional appeals should be handled sparingly and cau-
tiously. But for the favorable audience, you can hardly be too vivid or personalized as long as you avoid bad taste and redundancy.

Get your audience to make a public commitment.

Invite your listeners to offer suggestions, sign a petition, raise their hands to
volunteer, lend their names to a letterhead, or talk to others. People who
have made a public commitment—either oral, written, or physical—are less
likely to change their minds.

Provide several specific alternatives for action.

The following audience reaction is not enough: "Yes, somebody really should
do something about that situation. I should get involved myself one of these
days." Make it easy for listeners to take action by offering several specific
choices. For example, with people who have shown up at a rally for a candidate, do not say, "Stop by campaign headquarters sometime." Instead, say,
"I'd like everyone here either to walk a precinct or to spend an evening making phone calls. Sign-up sheets are being passed around now. If you can't
help out in either of these ways, Judy will be standing at the door and can tell
you about other things that need to be done to ensure our success." With a
favorable audience, do not settle for urging members to do "something." Tell
them what you want them to do, and make the execution easy and attractive:

If you want them to write letters, give them addresses; if you want them to reduce their sodium intake, give them low-sodium recipes.

Present your arguments in abbreviated form so that audience members actively participate in the reasoning process.

Being free to use motivational appeals with a favorable audience does not exempt you from building a strong argument with solid support. However, it does allow you to cast it in a special form. Because a favorable audience often shares your values and beliefs, it is not always necessary to spell out every step of your reasoning. In fact, classical rhetorical theory suggests that *enthymemes* (compact lines of argument) are very powerful. When audience members fill in parts of the reasoning you have not spelled out—be it major premise, minor premise, or conclusion—they are actively participating in making meaning with you. Just as members of a group feel that they are bonding when they use special jargon or initials or shorthand lines of speech, favorable audience members will establish an "in-group" feeling of commitment when a speaker takes some things for granted:

> If we elect this candidate, it will be like returning to the Carter years. [taking for granted that listeners agree that the Carter years were bad]

> We must support this bond issue, for if it fails, there will be no raises for teachers for five years. [assuming the audience agrees that raises for teachers are desirable]

To use these brief enthymematic arguments that create audience involvement, however, you must be sure that your listeners really do share your beliefs. Otherwise, the shortcut can backfire.

Prepare your audience to carry your message to others.

You can tap the potential of audience members as persuaders in their own right. Each of them may later discuss your topic with coworkers, neighbors, or friends who are neutral or hostile toward it. Give the less facile listeners ammunition for these interactions, and make that material as memorable and quotable as possible. When, in front of a favorable group, you offer examples, arguments, and statistics that support your position, your goal is not to persuade your immediate audience. Rather, you are aiming at the second generation of listeners. This second audience is a reason to consider not relying only on the compact argument of the enthymeme.

A part of this preparation involves providing your audience with ready answers to refute standard counterarguments. (See **22f**.) This also serves to inoculate your listeners against the persuasiveness of those counterarguments. Here's an example:

> You may meet people who tell you that the administration's economic policy is designed to help the average worker. Just ask those people why the greatest tax relief goes to the rich. Have them explain to you why a person who earns $300,000 a year will have a 50 percent reduction in taxes, but a person making $18,000 a year will see a reduction of only 6 percent. They may say, "Ah, but we are creating new jobs." Ask them this . . .

(2) Neutral audience

An audience can be neutral toward your position for one of three reasons: They are *uninterested,* they are *uninformed,* or they are genuinely *undecided.*

Stress attention factors with an uninterested neutral audience.

Listeners may be uninterested in a topic or position because they do not see how it affects them directly. With this sort of audience, draw on all the attention factors described in chapter **18,** but give special emphasis to the *vital.* Their interest and attention can be gained only through concrete illustrations of the impact of your subject on their lives:

> A lot of you are probably saying, "So what? So what if somebody across the room lights up a cigarette? It's a free country, and *he's* inhaling the smoke, not me." Would you say, "So what?" if I told you "secondhand" smoke can blacken your lungs just as badly as if you smoked 2 to 27 cigarettes a day?

Be sure the facts and statistics you use are relevant to your listeners' experience. Sprinkle your speech with humor and human interest. Make a special effort to have a lively and animated delivery and style to stimulate them.

With an uninformed neutral audience, emphasize material that clarifies and illuminates your position.

Before you can expect people to agree with you, they must have some comprehension of the issue. When they lack that essential background, you must spend a significant portion of your speech filling them in, even if it means sacrificing time better spent making points to support your position.

The main concern is clarity: Use explanation, definitions, examples, and restatement. (See **21.**) Visual aids can be helpful. Keep your language simple and your organization straightforward.

A direct persuasive appeal should be saved until the very end of the speech.

For an undecided neutral audience, establish your credibility by presenting new arguments that blend logical and emotional appeals.
The undecided neutral audience is both interested in and informed about your topic, but these listeners find the arguments for each side equally compelling. Let them know that you understand their ambivalence. Grant the complexity of the issue, and admit that there is truth on both sides.

Most listeners are uncomfortable with such uncertainty and seek to resolve it. They want to make a decision and are looking for a legitimate basis to do so. Offer yourself as the vehicle for reducing their discomfort. Establish your credibility by communicating expertise and integrity. As you present the arguments for your side, stress any recent evidence or new interpretations that might justify a decision. By definition, this audience finds sense in some aspects of the opposing arguments. This means that you must acknowledge and respond to the main arguments against your position, using the techniques in **22f**. Similarly, you need to inoculate listeners against arguments they may encounter later. When unanticipated, these arguments may tip the scales back to the balance point of indecision, or worse. When anticipated, these arguments can be dismissed by your listeners as having been dealt with already.

In short, a well-documented, logical presentation works best for the undecided neutral audience. Appeals to emotions, needs, and values are effective only if used sparingly and clearly interwoven with the logical argument of the speech.

(3) Unfavorable audience

Murphy's law: Anything that can go wrong, will. A corollary of this law, especially for speakers with an unfavorable audience, is: Anything that *can* be interpreted wrong, *will* be interpreted wrong.

An unfavorable audience is by no means a belligerent one—remember that *unfavorable* is defined to encompass anything on the disagree side of neutral, starting with slightly disagree. However, the more intensely the audience disagrees with you, the more members will be predisposed to reject both you and your message. Any idiosyncrasies of appearance and style of delivery will allow them to dismiss you as being on the lunatic fringe. A single joke that falls flat turns you into a buffoon. A stance expressed with conviction brands you as a fanatic.

At the same time, your audience realizes the disadvantage you are working under. If you handle the situation with grace and aplomb, you can earn their grudging respect. The results can be gratifying when you approach the speech to an unfavorable audience as a challenge to your skill.

Set realistic goals for a single speech.

Do not try to do too much with an unfavorable audience. Attitude change takes place slowly. If most of your audience falls at the strongly disagree end of the continuum, do not expect your 10-minute speech to change them to strong agreement. Sometimes, the measure of success is that they threw eggs and not bricks. Even if it means modifying your thesis statement, set a goal that you have a reasonable chance of achieving, such as easing those who strongly disagree over to moderately disagree, or those who moderately disagree over to neutral. Trying to do too much can alienate your audience and lead to a boomerang effect in which the attitude change that occurs is the opposite of what you were seeking. Do not make an express call for action when such action is highly unlikely. For instance, it would be self-defeating to ask a pro-choice group to contribute money to the campaign coffers of a right-to-life candidate. Better to ask members to think about the issues you have raised, or to ask them to work together to find a compromise.

Stress common ground.

However great the difference between you and your audience on any particular issue, there are bound to be places where your opinions and experiences overlap. When you think about the unfavorable audience you face, ask yourself what goals and values you share. Even the intensity of the disagreement between you and your audience over, say, school busing reveals a common concern for children's education. Or, if your listeners think unemployment can best be combated through government programs whereas you feel that private enterprise can deal with the problem successfully, you still both agree that unemployment is "bad."

Common ground is important to every speech, but it is crucial to the speech to the unfavorable audience. Stress it in your introduction and at several points throughout the speech. Make these points of commonality the major premises from which your arguments proceed. (See **16c**.) When you minimize the differences between you and your audience, you create the basis for communication to occur.

Base your speech on sound logic and extensive evidence.

The unfavorable audience is skeptical of your position and will reject most emotional appeals as manipulative. Your only chance to persuade these listeners is to build an iron-clad case supported by impeccable, unbiased evidence. With this audience, you must clearly indicate every step of your reasoning—nothing can be taken for granted. Discuss and defend even those assumptions that seem obvious to you. Spell out the logical links and connections that hold your argument together. Do not overstate your points; be careful not to claim more than the data allow. Say, "These examples suggest . . . ," rather than "These examples prove . . ."; say, "Smoking contributes to cancer," rather than "Smoking causes cancer."

Use factual and statistical evidence, and always cite your sources completely. If you mention the results of a survey, for example, tell when, where, and how it was conducted, and where it was presented or published. When supporting your points with testimony, quote reluctant experts if possible or highly respected unaffiliated authorities. Quotations from your own partisans are hardly worth giving. (See **15d**.)

Confront directly the arguments that are foremost in your listeners' minds. Do not be afraid to concede minor points that do not damage your basic case. State the remaining counterarguments fairly and answer them forcefully, but never stoop to ridicule. In fact, it has been shown to be advantageous to state your opponents' view *even more elegantly than they have,* before proceeding to refute it.

Pay particular attention to establishing a credible image.

Nowhere is the careful establishment of good character, good sense, and goodwill more important than in a speech to an unfavorable audience. (See **19b**.) Plan every detail of your speech content and delivery to project an image of a calm, reasonable, fair, well-informed, and congenial person. The judicious use of humor can bolster this image while releasing tension and putting the issue in perspective. Direct the humor at yourself, your position, a common enemy, or the ironic aspects of the confrontation. Never direct it at your listeners and their beliefs.

Although you do not want to seem combative, you should remain firm in your position. It is fine to build rapport by stressing common ground and granting minor points, but do not waffle or be overly conciliatory. Also resist the temptation to be snide, shrill, defensive, paranoid, outraged, arrogant, sarcastic, facetious, or patronizing.

Do not become frustrated by heckling or other indications that you are not getting through to the audience. (See **29c**.) Remember that attitude change is a slow process and that by maintaining your dignity and rationality you will not hurt and may help your cause in the long run.

Exercise 4. Examine a persuasive speech on the Sample Speeches Web site. Do you think the speaker perceived the audience as unfavorable, neutral, or favorable? What strategic decisions reflected in the speech content justify your conclusion? Name two specific adjustments the speaker should make if presenting this speech to each of the other possible types of audiences.

22d. Organize your points for optimal persuasive impact.

The speech organization patterns discussed in chapter **10**—topical, spatial, and chronological—grow out of analysis of the speech content. Other patterns can form from retracing the reasoning that led you to your conclusion—inductively, deductively, causally, or analogically. (See **16**.) Yet another way to think about ordering points is to consider how your speech unfolds for your listeners. So, if none of the familiar formats seems strategically adequate, here are some suggestions for alternative arrangements.

(1) Use the motivated sequence to engage your audience.

Developed by Alan Monroe several decades ago, the motivated sequence is one of the most widely used organizers for persuasive speeches.[4] This psychologically based format echoes and anticipates the mental stages through which your listeners progress as they hear your speech. Note that it includes the speech introduction and conclusion, unlike the sample outlines in the organization chapters in part **3**.

Attention: The speaker must first motivate the audience to listen to the speech.

Need: Listeners must become aware of a compelling, personalized problem.

Satisfaction: The course of action advocated must be shown to alleviate the problem.

Visualization: Psychologically, it is important that the audience have a vivid picture of the benefits of agreeing with the speaker or the evils of alternatives.

Action: The speech should end with an overt call for the listeners to act.

Here is an example of a speech that follows the motivated sequence:

Thesis: We need a light rail system in our country to reduce excessive commuter traffic congestion.

ATTENTION

Introduction

I was on my way to work, having left home earlier than usual so I could be there in plenty of time for my first important presentation. I heard screeching

---

[4]Raymie E. McKerrow, Bruce E. Gronbeck, Douglas Ehninger, and Alan H. Monroe, *Principles and Types of Speech Communication,* 14th ed. (Needham Heights, MA: Allyn & Bacon, 2000).

brakes. It turned out to be only a fender-bender a quarter-mile ahead of me. Nevertheless, I sat in my car, and sat, and sat, while my mood progressed from irritation to outrage to despair. I arrived at work an hour and a half late, just as the meeting was breaking up.

NEED

   I.   Excessive reliance on automobile transportation to the county's major employment areas is causing severe problems.
      A. Major traffic jams
      B. Pollution
      C. Stress to commuters

SATISFACTION

  II. A light rail system should be constructed to alleviate these problems.
      A. (Definition of light rail)
      B. (Proposed route)
      C. (Proposed funding)

VISUALIZATION

 III. The new system would be a vast improvement.
      A. (Scenario with the light rail system)
      B. (Scenario without the light rail system)

ACTION

Conclusion

Support the county initiative for a light rail system. Urge your friends to vote for it. Write to members of the county board of supervisors on this issue. Ask your employer to commit to providing free shuttle service from the proposed light rail station to your place of business.

This organization is rather similar to a standard problem-solution speech, but the presence of the visualization step makes all the difference. Instead of merely providing a logical need satisfaction in Main Point 2, this speaker has added another psychologically powerful step in Main Point 3. Two detailed narratives drive home the case for the listeners. The actual wording of the speech might go something like this:

If this proposal is adopted, picture yourself parking at a spacious parking lot, dropping your child off at the child-care facility right at the light rail station, and settling back in your comfortable seat. You can enjoy a cup of coffee, read the paper, review materials for your first business meeting, and arrive at work relaxed.

But, if this proposal is not adopted, picture your commute lasting longer and longer until you are spending nearly one working day a week driving to and from work. The smallest incident will cause gridlock. The pollution will become worse. Your stress-related health problems, such as high blood pressure and headaches, will increase.

It is essential that the attention step be engaging and that the action step be concrete. This does not preclude using the other parts of introductions and conclusions discussed in chapters **13** and **14** if they enhance clarity.

(2) Compare the advantages of two alternative proposals as a way of organizing your speech.

Sometimes, your persuasive task boils down to convincing an audience to choose between two alternatives. It may be that the need to do something is acknowledged or that the choice is "go/no go." In any event, your job is to show the comparative advantage of one choice over the other, which more or less dictates that you organize your speech around a sequence of head-to-head comparisons of the components of each proposal. You might have to compare energy policy based on conservation to energy policy based on expanding access to fossil fuel, or compare cost benefits for the long term and the short term. You are not compelled to say that one is perfect and the other awful. Rather, you strive to tip the scale toward your position. That is why a recurrent and highly effective phrase in comparative-advantage persuasive arguments is "on balance."

22e. As a general rule, place your strongest points first or last.

Ideally, all of the arguments and support for your thesis statement should be strong. In reality, however, you will find that you must use materials of varying strength. These should not be arranged randomly. Be aware that people will remember best what you say first (the *primacy* principle) and what you say last (the *recency* principle). In light of this, arranging your arguments either from weakest to strongest (climax) or from strongest to weakest (anticlimax) will be more effective than placing your best points in the middle (pyramidal).

The research on which one is stronger—primacy or recency—is far from conclusive. Our best advice regarding what to say first and last is that you consider the importance of your topic to your listeners, their attitude toward it, and your credibility. Also, remember that previews and summaries are essential in developing any complex argument. If you use these, your listeners will hear *all* your most significant points both first and last.

Exercise 5. Which of the speeches on the Sample Speeches Web site follow a climax order? An anticlimax order? Can you justify choices made by each speaker in terms of primacy or recency?

22f. In addition to presenting your own viewpoints, consider dealing with opposing arguments.

When time is limited, it is hard to decide whether to present only your own side of an issue or to bring up and refute opposing arguments. In the first instance, you run the risk of appearing to have a weak position. In the second, you sacrifice time to develop your own arguments, and there is always the chance that you will introduce a point against your case that would not have occurred to your audience otherwise.

Generally, it is a good idea to address counterarguments. On widely debated topics, these ideas will already be on listeners' minds, and they expect a response. Even on less familiar subjects on which you may have the first word, you probably won't have the last. At the end of a straightforward "pro" speech, your audience may agree with you. But if, a few hours or a few days later, listeners become aware of powerful opposing arguments, they may discredit your entire position. Speakers often inoculate their audiences by presenting a few counterarguments and answering them. Then, when these points are brought up later, the listeners will say, "Oh, yes, I was warned about this." Inoculation has created "antibodies" to resist the opposing position.

(1) Address the opposing arguments directly, using refutation techniques.

If you choose to respond to a point, you may follow these steps of refutation:

1. State the opposing view fairly and concisely.
2. State your position on that argument.
3. Document and develop your own position.
4. Summarize the impact of your argument and show how the two positions compare.

Here is a distilled example:

1. Many people argue that flexible work schedules lead to reduced productivity.
2. I challenge the underlying assumption that most people work only for money and will do as little as possible. Employees who are treated like responsible partners take pride in their work and are dependable and productive.
3. There are several research studies that support my point of view: [Speaker introduces and explains the studies.]
4. So, these examples refute the position that flextime will lead to decreased productivity. I have shown you how that argument is based on a false assumption about why people work.

Effective refutation can take various forms. In a speech against capital punishment, a speaker might follow the points supporting the thesis with this main point:

IV. Arguments in favor of capital punishment do not justify its continuation.
   A. It is argued that capital punishment deters crime: The facts do not support this.
   B. It is argued that it is very costly to provide life sentences for serious offenders: This is true, but expenditure of money is not a justification for collective murder.
   C. It is argued that dangerous criminals are released on parole and endanger lives: This may be a problem, but we can respond with stricter parole policies rather than execution.

Note that counterarguments may be handled in different ways. Point A is denied directly. Point B is conceded but labeled unimportant. Point C is partly conceded and then analyzed in a different light. Responding to a counterargument does not mean utterly obliterating it. You may concede it, minimize it, dismiss it as irrelevant, or attack the supporting evidence or underlying premise. Even if you grant the existence of a problem, you can differ on the best solution.

(2) In most cases, answer counterarguments after developing your own position.

Pro-to-con order is almost always more effective than con-to-pro. The only exception to this rule is when you know audience members are so preoccupied with an opposing position that they may not listen to you. In that case, respond to the point immediately.

Exercise 6. Do any of the speeches on the Sample Speeches Web site address opposing viewpoints directly? Identify the paragraphs that serve this function. In terms of what you know about the audiences of all of the speakers, evaluate the decision of each speaker to answer or not to answer counterarguments.

Exercise 7. Select a position you believe in strongly. Consider one widely used argument against that position. Write out your refutation of that point exactly as you would present it in a speech, following the four steps in **22f(1)** and including evidence and support you have garnered from a search of your InfoTrac College Edition.

Chapter 23

Adapting to Speaking Contexts

Adapt to the expectations and constraints of the context in which you speak.

This handbook emphasizes meanings rather than messages. What is important to a speaker is not what is said but what meaning is created through the saying. Any given message or *text* takes on meaning from the circumstances that surround it—from the *context*. (See **1b**.) Both speakers and listeners rely on the context to make sense of messages, and knowing the rules and customs of a given speaking occasion reduces the uncertainty they feel and helps to minimize fear.

23a. Learn all you can about the contexts in which you will speak: general expectations, specific formats, and unspoken norms for speakers and listeners.

Academic speech classes, presentation skills training programs, speech contests, and toastmasters' groups represent the few types of contexts in which the presentation of a public speech is treated as a primary activity rather than as a means to some other end. Where else, in the "real world," does one encounter a set of short persuasive speeches given sequentially on completely different topics or find a set of questions on a speaker's content intermingled with comments on presentation style and organization? Of course, classrooms, tournaments, and workshops are very real worlds. They provide particular contexts for speaking with the goal of practicing communication skills and celebrating excellence in speech making. As such, they impose their own set of rules and norms.

Outside of these settings, the skills and recommendations discussed elsewhere in the handbook are useful only to the extent that speakers adapt them to the expectations of a particular context. A speaker with excellent generic skills may still be at a loss if a situation requires knowledge of a particular format. For example, it does a concerned citizen no good to prepare an excellent persuasive argument if he cannot penetrate the rules of parliamentary procedure to gain recognition to speak. The dynamic presentation style that serves a politician so well at an outdoor political rally will seem ridiculously overdone on a television talk show. An engineer who gives a design review presentation without detailed visual support will suffer a major blow to her credibility.

In order to understand the demands of the multiple contexts in which speeches occur, speakers are well served by relying on analytic frameworks, not unlike those recommended in analyzing a specific audience. (See **7.**) Certainly, it is helpful to think about the primary purpose of speaking. Yet many occasions are a blend of informative, persuasive, and evocative goals, and each blend is quite distinctive. (See **6c.**) There are other dimensions that define the speaking context, which might be arrayed along several continua.

Public sphere   Private sphere

A context is established in part by the venue or domain in which speaking occurs. One set of expectations accompanies a meeting in a legislative hall, a large city square, or a cathedral. Even if the same topics are being talked about, quite different expectations will come into play if the speech takes place in a private office or a living room.

Formal demeanor   Informal demeanor

Some contexts carry the expectation of a high level of formality—dressy attire, use of titles and respectful forms of address, dignified word choice, and a setting that is orderly and perhaps adorned with symbols such as flags, official seals, or floral arrangements. The informality of other contexts is signaled by casual dress, use of first names, colloquial speech forms, and everyday physical arrangements.

Monologic   Dialogic

Contexts are also defined by the role of the participants. In *monologic* situations, it is assumed that a featured primary speaker will dominate the event, taking primary responsibility for what is talked about. In *dialogic* situations, other participants can direct both the topic and the form of the interaction. As with all the other continua, there are many contexts that fall between the extremes or that blend the norms. At a public lecture, for example, the expectation is that the main speaker will be listened to without interruption or heckling until the question-and-answer period begins. Then, the norms of dialogic speech take precedence, and it is considered inappropriate for the speaker to give another speech.

Highly prescribed rules of speaking   More open rules of speaking

All public speaking is rule-bound to some extent, but there is tremendous variation in how explicit or specific those rules are. Some contexts have very rigid rules about who may speak, for how long, and on what topic. In a formal parliamentary meeting, a speaker must receive recognition and then link the discourse to a particular motion before the house. In a legal proceeding, advocates can ask questions only in certain ways and at certain times, and they can present arguments only during opening and closing statements. Contrast this to a meeting of a small task force, in which participants might seize the floor at any time and change subjects at will. The rules in the latter case either are implicit—group members may subtly sanction those who talk too much or too long—or evolve on the spot—as when someone suggests that each person take a few minutes to state a position on the topic.

Power resides with speaker   Power resides with listeners

Power differences between speakers and listeners inevitably influence context. Sometimes, the power resides with the listeners: Bosses control paychecks, teachers assign grades, judges make rulings, and homeowners' association boards approve projects. Whether motivated by common sense, self-preservation, or genuine respect, speakers usually show a degree of restraint in addressing those in higher-power positions. At other times, power resides with the speaker. Here, the expectations differ: The speaker doesn't deny the power but often chooses to downplay it to avoid intimidating or seeming to threaten listeners.

Existing community   One-time assembly

The context of a speech differs based on the relationship among the participants. When an already established group comes together, speeches typically include in-group jokes, use of abbreviations and shorthand expressions, and references to shared history. There is no need to spend time building a sense of community as there would be in a situation in which individuals have gathered together for the first time, primarily because they are interested in a common topic or in the speaker.

Immediate audience   Extended audience

Most often, a speech is intended for those who are present. But there are occasions when everyone understands that the real context of the speech involves a much wider audience that will read it or hear it broadcast.

These dimensions illustrate the uniqueness and complexity of speech contexts. A speaker could be right on target in analyzing most of the relevant factors in a situation but, by misreading just one of these—say, the expected level of formality—could jeopardize effectiveness. Do not be afraid to ask questions about any new situation that you enter. If you are in charge of an event, be sure that invitations and announcements communicate shared expectations. People get grumpy if they come out for a one-hour "open discussion" on a topic and hear a 55-minute monologic presentation.

An additional and important determinant in each speaking context is culture. Mastering the marketing presentation in a U.S. business context will not prepare you to give a similar presentation in Japan. Knowing about different cultural norms and expectations also helps listeners to be respectful of international guests. A faculty member from Europe, invited to share his research with colleagues at a U.S. university he was visiting, was shocked and offended to find that many of them had brought their lunches and were eating during what he perceived to be a formal presentation.

The sections that follow offer some preliminary suggestions for three kinds of contexts: the business and professional, the civic and political, and the social and ceremonial. We do so with caution, because even these generalizations need to be adapted and combined for each specific event. For example, a retirement dinner within a company would combine the expectations of workplace communication and social communication.

Exercise 1. Classify the following events along the seven dimensions of context:

a. Pep rally
b. Union business meeting
c. Opening statement in a courtroom
d. Business retreat

e. Rehearsal dinner for a wedding party
f. Neighborhood crimestoppers meeting
g. Press conference to introduce a new university president

Exercise 2. What are other dimensions along which speaking contexts may vary?

23b. Become familiar with the workplace context.

Generally, presentations in business and professional settings are, well, businesslike. That is, in the formats that have been created and the norms that have evolved, the emphasis is on efficiency and clarity. Speech in workplace settings is expected to be streamlined and unadorned. A routine report to a work group typically does not begin with an attention getter, but rather features a detailed logical orientation step to locate the topic within the organization's multiple tasks. Visual aids (including handouts) are considered central to professional presentations, in part so that technical details can be available for examination and reference without having to spend a great deal of time going over them orally. Within organizations, because goals are assumed to be shared, listeners may ask each other tough questions and play devil's advocate. In a team environment, internal communication is a way to test ideas so that they can be improved before costly mistakes are made. Of course, organizational communication must include a healthy dose of team building, and sales and marketing presentations to persons outside the organization will involve a very different set of expectations.

Typical presentations in a business and professional context include the employment interview, the sales interview, the marketing presentation, the technical presentation, annual or periodic business reports, and the project status report. Discussions of two of these follow.

(1) Follow common guidelines for an employment interview and similar workplace interactions.

Traditionally, the job interview consists of an applicant and a personnel director, with a desk as a prop. However, more and more interviews are being done in a group, with a number of people from different departments and levels talking with the applicant. Other interview-like events are the performance review and the sales presentation to a committee. In any of these situations, you may not be successful if you come prepared only to answer questions.

When you speak to a group, even a small one, you should apply several public speaking concepts, of which the following are the most important.

Analyze your audience.

Learn all you can about the people who will be interviewing you. (If the organization has a Web site, mine it for information as your first step.) If possible, get a list with both their names, so you can learn to pronounce them, and their positions, so you can think about the various perspectives and interests they represent. When you are introduced, you can quickly associate faces with the names and roles you have studied. Throughout the interview, you can adapt your answers to their perspectives: "That brings up the whole question of the cost effectiveness of surveys. I'm sure that you confront that issue all the time, Mr. Keenan, being director of marketing research."

Prepare an opening statement.

The first question likely will be, "Well, tell us a little bit about your background—how you got to where you are now, and how you describe your orientation to our field." Hearing this, you do not want to seem startled or reluctant. Rather than being daunted by the breadth of the question, seize the opportunity to set the tone. Make a brief statement that serves the purpose that a speech introduction does: gets their attention, creates rapport, and establishes a framework for the main content to follow. Do not assume that on the day of the interview your résumé or sales brochure is fresh in the interviewers' minds. They may have read it a week ago and need a little memory jogging. Besides reiterating what you sent earlier, you can also update it if further developments would be of interest to the group.

You can use your opening statement to develop a general philosophy or position. Sometimes, you establish a vocabulary and theme in your initial remarks that you can keep referring back to as you answer questions. You may highlight aspects of your experience to show trends or directions that led you to the present interview. Whether you are selling yourself, a service, a product, or an idea, use this opportunity to establish credibility.

It seldom hurts to compliment their organization. Be as specific as possible to show your knowledge of it and its workings.

Answer questions directly and concisely.

Before any interview, review the guidelines for answering questions in chapter **30**.

Try to tie questions together in a group interview: "This question spotlights another side of the training issue Ms. Herman raised a few minutes ago." You can demonstrate your powers of synthesis by relating certain common threads to your opening position.

Prepare a repertoire of problem-solution-result (PSR) statements.

A PSR is a brief, memorable personal success story. In it, you succinctly state a *problem,* describe your *solution* to that problem, and then tick off the components of the beneficial *result* of your solution—and all in 90 seconds or less. Describing the problem should take about 50 percent of your time. You set the stage, laying out what was at stake, what the consequences would have been if the problem had not been solved, and what constraints you may have operated under. The solution should take no more than 25 percent— what actions you took and what skills and abilities of yours were brought into play. Summarize the key steps, and avoid the temptation to go into the kind of detail that comprehensively demonstrates your understanding of your field (save this for follow-up questions). The result should be brief as well, showing quantifiable results if possible, but it should be a concise and powerful description of the immediate and long-term benefit of your actions, along with any awards or recognition that came with them.

Here is a sample:

Problem

When I was the publications manager for a small software company, there was one time when my leadership, management, and organizational skills were really put to the test. We had a telecommunications management package under development and in trial at a large potential customer, and at a status meeting it was let drop that Sales had promised a complete documentation set for a week from Friday, eight days away, instead of the eight weeks agreed upon in the original development plan. Well, this was a problem, certainly, because the documentation consisted of 10 manuals, many of which were not started yet. But if we failed to produce the manuals, no matter how ridiculous the deadline, the image of the company would suffer, as would the chances for landing the customer.

Solution

I immediately pulled my staff off all other projects and divided the workload according to their various talents. I made the rounds of the other departments in the company, negotiating new delivery dates for their existing projects while gaining assurance of easy access to subject matter experts for my staff. As the days passed, I adjusted workloads to respond to evolving needs, did subprojects where necessary, and continued to work on interdepartmental cooperation.

Result

On the appointed Friday, three sets of a 10-manual, 800-page documentation suite went into the arms of DHL for delivery. As a result, my team was stronger, with the confidence that comes from meeting an impossible goal; the other departments knew they could count on us in a pinch; the potential customer was very pleased with the documentation, becoming a customer-in-fact not long after—which landed the company a $12 million receivable.

By preparing a collection of PSRs, you can ensure that in an interview you are primed to respond positively to a variety of questions concerning your skills and achievements. Ninety seconds is not much time at all, but for PSRs, brevity is important. By keeping them brief, you make them more memorable, and you also allow your interviewer to set the level of detail on any particular subject. If the interviewer wants to know more, she can ask more questions, and, of course, you will have prepared more PSRs to cover the more in-depth questions. In the preceding example, an interviewer could ask to find out more about how the speaker negotiated the new internal delivery dates or what the most difficult project assignment was.

PSRs are not only for job interviews. They are also very handy in performance reviews and salary adjustment meetings, in which having such a store of examples that demonstrate the benefits that accrue to the organization because of your presence can only work to your benefit.

Prepare the PSR when events are still fresh in the mind, or jot down enough notes to make sure you can recall all the crucial information later. Don't wait until the annual performance review, or until you start job-hunting, or until you've finished school.

Although by no means exhaustive, Table 23-1 lists a representative set of topics for PSRs.

Exercise 3. Look at the three categories in Table 23-1. Develop a PSR for one skill, asset, or achievement from each.

Maintain effective delivery skills throughout an interview.

You are "on stage" the entire time, even though you are seated and in an informal setting. Look at chapters **26** and **27** for a review of delivery skills.

When you answer a question from one group member, be sure to include the entire group in your eye contact.

(2) Follow common guidelines for designing and delivering a team presentation.

Often, teams form within an organization to present information on products, processes, or decisions to internal and external audiences. Usually, the information to be presented is complex enough to require an interdepart-

TABLE 23-1	Subjects for Problem-Solution-Result Statements	
Specific Personal Attribute	Decisiveness	Versatility
	Creativity	Leadership
	Spoken/written communication	Confidence
	Analytical problem solving	Fast learning curve
	Organization	Adaptability
Specific Work Skill	Report writing	Accounts receivable
	Supervision	Medical knowledge
	Manual dexterity	Government relations
	Crisis management	Facility with computers
	Negotiating experience	Budget preparation
Accomplishment	Designed and implemented *X*	Improved productivity
	Lowered costs	Organized and directed
	Staffed *X*	Enhanced customer relations
	Set record for *X*	Recruited and trained *X*
	Met goals and objectives	Devised new strategies

mental approach. This means that, in addition to good speaking skills, success depends upon planning, coordination, and teamwork.

As a group, establish an overall plan for preparation.

In the workplace, everyone is already overtasked, so it is crucial at the beginning of a project to make the investment in a plan that ensures people's time is used efficiently. This responsibility falls to the project manager, who should initiate the first planning session well before the date of the presentation. Key tasks include the following:

1. Clarify the purpose, including identifying who the stakeholders are, what their expectations are, and what constitutes success. (See **6b**, and **22a**.)
2. Agree on the core message, the equivalent of the thesis statement, which will serve as a touchstone against which all content will be evaluated. (See **6d**.)
3. Divide the labor among team members.
4. Establish the timeline, making sure to cover intermediate milestones and practice sessions.

Create an outline of the content and speakers' responsibilities.

If you have understood the benefits of the various steps in organizing an individual presentation (see **5, 9, 10**), you will see why we recommend that a team presentation be thought of as one "macrospeech" rather than as a series of individual presentations given at the same time and place. We have all heard group presentations in which the speakers contradicted each other, overlapped in content, left out some key points altogether, jumped ahead and stole the thunder of upcoming presenters, and even squabbled publicly about the order and coverage of points. To provide coherent content and project a professional image, it is crucial that each team member have a picture of the whole presentation and of how each piece relates to that whole.

Before an outline can be decided upon, the group will have engaged in initial brainstorming and preliminary decision making. When the topic is narrowed and focused, someone needs to create a detailed outline of the speech, complete with an introduction and conclusion, transitions, time limits for each segment, and a list of visual support and equipment needed.

In this process of decision making and outline crafting, the group should come to agreement on several issues.

How will the presentation be introduced? This may be done by the team leader, though it might be added to the responsibility of the first speaker. In any case, it should cover the basics of an introduction, making the audience want to listen, telling them what will be covered, and introducing the team members. (See **13**.)

What are the main points of the presentation? Thinking about it this way reinforces the need for each segment to serve a clear purpose in developing the core idea. If the group merely decides that Andrea will talk about her part of the project, and then Clint will talk about his, and so on, there is no guarantee that the components will be relevant and fit together. As with a speech, it is a good idea to have only a few key ideas and, generally, a few speakers. However, in an extended presentation, each group leader can present the main idea and additional speakers can present segments that function as subpoints under that topic. However simple or complex the organization, there needs to be prior agreement on the goal of each part of the presentation and on the time allotted for it.

How will transitions be handled? Listeners need to be reminded of the overall road map for the presentation. The transition from segment to segment can be handled by a group leader who acts as an emcee of sorts, or each speaker can be charged with building a bridge to the next. In either case, it is important to review the principles of transitions (see **12**) and to go beyond "Here's Johnny" to offer a statement like "Once the basic design is completed, it needs to be tested. Here is where John Carlton and his able group come in. John is now going to tell you about the steps they go through to make sure our clever designs actually work."

How will the presentation be concluded? Again, the functions of reviewing and integrating the material presented can be done by a group leader or by the final presenter. The important point is that there be a planned wrap-up that ties things together and ends on a positive note. (See **14.**)

How will questions be handled? The plan either needs to build in a question-and-answer period after each segment of a longer or more technical presentation or to allow for questions at the end. Decide who will field questions and direct them to the appropriate person. Sometimes, individuals are present who do not actually participate in the main presentation but are available as resources during the question-and-answer period. (See **30.**)

Agree on unifying elements.

A potential customer or client is greatly reassured by the overall sense that the organization is more than a set of talented individuals, that it is really a coordinated team. Think of projecting the impression of unity, mutual respect, and teamwork as one of the goals of each presentation. Having a clearly organized presentation is the most important way to make this point; however, there are a few additional steps a team can take to show they are "on the same page."

Make the segments parallel. This may involve common phrasing of the main idea of each piece: "With our technological innovations, we will own this marketspace next year. . . . With our dedicated and knowledgeable sales force, we will own this marketspace next year. . . . With our uncompromising support, we will own this marketspace next year." Or, in some cases, it may be appropriate to use the same suborganization in each part of the presentation. In a cross-departmental status report, each department might follow this pattern: (1) review of the goal, (2) report on progress to date, (3) report on problems encountered, (4) identify solutions, and, (5) provide a current timetable.

Use common themes and phrases. Develop a glossary of technical terms, abbreviations, and acronyms, and get agreement within the group to adhere to the "approved list," so that listeners aren't confused by multiple words meaning the same thing. Once the substance of the presentation is in place, look for ways to emphasize certain points that capture the unique approach of your organization or the special features you are offering. Just as the main ideas can have common phrasing, other integral concepts and themes can be consciously constructed in parallel language woven throughout the presentation.

Find opportunities for cross references. Speak of your copresenters with respect and admiration. Use terms like *colleague*. Briefly forecast or refer back to their points, and direct questions to them acknowledging their expertise.

Present a consistent visual message. Slides, presentation software, and diagrams should have a common look. Agree on a template at the beginning of a process, and have a designated specialist to polish and unify the material coming in from disparate sources.

Practice the presentation.

Busy professionals who know their topic well and talk about it often are reluctant to have formal practice sessions. Practice is important for an individual talk, but it is *essential* for pulling together a team of speakers.

Schedule at least one early run-through even if some pieces are still under construction. The goal is to get a sense of how the presentation fits together and to find opportunities to improve it.

Schedule at least one final run-through. This will serve to polish the transitions and to familiarize the speakers with the equipment and visual aids used.

Arrange for feedback on the presentations during the practice stage. Participants may comment on one another's content and clarity. It is also common for managers or other organizational members to sit in on practice sessions to make suggestions. For very important presentations, simulations may be staged with persons role-playing potential audience members, and communication consultants may be brought in to videotape the rehearsal and even coach individuals on presentation skills.

Pay attention to the timing of the overall presentation, whatever the level of rehearsal. It is not inappropriate to have someone give time signals during the actual presentation to keep the team on track.

Debrief each presentation to learn from the experience.

Shortly after a presentation, whether it was successful or disappointing, the team should meet to talk candidly about what worked and what can be improved in the future.

23c. Become familiar with the civic and political context.

When you speak as a member of a community or a political unit, you may be entering a context in which there are conflicts of interest. For a diverse group to come to consensus, communicators have to work to build bonds. These contexts are often characterized by explicit affirmations of respect and common ground. Notice, for example, how representatives from opposing political parties continually say things like "My highly distinguished colleague from South Carolina . . ." and "The esteemed senator and I have cosponsored legislature in the past, and it is with regret that I must reluctantly disagree with her remarks." In a democratic society, we allow for the testing of ideas through vigorous debate and argumentation. We maintain social order by setting fairly strict rules constraining the form of speech. The ideal is that personal attacks are taboo, as are arguments from pure self-interest. We do not argue for restricted parking in the neighborhood around a university campus by saying, "I am inconvenienced, and my property value may be jeopardized." Instead, we state that the community needs to maintain its special character and to continue to attract residents who will be good neighbors to the university.

Passion and eloquence are not out of place in this context. Sound argument and evidence are frequently combined with appeals to common values.

Typical speaking situations in this context include public debates, community forums, legal arguments, panel discussions, political conventions, appearances before community agencies, rallies, and talk shows.

(1) When participating in a symposium, panel, forum, or debate, tailor your individual presentation to the group format.

Be sure of the format of the program, and clarify expectations about your responsibilities.
There are many versions of group presentations, and too often, their standard labels are used interchangeably and inconsistently. You may be invited to be part of a "panel" and prepare accordingly, only to discover that the organizer has actually set up a debate. Here are the definitions most commonly used by speech communication texts:

Symposium: A series of short speeches, usually informative, on various aspects of the same general topic. Audience questions often follow.

Panel: A group of experts publicly discussing a topic among themselves. Individual prepared speeches, if any, are limited to very brief opening statements.

Forum:	Essentially a question-and-answer format. One or more experts may be questioned by a panel of other experts, journalists, and/or the audience.
Debate:	A structured argument in which participants speak for or against a preannounced proposition. The proposition is worded so that one side has the burden of proof, and that same side has the benefit of speaking first and last. Speakers assume an advocacy role and attempt to persuade the audience, not each other.

Do not assume that the person arranging the program uses the terms this way. Find out as much as possible about the program, asking such questions as:

- What is the purpose of the group presentation?
- Who is the audience?
- How much time is allotted? How will it be divided among speakers?
- Will there be discussion among participants? Will there be questions from the audience?
- Who are the other speakers? What will they talk about? In what order?
- Is there a moderator or discussion leader?

Prepare as carefully for a group presentation as for a speech.

Do not be lulled into thinking a group presentation is merely a conversation. Even if you already know your topic very well, brush up on your research, plan a general outline, and bring along notes with key facts and statistics. Prepare visual aids if appropriate. Plan an introduction and conclusion for your formal part of the session.

Be prepared to adapt, however, in your best extemporaneous style. Because you are in a group, do not give your talk in isolation; make frequent references to the other panelists: "Ms. Larsen has pointed out some of the reasons mental health care is so expensive" or "I won't get into the medical details. Dr. Nguyen is the expert on that." Also, unless the panelists coordinate beforehand, overlap is inevitable on related topics. When you hear your favorite example or best statistic being presented, quickly reorganize and substitute the backup material you wisely brought along. Review the principles in chapter **30** for use in the question-and-answer exchange.

Be aware of your nonverbal communication throughout the entire group presentation.

When you speak in a group, you should still follow the guidelines for effective delivery. The fact that you might be seated does not allow you to be off-hand or overly casual. On the contrary, you may need to project a little more energy to compensate for the lack of visibility and movement.

What far too many speakers seem to overlook is that they are "on stage" during the whole presentation. While other speakers are talking, look attentive and be courteous. Nod and respond facially in ways sufficiently subtle that you do not upstage the speaker. Above all, do not distract the audience by whispering, fidgeting, or grimacing in disbelief. Do not hurt your own credibility by looking bored or by frantically going over your notes.

The previous suggestions, combined with general speaking skills, should get you through most group situations. The public debate presents some additional challenges.

(2) Follow common guidelines for a public debate.

Formal academic debating and competitive tournament debating require skills beyond the scope of this handbook. Excellent texts and classes are available. Any good public speaker, though, can handle informal debates—such as are held during election campaigns or at public meetings or club functions—by remembering and applying the following prescriptions.

Prepare by considering the opposing point of view.

Research both sides of the topic to see what evidence you will encounter. Look at the strongest points of your opponent's case and the weakest points of your own. This helps you anticipate the arguments and prepare for them.

Organize your ideas, arguments, and evidence into three general areas.

First, develop your own best case for your position, which will be your opening statement or constructive speech. Next, plan attacks on or challenges to the opposing position, which you will use to respond to or refute their case. Finally, compile defense material, which you will probably need to answer challenges to your position.

Prepare your opening speech with particular attention to organizational clarity and sound support of assertions.

Follow the general suggestions for speaking to an unfavorable audience. (See **22c(3)**.)

In the refutation phases of the debate follow the guidelines in 22f(1).

Time is usually limited, so address yourself to major issues. Explain the argumentative impact of your points. Show what damage you have done to the underlying logical structure of your opponent's argument.

When you weaken an opponent's case, drive home the point by issuing a specific challenge.

Save time for a clear and persuasive summary of the argument.

Debates can be confusing, with points flying back and forth. So, even if you have to skip some additional specifics, use the final few minutes to focus the controversy, interpreting how it has emerged during the discussion. End with a persuasive closing statement and a clincher that capitalizes on your strongest point.

Maintain a calm and professional demeanor throughout the debate.

As with sports, poker games, or any other competitive activity, emotions can sometimes get out of hand. Do not lose perspective: Getting the last word on every single point is less important than maintaining your long-term credibility. Even if another debater distorts or misleads, you should remain courteous and unflappable. Your tone may be vigorous, but it should never be hostile. Address your arguments to the audience, and refer to the other speaker by name, and not as "my opponent." Treat her or his arguments respectfully, and grant good points that are made. Always assume the honesty and good intentions of the other speaker. Never say, "That's a lie;" rather, say, "I think those figures are inaccurate. Here's what I found."

23d. Become familiar with the social and ceremonial context.

Arguably, the most ancient forms of speech are those that people developed simply to affirm their connectedness. We make small talk to share our everyday experiences, and we draw together to share joy, grief, outrage, and reverence. The expectation in social and ceremonial contexts is that the participants are united. This is not a time to mention difference or to actively build consensus. Just assume consensus and celebrate it.

Some speeches, classified in this book as evocative, are designed more to fill a ritualistic function than to transmit information or change behavior. These follow standard forms, and as with all rituals, the familiarity of the form is one source of the emotional satisfaction participants derive. Happy moments like winning an Olympic medal and sad ones like mourning a death take on added meaning when accompanied by traditional, familiar ceremony. Certain words, gestures, and acts are expected—the Olympic athlete would undoubtedly be disappointed if the medal award ceremony and playing of the national anthem were replaced by a gift certificate presented at a pizza house get-together. As you might imagine from the preceding, you are by necessity forced to tread near that line separating tradition and triteness when you give a ceremonial speech.

Cover the expected bases no matter how predictable they are. Do not be *too* creative, but at the same time, strive to find ways to make these ceremonial moments special and fresh. Above all, this means avoiding overused phrases and constructions. Unless you prepare carefully, you will hear yourself ad-libbing clichés you would never use otherwise:

> On this auspicious occasion . . .
> It is indeed an honor and a privilege . . .
> . . . this small token of our esteem.
> With no further ado . . .

Information exchange is of secondary importance in these speeches; style becomes crucial. Because the two or three ideas you transmit will be fairly basic, you should expend your energy crafting ways to express them, polishing your language and timing. This is made easier by the fact that ceremonial speeches are usually short. Frequently, a memorized or partially memorized mode of delivery is best. (See **24d**.) Your language should be more elevated than in everyday speech, but not so formal as to seem stiff or unnatural.

(1) Identify the needs of the people involved.

In preparing all ceremonial speeches, consider two questions.

What are the needs of the person to whom or about whom I speak?

Suppose that as company president you give a safety award each year, and so for you it is old hat. However, it is a special moment for the recipient. What can you say that he or she will remember with pride? Address the uniqueness of that person. Although the form of the speech may be stylized, the content should be personalized.

What are the needs of the people for whom I speak?

In most ceremonial or ritualistic addresses, you can think of yourself as speaking on behalf of some group or community and not just for yourself. People have come together to share emotions as well as—or instead of—information. Yet these emotions may be unfocused. When you deliver a thoughtful and moving speech, you symbolize the feelings of audience members, thus bonding them. You also help them gain perspective and find deeper meanings in their experiences. Early in the preparation for this sort of speech, envision yourself as a vehicle for group expression. The following internal monologues are examples of this search for group motivations: "All of us feel such affection for Gary. What is the best way to say what each of us would like to tell him as he retires?" and "So many people in our city have worked hard to arrange a successful visit for these exchange students. What words can I choose to portray that warm welcome?"

Typical speaking situations in this context include presenting an award, welcoming delegates to a convention, proposing a toast, and nominating a candidate.

(2) Follow common guidelines for various contexts.

When presenting an award or honor

1. Unless a surprise is part of the tradition, announce the person's name early in the speech.
2. Explain how the person was selected for the honor, and by whom.
3. Besides listing achievements or qualities, try through a brief anecdote or description to capture some unique qualities of the person.
4. If a tangible object—plaque, certificate, key to the city—is presented, explain what it symbolizes.

When delivering a eulogy or memorial address

1. Do not accept this assignment unless you feel able to keep your composure.
2. Acknowledge shared feelings of sadness, loss, and anger, but do not dwell on them.
3. Highlight and celebrate the value of the one being eulogized. Some people present may have known the person only professionally or only socially, or only long ago or only recently. Touch on several aspects of the person's life. Do not be reluctant to share light, and even humorous, moments.
4. Use phrases that bond the group together: "All of us who cared for Eleanor . . ." or "I see many people here who . . ." or "We all know how persistent she could be when she believed in an idea."
5. Try to place the loss in some larger, more optimistic perspective. Themes of the continuity of life, appreciation of each moment, and growth through pain are timeless and universal. These philosophical concepts are still a source of comfort.
6. Do not play on the grief of a captive audience to promote a specific religious belief or social or political cause.

When giving a toast

1. If the toast is a formal part of the event, make arrangements ahead of time so that everyone will have a beverage in hand at the proper point. Be sure that nonalcoholic beverages are available so that everyone can participate.
2. Refine your basic idea into a short message of goodwill, and memorize it.
3. Choose the words carefully. Humor, wordplay, rhymes, metaphors, and proverbs all find their way into toasts. If no witty inspiration comes to you and if the toasts in books all seem corny and contrived, then there is absolutely nothing wrong with taking a sincere thought and stating it gracefully.
4. If the toast is more than a few sentences—really, a short speech—do not make listeners hoist their glasses the full time. Start out as a speech. Then at the end say something like, "Let's raise our glasses to our new laboratory director. Sheila, we wish you luck, and success, and may all your troubles be microscopic!"

When accepting an award or tribute

1. Unless asked in advance to prepare a major acceptance speech, limit your remarks to a few sentences.
2. Accept the honor with pride.
3. Do not let humility and embarrassment make you seem to reject the gesture.
4. Share the honor with those who deserve it. But do not get into an endless thank-you litany of the sort that always makes the Academy Awards presentation run overtime.
5. Give a gift back to the audience. Can you offer them a genuine tribute, an insight, or even a funny story related to your relationship with them?
6. End with a future-oriented statement about what the honor means to you.

23e. Be prepared to assume leadership roles in a variety of contexts.

The recommendations so far have dealt with situations in which you as an individual speaker will need to fit into an existing context. Often, people are lucky enough—or unlucky enough—to find themselves in leadership roles, in which they can shape a context for speaking. In this case, others will look to the leader to define the ground rules and to facilitate the interactions. There are as many leadership roles as there are contexts, but we present here suggestions for a few common ones.

(1) Prepare carefully when you chair a program or meeting: Clarify the format, coordinate the participants, and anticipate contingencies.

Plan the agenda carefully.

Determine what will occur and in what order. In some cases, you will find that a format is already set by bylaws and custom. Regardless, try to establish mechanisms whereby all potential agenda items are submitted to you well in advance. How many business meetings and banquets have been thrown off schedule by the surprise request to make a "brief announcement"—one that turned into a 15-minute speech followed by a half-hour debate? It is your responsibility to manage the communication so that the group's goals are met efficiently. Be firm in sticking to the agenda and moving the proceedings along.

Generally, an agenda should follow a climactic order. Take care of routine reports, announcements, or introductions early and lead up to the major speaker, presentation, or discussion.

Sample Agenda for a Project Status Meeting

1. Welcome, introductions, overview
2. Goal review
3. Progress to date
4. Problems encountered
5. Identified solutions
6. Impact on timetable/budget
7. Summary, Q&A

Sample Agenda for a Banquet or Ceremony

1. Greeting: brief statement of purpose by emcee
   *Invocation, song, patriotic ritual, group ritual [*indicates optional]
   *More extended theme-setting remarks by emcee
   *Formal welcome (from mayor, governor, etc.)
2. Introduction of honored guests at platform or head table
   *In audience
   *Telegrams, messages from those not present
3. Ceremonial event
   *Thanks to committees, planners
   *Announcements of elections and so on
   *Awards, presentations
4. Introduction of featured speaker or event
   Featured speaker or event
5. Closing by emcee
   *Quick announcements
   *Benediction, song, ritual

Light entertainment—comedy, skits, musical interludes—may be interposed before items 2, 3, or 4. When a ceremony is the very purpose of the event, as in presenting the Heisman Trophy, items 3 and 4 are usually reversed.

Sample Agenda of a Parliamentary Session

1. Call to order
   *Check credentials; call roll; introduce observers, parliamentarian; any ceremonial functions
2. Approval of agenda
3. Reading (or distribution) and approval of minutes of previous meeting
4. Treasurer's report
5. *Reports of other officers
6. Reports of standing committees
7. *Reports of special committees, task forces
8. Old business
9. New business
10. Announcements
11. Adjournment

Be sure all participants in the meeting or program understand the agenda and the roles they are expected to play.

Give a *written* copy of the agenda to all participants in a formal business meeting. Confirm how and when they will participate: "I'll call on you for the treasurer's report right away. Save your idea for fund-raising, though, and introduce it under new business." For a decision-making session, let every participant know what to expect, so each can come prepared with the right information and some prior thoughts. For an informal program such as a banquet, you might not write out the agenda, but you should still apprise each person of your plan: "Right after the ventriloquist performs, I'll introduce you for the presentation of the Scholarship Award."

Be prepared for all contingencies.

As chair of any event or session, you are a coordinator, facilitator, and host. You are not the "star"; you are there to serve the group by helping members meet *their* goals efficiently and pleasantly. To this end, prepare by visualizing the event that you will chair. Anticipate any issues that may arise. Will the group need information for its discussion? Perhaps you should bring minutes, policies, reports, and data for reference. Prepare handouts, slides, or charts to put key information before the group. Consider the comfort and convenience of those assembled. At a business meeting, are there writing materials, name tags, refreshments, and scheduled breaks? At a banquet or public program, oversee or delegate even such small details as seating arrangement, water at the speaker's table, and audiovisual equipment.

Carefully plan your opening and closing statements. Try to develop coherent, and even graceful, transitions to bridge the parts of the program so that you do not fall back on "moving right along" or "last, but not least."

When moderating a forum, panel, or debate

1. Be sure the format and ground rules are clear to all participants well in advance. Let them know who the other speakers are and what they will cover.
2. Plan an introduction. Engage and motivate the audience toward the topic to be discussed. (See **13**.)
3. Make a *brief,* one- or two-sentence transition between each segment of the presentation.
4. Strictly enforce time limits. Emphasize the importance of this to speakers before the program, and arrange an unobtrusive signal for when the time is almost up. If a speaker goes way overtime, you should interrupt politely but not apologetically.
5. Moderate discussion aspects of the session by keeping the participation balanced. If one topic, speaker, or audience member is consuming too much time, again interrupt politely and move the discussion along. Do not, however, take over the discussion to develop your own ideas.
6. Wrap up the parts of the presentation with a conclusion. (See **14**.) The logical closure should be an extemporaneous summary of the points that have actually emerged.

When acting as emcee of a ceremony or banquet

1. Plan opening remarks that establish an appropriate mood. Whether the occasion is a solemn one, a celebration, or a regular monthly luncheon, make guests feel welcome and set the tone for the events to follow.
2. Make gracious and concise introductions. Learn to control and invite applause at appropriate times. When you introduce people, you will not have applause cards to regulate audience response. Direct it by asking them to hold their applause or by signaling for it through your phrasing and inflection.

(2) Take responsibility for establishing a positive and helpful environment.

Beyond the logistical concerns of agenda setting and troubleshooting, an effective leader can shape a context that helps a group meet its goals for communicating.

Set the tone through modeling communication that is appropriate to the context.

As the person who speaks first and from a position of leadership, you can let a group know about a situation by the way you present yourself, the tone you take, and the level of formality you assume. Most astute observers will read the communicative norms and feel at ease.

Set communication ground rules.

Sometimes, it is necessary to be more explicit about the way communication will proceed. In these cases, a leader should *metacommunicate,* or talk about talk. For example, you might say:

> At our meetings we agree to seek the floor by raising a hand and letting the speaker call on people.

> Because of the sensitive nature of our topic, we request that you not use names or identifying information when you share examples from your organization.

> So that more people have time to participate, we request that you keep questions and comments brief.

> This morning, we will only be discussing the problems that have brought us together and the causes we can identify. After lunch, we will get into possible solutions. If we start to jump ahead of ourselves, I will remind you to hold the thought until later.

Deal promptly and diplomatically with violations of rules and norms.

Remind the entire group of the ground rules: "Remember, we agreed not to make any personal attacks in this discussion." If there have not been explicit ground rules, ask the group if it wishes to set some: "I notice that we've covered only two points on our agenda. Because we have to finish by four o'clock, would the group like to set a policy of limiting discussion to 10 minutes per point, and then we can return to discuss any in more depth once we've covered everything?"

If you must single out an individual, try to do so with a compliment: "Mr. Pour, you have so many experiences to share that you have already given us a great deal to think about. Now we need to move on to the next area of discussion."

Exercise 4. Under what circumstances can a group rely on implicit understandings of communicative norms and rules? When are members likely to need more explicit discussions and metacommunication?

Exercise 5. If you were leading a communicative event, what would you do in each of the following situations?

1. One person engages in angry refutation and personal attacks on the invited primary speaker.
2. Three individuals in the back of the room continue to whisper and carry on private conversations that distract the group.
3. In a general discussion of a social issue, one participant reveals very personal information and becomes extremely emotional.
4. At a business meeting, one employee begins to link a concern to the general economic climate and proceeds to advocate for the election of a particular political candidate.

Part 5

Presentation

Introduction

A face-to-face speech puts heavy demands on speakers and listeners. However, "keynote handouts" have not replaced keynote speeches at conventions, nor have memos usurped the role of conferences. This is because information transmission is but a small part of the total communicative event. People meet in public spaces to affirm their sense of community and to act collectively. The combination of voice, body, and personality— as well as on-the-spot chemistry—makes speech a form of communication with compelling vitality. It is exciting to listen to a good speaker.

By "good speaker," we mean someone who has something to say and says it well. Too often, when people describe a speaker as good or poor, the reference is to the speaker's delivery only. "He didn't have anything to say, but he was a very good speaker" is a contradiction that points up how necessary it is for speakers to have strong presentation skills if they expect to have their message heard. An audience will listen avidly to a well-delivered speech even if, at the end, they discover there was little of substance in it. They will not afford the same consideration to a poorly delivered speech, no matter how exciting or important the content.

Recognizing the importance of the performance aspects of a speech, some speakers prepare as actors do—blocking out each movement, and planning every vocal change. Carried to its extreme, in a movement known as *elocution,* this approach entails the detailed marking of a manuscript or outline, so that a typical sentence might look like this:

point to audience   *point to self*   *hands*   *pleading*   *hands clenched*   *voice louder*   *one hand forward*   *frown*

You and I must work/ together/ to *solve* this *dreadful*

drop in inflection   *two steps to left*

problem.//

It is almost impossible to find the words among all the stage directions! When voice and bodily action are consciously orchestrated to this degree—whether or not they are written down—the ideas of the speech are lost to both speaker and listeners.

As we explained in chapter **1,** borrowing too directly from the performative repertoire of the actor can be inappropriate because being in a play and giving a speech are fundamentally different. As an actor, you assume the role of someone else, speak words written by another person, and strive to perform each line exactly as rehearsed. As a speaker, you present your own personality, speak your own words, and try to adapt to the response you receive. Thus, public speaking is far more like conversation than like acting.

We advocate an approach to speech delivery called the *natural theory of delivery,* which emphasizes speech as an interaction of ideas as opposed to speech as a performance. However, this does not deny the performance aspects of a public speech. It does claim that the performance will be most effective when conceptualized as amplified conversation, rather than as a whole new kind of speaking.

Your consciousness can be directed—consciously—toward your speech goals rather than yourself. Paradoxically, the less you think about your speech delivery, the more effective it becomes. Perhaps you have heard a speaker give a speech presentation stiffly and mechanically and then heave a sigh of relief and ask for questions. Suddenly, a great transformation occurred! In the question-and-answer period, while clarifying points, the speaker had more facial expression, more variety of tone, and more body language. It was as if the speaker thought, "I'm through with 'my speech.' Now I can really talk to these people." The delivery became much better as the speaker's attitude toward the situation shifted from a performance orientation to an interaction orientation.

There is an explanation, if oversimplified, for this change. We all have had more practice communicating than performing. The natural theory of delivery is based on the assumption that you communicate well many hours of every day without consciously thinking about speech mechanics. When you are intensely involved in conversation, you do not stop and think, "Now I'll furrow my brow and point my finger." Changes in your voice and actions just happen naturally when you are wrapped up in communicating your message. If you are similarly wrapped up in the content of your speech, your delivery should take care of itself. The single most important delivery goal for any speaker is to internalize this conception of speech as conversation. Once you feel the sense of interaction with an audience—the sort of give-and-take you experience in other conversations—your enjoyment of speaking will increase along with your confidence and skill.

Are we saying that a successful speech will result from talking just as you do every day? Certainly not, if your everyday speech is listless, and ungrammatical, and marred by distracting habits. What we are saying is that this natural theory of delivery ought to ensure that your public style is *no worse* than your private style. Ideally, your speech delivery should be lively and unobtrusive, but this can be difficult: A conversation with 50 people is very different from a conversation with 3. Projecting your voice and personality in this setting may seem and sound strange at first. But you can amplify and exaggerate your conversational style without acting like a different person. Be yourself. There are many sides to a person's self, of course, and different ways of speaking associated with each. Neither the intimate shorthand of lovers nor the rambling style of a telephone conversation between best friends is an appropriate model for public speaking. We suggest that you picture the way you describe an exciting event to friends, or picture yourself as you talk about a strongly held opinion. That is, imitate yourself as you are in your liveliest and most animated conversation. Disregard for now the more reserved and introspective aspects of yourself. You have chosen to be (or have been thrust into) the center of several people's attention, so call on that side of you that is most outgoing and expansive.

This may not be easy, because the fears surrounding public speaking can put you in touch with the facets of yourself that are most shy, apologetic, and self-protective. Thus, a lively delivery may not feel really "natural"—hiding under the podium could feel more in character. Nevertheless, learn to assume a role as you speak—the role of yourself, at your most confident, poised, and expressive. Quite literally, call up past triumphs of lively and effective speech. Think to yourself, "I want to communicate as I did at lunch the other day telling about my trip. I don't really feel comfortable here, but that's the sort of speech personality I want to project."

Effective, natural delivery is also unobtrusive. Your listeners should be thinking neither "what an awkward gesture" nor "what a beautiful voice." Instead, they should attend to what you are saying. If you do have problems of a vocal, verbal, or physical nature, by all means work on them. Be realistic, though, about how many goals you can set for conscious competence at one time. It is a good idea to select one goal in the area of physical delivery and one goal in the area of vocal delivery to work on at a time. When you master these and become unconsciously competent, entrust them to habit and then move on to another area of improvement. That way, most of your conscious attention during a speech can be directed where it belongs—to your message and your audience.

Chapters **24–30** deal with the diverse aspects of speech presentation. Depending on the situation, you will use one of four standard *modes of delivery. Practice sessions* help you shape your presentation and sharpen your message. Whatever the mode, to transmit your message effectively, you must understand the dynamics of *vocal delivery* and *physical delivery.* The successful speech will have even greater clarity and impact if you support it with *visual aids.* Another skill in effective transmission is being able to *adapt to the speech situation* and modify your presentation to account for differences between how you envision a given speaking event and how it really turns out. Finally, if you go about *answering questions* properly in the question-and-answer period, you have more chances to reinforce your message.

Chapter 24

Modes of Delivery

Select a mode of delivery that is appropriate to your topic, audience, and occasion.

Decide early if your speech will be *impromptu* (off-the-cuff), *extemporaneous* (given from notes), *manuscript* (written out and read), or *memorized* word for word. Settle on the predominant mode you will use, but be aware that no speech is purely *one* mode. As we've seen, each speech is a unique blend of conversation, writing, and performance. Even in an extemporaneous speech, for example, it is often advisable to write out the introduction and conclusion and to partially memorize them. And any speaker who encounters hecklers must be prepared to offer some impromptu retorts.

24a. For most speaking situations use the extemporaneous mode.

Extemporaneous speaking is the most common mode of delivery and is the one you should use in all but a few special cases. This mode is sometimes confused with impromptu speaking. Although it shares some aspects of spontaneity with the impromptu, the extemporaneous mode is considerably more structured. In this mode, you prepare extensively, constructing the progression of ideas with the aid of an outline, planning your content thoroughly, and practicing until you are comfortable and conversational. But you never commit yourself to a rigid, exact sequence of words.

Preparing a set of ideas rather than a set of verbatim paragraphs is the only practical and realistic method for most teachers, trial lawyers, salespersons, and others engaged in speaking for hours at a time or for large portions of the day. But even for the occasional public speaker, the extemporaneous mode, once mastered, gives a sense of power and confidence. You will sound more natural and conversational if you phrase your sentences as you go along. Your mind will be on your ideas and on your audience's reaction to them—so you are less likely to go blank than if you are focusing on recalling certain words. You will also find that speaking extemporaneously lets you be flexible and adjust to audience response. If you find your listeners nodding knowledgeably at points you thought would be confusing and in need of clarification, you can drop your extensive examples and move on. Conversely, you can spend more time on points where you hit unexpected resistance or do not get the response you anticipated.

Prepare an extemporaneous speech in four steps:

1. *Begin with a fully developed outline.* Follow the recommendations in chapters **9, 10,** and **11** to arrange your material in a logical and effective manner.
2. *If you have used a full-sentence outline, convert it to a keyword or key-phrase outline.* The full-sentence outline is a tool to ensure that you develop your speech content adequately and logically. The full-sentence outline is not the written version of the words you will use in your speech, however. The declarative sentences that characterize a full-sentence outline are written English, not spoken English, and if you follow them too closely as you develop the wording of your speech, the result may be dull and lifeless. In other words, you may find your expressiveness being limited by what you see on the page. For this reason, we suggest that you convert the full-sentence outline to a keyword or key-phrase outline. For instance, Main Point IV of the full-sentence outline in **11b** is "During World War II and after, women were used as a dispensable and secondary source of labor." This could be converted to "WWII—dispensable labor." An outline constructed of such phrases retains the structure derived from the full-sentence outline while enabling you to improvise as you proceed through Step 3.
3. *Word the speech.* Working from this brief outline, practice putting your ideas into words. Listen to yourself carefully to detect a clumsy sentence or an exciting turn of phrase. The second time through, some of the clumsy phrases will have disappeared (and some of the exciting ones, maybe) as you play with sentence structure, rhythms, and so forth. Third time, fourth time, fifth time through—your topic is becoming more and more familiar, giving you the freedom to relax and to allow yourself to really experiment with construction. You will also discover that no one way of expressing a set of thoughts is necessarily better than another:

You have said the same thing five times, differently each time, but each of the last three ways works equally well.

4. *Convert your brief outline to speech notes.* See **25c** for directions on how to transfer your content to a format that provides easy visual cues to which you can refer.

24b. When formal preparation is impossible, remember four simple steps for successful impromptu speaking.

No one should set out to give an important speech in the impromptu mode. Those good speakers who seem to be able to speak fluently on the spur of the moment are usually speaking extemporaneously, stringing together practiced "bits" to fit the subject that has been dropped into their laps. Do not let this illusion of spontaneity mislead you into underpreparing.

There are several sets of scenarios that can result in impromptu speaking:

- *No excuse:* A lazy or overconfident speaker may decide to "wing it" even though there has been plenty of time to prepare. The resulting shoddy word choice, lack of organization, repetition, generalities, and unsupported assertions will be a monumental waste of the audience's time.
- *Should have seen it coming:* Many impromptu speeches could have been extemporaneous if the speaker had analyzed the requirements and potentials of the situation. An expert caught flat-footed by a question at a news conference probably could have seen it coming by visualizing the event and anticipating the varied perspectives of the questioners. The best man at a wedding who has not prepared a toast is guilty of failing to investigate his responsibilities.
- *Legitimately unexpected:* There are some instances in which no realistic amount of preparation or anticipation will lead one to think that he or she will have to speak. The executive who finds 50 demonstrators in the boardroom can be excused for not having a prepared statement. Similarly, it would be a bit conspicuous if the recipient of a surprise award proceeded to give a two-hour speech of acceptance. In a meeting, you might innocently agree to a whispered request to nominate a colleague, and to your dismay, the chair then announces, "Now we will have the nominators make statements about their candidate's qualifications."

If you too often find yourself in the no-excuse or should-have-seen-it-coming scenarios, the solutions lie in other chapters of this book, especially chapters **5, 8,** and **11.** The suggestions that follow pertain to the third, legitimately unexpected, case.

(1) Keep your composure.

Do not apologize. Knowing the situation is truly a surprise, the audience will have realistic expectations of you. You should have realistic expectations yourself and not fall apart if what comes out is not your most polished performance. Speak slowly and confidently. Remind yourself that you speak all the time without extensive preparation. In any casual conversation, not only are you speaking, you also are planning what to say next. You do mental composition *all the time.* Do not let the stress of a speaking situation make you forget that!

By maintaining your composure, you can take full advantage of the time between the surprise announcement of your speaking and the actual beginning of that speech. Whether you have the 30 seconds that it takes to walk to the podium, or the 10 minutes after hearing that the featured speaker is stuck in a snowbank in the next county, use the time to do accelerated speech preparation. However short the period, the steps should be the same: Pick a theme, an organizational pattern, and a beginning and ending sentence.

(2) Select a theme.

Very quickly list several possible approaches to the topic. Do it mentally or, if time permits, with pencil and paper. By thinking beyond the most obvious approach, you may discover a way to link your topic to a subject you are conversant with.

(3) Select an organizational framework.

You will not have time to make an extensive outline, obviously, but that does not mean you are justified in bouncing erratically from point to point. You can hook your topic to a simple framework like one of the following:

> Past-present-future
> Pros and cons
> Problems and prospects
> Concentric rings, with main points progressing from immediate concerns to universal concerns (e.g., in the home, in the school, in the community; or locally, regionally, nationally, internationally)
> Domains, developing the different spheres touched by the topic (e.g., politically, socially, economically; or practical implications, theoretical implications, or moral implications)

After you have divided your topic along the lines of one of these frameworks, find one means of support or development for each idea, such as an explanation, example, story, fact, or statistic.

If time permits, make a rudimentary outline. Even a few keywords on a napkin can reassure you and keep you on track once you have started to speak.

(4) Whenever possible, plan your first and last sentences.

The beginning and ending are the most difficult parts of any speech, and this is especially true in impromptu speaking. Even the simplest attention getter can propel you through that awkward first moment. When you know what your concluding sentence is, you avoid the panicky search for an ending when you run out of steam. By having introductory and concluding sentences, you avoid the aimless rambling so characteristic of impromptu speaking. When you know your task is to start with Sentence A and work your way to Sentence B, you have a ready reference against which to judge ideas that occur to you as you are speaking.

24c. Speak from a manuscript when precise wording and exact timing are essential, but maintain oral style and conversational delivery.

There is a widespread misconception that speaking from a manuscript is the easiest and safest mode of delivery ("I'm not an experienced speaker, so I'd better write it out"). This is no excuse for avoiding the extemporaneous mode. A bad manuscript speech is much worse than a bad extemporaneous speech. Stilted phrasing, monotonous vocal delivery, and lack of eye contact are all perils facing a novice speaking from a manuscript.

Limit your use of manuscripts to the following situations:

- *The time allotted is specific and inflexible.* This is mostly the case in the broadcast media. Short replies to editorials need to be precise and compact, with only a few seconds of leeway in the scheduling.
- *The wording is extremely critical.* Many ways of phrasing a thought are acceptable, but there are occasions when slight differences in phrasing are *not* acceptable. Sometimes, poor word choices can have severe consequences. The most visible examples of this are the public statements made by world leaders during a crisis. As the crisis deepens, the wording of

these statements becomes more and more precise to forestall the misinterpretation that could trigger a holocaust. There are also times when the lack of precision in speaking can lead to lawsuits. On some sensitive and emotionally charged topics, the consequences of an ill-chosen word can be hostility, hurt feelings, or loss of business. A speaker would also be best advised to use a manuscript for technical or research reports in which there is a lot of complex data and specialized denotations for many words.

- *The style is extremely important.* There are occasions when, although World War III is not a possible result, precision is required all the same. The necessity of precision springs from matters not so much of content but of style. It is expected that your language will be more compact, elevated, witty, or elegant than your everyday speech. For instance, though you still want to sound conversational in a major speech of tribute, the desire for the best possible word choice, sentence rhythm, and polished tone might lead you to use a manuscript.

(1) Prepare an easily readable manuscript in the oral style.

Do not let the fact that you are writing out a manuscript lure you away from the tenets of good organization and composition. Work from a full-sentence outline. (See **11.**) Remember that the sentences of the outline are meant to be logical guides, and not the actual wording of the speech. To get from the outline to the manuscript, "talk" the speech out and onto the paper. You need to check your composition against your ear more than your eye. As you write, and rewrite, keep saying it aloud, listening for the rhythms of oral style. (See **17.**)

A tape recorder is helpful here. Listen to yourself and identify the stiff, unwieldy phrases that need revision. To get a second opinion, have a friend listen.

When you have settled on the final version of your speech, produce the copy you will read from, following these guidelines:

1. Don't write it out by hand; print it out on a printer, triple spaced, with wide margins. Some speakers prefer to use oversized type.
2. Use capital and lowercase letters in standard sentence format. Text done using all capitals is more difficult to read.
3. Print it on heavy paper. Avoid crinkly or flimsy paper.
4. Make sure the letters are dark and legible. Do not counteract the benefit of typing or printing something out by then having a product that is too faint to read easily.

Figure 24-1 gives an example of a manuscript page prepared along these lines. Note that the speaker has included marginal notations to help him find his place and has marked up the text to indicate areas for emphasis.

FIGURE 24-1   Easy-to-Follow Manuscript

①

Everybody knows it: if you want to get
anywhere these days you've got to have a

58   specialty. And when, at the age of fifty-eight,

you become associated with a large and active

B of R
Naples   Board of Realtors like the one at Naples,

Florida, and you're making an entirely fresh

start in what is for you a new and challenging

business, you have a problem.

acreage   One man is a specialist on acreage. One   **(Names**

m & h   knows all about motels and hotels. A woman I   **from**
audience?)

? condo   know has picked condominium apartments.

Waterfront houses are the principal interest of

another. Everywhere I looked someone was

there before me. Reluctantly, I accepted the

truth: all of the good specialties were taken. !

/ min.

331

In some speaking situations, you will not have your manuscript in your hands, but will be reading it from a TelePrompTer or similar machine.

(2) Be familiar enough with your manuscript to look and sound as though you are speaking extemporaneously.

The two biggest problems in delivering a manuscript speech are a lack of conversational inflection and a lack of eye contact. Even though every word is written out, you should not sight-read. Practice reading your manuscript out loud often enough that you are comfortable with it. Do not memorize them, but become familiar with the flow and rhythm of the words. If you follow the hints for composing in the oral style, you will avoid slipping into a singsongy cadence or gasping for breath between overlong sentences.

The printed, easy-to-follow page discussed in **24c(1)** is essential to maintaining good eye contact during a manuscript speech. The spaces and visual cuing make you less likely to lose your place while looking out at the audience regularly. Only through sustained eye contact can you reap prime benefits: connection and feedback. An occasional quick glance up from the page will not provide you with much information about what is going on in the audience, and such jerky movements can be just another distraction for listeners. If you have practiced your speech enough, you will be comfortable raising your head and engaging the audience with unhurried and unchoppy looks.

Never read your first or last few sentences. Have them memorized so that you can start your speech making eye contact with your audience. And never read your punch lines.

24d. Memorize a short, important speech only on those occasions when holding a manuscript would be out of place.

By definition, giving a memorized speech entails a manuscript speech—without the manuscript. The only times you should give a memorized speech, therefore, are the same as put forth in **24c,** with the added limitations that the speech should be a short one and the situation inappropriate for reading. These occasions are most often ceremonial: giving a toast, presenting a plaque, or accepting an honor.

(1) Memorize the structure of the speech before memorizing the speech word for word.

Learn a few keywords that help you internalize the main sequence of ideas. For example, if you are presenting an award to your company's salesperson of the year, you might learn this outline for your brief speech:

    I.   Selection process for the award
    II. Chris Welch's sales record for this year
    III. Chris' qualities as a successful salesperson

Or even more simply:

    Process
    Record
    Qualities

(2) Read the speech aloud several times and then work on learning it paragraph by paragraph.

Always keep your mind on the meaning. Do not try to learn sentences in isolation, but rather work on whole paragraphs at a time, reinforcing their logical and conceptual unity.

(3) As you practice, visualize giving the speech.

Avoid thinking of your speech as lines of text in a social vacuum. You do not want to be startled and lose your concentration when you realize that you are actually facing a roomful of people.

(4) Do not go into a trance when delivering the speech.

Once again, be comfortably familiar with your material so that you can maintain eye contact and establish a rapport with your audience, instead of having your eyes glaze over and your voice and body tighten with concentration.

(5) If you go blank, switch to the extemporaneous mode and recall the structure of the speech rather than groping for the next word.

Speaking along the general lines of the point you know you were trying to make, you can collect your thoughts and click back into what you have memorized.

Chapter 25

Practice Sessions

Use practice sessions to help compose and polish your speech. Allow time for three stages of practice.

Start practicing your speech aloud well before the presentation; this enables you to finalize your points, get feedback from others, and polish the delivery.

25a. Optimize your sources of effective feedback.

(1) Whenever possible, form a support group of other learners or a network of colleagues and friends.

Although you can get feedback from a number of sources, it is most desirable to establish an ongoing relationship with people who have similar goals. In a speech class, this may be a group of classmates who meet to discuss ideas and practice speeches. The value of peer collaboration is acknowledged in business and professional settings and by politicians and citizens' groups. The most effective speakers routinely test their presentations on one another throughout the phases of development.

(2) Set guidelines for effective feedback and speech criticism.

Within any group of speakers, it is desirable to establish some ground rules for commenting on each other's speeches. Often, the speaker can lead the discussion, asking for comments on the areas of greatest concern to her or him as recommended in **25b(2)**. See **2d** for a discussion of constructive feedback.

25b. Use three stages of practice sessions to convert your speech from outline to finished product.

Your practice sessions need a timetable. It is not necessarily true that more is better. In the case of your speech or report, too much practice may make your delivery stale, and you run the risk of becoming bored with your topic. Most speakers err in the opposite direction, however, and the result can be even more disastrous. To avoid falling into either of these traps, you should plan your practice sessions, write down a timetable of steps and phases, and adhere to it.

Your speech is not going to be static during these sessions. The creative process, as outlined in **5a,** will continue, and the practice timetable should not be so rushed that the periods of incubation between sessions are squeezed out. Doing a stand-up, full-scale practice once in the morning and once in the evening for three days is immeasurably better than running through the speech six times in a row. With your practice sessions spread out, you are more likely to benefit from the illumination and refinement that follow incubation.

There is no one, arbitrary timetable to adopt. The variations in type of speech and in lead time for preparation make it impossible to prescribe an exact number of practice sessions. Table 25-1 shows possible timetables for three speeches in which the advance notice is different for each. This can be used as a guide to help you create a schedule unique to your circumstances.

A practice timetable can also be influenced by personal differences in speaking ability. For instance, an experienced speaker giving a classroom speech may not need three final practices a day—one may suffice. Adapt your timetable based on an honest evaluation of your speaking skills.

(1) Use early practice sessions to flesh out your outline.

During these early developmental sessions, you transform your outline of ideas into a speech by adding the elements of language and delivery to the logical framework erected by your outline.

Begin by internalizing your outline. Read it over a number of times, becoming familiar with the flow of the logic. Sit at your desk or a table and talk your way through the outline. Try to explain the ideas to yourself—half-thinking, half-talking it out.

At this point, pick a quiet spot and start to put together the speech as it will actually be given. Stand up and give the speech out loud in your speaking voice. Include everything. Do not say to yourself, after making a point,

TABLE 25-1   Possible Practice Schedules

Type of Speech	Commitment Made to Speak	Preliminary Analysis, Research, and Outline Completed	Early Practice Sessions (Development)
Major policy address	Several weeks before	1 week before	1–2 weeks before: Discuss ideas with colleagues. 5–6 days before: Talk through speech once a day.
Classroom speech	10 days before	4 days before	4–10 days before: Talk about speech with friends. 4 days before: Read outline several times; practice aloud twice.
Routine oral report in a business meeting	24 hours before	Evening before	Afternoon or evening before: Talk through basic ideas with friends or colleagues. Evening before: Practice aloud one to three times.

"and then I'll give a few examples." Actually give them. You want to discover awkward phrases and constructions and poor word choices sooner rather than later. Visualize the speech situation and mentally put yourself there. Do not think, "This is a practice session." Make it real—envision the faces out there and talk to them. At this point, do not worry about refining your gestures and vocal inflection.

Sometime during this stage, you will have made the first draft of your speech notes. Do not carve them in stone. They are mutable according to how things shape up as you tinker with the wording. Remember, you do not want to lock yourself irreversibly into one exact sequence of words.

(2) Use one or more middle practice sessions for receiving feedback.

After you have become comfortable with your material but before doing the final polishing, you should seek feedback on your speech. This is usually sometime in the middle of your timetable. If you solicit feedback on content, style, and delivery too soon, when you have not finished shaping your basic speech, you will miss getting help on those parts that have not yet been crys-

Middle Practice Sessions (Feedback)	Final Practice Sessions (Refinement)
4 days before: Give speech on videotape, review with advisors, repeat.	Beginning 3 days before: Practice aloud once a day; read notes or outline once a day. Day of speech: Practice aloud once; review notes just before speaking.
3 days before: Give speech to friendly critic, receive feedback, practice aloud one other time.	Beginning 2 days before: Practice aloud one to three times a day; read over outlines and notes several times. Day of speech: Practice aloud once; review notes just before speaking.
Morning of meeting: Give report to colleague if possible.	Day of presentation: Practice aloud once; review notes just before leaving for meeting.

tallized. If the feedback comes too late in the schedule, you will not have the time to incorporate comfortably the useful information you have received.

Practice your speech in front of others and ask for their feedback.

Just as people are good sounding boards for the development of your ideas, as stated in **5c,** so they are the best source of feedback. Seek a variety of responses from others—colleagues, family members, friends. Take what you can get, but if possible, move beyond your support group and find critics as close to being representative of your potential audience as possible. If you are going to speak to a high school audience, for instance, ask your teenage cousin, niece, or friend to listen to a practice session. As you rehearse your speech imagine that you are in front of your actual audience, and skip the nervous clowning. Do not make it more informal simply because they are friends. Do not leave things out and say, "You've heard this story." Tell it. Do not talk about your speech. Give your speech.

Ask for honest feedback on content and delivery, but do not necessarily take any single person's comments as the last word. He or she has quirks and prejudices just like everyone else. This is why a group of people is preferable, giving you a sampling of responses.

You should not ask, "How'd you like my speech?" Answers like "It was nice" or "I thought it was okay" certainly do not help you much. Lead your critics with a few questions and seek clarification of their answers. Here are some specific questions you can ask:

- "What did you see as the single most important thing I was trying to say?" If they do not come up with your thesis sentence, then you must look at your structure again.
- "What were the main ideas I was trying to get across?" They should answer with your main points.

It is important to get answers to these first two questions before moving on to finer points of development and delivery. You are speaking for a specific purpose, and everything else is insignificant if your whole reason for speaking is not being understood. If you are satisfied that your purpose is clear, then you can ask questions along these lines:

- "Did my ideas flow in a logical sequence?"
- "Did the speech hold your attention? What parts were boring? Confusing?"
- "Did I prove my points?"
- "Did my introduction show you where I was going?"
- "Did the conclusion tie the speech together?"
- "Did I sound natural?"
- "Did I have any distracting mannerisms?"

Record your practice session on audiotape or videotape and analyze your performance.

A videotape is the next best thing to a human critic. If you don't own a video camera, there are sources for the casual user. Video clubs usually have rental equipment available. If you are taking classes, your school may have machines you can use. Some speech consultants offer a videotape service. Your company may have videotape equipment for training.

When you view your performance on playback, try to get outside yourself and see the image as that of a stranger. In this case, you may temporarily shift your focus from your message and your imagined audience to yourself as a speaker. Become the audience and ask yourself the same questions raised previously. You might not believe it when a friend tells you that you start every other sentence with "I mean" and that you are always picking at your sweater. The evidence is inescapable when you watch yourself do it on tape. A hazard to avoid here is being too self-critical. Seeing yourself on tape can be devastating if you notice only the aspects that need improvement. Look also for things you are doing right. Do not get caught up in examining physical attributes—worrying about the shape of your nose or the fact that your ears stick out or that your taped voice sounds different from the way you normally perceive it. This is where it can be helpful to watch the tape with a friend or coach who can give you a more balanced perspective.

If a video camera is not available, your next best source of help is, of course, the tape recorder. You will not receive the visual information, but you certainly will be able to get feedback on content, pacing, voice, and so on. Occasionally, you may want to use a tape recorder earlier in the schedule, especially if you are blocked creatively. The recorder can help you remember good ideas and possible wordings, and hearing your own ideas and phrasings complements talking your ideas out with friends.

Practicing in front of a mirror should be limited to a single session, if done at all.

It is our opinion that practicing in front of a mirror often does more harm than good. The methods just described allow the feedback to be *delayed:* After speaking, you can shift your focus away from ideas to a more detached assessment of the details of your presentation. With a mirror, however, you are constantly compelled to divide your attention between what you are saying and how you are saying it. If you have no other way to check on the visual impact of your posture, gestures, and facial expressions, it may be worthwhile to practice before a mirror just once.

(3) Use the final few practice sessions for refinements of style and delivery.

By this time, you should be committed to a basic version of your speech while maintaining the flexibility of the extemporaneous mode. You should not be making radical changes.

Make the final practice sessions as realistic as possible.

If you are going to use visual aids, they should be ready early enough that you can include them in your final practice sessions. The same holds true for the final draft of your notecards. Check yourself against your time limit. Practice your speech, standing up, at the rate and volume you will be using. Speaking with rudimentary mechanical amplification to a large audience, for example, will use more breath than will the conversational volume used in early practice. You need to unabashedly boom out your speech in the final practice sessions if that is what it will take to be heard when you actually give the speech.

Continue reading through your notes and outline, but do not think of these activities as a substitute for the formal practice sessions.

25c. Prepare speech notes to act as a guide and a safety net.

You should not confuse speech notes with your outline, as they serve different functions. An outline is used to ensure that the speech has a logical organization. Speech notes, in contrast, are used as an aid while you are actually speaking.

Like your outline and wording, your notes can go through several drafts. Work on them, doodle on them, and then copy them over. Do not feel committed to the first thing you write. The kinesthetic act of copying over your notes is an excellent way to firm up your speech in your mind.

(1) Include in your speech notes keywords, key phrases, and material that is to be cited directly.

Unlike your outline—in which your points must be parallel, mutually exclusive, and in full sentences—your speech notes do not have a rigid, regulation form. A point can be represented by a word, a sentence fragment, or an actual sentence or two. What goes into your notes depends on what you find you need during practice.

For example, perhaps one point of your speech, which in your outline was developed to the second level of subordination, with all its accompanying A's and B's and 1's and 2's, is one with which you are so familiar that it can be represented in speech notes resembling those in Figure 25-1.

While practicing, you may also find that you want more than just a keyword reminder to get through an important but tongue-twisting sentence or to ensure that you remember an especially eloquent turn of phrase that has a delicate rhythm. Your notes may also contain material that you will be citing exactly as written out, such as long quotations or complicated statistics.

Keep in mind, however, that your notes should remain *notes*. If you make them too extensive and detailed, you risk moving out of the extemporaneous mode and into the realm of the manuscript speech. Your notes should be referred to, not read from.

(2) Prepare your speech notes in a format that aids your delivery.

There are many contexts in which your speaking can occur (see **23**), and these will dictate to some degree the format your notes take. The invited

FIGURE 25-1   Speech Notes

---

⑤

  B. Recurring experiments with Protectionism
    1. Just doesn't work
        ―――――――――――― -- F Co's absorb, cut profits
    2. Pass to consumer
                      $66 B   Gary Hufbauer
                                   (Prof of finance GT U)
    3. Hurt US Co's
                      15% imports multinat.
                      need cheap F mat'ls & components
  ⭐ 4. Retaliation
                McFadden (Fortune)
                trade war ――→ recession ――→ depression

                      CHECK TIME *(about 8 min)*

---

speaker at a world affairs forum may use 4″ × 6″ cards. An attorney in court does not look out of place referring to a legal pad while speaking. A project manager can glance at the PowerPoint note page on her laptop screen covering the content of her slides. For all of these instances, however, the advice in **25c(1)** still applies.

In addition, there are formatting suggestions applicable to notes in any layout. The words and phrases should be large, well spaced, and uncluttered. There should be a lot of visual cues—large card numbers, underlining, indenting, stars, highlighting, different colors—all for the purpose of making it easy for you to find what you want at a glance. Speech notes should also be cued to choices you will make during the speech. Time notations are essential. You might write at one point, "If more than 8 minutes, skip to [card 6/point 4/slide 10]." You might use a special color to mark optional sections of the speech. Examples highlighted in yellow could mean: "Include this if the audience seems uncertain about my point. Otherwise omit it."

Preparing speech notes on notecards

Many speakers prefer to put their notes on 4″ × 6″ or 5″ × 8″ cards. The 8½″ × 11″ sheet of paper has the disadvantage of being large and floppy, inhibiting your gestures and limiting your movement by effectively tying you to the lectern or table. (One way around this, for the case in which your keyword outline can fit on one page, is stapling the $8^{1}/_{2}'' \times 11''$ sheet to a manila folder, giving it enough stiffness to stand up to gesturing and whatnot.) Whereas the $8^{1}/_{2}'' \times 11''$ sheet is too large in most cases, the $3'' \times 5''$ card is too small. If you make your notes on them properly, large enough to be read, you will end up with a huge stack of cards through which you are constantly flipping.

If you choose to go the notecard route, a few medium-sized cards can easily become an extension of your hand as you gesture and move about. They will not be distracting to your listeners if you seem comfortable with them. Do not be coy about using your notes—refer to them honestly. A surreptitious peek at protectively cupped hands will not fool your listeners into believing that you are speaking without aids.

Do not go to the other extreme and get lost in your notes. You should be able to look down, see what is next, and then talk about it. If you find yourself burying your nose in your notes, you have not prepared them correctly.

Preparing speech notes in a presentation software package

Presentation software gives you the option of entering notes to accompany the slides you create. Here is where you can put the tongue twister, the precise data, or the quotation mentioned in **25c(1)**, but don't be constrained by the default font settings to make everything too small to read easily. Also, feel free to mark up the output with the other visual cues as illustrated in Figure 25-1 and noted previously. If you don't want to have to deal with $8^{1}/_{2}'' \times 11''$ sheets, use a paper cutter to lop off the top part of the printer output with the image of the slide—assuming you have prepared your notes with adequate keywords to cover the content.

25d. Fit your speech into the time limit.

The section on preparation admonishes you to limit your topic according to the time allowed. Often, you cannot tell for sure how much time your speech will take until you have gotten well into the practice sessions. In extemporaneous practice, you will experience variations in length as you work with the form of your ideas and the style and rhythm of your speaking. This, again, is where envisioning audience response is helpful. Most first-time speakers practice at a speaking rate faster than the one they find necessary for clarity during the speech itself. The more realistic your practice, the less likely you are to misestimate your time.

To clock your speech, do not glue your eyes to the sweep hand of your watch. Merely note the time when you begin and when you finish. A sweep hand can induce unnatural behavior, such as speaking at twice your normal rate for the last minute if you think you are running long, or, in the opposite case, slowing your delivery to a tired shuffle. There are more sensible ways to address problems of length. The first step is to time the parts of your speech. Two possible ways of doing this are to have a helper jot down the times of your main points on your outline as you practice or to do it yourself with a tape recorder.

Look at the relative proportions of the parts of your speech: introduction, body, conclusion. Generally, the body should make up 75 percent of your speech. Does an extended story make the introduction too long? Look, too, at the relative proportions of your main points. Are you spending half your time on only the first main point? Is it worth it?

If Your Speech Is Too Long

1. Consider cutting out an entire main point. (Adjust your thesis accordingly.)
2. Look at your supporting evidence and examples, and cut those that duplicate effort. (But save the ones cut, as they may be needed for the question-and-answer or discussion period.)
3. Turn some of your illustrations into examples; instead of telling the whole story, toss off a one-liner that capsulizes it.
4. Eliminate any long stories, jokes, or narrations unless they are absolutely essential to the theme of the speech.
5. Consider using means other than speech, such as handouts and visual aids, to transmit technical or detailed information.
6. Polish and tighten your language and phrasing. Speak simply.

If Your Speech Is Too Short

1. Find out if there are important ideas that are not sufficiently developed relative to the other points.
2. See if you are too concise for your own good. As is explained in many other places in this handbook, the spoken word is fleeting, and it needs repetition and embellishment and illustration to bring home to each and every member of the audience the emphasis that you want to deliver.
3. Make sure you have proved all your points. Double-check your evidence to make sure that you have not assumed too much or made some logical leaps that are not justified.
4. Do some more research. You may have given up too soon at the library.

In a speech class, there may be penalties for not reaching a minimum time limit. In most other settings, no one is going to be awfully upset if you take only 15 out of the 20 minutes you have been given. However, taking

40 minutes when you have been allotted 20 can disrupt the schedules of countless other people.

The experienced speaker always knows the duration of each element of the speech. Even if the first clocking run-throughs show that the speaker meets the time requirements, she or he still wants to have a point-by-point time breakdown. This knowledge aids adaptation to changes that might crop up in the speech situation itself. (See **29**.)

When you reach that point in your practicing at which the speech consistently comes out the same length, mark the cumulative times of the parts in your notes. For example, you might print "2 mins" at the bottom right of your notes on the introduction, "5 mins" after the first main point, "8 mins" after the second, and so on. (See Figure 25-1.)

Here, as examples, are two situations in which knowing the timing of the elements of your speech will help you adapt without panic:

> You planned to spend 5 minutes on your first main point. Feedback from the audience convinces you to use 8 minutes to make certain they are getting it. You decide to drop anecdotes from your second and third points to make up the 3 minutes.

> You are on a program that is running late but can't go overtime because of scheduling conflicts. The moderator asks you to trim your presentation from 30 minutes to 10. You begin doing mental arithmetic, subtracting combinations of points until you arrive at a plausible shortened version of the speech.

Some people have internal clocks that are accurate enough that they do not need external cues. If yours is not that well developed (and most of ours are not), feel free to take off your watch and lay it where you can see it or to have a colleague in the audience give you prearranged time signals. Avoid excessive reliance on the clock, though. Become comfortable with your presentation by practicing and timing your speech.

25e. Save the hours just before the speech for one final run-through and for getting into the proper, relaxed frame of mind.

Imagine that you are giving an important speech one afternoon or evening. You should have planned your practice sessions so that, by the night before, your speech is polished and you are comfortable with it. Remember that it is never a good idea to compress your practice into a few frantic hours. On the morning of the event, allow for one unpressured practice session. As you go about the day's activities, you may want to look over your outline or notes one time. If you feel yourself becoming anxious, try some of the relaxation or visualization techniques recommended in **4c** and **4d.**

The last quiet, private moment before the speech is the time to go through your notes and outline once again.

This could be done just as you leave your home or office or as you sit on a bench outside the building. In the final minutes before your presentation, go through your introduction and conclusion. Visualize the basic structure of the speech, a macroview of the ideas.

Throughout the construction of your speech, you should keep in mind what preparation it will take to get yourself to the podium in a relaxed frame of mind. Take time well before the speech to think about those possible situations that might throw you off your pace, and develop strategies to avoid or dilute them. Try to arrange your day so that you are not rushing around picking up dry cleaning or trying to cash a check. Get the logistics of your life in order early. If you have a meeting just before the speech, one that you know is usually tense and upsetting, do not go. Be conscious of your idiosyncratic responses to a number of stimuli. If you know you do not function well on a full stomach, do not eat the rich banquet—have just the salad. In short, be a little selfish and take care of yourself in the ways you have learned work best. You owe it to your audience and to yourself to be feeling comfortable, confident, and composed when you present the speech you have worked so hard to prepare.

25f. Avoid common practice pitfalls.

(1) "Mental" rather than oral practice

Sitting and thinking about your speech, or reading over your outline or notes, is no substitute for rehearsing the speech aloud. Oral practice is essential to get comfortable with phrasing and to check your timing. Do not let "speaker's" block make you put off working orally until the last moment.

(2) Too many critics

Some speakers seek feedback from everyone they know, and most of these people are happy to oblige. Although it is good to get a variety of opinions, it can be confusing to receive contradictory advice: "Make it longer." "Make it shorter." "You seem too serious." "You seem too casual." It is *your* speech; after receiving comments from a few people whose judgment you trust, decide what advice to take, and move on to finalizing your speech.

(3) Overpreparation

This is rare, but some speakers rehearse their speech so much that it becomes mechanical. As noted in **1c(5),** by drawing too heavily on writing or on performing, or on both, speakers can lose all sense of the original meaning of the words and ignore audience reactions.

(4) Self-consciousness rather than audience consciousness

Except for a few middle practice sessions in which you receive feedback from others or from recordings, try to keep your attention off yourself as a speaker and on your message and the audience response you desire. Remember to visualize *them* when you practice. Again, don't let the performer upstage the conversationalist.

Chapter 26

Vocal Delivery

Speak clearly, correctly, and conversationally. Vary your vocal delivery for interest and emphasis.

As important as preparation, organization, content, and style are, the essence of the speech is still your utterings. What a waste of time and brainpower if what you have to say cannot be heard or understood at the critical moment of speaking. You must be aware of the mechanics of transmitting sound: articulation, breath control, projection, and so on. At the same time, your most important goal is to develop a style of vocal delivery that sounds natural and conversational. The "orator," with trilling *r*'s and shuddering pauses, can really set listeners' teeth on edge. Except for the stylized chants of the auctioneer and revival minister, most public speech should sound like private speech, only exaggerated to fit the size of the room.

Voice prints are as distinctive as fingerprints. "Finding a voice" is a powerful metaphor for achieving a social identity. Your way of speaking reveals your ethnic and cultural heritage, as well as your personality. In a multicultural society, the sounds of everyday speech are always changing to include new voices. As you develop your public speaking skills, stay attuned to your distinctive sound.

26a. Speak so that you can be heard and understood.

(1) Speak loud enough to be heard by the entire audience.

For the inexperienced speaker, just about *any* volume level will sound too loud. This is understandable. There are few occasions for speaking above a conversational level, and even on such occasions, as when we scream our heads off at a football game, we rarely care if we are being understood. For the most part, being loud and conspicuous is, in Western cultures, considered boorish behavior. This adds another dimension of difficulty to using your voice properly when you speak before an audience.

The only thing that will make loud speaking more comfortable and natural is, of course, practice. In the early stages, you have to ignore the feedback on volume that you receive from your own ears and rely on a friend or perhaps a tape recorder set some distance away. What you are aiming for is a louder voice that retains the rhythms and inflections of your normal conversation. You want to be loud, but not to yell like a drill instructor. As you practice, you will discover that this requires more air for each phrase and that you need to develop breath control to permit you to keep your breathing pauses in normal patterns.

Maintain a mental image of broadcasting or propelling your voice to the far corners of the room. You will then find yourself doing those things that naturally aid projection, such as keeping your head up and opening your mouth wide.

Know how large an audience you can address without sounding strained. Can you speak for an hour at an outdoor political rally, or do you reach your limit speaking to 12 people in a boardroom for 10 minutes? (Insist on a microphone if you know that the audience or room will be too big for your voice.) Continue to practice increasing your speech volume. A good goal for the average person is to be able to speak conversationally, without amplification, to 50 or 60 people in a room with average acoustics.

(2) Speak at a rate your audience can follow.

Although there are speaking-circuit veterans who have a 250-words-per-minute rate as one of their gimmicks, most people lose intelligibility far short of that. An average rate of speaking is around 150 words per minute. To check your rate, select a fairly easy newspaper or magazine article. Then time yourself for three or four minutes of reading aloud. Next, count the number of words in the passage and divide by the number of minutes you read. Be sure to read in as natural and conversational a manner as possible. If you speak faster than 200 words per minute or slower than 100 words per minute, you may be endangering your comprehensibility by overworking your audience. The extremely fast speaker asks his listeners to decode and process information more rapidly than is their custom. The plodding speaker, who seems to avoid phrases and slowly lays out each word as if it were unrelated to any other, keeps her listeners in a state of bored suspension as they wait for the words to gel into some sort of context.

Generally, when giving a speech, plan to speak a little slower than you do in daily conversation. The need to speak a little louder and a little more distinctly will require extra breath. It will be more natural to pause to breathe between phrases than to rush through the last few words of a sentence and gasp for air. To be sure you have timed the speech realistically, practice at the rate and volume you will actually use.

(3) Enunciate words distinctly and naturally.

When speaking, either publicly or privately, people rarely enunciate *every* sound in *every* word. The phrase "jeetyet?" can be deciphered as "did you eat yet?" by a friend who has a context for the remark. In public speaking settings, much information can be lost due to distance from the speaker and to distracting noise. Thus, it is important to work on crisp, precise articulation. Use your tongue, teeth, and lips to pronounce every sound. Be sure you say "gover*n*ment" rather than "goverment" and "hundred" rather than "hunnerd." Do not mumble, run words together, or swallow whole phrases. (See **26d(2)** for a discussion of chronic articulation problems.)

You can enunciate properly and still sound natural. It merely takes some practice incorporating precision into your normal conversation instead of creating a separate "speaking persona." Some people, in a misguided attempt to sound more formal or "literate" during a speech, will overarticulate words or take on affected mannerisms or pronunciations. The result is quite the opposite of what they wish. Rather than sounding erudite, they—with their grimaces and popping consonants—come across as patronizing, melodramatic, and just a little silly. Do not say "thee" in a place where "thuh" is natural. Do not use "would not" where "wouldn't" feels right. (Just be sure to say "wouldn't" rather than "wunt.") Standard usage dictates that some syllables are truncated. Do not reverse this procedure. "Con grat you lations" is an overly precise pronunciation of "congratulations," which most speakers say like "con grad ja lations."

(4) Make special adjustments, if necessary, to compensate for having an accent that your audience may have difficulty understanding.

If you have a regional accent or if you are not a native speaker of American English, you may be concerned about being understood. Do not try to eliminate or hide your accent. Your manner of speaking is part of your unique personality. The differences can add interest and charm to your presentation. To ensure comprehension, follow these suggestions:

1. Do not start out with the most important material. Use your introduction to let the audience adjust to the pronunciations and patterns of emphasis that differ from their own. Usually, this will take just a few minutes.
2. Speak more slowly and distinctly than you do in conversation.
3. Be very alert to feedback. If you see confused faces, repeat ideas slowly. Unclear vocabulary or mispronunciation of one key word may mystify your listeners. Try several synonyms for important words.

If you are a non-native speaker of English, you may find these two simple tips useful in increasing your intelligibility:

1. Prolong your vowel sounds. In contrast to many other languages, spoken American English carries more meaning in vowels than consonants. It will sound odd to you, but make a conscious effort to extend your vowels. Maaaaake eeeeeach laaaaaast a looooooong tiiiiiime.
2. Also blend the end of one word into the beginning of the next so that each phrase sounds like one long word. This reduces the perceived choppiness of much accented English.

For more detailed suggestions, refer to:

Porter, Patricia A., and Margaret Grant. *Communicating Effectively in English: Oral Communication for Non-Native Speakers,* 2nd ed. Belmont, CA: Wadsworth, 1992.

Raifsnider, Barbara. *American English Pronunciation Program for Speakers of English as a Second Language and Native Speakers with Strong Regional Accents.* New York: Living Language, 1999.

26b. Reinforce meaning and make your speech more interesting through vocal variety.

The speaker who has a clear speaking voice devoid of vocal tics wastes these good qualities if she or he speaks hypnotically, with no variation in pitch, rate, or volume. Change and movement are intrinsically more interesting than the static or predictable. In chapters **17** and **18**, we stress the importance of variety in word choices and examples in maintaining a high level of audience attention. Vocal variety is equally important, and the need for it goes beyond a mere desire for novelty. Your voice should not simply transmit words; you can use it to underscore and reinforce your message. Suppose your speech on air pollution contained these two sentences:

> When the pollution levels are high, my hair feels gritty, and I have to wash it more often.

> Every time pollution reaches the Alert level in our city, more people with chronic respiratory problems die.

Delivering these sentences in the same tone of voice could imply that they are of equal importance. Changes in pace and emphasis show your audience what is significant and can signal humor, seriousness, irony, and a range of emotions.

(1) Vary your pitch.

Speaking in a monotone says this to an audience: "I have little interest in the subject or confidence in my ability to interest others in it." A listless vocal performance will negate any dynamism that ordinarily would spring from your word choice and content. Varied inflection implies a high energy level and self-confidence, and generally aids your credibility. The pitch you use for the delivery of a word or phrase can underscore its meaning or imply its opposite. For instance, it is common to indicate disagreement with an assertion or statement merely by speaking it in the inflection used for questions.

If you can sing an octave, on key or not, you can speak an octave. Do not be afraid to use the full range of your voice.

(2) Vary your rate of speaking.

The average pace of your delivery should be geared toward comfortable listening. However, changes in rate at different times during the speech can be effective in establishing moods or in adding emphasis. Speaking slowly can make you seem thoughtful and deliberate, and it can also impart a sense of drama. Similarly, an extended pause at the end of a sentence signals to your audience that you consider what you just said important and worth some thought. Rapid delivery shows excitement and activity. A climactic effect is achieved by presenting a series of ideas or examples at a rapid clip, as in the following example:

> [slow] Since we adopted this management system, [fast] absenteeism is down, productivity is up, morale is up, sales are up, profits are up.

The preceding example also demonstrates that the shift in rate (in this case, slow to fast) is as important to creating a climactic effect as the rate itself. The following passage shows what a fast-to-slow shift can achieve. Were you to read this aloud, you would speak faster and faster through the first sentence but would speak the second sentence very slowly.

> In the next hour they looked in her room, checked the tree house, went over to the playground, called several of her friends, drove around the block, asked all the neighbors. No one—had seen—Emily—since—she—got off—the school bus.

The accelerating pace of the first sentence communicates mild concern turning to frantic worry, which leads to the sudden moment of grim acceptance contained in the measured delivery of the last sentence.

(3) Vary your volume.

You should speak loud enough that you can drop your voice for effect and still be audible to the listeners in the far corners. At the same time, you should hold some volume in reserve so that you can raise your voice for emphasis.

Notice how a drop in volume can pique interest by evoking an air of confidentiality:

> I was having an awful week. Few prospects, no sales. It was hard on a young, eager guy just out of school. On the other hand, I never saw old Jones without a customer at his side or a signed contract in his hand. I guess he saw my hangdog look and took pity on me, because he walked over and said, "Smith, you've got the makings of a great salesman, but you're doing one thing wrong."
> [in a softer voice] Now, this is what he said: . . .

Here is an example of raising one's voice for emphasis:

> The city council has approved yet another halfway house in the neighborhood. The university is using our streets for its parking lot. The state parole board dumps its parolees downtown. Prostitutes from miles around converge each night on Second Street.
> [in a louder voice] Do you want to know what's coming next?

26c. Use standard, acceptable pronunciation.

(1) Identify words that you habitually mispronounce.

Some differences in the ways people pronounce words are inevitable and cause no problem for public speakers. A person from New England might say, "I went to a pahty," a Pennsylvanian may have "cot a cold," and a Texan may tell you to come "ovah heah." Unless they have strong biases against some part of the country, listeners rarely make negative inferences about the speaker on the basis of regional pronunciations like these. If, however, a person says "warsh" instead of "wash" or "ax" instead of "ask," many listeners will consider this substandard and draw conscious or unconscious conclusions about the speaker's educational level, competence, and intelligence. This sort of linguistic snobbery can be unfair, but a speaker can change some pronunciations more easily than everyone else's attitudes.

Look over the list in Table 26-1 and see if you are guilty of any of these pronunciation errors. If you find one or two words that you mispronounce, you can easily work on correcting them. If you find five or more, you may need more extensive help in the form of coaching or coursework. Due to

TABLE 26-1	Pronunciation Errors	
Word	Proper	Improper
get	get	git
just	just	jist
across	a cross	a crost
nuclear	nu clee ar	nu cyou lar
perspiration	pers pir a tion	press pir a tion
strict	strict	strick
escape	es cape	ex cape
compulsory	com pul sory	com pul so rary
recognize	rec og nize	reck a nize
library	li brar y	li berry
mischievous	mis che vous	mis chee vious
theater	THEE a ter	thee A ter
picture	pic tchure	pit chure
surprise	sur prise	sup prise
comparable	COM per able	com PARE able
larynx	lar inks	lar nix
relevant	rel a vant	rev a lant
drowned	drowned	drown ded
et cetera	et cet era	ek cet era

factors in your background or perhaps a lazy ear for the finer distinctions of speech, you probably are also mispronouncing several other words and impairing your effectiveness in communicating with certain groups of people. Here, too, feedback from your practice audience can alert you to errors of which you were unaware.

(2) Check the preferred pronunciation of unfamiliar words.

Your reading vocabulary and your speaking vocabulary are different. There can be words you frequently see and understand yet rarely speak or hear spoken. Without exposure and feedback, you might develop your own way of mentally pronouncing such a word that involves a mistake like adding a sound or reversing sounds. The incorrect pronunciation will feel right to you because you have said it to yourself so often as you read and did research. If you give a whole speech about the Electorial College (instead of Electoral), your listeners might wonder just how knowledgeable you really are. Or they may be confused or amused if you constantly refer to the need for a counselor to listen "emphatically" when you think you are saying "empathically," a word that means something entirely different. Check words you encounter in research, but do not use regularly, to be sure you have them right.

As a child, you may have been taught to "sound out" unfamiliar words. You also discovered the perils of this technique the first time you pronounced *island* "iz-land," and wrestled with *pneumatic*. You learned then that it was unwise to make assumptions about unfamiliar words; this is still true, especially for the speaker.

Place names are always an area for careful investigation. Looking at the word *Beaulieu*, you might expect to say it "Bowl yew." However, the village by that name in Britain is pronounced "Byew lee." Similarly, Leicester is "Lester." The Cairo in Egypt we call "Kie row"; the Cairo in Illinois, is "Kay row." Houston Street in New York City is "How ston," but Texans have "Hyew ston."

There are minor differences in pronunciation that can be troublesome. "Apricot" or "aypricot"? "Har *rass*" or "*har* rass"? Which pronunciation of *Vietnam, Peking,* or *Caribbean?* A dictionary is not much help when there are several correct pronunciations, or changing ones; or when words become more or less anglicized; or when unusual proper names like *Nagorno-Karabakh* spring upon the scene. It has been said that the arbiters of the most current acceptable pronunciation are the anchors of national news programs. You are usually safe to follow their lead or that of other such models as the most articulate and respected leaders of the community.

Refer to these sources for questions of pronunciation:

Dauer, Rebecca M. *Accurate English: A Complete Course in Pronunciation.* Englewood Cliffs, NJ: Prentice-Hall/Regents, 1994.

Prator, Clifford H., Jr., and Betty Wallace Robinett. *Manual of American English Pronunciation,* 4th ed. New York: Holt, 1985.

Silverstein, Bernard. *NTC's Dictionary of American English Pronunciation.* New York: McGraw-Hill, 1994.

Yates, Jean. *Pronounce It Perfectly in English* (with 3 cassettes). Hauppauge, NY: Barrons Educational Audio, 1995.

26d. Identify and eliminate distracting characteristics of your vocal delivery.

Your reason for speaking is undermined when your listeners begin to pay less attention to what you are saying and more to how you are saying it: "That's the fifteenth time she's said 'quite frankly'" or "Why doesn't he clear his throat?" or "That repetitious inflection is really irritating." Your voice and speech style should be unobtrusive vehicles for your ideas.

Distracting speech habits are difficult to identify and even more difficult to change. Vocal mannerisms become so familiar to you and your closest associates that they are overlooked and cease to distract, but to a new audience they are blatant. Follow the suggestions in chapter **25** for receiving feedback. Use videotape, audiotape, and critics to get some objective perspective on your performance. When you isolate a problem, do not view it as simply a public speaking problem. An overused phrase and a harsh, raspy voice reduce your effectiveness in daily conversation as well. Resolve to correct problems gradually and permanently by modifying your everyday speaking habits.

(1) Identify problems of voice quality.

The resonant, musical voice you view as an ideal may be beyond your reach, but there is, of course, no one perfect voice for effective speaking. Rather, there is a range of pleasing voices. Although the quality and timbre of your voice are determined to a great extent by your larynx and by the size and shape of your nasal cavities, you can find yourself within that range unless you are hampered by one or more of the following problems.

Harshness, hoarseness, or stridency

These qualities are caused by constriction of the throat or by tension in or damage to the vocal folds. The voice may sound husky, rough, or shrill and so give an impression of anger or gruffness.

Breathiness, thinness, or weakness

These qualities are caused by having an inadequate airstream, by releasing excessive air, or by speaking in an unnaturally high falsetto. The result is a soft, childish-sounding voice that lacks authority and power.

Nasality and denasality

Incorrect flow of air through the nasal passages creates these problems. With nasality, too much air escapes through the nose; with denasality, too little air escapes. These problems primarily affect *m, n,* and *ng* sounds, and produce either whiny or stuffed-up qualities.

(2) Identify problems of articulation.

Many people have speech problems that are not severe enough to be considered disabling but that are still sufficiently distracting to impede good communication. A stutterer will certainly be aware of her or his condition, whereas people with lesser problems are usually not conscious of their misarticulations.

Listen closely to your speech for irregularities in the way you produce consonant sounds or blends of consonants. Many articulation errors take the form of *substitutions,* such as "*th*olution" for "*s*olution" or "*dese*" for "*these.*" Also common are sound *distortions:* the slushing, hissing, or whistling *s,* or the lazy *l* or *r.* Less frequently encountered articulation errors are *additions* ("ath*a*lete" for "athlete," "real*a*tor" for "realtor"), and *omissions* ("doin'" for "doing," "reglar" for "regular"). If you discover any of these errors, notice whether they occur every time you make the sound or only in the initial, middle, or final positions in a word. For instance, a lazy *r* may show up in the middle but not the initial position: You can say "rabbit," but "turkey" comes out as "tuw-key." Also, consonant sounds that you produce well in isolation may tend to be distorted in consonant blends: That same *r* sound may give you trouble only in *cr, gr,* or *dr* combinations.

The real distraction caused by these misarticulations is not the minor aural irritation it may arouse in your listeners. Rather, these speech problems can create a contradictory message that works against the credibility you want to project. Sound substitutions are a part of a child's language development and disappear after the child learns to discriminate more precisely among sounds. An audience listening to a speaker who says "wange of pothibilities" will experience conflict between the image of competence and intelligence conveyed by the words and the image of incomplete development triggered by the sounds. Similarly, sound distortions can produce an image of sloppiness that conflicts with an otherwise crisp and concise presentation. Consider the image discord created by the accountant who presents precise facts while slushing his s's in phrases like "the projections for the next fishcal year sheem to shupport our prediction of sholid growth potential." It may be illogical and unfair to associate certain articulation errors with baby talk and drunkenness, but you had best be aware of the unconscious tendency of listeners to do so.

(3) Identify vocalized pauses and other irrelevant sounds and phrases.

Do not be afraid to pause between sentences or thoughts when you speak. But avoid filling those pauses with distracting and meaningless sounds and phrases. When a speaker is nervous, a 1-second pause can seem like a 10-second stretch of dead air, and the temptation to fill it with something can be great. Consider these questions:

- Do you use vocalized pauses: "uh," "um," "err"?
- Do you fill pauses with other nonspeech sounds: lip smacking, tongue clicking, throat clearing, snuffling?
- Do you unconsciously insert a giggle after every sentence?
- Do you repeat to excess certain words or phrases in nonsensical places?

In the latter case, these may have originated in requests for feedback. The coherent question "Do you know what I mean?" following a complicated idea turns into "y'know" tossed in whenever the speaker feels uncertain. From there it is a short step to using it as just another pause filler. In the following example, the phrase "y'know" has no more meaning than "uh":

> One of the, y'know, advantages of joining a credit union, y'know, is the low-interest auto loans, y'know.

Other irrelevant repetitions may grow out of an unconscious need to apologize for inadequacies of expression. Tacking on "or whatever" at the end of every sentence is an example.

Here is a list of words and phrases that lose their original meanings when allowed to spread cancerlike through a speech:

okay?
y'know
see
like
I mean
or whatever
and so on and so forth
et cetera
in other words
so to speak
you might say
right?

(4) Identify repetitious patterns of inflection.

While growing up and listening to other people, you learn very early that there are logical and natural places in sentences to vary the pitch of your voice. For instance, in English, your voice usually goes higher in pitch at the end of a question or deepens for an emphatic statement. In normal conversation, we use a variety of inflections without having to think about it. In public speaking, however, there can be a tendency to deliver every sentence with the same inflectional pattern regardless of the sentence's meaning or grammatical structure. This happens when the speaker is not thinking about the content of the speech, is nervous, or is reading from a manuscript or recalling a memorized text. A singsongy, hypnotic pattern of inflection can easily lead to drooping eyelids in the audience.

(5) Eliminate your distracting habits through a systematic self-improvement program or with professional help.

Self-improvement
When you identify a problem and your motivation to correct it is strong, you may devise a simple plan of action, as Demosthenes did in ancient Greece when he was troubled by problems of articulation and enunciation. His solution was to practice being understood while speaking over the roar of the ocean with his mouth full of pebbles. This may not suit many modern speakers, especially if they live in Kansas on sandy soil, but there are other sources to tap. Books and recordings are available to provide exercises in breathing and projection. These also have exercises, like tongue twisters, that make

apparent the muscle groups used to produce certain sounds properly. You can start with such books as these:

Hahner, Jeffrey C., Martin A. Sokoloff, and Sandra L. Salisch. *Speaking Clearly: Improving Voice and Diction,* 6th ed. (with pronunciation CD-ROM). New York: McGraw-Hill, 2002.

Modisett, Noah F., and James G. Luter, Jr. *Speaking Clearly: The Basics of Voice and Articulation,* 3rd ed. Minneapolis: Burgess, 1988.

Wells, Lynn K. *The Articulate Voice.* Scottsdale, AZ: Gorsuch Scarisbrick, 1989.

For a deeply ingrained habit, you may choose to map out a program of behavior modification. This approach, which has been quite successful in helping people to lose weight or quit smoking, is based on the premise that habits that develop gradually are best eliminated gradually. New behaviors are substituted for old ones, and the new behaviors are rewarded. The steps are simple:

1. Assess your present behavior. Quantify the exact frequency of the distracting habit.
2. Set a specific, realistic goal. If you say "okay?" after nearly every sentence, perhaps 20 times in a 10-minute speech, resolve to cut down to 10 times in a 10-minute speech.
3. Monitor your behavior. Do not simply estimate your progress. Have a friend tally the occurrences, or tape each speech yourself. Keep a written chart of your progress.

For most motivated adults, knowledge of results is an adequate reward. Just seeing the progress in quantified form keeps you working toward the goal. Feel free, though, to use more tangible rewards. You can promise yourself a special treat of some sort when you reach your goal, if you think that such an incentive will be useful in helping to keep you on track.

Professional help

Some problems of vocal delivery are difficult to diagnose or solve without professional help. In seeking help, consider the nature and seriousness of your vocal problem, as well as the time and money you are able to commit. Then consult the appropriate professional person from the following list:

- *Speech therapists* are the best source of help for fairly serious or persistent articulation and voice problems.
- *Voice coaches* may be affiliated with theater, radio, or television. They can help you improve voice quality, diction, and pronunciation. If you also

want to work on regionalisms or accents and want to develop greater variety and expressiveness, consider a course in voice and diction or oral interpretation. An acting course will help in these areas and also improve your physical movement.

- *Public speaking teachers* and *consultants* can provide help with voice, articulation, emphasis, and expressiveness within the context of public speaking. Usually, work on speech delivery is integrated with the development of speech content.

Chapter 27

Physical Delivery

Use your physical delivery to create a visual effect that complements the content of your speech.

Much of how your listeners respond to you is a result of what they see rather than what they hear. The words may be confident, but shaking knees and fidgeting fingers tell another story. A slumped posture and a sour expression can give the lie to the statement "I'm so happy to be here!" When practicing and delivering your speech, be aware of the visual image you are creating. As with vocal delivery, the goal is to be natural and to avoid any actions that will distract your audience from your message.

27a. Be conscious of your appearance.

What kinds of first impressions do people have of you? Are they initially intimidated by you because you are big and burly? Do people dismiss you because you look 10 years younger than you are? Obviously, you cannot trade in your body; but if such impressions get in the way of your speech goals, you can try to compensate. Correct false impressions, especially in the opening minutes of your presentation, by using speech content and all those physical characteristics you have control over.

As you get ready for a particular speech, consider what your hairstyle, grooming, and clothing might communicate to your audience. You do not need, nor do you necessarily want, to mimic the dress of your audience. Regardless of differences in sense of style, however, you should show that you took care in preparing, that you consider the event important enough to expend some energy in trying to look good.

Ideally, your clothes should provide a tasteful and unobtrusive frame for your personality and your remarks. Be aware of regional, cultural, and occupational norms. In some parts of the country, and in certain professional or social settings, jeans and a sport jacket may be considered formal enough for a presentation. When in doubt, though, lean toward conservative business attire. There is no need to be drab, but remember that your audience could be distracted by gaudy colors, busy patterns, eye-catching jewelry, unorthodox combinations of apparel, and any clothing they associate with seduction or courtship.

27b. Eliminate distracting mannerisms.

Distracting mannerisms fall into two categories: those you have all the time (pushing your glasses up on your nose, tucking your hair behind your ear, cracking your knuckles), and those you have only when giving a speech (noisily fanning and squaring up your notecards, rocking back and forth on your heels, tapping your pencil on the lectern). These are physical equivalents of saying "y'know . . . y'know . . . y'know." Few acts are inherently distracting—it is the repetition of some act that becomes distracting. As with vocal mannerisms, you are probably unaware of the frequency of the act until someone points it out. Thus, the biggest step toward eliminating the problem is becoming aware of it; sometimes, this awareness is sufficient to resolve it. Commit yourself to using the practice techniques laid out in **2d** and **25a** to get feedback on your delivery.

Distracting mannerisms do not spring up overnight, and it is unrealistic to think that they can be eliminated overnight. The primary goal should be a reduction in the frequency of a given mannerism by adapting the behavior modification techniques described in **26d(5)**.

27c. Stand or sit with a relaxed but alert posture.

As a general rule, you should stand when speaking. This focuses audience attention on you and gives you a better view of your listeners. There are exceptions, of course. In an intimate setting, such as a circle of a dozen people, you might choose to speak seated. As a member of a panel discussion, you may be constrained to follow the sedentary lead of the moderator. If, however, you can learn to be comfortable speaking without a lectern—with your weight evenly distributed, and your notes grasped casually in one hand at waist level, supported by no props of any kind—then you can easily adapt to any setting. Appropriate variations might include leaning across the lectern to show deep involvement or sitting on the edge of a desk or table to signal the shift to an informal mood. Draping yourself across the lectern, lounging at the side with one elbow extended, or standing in an off-center posture are incompatible with the energetic and controlled image of a polished public speaker. But avoid as well the rigid, petrified stance of a military academy cadet. Specifically, be careful never to lock your knees—you risk becoming light-headed or even toppling over.

27d. If you move about during the speech, make the action purposeful and relevant.

You can give a perfectly good and proper speech standing behind a lectern. However, most speeches can be aided by movement at appropriate times. Taking a few steps to the left or right, or moving closer to your listeners can add variety and emphasis to your speech. You also establish contact with that segment of the audience that you move toward. Moreover, physical movement during a speech is a constructive way to release tension.

Make your movements purposeful. Pacing nervously around the room is distracting. So are the tentative dance steps of the speaker who cannot really decide whether to move or not. This speaker shuffles, rocks from side to side, extends a toe as if testing the water, and then darts back, as if chilled. If you are going to move at all, be decisive. Take at least two or three normal paces diagonally or directly forward. When you stop, keep your body orientation and eye contact toward the most concentrated part of your audience.

The timing of your movement can reinforce your ideas. Generally, it is not effective to move around when explaining complex material or when delivering your most emotional examples or powerful arguments. Physical movement works best at transitional points, where it signals a change in mood, content, or form.

27e. Keep your hands free so you can gesture if it feels natural.

"I don't know what to do with my hands" is perhaps the most frequently expressed concern about delivery. People who use their hands to gesture naturally and comfortably in everyday interaction stare with consternation at the two frying pans dangling from their wrists when it is time to give a speech. What you should do with your hands in a speech is exactly what you do with them in normal conversation. For some people, using their hands in this manner means hardly using them at all. For others, it means gesturing a great deal. Whether you gesture a little or a lot, you do it to describe, to point out, to enumerate, to emphasize, to entreat, and so on.

There is no need to plan what gestures go with your speech. If you have ever seen a speaker who prepared a gesture for nearly every word in the speech, you probably began to feel that you were watching a game of charades or a person signing for the hearing impaired. Inevitably with such a scheme, the carefully planned gestures get a little ahead of or behind the words, and the unfortunate result resembles a movie with its sound track out of sync.

If you are absorbed with your topic and with communicating it to your listeners, your gestures will emerge spontaneously at the appropriate points. But this will happen only if your hands are free to move. Too many speakers immobilize their hands completely, both out of the panicky need to cling to something and the desire to prevent uncontrolled movement. Do not lock yourself into any of these gesture-inhibiting stances:

The bear hug:	Arms across the chest—one of the most common ways of getting a grip on yourself
Ten-hut!	Arms stiff, wrists firmly nailed to hips
The flesh wound:	One arm hanging useless at the side, the other hand serving as a tourniquet above or below the elbow
The firing squad:	Legs slightly spread, hands clasped behind back
The choirboy/girl:	Hands clasped at waist level, with fingers entwined
The supplicant:	Same as the choir, but higher, at chest level
The fig leaf:	Demurely crossed hands, strategically placed

Actually, all of these are perfectly acceptable *transitory* postures. The problem with them lies not in the position of the limbs, but in the temptation to remain in one stance, statuelike, while concentrating on what is coming out of your mouth. As you become more involved in your message and the audience's response to it, your natural gestures will come back to you. When these natural impulses collide with the unnatural posture you have locked yourself into, the results can be bizarre:

- The supplicant, who cannot get her fingers untangled when she wants to forcefully jab a finger in emphasizing a series of points, looks as if she is holding a pistol in a two-handed police grip and taking potshots at the audience.

- Another speaker, trying to describe a complex process while in the ten-hut! position, finds himself flapping his hands uselessly at his thighs, like a penguin trying to fly.
- The choirboy starts a dramatic elevating gesture to emphasize his point on the rise in inflation and discovers that, because he cannot unclench his hands, they have come to a stop against his chin and his elbows are twitching out in the vicinity of his ears.

So, what *do* you do with your hands? First, do nothing distracting such as nervously shredding notecards, drumming on the table, or other kinds of unproductive hand movements:

The Lady Macbeth:	Hands wrung compulsively and continuously to wash out the "stain" of having to speak
Happy pockets:	Keys, change, and other pocket articles set to jingling by restless hands, the sound competing with the speaker's voice

Second, do nothing contrived—no rehearsed gestures. A hand can be at your side, or holding cards at waist level, or resting lightly on the other, or *gently* grasping the lectern, or casually resting in a pocket (no change jingling). What matters most is that your arms, wrists, and fingers are relaxed so that your hands can move if you find a need for that movement arising naturally.

27f. Maintain eye contact.

Be familiar enough with your material that you can look at as many members of your audience as possible, as often as possible. In our culture, looking into another's face connotes openness and interest, whereas looking away or down is interpreted as a sign of insincerity or shiftiness. People would much rather look at your face than the top of your head. Moreover, it can distract them from what you are saying if you stare fixedly out the window or up at the ceiling. After a while, listeners' attention begins to shift in those directions, and they wonder if cue cards are taped to the rafters or if a major crime is in progress outside. But more essentially, maintaining eye contact allows you to read your listeners' faces to get feedback on how your message is being received. Advice to fake eye contact by looking between heads or just over the heads of the people in the back row misses the whole point.

At the beginning of your speech, when you have not yet hit your stride, find a few listeners who are responding supportively with nods and positive facial expressions. Look at them and use their support to help you through this uncomfortable period. As soon as you start to roll, however, broaden your eye contact to include everyone.

Actually look into the eyes of the individual audience members, and hold that contact for at least three seconds. Do not skim across rows of faces. Move your eye contact randomly throughout the room. Do not fall into a head-bobbing pattern: left, center, right, center, left . . . Have a friend or colleague observe and tell you if you scan mechanically or if you have a tendency to neglect any one segment of the audience.

In any speech, even a manuscript speech, you should have eye contact 85 percent of the time, looking down only to read technical material or to refer briefly to your notes. Most important, be sure to maintain eye contact throughout your introduction and conclusion and during the most telling points and pivotal arguments.

27g. Use facial expression to reflect or forecast mood and tone.

Do not let the tension of a speaking situation force you into a deadpan face. Your natural facial expressions serve as one more channel for effective communication. Generally, changes in facial expression precede and forecast shifts in tone or mood. Replacing your cheerful countenance with a concerned frown can be a better transition than that hoary old cliché "but seriously, folks."

You should not plan a series of mugs, smiles, and grimaces—all you need do is exaggerate slightly those expressions that arise normally. The subtle nuances that work in face-to-face contact will not reach the back row.

The *one* expression that has the same meaning in every culture is the smile. Most public speakers underuse or misuse this powerful tool. A constant, fixed, jaw-aching grin is as bad as a deadpan expression. A smile at a sad or serious moment is inappropriate. However, remind yourself to smile genuinely whenever it can reinforce your message. It is one of the easiest ways to establish rapport, show your goodwill, and put you and your audience at ease.

Chapter 28

Visual Aids

Use visual aids appropriately and effectively to support your message.

There are places in a speech where a visual aid can help you make a point more clearly and quickly than if you used words alone. Conversely, visual aids poorly used or overused can make your ideas obscure and slow the pace of your speech. Overreliance on visual aids cuts into time better spent on analysis or development of points and ideas.

A visual aid is best used in two places: when you are attempting to explain a complex or technical idea and when you want to reinforce a particular message. For example, a geneticist might find it useful to have a model of the DNA double helix when talking about how that remarkable molecule duplicates itself. Or the speaker wishing to impress upon his or her audience the importance of stiffer drunk-driving penalties may choose to reinforce a recitation of traffic fatality percentages with a "pie" graph that demonstrates the overwhelming predominance of drunk driving over other causes of traffic deaths.

28a. Select a visual aid appropriate to the point you wish to illustrate or clarify.

We can put visual aids into three categories.

(1) The object or a physical reproduction of it

While demonstrating the simplicity of a new lens-to-camera attachment system, a speaker can put force behind her or his words by using the actual camera and lens to show the ease of coupling. It would take many more words by themselves to convey the same message. With a large audience, however, this sort of demonstration might not work, because of the smallness of the equipment. In this case, the speaker might use larger-than-life-size models to make sure the message is clear. Other objects are obviously too small or large to use, like a microchip or the *Queen Mary,* so scaled-up or scaled-down reproductions are necessary.

There are other considerations when deciding between an object and its reproduction. Most audiences (other than groups of medical professionals) will be grateful if the speaker explains valve structures and their functions by using a plastic replica of a human heart rather than the real thing.

(2) Pictorial reproductions

These can include photographs, sketches, plans, pictures, slides, overhead transparencies, computer animations, film clips, and videotapes. If the mechanical device that makes the lens-to-camera coupling so easy is in itself complex, the speaker might use an exploded three-quarter-view schematic drawing to show the interaction of all the pieces. The speaker wishing to show the musculature might prefer a large photograph of the human heart. Again, object size and audience size are important factors in determining which to use.

(3) Pictorial symbols

Pictorial symbols are used with more abstract concepts and can include graphs, charts, diagrams, maps, and lists of important words and phrases.

Bringing a derelict in off the street will probably get an audience's attention, but it will not be as useful, when speaking on the declining state of the economy, as a line graph showing the buying power of the dollar over the past two decades. An aerial photograph of San Jose will not be as appropriate in a speech on local politics as a map showing city council district boundaries. If a speaker wants to highlight a motto, inspirational phrase, or name of a product, then suitably lettered posters can help. Figure 28-1 shows some common pictorial symbols.

28b. Prepare clear and manageable visual aids.

(1) Prepare visual aids large enough to be seen by the entire audience.

The nature of the place in which you will be speaking and, as stated in **28a(1)**, the size of the audience determine to a great extent the type and size of your visual aids. It helps to look over the facility in advance if possible. Stand at the back of the room and envision the scene, or, if you already have a rough mock-up or draft of one of your aids, place it where you expect it to be when you speak. Obviously, if the aid is too small, you need to enlarge it. One option is to design transparencies to show on an overhead projector; another is to use presentation software. Reduce any aid that is larger than it need be, considering the size of the room, or that is so unwieldy you will have to wrestle with it.

FIGURE 28-1   Pictorial Symbols

Pie Graph

Line Graph

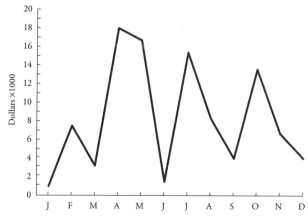

continued

FIGURE 28-1   continued

Bar Graph

Annotated Map

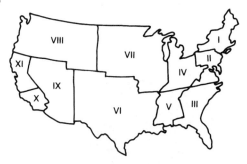

Slogan or Memorable Phrase

The "Four D's"
- Drop it
- Delay it
- Delegate it
- Do it

Lines on charts should be thick and bold. Model parts should be large enough to be distinguishable. Screens for slides, projected presentations, and filmstrips should be large enough for the size of the room, and projectors should have focal lengths great enough to fill the screen. If you are showing a videotape, make sure that the monitor can be mounted high enough to be seen by people in the back row or that there are enough monitors for everyone to get a good view.

(2) Keep your visual aids simple and clear.

Do not design overelaborate aids. They should contain just enough detail to allow your listeners to distinguish easily one part from another. Look at the two cutaway drawings of a car engine in Figure 28-2. The one on the right will be the better one to use if you want to demonstrate the ignition system. It provides information on where the ignition system is in relation to the rest of the car's engine, without forcing the audience to try to distinguish it from the fuel system, the cooling system, the air conditioning system, and so on.

FIGURE 28-2   Overelaborate Versus Clear Visual Aid

Ignition System

Similarly, do not crowd maps, charts, graphs, models, and photographs with so much data that your audience is confused about which part you are referring to. For instance, you should have one map showing only city council districts and another only county supervisorial districts in the city. Avoid having so many lines on a line graph that audience members are at risk of taking a "wrong turn" while following one line across. With photographs, try to find one that shows the object in isolation or in sharp focus in relation to other objects.

Keep the wording on any visual aid simple and familiar, printed in clear block lettering if you letter by hand. Use no more words than strictly necessary to label parts and ideas.

Maintain continuity when you spread your information out. If you use a pie graph for your first aid, any following aids dealing with similar or related information should also be pie graphs.

Use color to delineate different aspects of the object or symbol. A large model heart with bright blue, red, and yellow parts may not look totally realistic, but audience members will find it a lot easier to keep the parts separate in their minds as they follow the explanation.

Presentation software packages enable you to create slides that you can either print and project or project directly using a computer projection system. Keep the following suggestions in mind to ensure that the overheads and slides you create are effective:

1. Use simple typefaces. Do not mix more than two typefaces on a sheet. Avoid ornate or showy type, and stay away from drop shadows, outline fonts, and other decorative type modifications that add visual "noise."
2. Use uppercase and lowercase letters in the titles and text. Sentences printed exclusively in capital letters are harder to read.
3. Use a lot of white space. Do not crowd too much information on one sheet. Keep the information simple; use your speech to fill in the details.
4. Maintain continuity throughout the transparencies. Settle on a design theme and carry it out for each sheet. For instance, if you use a border, put it on all sheets; if you use bullets for a list on one sheet, do not use numbers or dashes for a list on another sheet.

(3) Design visual aids for maximum audience impact.

The design and form of your visual aids can enhance your credibility, add humor, provide information beyond the data presented, or simply maintain the interest of your listeners.

A professional-looking aid can do much to lend a polished tone to a speech. You need not hire a professional to prepare one, however, nor do you need a computer. Art supply stores stock transfer letters, stencils, colored plastic in various geometric forms—all sorts of simple graphic materials that even the unartistic can use to produce a neat and attractive visual aid.

If you do use a computer to make a two-dimensional aid, a number of presentation software packages offer templates with predetermined design attributes: colors, borders, typefaces, and the like. These are handy to ensure that continuity is maintained between sheets and that the type is large enough to read. The manuals describing these templates usually categorize them by method of display: Some are appropriate if you are going to make overheads off a laser printer, others if you are going to produce 35mm slides, and still others if you are going to present the material on-screen. Follow the guidelines; a laser print of an overhead produced from a 35mm-type template will probably be dark and hard to read, with murky graphic elements. Within a particular category, choose one of the simpler designs. Many of the templates can be overly complex, and some have design elements that detract from the material presented—the visual equivalent of a dog barking at your feet while you speak.

For whatever type of visual aid, basic, unexotic colors are best to use, unless a certain color is popularly associated with the object or idea being depicted. And, of course, there are standard uses, like green for forests, blue for water, and so on.

Along this line, you can construct your visual aids in a manner that underscores the theme of your speech. For instance, instead of using bar graphs to indicate yearly differences in logging revenues, substitute tree outlines with the proper relative dimensions. (Be careful here—if you go by relative height alone, the relative volume of the objects will be out of scale, and the graphic will be misleading.) Or compare rows of objects—houses, missiles, stick figures with dunce caps—where each object represents a certain number of housing starts, strategic warheads, or failing students. A particularly subtle way of using visual material to drive home a verbal message was demonstrated by former President Reagan when he went on television to present his tax plan to the American public. He displayed a line graph depicting the projected government spending that would result from his plan and the spending that would result from his opponents' plan, explaining it by saying, "Our plan, shown here by the *solid* line . . ." and "the Democrats' proposal, which is the *dotted* line . . ." The solid line on the graph invested his position with the semblance of stability and careful planning; the insubstantial dotted line seemed to represent the lightweight, disjointed thinking of the opposition.

28c. Introduce your visual aids so that they blend smoothly into the speech.

(1) Practice with your visual aids.

Your aids should be prepared early enough that you can practice with them several times. (See **25b(3)**.) This will alert you to any changes that might be necessary. Become comfortable with them so that you do not fumble around during the presentation.

(2) Maintain eye contact.

Be so familiar with your material that you can look at your listeners while explaining the visual aid. Often, a speaker will turn away from the audience and talk directly at the visual aid. This deprives the speaker of feedback and strains the listeners' hearing.

(3) Keep talking.

Avoid long pauses when demonstrating a process. If there is some complexity, or if many steps are needed to produce your desired result, you might take a hint from television cooking shows and prepare a series of aids to demonstrate the various phases. Doing so will eliminate those periods when both you and the audience are waiting for something to happen. For example, a speaker could say, "Then you apply glue to the two blocks, press them together like this, and let the bond dry. Here are some that have already dried. Now, I'll show you the next step . . ." When you cannot avoid a time lag introduced by some process, have a planned digression—some bit of history related to the process, perhaps—to fill the gap.

(4) Do not let your visual aids become a distraction.

Keep your visual aids out of sight, turned off, covered, or turned away from your audience until you are ready to use them. Remove or re-cover them immediately after they have served their purpose. If you are using a projector, turn it off whenever you can to eliminate the cooling fan noise.

Refrain from passing objects around the room, as that will cause a ripple of inattention. This rule is flexible, especially when you are dealing with an unusual object and a small audience, but still it is probably best to share the item *after* the speech—say, during the discussion period. By the same token, handouts should be distributed after a speech. You want the audience to listen now and read later.

Finally, visual aids are most distracting when you are clumsy with them. Be sure that your charts are in the right order, your models are set up, and your equipment is in perfect working order. Avoid visual aid fiascoes by practicing carefully, arriving in plenty of time for setup, and bringing pins, tape, extension cords, extra projector bulbs, CD-ROM backups, and the like to ensure that what you envision comes to pass.

28d. Understand the benefits, constraints, and perils of using presentation software.

Presentation software can be considered a mixed blessing to the speaker. On the one hand, it is possible to create transparencies and handouts that are consistent and attractive. On the other, it is possible to be put in a position in which you are narrating your outline rather than giving a speech.

(1) Keep your text slides simple.

The templates that come with the presentation software application are designed to keep your slides simple. That is, if you use the typefaces in the sizes that come as the default, it will be difficult for you to clutter up a slide with too many words and ideas. This is good; avoid the temptation to finesse your way around the constraints of the type size. Instead, look for better ways to organize your material, and pare down your language to the minimum. (See **9** and **10**.)

You can use animation effects or "builds" to expose certain elements of a slide in a particular order for dramatic effect or to keep the focus on the most immediate point. If you do take advantage of this capability, do so with restraint; the efficacy of the effect will diminish with overuse. Similarly, exercise restraint with the sound effects that come with the package—"zoop"-ing sounds may be fun with 5 slides, but with 30 they will move beyond being irritants.

(2) Maintain consistency.

Used properly, presentation software can help you maintain a consistent look throughout your slides. While templates work for keeping the type consistent, the program's settings for color schemes, slide backgrounds and patterns, and so on work to keep other elements consistent. Even with this help, though, you need to review your slides to make sure no discrepancies have crept in. Look at the captions. Are they all in burgundy 14-point bold Helvetica? Or has one somehow ended up in green 14-point Arial Narrow? How about the placement of elements? Click through the slide show quickly to see if elements seem to jump from place to place in relation to other instances. Also, check other features, like transition effects and builds, for consistency. Sometimes, especially if a presentation is being created from a number of earlier ones, these may get mixed up, so that you end up with most slides using a "fade through black" transition and a few using a "wipe right."

(3) Be judicious in your use of clip art.

Avoid the temptation to "pretty up" your slides with a lot of clip art graphics that come with the software. Because the popular software packages have such wide exposure, the use of a familiar clip art image—for example, of businesspeople standing around a table or the ubiquitous business handshake—makes your message seem less than unique. Additionally, too many images can be distracting. Images in different styles (a line drawing of person followed by cartoon image of person, for instance, or a low-resolution bitmap image followed by a sharp PostScript image) can be distracting as well. (See **28d(2)**.)

(4) Do not become secondary to your slides.

It is a common scene in conference and convention settings: One or two large screens dominate in a room holding dozens or hundreds of people; dwarfed by the screens, a speaker is partially hidden behind a bank of computer monitors, hunched over in the dim light, clicking away at the mouse while talking into the body mike, and often commenting on some glitch with the system. Obvious problems here are lack of connection with the audience because of the darkened room and the focus on the machine, confinement of the speaker to the space in front of the computer, and the "aid" becoming an impediment.

If you are in a situation in which this sort of projection will be used, take steps to counteract the potential difficulties. Enlist a colleague or friend to work the computer (make sure you have practiced enough; see **28c(1)** and **29b**) so that you are free to move around and to make eye contact with the audience. If you cannot avoid working the equipment, or if you must compensate for dim lighting, use vocal variety to counterbalance immobility and lack of visibility. See (**25b.**) If possible, use the slides for key illustrations and points, but leave the screen blank the rest of the time.

Exercise 1. Suggest three different kinds of visual aids that might be used for speeches on each of these topics:

Car Pool Lanes
How a Check Is Processed
The Workings of a Lock
Instituting Mandatory National Service

Exercise 2. Rank-order the speeches on the Sample Speeches Web site by the need for visual aids. Explain your decision in terms of audience, occasion, and topic. If you decide that visual aids would complement some of the speeches, recommend what kinds of aids, and indicate where in the speech they should go.

Chapter 29

Adapting to the
Speech Situation

Anticipate that the actual speech situation may be different from your visualization of it. Be prepared to take advantage of the good variations and to cope with the bad ones.

What do you do if 20 people show up for your speech when you were told there would be 300? What if you expected a homogeneous audience and find a mixed one waiting—or assumed an audience to be favorable but discover they are unfavorable? How will you handle distractions or hecklers during your speech? To cope with these turns of events, you must resist the temptation to go on automatic pilot and spew out the speech exactly as practiced. Do not stop thinking the second you start speaking. Despite all your hours of preparation, the actual creation of the speech occurs *now,* as you talk. Dozens of strategic choices cannot be made until during the speech. But you can avoid some unpleasant shocks if you spend some time thinking about the contingencies you might face. When you prepare for and practice a speech, consider not only the probable but also the possible.

29a. Adapt to the audience response as you give your speech, and plan alternative strategies for reactions you may receive.

The give-and-take between speaker and listeners is one thing that makes giving a good speech more than merely reading aloud. A speaker can present the same report 12 times and not become boring and flat, because she or he experiences the excitement each time of interacting with a different audience. The changes and adaptations sustain the vigor of the speech. Adaptation is not a new skill you must laboriously learn; it is nothing but a more structured version of the mood sensing and editing you do all the time in ordinary conversation.

(1) Follow some common guidelines for making adjustments.

If your audience seems bored or restless

1. Use more humor and novelty.
2. Use more concrete examples.
3. Use more direct references to the audience.
4. Invite direct participation—by asking listeners to give examples or to raise their hands to denote agreement, and so on.
5. Cut out or simplify technical descriptions and statistics.
6. Make your delivery more animated.
7. Make a physical change—for example, walk around the lectern and sit on a desk.
8. Cut it short. The program might be running late, so cut out subpoints, drive home your thesis, and stop.

If you are not getting the agreement you expected

1. Stress common ground.
2. Modify your goal; do not try to do so much.
3. Spend extra time establishing your credibility.
4. Appeal to your listeners' sense of fair play: "Whether you agree with me or not, I'm sure you will hear me out."

If your audience is less informed than you expected

1. Check your perceptions. Ask questions like "How many of you know the difference between fission and fusion?" or "How many of you know the secret of Damascus steel?"
2. Use more supporting materials that are geared toward clarification: definition, explanation, examples, illustration, restatement, and analogies that compare the unknown to the known.
3. Delete the more technical materials.

If your audience is more informed than you expected

1. Condense your basic material and call it a review: "As most of you know . . ."
2. Recall and insert the more technical or abstract materials you encountered in your research.
3. Introduce the questions and issues that you see as unresolved aspects of the topic.
4. Cut the speech short and invite discussion of your topic.

If your audience is more heterogeneous than you expected

1. Gear your supporting material and language to what seems to be the typical audience member. Identify the predominant ethnic group, for example, or estimate the average age.

2. Add materials that acknowledge the presence of the full range of listeners, but do not change the main thrust of your speech. For example, add a reference to a television show that children in the audience can relate to, or spend a few minutes establishing your credibility for the 10 percent of the audience that disagrees with you.

Caveat: Do not overreact in categorizing your audience. Give your listeners time to adjust to you and give your speech time to make an impression on them. Keep in touch with the mood of the audience, and do not play to the extremes.

29b. Take several steps to prevent distractions, and if distractions do occur, be familiar with the strategies to deal with them.

Murphy's law is an especially potent force to reckon with in facing the physical setting and the mechanical apparatus of the speech situation. Here are some suggestions on how to avoid or mitigate its effect.

(1) Check your presentation's setting and equipment to detect possible sources of distraction.

Arrive early and survey the room where you will speak. Make whatever changes necessary to ensure that attention will be focused on you and your message. For instance, if the room has windows, you may have to draw the blinds or modify the seating arrangement to prevent sunlight from blinding your listeners. An obtrusive object or chart should be covered or turned around. The chairs should be shifted to suit your type of presentation. Test the acoustics to see if you need to close windows against outside noise or need amplification to counteract an undercurrent of environmental sounds.

If you are using electronic aids, find the outlets in the room and actually test both your aids and the outlets for proper functioning. Have backups for your equipment or, if you are being provided with equipment, insist that it come with spare bulbs, batteries, and so on. Now, and not after being introduced, is the time to check the sound level of your microphone.

If you are using a computer, make sure it is compatible with the projection system.

Inevitably, there will be some sources of distraction that cannot be controlled. The FAA will doubtless be unwilling to cancel all commercial flights over the building in which you will be speaking, but you should take every opportunity to change what you can. Katharine Hepburn, during the run of the musical *Coco,* was able to convince the construction workers across from the theater to cease riveting during her big solo each matinee.

(2) Deal with fleeting or low-level distractions during your speech by not acknowledging them.

The first rule of dealing with distractions is, naturally, that you yourself must not become or seem distracted. At the same time, though, you should subtly raise your energy level to keep your listeners' attention. When all heads turn as a latecomer enters through the door behind you, do not legitimize the interruption by turning your head also. Do not appear to be flustered when a fluorescent bulb starts to flicker overhead—simply speak a little louder, become a bit more animated, or add some extra attention-getting devices such as humor or storytelling.

(3) Turn distractions to your purpose by incorporating them into your speech.

One frequently told story is of the politician whose campaign speech was interrupted by a crying baby. "I can't blame that youngster," he remarked. "She's just thinking about four more years of a Republican administration." In another instance, a speaker had to pause when a waiter noisily dropped a tray of dishes. He continued with, "That's about how the intercollegiate athletics' department came crashing down when the scholarship scandal hit the press. Guess who got elected to pick up the pieces?"

(4) When it is actually necessary to interrupt the continuity of your speech, do so as quickly as possible and then draw your listeners back in.

Your job is to give the speech—not to close doors, answer telephones, adjust the thermostat, and so on. If no one seems to want to take care of a problem, then you must interrupt your speech and deal with it so that everyone can quickly return to the business at hand.

There are two levels of interruption. In the first, you do not stop speaking: "... which would justify that course of action. Would someone please unlock that door? There are people wanting to get in. For my second point, I would like you to consider ..."

In the second case, circumstances require that you stop speaking while certain actions are taken by you or members of the audience. After you are satisfied with the result of that action—as, for example, when a victim of heat prostration has been cared for and helped from the room—you may continue, backing up in your organization to summarize the progression of your points prior to the interruption: "Thank you for handling that so competently. Now, as you will remember, I was just a moment ago talking about ..."

29c. Do not hand control of the situation over to the verbal or nonverbal heckler, but rather respond to such interruptions calmly and firmly.

The worst distraction a speaker can face is the intentional interrupter. The problem can range from the listener who has had a little too much to drink and has delusions of wit, to the person who makes a systematic attempt to undermine your speech goal or even to prevent you from speaking. Generally, respond to them by progressing through the steps in **29b:** Ignore; if you cannot, incorporate; if you cannot, confront.

Always keep in mind your credibility with the audience, and remember that you do not want to do anything that will interfere with achieving your speech purpose. You never want to lose your composure, dignity, or temper; you do not ever want to sink to the heckler's level.

(1) The verbal heckler

If you start justifying yourself to a heckler, you have lost control of the situation and have put it in his or her lap. Do not get into a defensive posture. For example, do not defend yourself against name-calling: "You're a crook!" or "You don't care about the environment." Do not waste time with denials. Deal with the substance, not with the accusations.

First-level tactics
Establish an image or tone of reasonableness or fairness. Make it clear that you are not opposed to dialogue, even if the heckler is disregarding the polite convention that gives the floor to you. Give the heckler the benefit of the doubt in terms of her or his sincerity.

Appeal to fair play. Say, "I base my opinions about China on my three months travel there. Will you hear me out while I describe those experiences? *Then* we'll listen to your objections."

Build on common ground. Say, "We both want the best schooling for our children. If we didn't think it was vitally important, neither of us would be here."

Never seem to shut out the heckler or his or her point of view completely. Each does represent a point of view, and you want the audience to view you as a reasonable person. Of course, if you believe that the heckler, though sincere, has adopted a vastly oversimplified analysis of a complex issue, you should communicate that to your listeners.

Second-level tactics

In the course of being polite, you do not want your audience to think that you are glad that you have been interrupted and are enjoying the byplay. There comes a time where you have to cut the person off and get on with the speech.

Enough is enough. If the heckler has not been mollified or deflated by your reasonableness, then you can say something like, "I think you've made your point. Now I really must ask you to sit down and let me continue my speech." Even if the heckler does not, this will give the audience permission to tell the person to shut up or security permission to remove her or him.

The zinger. As a last resort, it is sometimes appropriate to flatten a heckler with a pithy and pointed comeback. Effective use of the "zinger" depends on two factors: your ability to think of a wise and witty retort (not one of the "your mother wears combat boots" variety), and your correct reading of the audience. If your listeners are irritated and impatient with the heckler, they will welcome your initiative. If you have misjudged their mood, however, you run the risk of seeming nasty or petty.

(2) The nonverbal heckler

These are the hecklers you will run into more frequently. Rolling their eyes, fidgeting, sighing, whispering, passing notes—these are their trademarks. They do not quite have the nerve to heckle you out loud, but they want you to know that they disagree or are bored. If you focus on their behavior, your self-confidence may start to erode. These people can absorb all your attention as you start playing to them.

By and large, the way to deal with the nonverbal heckler is to ignore him or her. Sometimes, you might have to cut off eye contact completely with that section of the audience. Instead, make eye contact with the people who are displaying positive signs, and avoid allowing your eyes to drift back to the heckler.

If you find it difficult to ignore the heckler, you may want to try one of the following:

1. If you know the person by name, throw the name, in a complimentary sense, into the speech. This may either get the heckler's interest or embarrass her or him into being polite.
2. If you are sufficiently self-assured, maintain eye contact with the nonverbal heckler until he or she defers.

If the heckling is an ongoing problem—in a class, say, or in a series of business meetings—you might want to talk to this person privately and ask for feedback. He or she may be gratified enough by the attention to modify the annoying behavior.

You should avoid, however, projecting your own interpretations too freely onto the audience. Often, teachers have been surprised when the student who has been sitting in class all year with crossed arms and a sour expression comes up at the end and says, "This was the best class I've ever had." The frown may be the result of a headache, or indigestion, or merely concentration. Do not leap to conclusions about the nonverbal messages your audience is sending you.

Chapter 30

Answering Questions

Use the question-and-answer period to ensure that your message was understood by as many people as possible. Prepare fully, answer questions directly, and maintain control of the interaction.

The question-and-answer period is a great opportunity to further the goals of your speech. While you spoke, you attempted to address the needs of your audience, and now you can see how close you came. From your listeners' questions, you can learn what points are unclear or what arguments and objections they have. Do not approach the question-and-answer period as if facing a firing squad. Communicate an eagerness to interact with your listeners and to hear their ideas on your topic. Express your enthusiasm through such reactions as, "I'm glad you brought that up," "That's a good question," and "That's intriguing. I never thought of it quite that way."

Do not lose your delivery skills just because the speech is over. Maintain eye contact, and avoid fidgeting or mumbling. Actually, some speakers' delivery improves during the question-and-answer period because they become more relaxed.

30a. Come prepared for a question-and-answer period.

Keep in mind the importance of the question-and-answer period throughout the stages of preparing your speech. Anticipate the questions that will arise naturally from each of your points. One aid to this is to have the friends who listen to your practice sessions ask you questions afterward. Although you can never predict the exact questions that will come up, certain ones are more probable than others. Rehearse aloud possible answers to the most complicated and difficult ones. This is how public figures prepare for news conferences.

Ideally, your research has been so extensive that you have much more material than you were able to use, considering the time constraints surrounding your speech. You should not shove this extra material into a drawer and forget about it. Continue to review it so you are familiar enough with the content to weave it easily into elaboration and explanation in response to questions.

Think of possible applications of particularly effective evidence. For instance, for your speech on women in the labor force (see **11b**), you do not use a delightful story you found about a Japanese woman worker because your speech concentrates on conditions in the United States. The day before the speech, though, you go over the details of the story so you can tell it accurately should any of the audience question you about how your observations may relate to women in other cultures. Similarly, it takes a minute to memorize Flo Kennedy's wonderful insight—"I know we're termites. But if all the termites got together, the house would fall down"—which you realize might fit into a discussion of the need for women to use their potential power. The statistics used in your speech relating income differences between men and women in Woodside city government jobs may be challenged by some in the audience, so put together a backup notecard that (1) explains the sampling frame for the survey, (2) breaks the statistics down by occupation group, and (3) lists comparable statistics for eight other major cities.

30b. Invite and answer audience questions in a straightforward manner.

Do not worry if there are not any questions immediately, or if at first there are long pauses between questions. It usually takes your listeners a moment to collect their thoughts. In some cases, you can start the ball rolling yourself by asking a question of the audience. "What problems have you encountered setting up affirmative action programs in your companies?" can generate counterquestions.

Call on questioners in the order they sought recognition, and maintain eye contact while the question is being asked. If you are not sure you understand the question, paraphrase it according to your own interpretation and ask the questioner if it is accurate. When both of you are satisfied, restate or paraphrase it for the entire audience and direct the answer to them.

Be sure you *answer* the question. To avoid oversimplification, you want to elaborate, expand, or qualify your answer, but if your discussion becomes too diffuse, you will appear to be avoiding the issue. Consequently, always include a one-sentence, direct answer in your response to a question. For emphasis, place this sentence first or last, as in these examples:

First:	*Yes, I do oppose building nuclear power plants,* at least until several safety questions are answered satisfactorily. My reasons include . . .
Last:	. . . so, because of all these serious problems I see, my answer to your question would be *Yes, I do oppose building new nuclear power plants at this time.*

What if you are asked a question for which you do not have an answer? Do not try to bluff your way through. Rather, admit that you do not know. If you have some idea where the answer might be found, tell the questioner of the source. Ask other audience members to help you out by volunteering what they know. Or you might promise to look it up if the listener wants to get in touch with you later.

30c. Do not allow self-indulgent questioners to distort the function of the question-and-answer period.

The purpose of a question-and-answer period is to clarify issues for the entire audience. When individual audience members attempt to use this time for detailed consultation on a specialized problem or to get on their favorite soapbox, you have an obligation as speaker to bring the interaction back on its true course.

Be prepared to keep control of the situation by dealing in a firm and tactful manner with several types of distracting questioners.

(1) The person who wants to give a speech

This person may agree or disagree with you, or may have a favorite ax to grind that is only tangentially related to your topic. The distinguishing characteristic is that it becomes obvious that she or he has no real question to ask you but rather is taking advantage of an assembled audience to hold forth. It is rarely effective to ask, "What is your question?" The person will just say, "Don't you agree that . . ." or "What do you think of the position that . . ." and take off for another five minutes. You have to jump in at the end of a sentence, manufacture a question somewhat related to the person's ramblings, answer it, and recognize another questioner on the opposite side of the room: "So, you're saying that there is so much inefficiency in government that you wonder how this or any other problem can be solved? That is a tough question to answer, but I am hopeful that the recent reorganization of our agency will permit us to be successful in our efforts. Next question over there?"

(2) The person who wants to have an extended dialogue

This person might start out with a genuine question, but refuse to relinquish the floor when you respond. Rather, he or she counters with follow-up questions, comments on your answer, or opens new lines of discussion. Sometimes, this sort of person wants free professional advice or therapy and does not mind seeking it in public. Other times, the person simply finds you and your ideas fascinating and wants to converse at length, as though you were both guests at a cocktail party instead of speaker and audience member in a formalized setting. The best way to deal with this sort of person is to end the exchange firmly but with a compliment and/or invitation: "Thank you, you've given me quite a number of interesting insights here. Maybe you can come up and talk to me about them some more later."

(3) The person who wants to pick a fight

Intellectual confrontation and probing, penetrating questions are to be expected, and even welcomed, from audience members who disagree with you. But sometimes questioners become inappropriately argumentative and mount hostile, personal attacks against a speaker. It becomes obvious that they are not really seeking an answer to a question, but are trying to destroy your credibility. Do not let them succeed by becoming angry or by defending yourself against generalized name-calling. (See **29c** on heckling.) Pick out the part of such a person's diatribe that contains the kernel of a question, paraphrase it, and answer it calmly and reasonably.

Q: What about all this poisonous junk that you greed-crazed despoilers
       dump into our rivers to kill our children and whole species of animals?
A: The questioner has brought up the valid and difficult subject of toxic
       waste disposal. What is our company doing about it? Well . . .

In short, respond to these disruptive people diplomatically. Remember that, unlike hecklers, their participation has been invited. Do not take cheap shots or direct humor at them to shut them off. Likewise, when you are taken aback by incomprehensible questions or questions that demonstrate gross ignorance or misinformation, you should react positively. Avoid language that embarrasses the questioner or points out errors:

Not:	Well, *as I said* in my speech . . .
But:	Let me go over these statistics more slowly. . . .
Not:	You've totally confused fission and fusion!
But:	Many of those problems relate to nuclear *fission*. The *fusion* reaction is quite different. It works like this . . .

Try to find ways to dignify bad questions and turn them into good ones. Your listeners' empathy is with the questioner, who may be nervous or confused. Your efforts to put others at ease will earn you an audience's goodwill.

Index

References to sections of this book are printed in boldface type.

R

S

W